CHRISTIANITY

A READY DEFENCE

For more information about the ministry of Campus Crusade for Christ, write to:

United Kingdom: Agapé
4 Temple Row
Birmingham B2 5HG

Australia: LIFE
PO Box A399
Sidney South 2000

Canada: Campus Crusade for Christ
Box 300
Vancouver, BC V6C 2X3

New Zealand: Lay Institute for Evangelism
PO Box 8786
Auckland 3

West Africa: Great Commission Movement of Nigeria
PO Box 500
Jos, Plateau State
Nigeria

Republic of South Africa:
Life Ministry
PO Box/Bus 91015
Auckland Park 2006

USA: Campus Crusade for Christ International
Arrowhead Springs,
San Bernardino CA 92414

Ireland: Agape—Ireland
264 Merrion Road
Dublin 4

JOSH McDOWELL

COMPILED BY
BILL WILSON

Over 60 VITAL LINES OF DEFENCE FOR CHRISTIANITY

With EASY REFERENCE GUIDE

First Published by
HERE'S LIFE PUBLISHERS, INC.
P.O. Box 1576
San Bernardino, CA 92402

First British edition 1991

ISBN 1 872059 56 2

Production and Printing in England for
SCRIPTURE PRESS FOUNDATION (UK) LTD
Raans Road, Amersham-on-the-Hill, Bucks HP6 6JQ by
Nuprint Ltd, Station Road, Harpenden, Herts AL5 4SE.

Contents

Part Two ANSWERING THE BIBLE'S CRITICS

SECTION 2 JESUS

His Humanity and his Deity

SECTION 3

OTHER RELIGIONS
Compared with Christianity

Part One NON-CHRISTIAN RELIGIONS

Part Two SECULAR RELIGIONS

Part Three CULTS

Part Four THE OCCULT

CHRISTIANITY
Questions Asked

THE CHRISTIAN EXPERIENCE
Its Uniqueness

How to Use This Book

THIS BOOK is a powerful compilation of passages from all Josh McDowell's books on historical defences for the validity of the Christian faith. The table of contents will help you find major blocks of material that interest you. To help you locate more specific quotes and information, three different indexes (Subject, Author, and Scripture) are provided in the back of the book.

If you desire more detail on a particular subject, we recommend you consult the source volume. The original works also contain additional bibliographic references and may provide additional information in foot-notes that were not carried over to this edition.

The *'Easy Reference Guide'* overleaf will help you to quickly locate the relevant sections and the marginal tabs will remind you what section you are in.

In order to determine the original publication, notice the references—e.g., C/24-26–usually found after a unit or chapter title. The "C" here refers to Josh's book, *More Than a Carpenter*, and the "24-26" refers to the page numbers in that book. Following is a list of the codes and the books to which they refer:

A *Answers to Tough Questions*, Scripture Press, 1988.

C *More Than a Carpenter*, Kingsway, 1984.

D *Daniel in the Critic's Den*, Here's Life Publishers, 1979.

E *Evidence That Demands A Verdict Vol I*, Scripture Press, 1990

HW *He Walked Among Us,* Scripture Press, 1989.

ME *Evidence That Demands a Verdict, Volume II*, Scripture Press, 1990

R *Reasons Skeptics Should Consider Christianity*, Scripture Press, 1988.

RF *The Resurrection*, Scripture Press, 1988.

UC *Understanding the Cults*, Here's Life Publishers, 1982.

UNR *Understanding Non-Christian Religions*, Here's Life Publishers, 1982.

UO *Understanding the Occult*, Here's Life Publishers, 1982.

USR *Understanding Secular Religions*, Here's Life Publishers, 1982.

NOTE: Separate bibliographies are found at the end of each Part of each Section, NOT at the end of the book.

After each quote you will find two sets of numbers divided by a slash (example: 54/221). The number on the left of the slash refers to the source in the bibliography for that part of the book. The number on the right refers to the page(s) within that source. Where there is only one number, only the source is referenced–no page numbers.

Easy Reference Guide

From the Editor

"Make me an offer I can't refuse." That was my fill-in-the-blank answer to the question: "Where would you most like to be assigned for the 1978-79 school year?" on Campus Crusade for Christ's annual Placement Preference Questionnaire. I was up for any exciting assignment God wanted to give me.

My assignment turned out to be even more exciting than I could have imagined: personal traveling assistant for Josh McDowell.

That year I traveled thousands of miles—in planes, cars and vans, making phone calls and photocopies, running down details, setting up meetings, and handling a multitude of other tasks, all to help Josh do what he does best: introduce skeptics to Jesus Christ. Not just one here and another there . . . but thousands of them, students and professors alike, on campuses all over the United States and beyond. Many of these people are fed up with "religion" and appreciate hearing from someone else who also was fed up with "religion," so much so that he did his homework in order to get rid of it. To say the least, my assignment was a thrill!

It was also exhausting. I found Josh to be the most dedicated, hard-working man I had ever met. After speaking at various functions throughout the day and to thousands of students each night, he would return to his hotel room and make phone calls or write until 2 in the morning. At 6 A.M. the process would start all over again.

Most of all, it was just plain fun. Josh has the most positive yet down-to-earth attitude I've ever seen. Even though he has studied all the intellectual arguments surrounding the Christian faith, he has the innocence of a little child when it comes to the thrill of knowing and appreciating God. I still relish fond memories of driving through the New England states . . . Josh, his wife Dottie and their first two children, Kelly and Sean, and myself . . . all peering out the windows at the changing autumn leaves. About every ten minutes Josh would yell out, in that expressive manner you know only if you have been around him, "Oh! Just goooooorgeous!"

At the end of that year Josh challenged me to go to seminary. So I did. I can still remember him sending me off with, "Maybe we'll be working together again sometime." At the time I didn't think it was anything more than just a kind, parting comment. Actually it was prophetic.

A year after I graduated from seminary our paths crossed again. One thing led to another, and before long my wife Sharon and I, and our six-week-old first child, were on our way to Dallas to join Josh's ministry team. What a privilege it has been for me to serve the Lord as Josh's director of research these last six and a half years. Which brings me to this book.

In response to the many questions we receive in the mail, someone hatched the idea of pulling together in one book the most powerful of Josh's recorded evidences for the Christian faith. The end product would be of tremendous service to believers and non-believers alike. His material fills more than fifteen books, and bringing the most pertinent discussions together into one volume seemed a good way to help people find the answers they sought, whether for themselves or to help them in their witness to others. *A Ready Defense* is that end product.

At an even deeper level, my excitement for the project went all the way back to my college years as an agnostic. When my brother's life was radically changed by his becoming a Christian, I decided to investigate Christianity. I read everything I could find. How helpful a volume like this would have been to me at that time.

So, to make a not-so-long story even shorter, when Josh graciously gave me the opportunity to take on this project, it was another offer I couldn't refuse!

Bill Wilson, Editor

Bill Wilson is a cum laude graduate of Trinity Evangelical Divinity School. He serves as director of research for the Josh McDowell Ministry, and he is co-author of HE WALKED AMONG US.

CHAPTER 1 *He Changed My Life*

(C/117-28)

Jesus Christ is alive. The fact that I'm alive and doing the things I do is evidence that Jesus Christ is raised from the dead.

Thomas Aquinas wrote: "There is within every soul a thirst for happiness and meaning." As a teenager I wanted to be happy. There's nothing wrong with that. I wanted to be one of the happiest individuals in the entire world. I also wanted meaning in life. I wanted answers to questions like, "Who am I?" "Why in the world am I here?" "Where am I going?"

More than that, I wanted to be free. I wanted to be one of the freest individuals in the whole world. To me, freedom is not just going out and doing what you want to do. Anyone can do that, and lots of people are doing it. Freedom is "having the power to do what you know you ought to do." Most people know what they ought to do but they don't have the power to do it. They're in bondage.

So I started looking for answers. It seems that almost everyone is into some sort of religion, so I did the obvious thing and took off for church. I must have found the wrong church though. Some of you know what I'm talking about: I felt worse inside than I did outside. I went in the morning, I went in the afternoon, and I went in the evening.

I'm always very practical, and when something doesn't work, I chuck it. I chucked religion. The only thing I ever got out of religion was the twenty-five cents I put in the offering and the thirty-five cents I took out for a milkshake. That's about all many people ever gain from "religion."

I began to wonder if prestige was the answer. Being a leader, accepting some cause, giving yourself to it, and "being known" might do it. In the first university I attended, the student leaders held the purse strings and threw their weight around. So I ran for freshman class president and got elected. It was neat knowing everyone on campus, having everyone say, "Hi, Josh," making the decisions, spending the university's money, the students' money, to get speakers I wanted. It was great but it wore off like everything else I had tried. I would wake up Monday morning, usually with a headache because of the night before, and my attitude was, "Well, here goes another five days." I endured Monday through Friday. Happiness revolved around three nights a week: Friday, Saturday, and Sunday. Then the vicious cycle began all over again.

Oh, I fooled them in the university. They thought I was one of the happiest-go-lucky guys around. During the political campaigns we used the phrase, "Happiness is Josh." I threw more parties with student money than anyone else did, but they never realized my happiness was like so many other people's. It depended on my own circumstances. If things were going great for me, I was great. When things would go lousy, I was lousy.

I was like a boat out in the ocean being tossed back and forth by the waves, the circumstances. There is a biblical term to describe that type of living: hell. But I couldn't find anyone living any other way and I couldn't find anyone who could tell me how to live differently or give me the strength to do it. I had everyone telling me what I ought to do but none of them could give me the power to do it. I began to be frustrated.

I suspect that few people in the universities and colleges of this country were more sincere in trying to find meaning, truth, and purpose to life than I was. I hadn't found it yet, but I didn't realize that at first. In and around the university I noticed a small group of people, eight students and two faculty members, who had something different about their lives. They seemed to know why they believed what they believed. I like to be around people like that. I don't care if they don't agree with *me*. Some of my closest friends are opposed to some things I believe, but I admire a man or woman with conviction. (I don't meet many, but I admire them when I meet them.)

That's why I sometimes feel more at home with some radical leaders than I do with many Christians. Some of the Christians I meet are so wishy-washy that I wonder if maybe 50 percent of them aren't masquerading as Christians.

But the people in this small group seemed to know where they were going. That's unusual among university students.

The people I began to notice didn't just *talk* about love. They got involved. They seemed to be riding above the circumstances of university life, while it appeared everybody else was under a pile. One important thing

I noticed was that these people seemed to have a happiness, a state of mind not dependent on circumstances. They appeared to possess an inner, constant source of joy. They were disgustingly happy. They had something I didn't have.

Like the average student, when somebody had something I didn't have, I wanted it. That's why bicycles at colleges have to be locked up. If education were really the answer, the university would probably be the most morally upright society in existence. But it's not. So, I decided to make friends with these intriguing people.

Two weeks after that decision several of us were sitting around a table in the student union, six students and two faculty members. The conversation started to get around to God. If you're an insecure person and a conversation centers on God, you tend to put on a big front. Every campus or community has a big mouth, a guy who says, "Uh . . . Christianity, ha, ha. That's for the weaklings. It's not intellectual." (Usually, the bigger the mouth, the bigger the vacuum.)

They were bothering me, so I finally looked over at one of the students, a good-looking woman (I used to think all Christians were ugly), and I leaned back in my chair because I didn't want the others to think I was interested, and I said, "Tell me, what changed your lives? Why are your lives so different from the other students, the leaders on campus, the professors? Why?"

That young woman must have had a lot of conviction. She looked me straight in the eye, no smile, and said two words I never thought I'd hear as part of a solution in a university. She said, "Jesus Christ."

I said, "Oh, for God's sake, don't give me that garbage. I'm fed up with religion; I'm fed up with the church; I'm fed up with the Bible. Don't give me that garbage about religion."

She shot back, "Mister, I didn't say religion; I said Jesus Christ."

She pointed out something I'd never known before. Christianity is not a religion. Religion is humans trying to work their way to God through good works. Christianity is God coming to men and women through Jesus Christ, offering them a relationship with Himself.

There are probably more people in universities with misconceptions about Christianity than anywhere else in the world. Recently I met a teaching assistant who remarked in a graduate seminar that "anyone who walks into a church becomes a Christian."

I replied, "Does walking into a garage make you a car?"

There is no correlation. A Christian is somebody who puts his trust in Christ.

My new friends challenged me intellectually to examine the claims that Jesus Christ is God's Son; that taking on human flesh, He lived among real men and women and died on the cross for the sins of mankind; that He was buried and He arose three days later and could change a person's life in the twentieth century.

I thought this was a farce. In fact, I thought most Christians were walking idiots. I'd met some. I used to wait for a Christian to speak up in the classroom so I could tear him or her up one side and down the other, and beat the insecure professor to the punch. I imagined that if a Christian had a brain cell, it would die of loneliness. I didn't know any better.

But these people challenged me over and over. Finally, out of pride, I accepted their challenge. I did it to refute them. I didn't know there were facts I didn't know there was evidence that a person could evaluate.

Eventually, my mind came to the conclusion that Jesus Christ must have been who He claimed to be. In fact, the background of my first two books was my setting out to refute Christianity. When I couldn't, I ended up becoming a Christian. I have now spent fifteen years documenting why I believe that faith in Jesus Christ is intellectually feasible.

At that time, though, I had quite a problem. My mind told me all this was true, but my will was pulling me in another direction. I discovered that becoming a Christian was rather ego-shattering. Jesus Christ made a direct challenge to my will to trust Him. Let me paraphrase Him: "Look! I have been standing at the door and I am constantly knocking. If anyone hears Me calling him and opens the door, I will come in" (Revelation 3:20).

I didn't care if He did walk on water or turn water into wine. I didn't want any party pooper around. I couldn't think of a faster way to ruin a good time. So here was my mind telling me Christianity was true, but my will was somewhere else.

Every time I was around those enthusiastic Christians, the conflict would begin. If you've ever been around happy people when you're miserable, you understand how they can bug you. They would be so happy and I would be so miserable that I'd literally get up and run right out of the student union. It came to the point where I'd go to bed at ten at night and I wouldn't get to sleep until four in the morning. I knew I had to get it off my mind before I went out of my mind! I was always open-minded, but not so open-minded that my brains would fall out.

But since I was open-minded, on December 19, 1959, at 8:30 P.M., during my second year at the university, I became a Christian.

Somebody asked me, "How do you know?"

I said, "Look, I was there. It's changed my life." That night I prayed. I prayed four things to establish a relationship with the resurrected, living Christ which has since transformed my life.

First, I said, "Lord Jesus, thank You for dying on the cross for me."

Second, I said, "I confess those things in my life that aren't pleasing to You and ask You to forgive me and cleanse me." (The Bible says, "Though your sins be as scarlet they shall be as white as snow.")

Third, I said, "Right now, in the best way I know how, I open the door of my heart and life and trust You as my Savior and Lord. Take over the control of my life. Change me from the inside out. Make me the type of person You created me to be."

The last thing I prayed was, "Thank You for coming into my life by faith." It was a faith based not upon ignorance but upon evidence, upon the facts of history and God's Word.

I'm sure you've heard various religious people talking about their "bolt of lightning." Well, after I prayed, nothing happened. I mean, nothing. And I still haven't sprouted wings. In fact, after I made that decision, I felt worse. I literally felt I was going to vomit. I felt sick deep down. "Oh, no, what'd you get sucked into now?" I wondered. I really felt I'd gone off the deep end (and I'm sure some people think I did!).

I can tell you one thing: In six months to a year and a half I found out that I hadn't gone off the deep end. My life *was* changed. I was in a debate with the head of the history department at a midwestern university and I said my life had been changed, and he interrupted me with, "McDowell, are you trying to tell us that God really changed your life in the twentieth century? What areas?"

After forty-five minutes he said, "Okay, that's enough."

One area I told him about was my restlessness. I always had to be occupied. I had to be over at my girl's place or somewhere else in a rap session. I'd walk across the campus and my mind was like a whirlwind with conflicts bouncing around the walls. I'd sit down and try to study or cogitate and I couldn't. But a few months after I made that decision for Christ, a kind of mental peace developed. Don't misunderstand. I'm not talking about the absence of conflict. What I found in this relationship with Jesus wasn't so much the absence of conflict but the ability to cope with it. I wouldn't trade that for anything in the world.

Another area that started to change was my bad temper. I used to blow my stack if somebody just looked at me cross-eyed. I still have the scars from almost killing a man my first year in the university. My temper was such a part of me that I didn't consciously seek to change it. Then one day I arrived at a crisis of losing my temper only to find it was gone! Only once in fourteen years have I lost my temper—and when I blew it that time, I made up for about six years!

There's another area of which I'm not proud. I mention it only because a lot of people need to have the same change in their lives, and I found the source of change: a relationship with the resurrected, living Christ. That area is hatred. I had a lot of hatred in my life. It wasn't something outwardly manifested, but there was a kind of inward grinding. I was ticked off with people, with things, with issues. Like so many other people, I was insecure. Every time I met someone different from me, he became a threat to me.

But I hated one man more than anyone else in the world. My father. I hated his guts. To me he was the town alcoholic. If you're from a small town and one of your parents is an alcoholic, you know what I'm talking about. Everybody knows. My friends would come to high school and make jokes about my father being downtown. They didn't think it bothered me. I was like other people, laughing on the outside, but let me tell you, I was crying on the inside. I'd go out in the barn and see my mother beaten so badly she couldn't get up, lying in the manure behind the cows. When we had friends over, I would take my father out, tie him up in the barn, and park the car up around the silo. We would tell our friends he'd had to go somewhere. I don't think anyone could have hated anyone more than I hated my father.

After I made that decision for Christ – maybe five months later – a love from God through Jesus Christ entered my life and was so strong it took that hatred and turned it upside down. I was able to look my father squarely in the eyes and say, "Dad, I love you." And I really meant it. After some of the things I'd done, that shook him up.

Shortly after I transferred to a private university, I was in a serious car accident. My neck in traction, I was taken home. I'll never forget my father coming into my room. He asked me, "Son, how can you love a father like me?"

I said, "Dad, six months ago I despised you." Then I shared with him my conclusions about Jesus Christ: "Dad, I let Christ come into my life. I can't explain it completely but as a result of that relationship I've found the capacity to love and accept not only you but also other people, just the way they are."

Forty-five minutes later one of the greatest thrills in my life occurred. Somebody in my own family, someone who knew me so well I couldn't pull the wool over his eyes, said to me, "Son, if God can do in my life what I've seen him do in yours, then I want to give Him the opportunity." Right there my father prayed with me and trusted Christ.

Usually the changes take place over several days, weeks, or months, even a year. My life was changed in about six months to a year and a half. The life of my father was changed right before my eyes. It was as if somebody reached down and turned on a light bulb. I've never seen such a rapid change before or since. My father touched whiskey only once after that. He got it as far as his lips and that was it. I've come to one conclusion. A relationship with Jesus Christ changes lives.

You can laugh at Christianity; you can mock and ridicule it – but it works. If you decide to trust Christ, start watching your attitudes and actions, because Jesus Christ is in the business of changing lives.

Christianity is not something you shove down somebody's throat or force on someone. You've got your life to live and I've got mine. All I can do is tell you what I've learned. After that, it's your decision.

Perhaps the prayer I prayed will help you: "Lord Jesus, I need You. Thank You for dying on the cross for me. Forgive me and cleanse me. Right this moment I trust You as my Savior and Lord. Make me the type of person You created me to be. In Christ's name. Amen."

The remainder of this book contains some of the most important facts I discovered when I originally set out to disprove Christianity and ended up becoming a Christian. Other clear evidence discovered since that time has also been included.

If you have not yet come to know Christ personally, consider – with an open heart and an objective mind – the information provided here. It is my prayer that you will make this greatest of all discoveries.

If you already have a personal relationship with Christ, be encouraged by what you read here to share your faith boldly with other people. This information will give you "A Ready Defense" when witnessing and dealing with others who perhaps are like I was. Helping other people come to know Christ is one of the most thrilling adventures a Christian can experience.

THE BIBLE
Its Reliability

Part One CAN IT BE TRUSTED?

Part Two ANSWERING THE BIBLE'S CRITICS

Part One

CAN IT BE TRUSTED?

CHAPTER 2 Is the Bible Relevant Today?

Have you ever noticed that some things relevant to one generation are completely outmoded and useless to another? Can you imagine how incredibly difficult it would be to write a book that would be applicable, not only to all cultures and nationalities but to all generations as well?

Our purpose here is to present compelling evidence that the Bible, though written centuries ago, **is** pertinent to us today. The Bible repeatedly speaks in terms that involve all generations. Jesus claimed, "Heaven and earth will pass away, but My words shall not pass away" (Matthew 24:35). The prophet Isaiah said, "The grass withers, the flower fades, but the word of our God stands forever" (Isaiah 40:8).

The only reason the Bible can be relevant today, as well as at all other times, is that it is true. It claims within itself to come from an all-knowing, all-powerful, personal and only existing God. If it did not come from the one, true, living God, we could not expect it to be true or relevant to all people for all time. So consider the following:

Does the Bible Give Evidence of Being From God?

(R/77-79)

To be considered to have come from an all-powerful God, a book must meet certain requirements. **First**, it must be transmitted to us accurately from the time it was originally written so that we may have an exact representation of what God said and did. **Also,** it must be correct when it deals with historical personages and events. A book that confuses names, dates and events has no right to claim it comes from an infallible God. **Furthermore,** any revelation from God should be without any scientific absurdities which would betray that it came by mere human authorship.

At the very least, any work coming from God must meet the above requirements. The Bible does this and much, much more.

The text of the Bible has been transmitted accurately. In fact, there is more evidence for the reliability of the text of the New Testament as an accurate reflection of what was initially written than there is for any ten pieces of classical literature put together. We may rest assured that what we have today is a correct representation of what was originally given.

If one will judge the New Testament documents with the same standards or tests applied to any one of the Greek classics, the evidence overwhelmingly favors the New Testament. If a person contends that we have a reliable text of the classics, then he would be forced to admit we have a reliable text of the New Testament.

Not only does the New Testament text have far superior evidence for reliability than the classics, but it also is in better textual shape than the thirty-seven plays of William Shakespeare written in the seventeenth century, after the invention of printing. In every one of Shakespeare's plays there are *lacunae* (gaps) in the printed text, where we have no idea what originally was said. This forces textual scholars to make conjectural emendations (a fancy term for "good guesses") to fill in the blanks. With the abundance of existing manuscripts (handwritten copies) of the New Testament (more than 25,000), we know nothing has been lost through the transmission of the text.

The history recorded in the Scriptures also proves to be accurate. As far as we have been able to determine, the names, places and events mentioned in the Bible have been recorded accurately.

For example, the book of Acts, once considered spurious, has been vindicated by modern discoveries. As the Roman historian A. N. Sherwin-White says, "For Acts the confirmation of historicity is overwhelming. . . . Any attempt to reject its basic historicity even in matters of detail must now appear absurd. Roman historians have long taken it for granted." 120/189

Those who contend that the Bible is unreliable historically are not professional historians. This is the reason the great archaeologist William F. Albright said, "All radical schools in New Testament criticism which have existed in the past or which exist today are prearchaeological, and are, therefore, since they were built 'in der Luft' (in the air), quite antiquated today." 4/29 The testimony of the historical evidence is that the Bible can be trusted as an accurate document.

Where the Bible speaks on matters of science, it does so with simple yet correct terms devoid of absurdities. While some nonbiblical accounts of the formation of the universe and other scientific matters border on the ridiculous, the Scriptures nowhere are guilty of this. This is not what would be expected from a book written by men during prescientific times.

Matters dealing with science also are written with restraint (such as the Genesis account of creation). The biblical narrative is accurate and concise in direct contrast to the crude Babylonian story which contends the earth was made from a dismembered part of one of the gods after in-fighting in heaven.

Likewise, the flood of Noah's day is given in simple but accurate terms which are sensible scientifically. (See *The Genesis Flood,* by John C. Whitcomb and Henry Morris [Philadelphia: Presbyterian and Reformed Publishing Company, 1961], regarding such matters as the seaworthiness of the Ark, etc.) The clarity and restraint which the Bible shows toward the scientific is exactly what we should expect of a book inspired by God.

Not only does the Bible meet the minimum requirements for being a book coming from God, but it also contains powerful additional evidence of having a divine origin. In the remainder of this section, we will explore some of the evidence which supports the claim the Bible makes that it is the Word of God.

CHAPTER 3 The Uniqueness of the Bible

(E/15-24)

Over and over again, like a broken record, I hear the question, "Oh, you don't read the Bible, do you?" Sometimes it is phrased, "Why, the Bible is just another book. You ought to read . . . ," etc.

There is the student who is proud because his Bible is on the shelf with his other books, perhaps dusty and not broken in—but it is there with the other "greats." Then there is the professor who degrades the Bible before his students and snickers at the thought of reading it, let alone of having it in one's library.

The above questions and observations bothered me when I tried, as a non-Christian, to refute the Bible as God's Word to man. I finally came to the conclusion that those sayings were simply trite phrases from either biased, prejudiced or simply unknowledgeable men and women.

The Bible should be on the top shelf all by itself. The Bible is "unique." That's it! The ideas I grappled with to describe the Bible are summed up by the word *unique*.

Webster must have had this "Book of books" in mind when he wrote the definition for *unique:* "1. one and only; single; sole. 2. different from all others; having no like or equal."

Professor M. Montiero-Williams, former Boden professor of Sanskrit, spent 42 years studying Eastern books and, in comparing them with the Bible, said,

> Pile them, if you will, on the left side of your study table; but place your own Holy Bible on the right side—all by itself, all alone—and with a wide gap between them. For . . . there is a gulf between it and the so-called sacred books of the East, which severs the one from the other utterly, hopelessly, and forever . . . a veritable gulf which cannot be bridged over by any science or religious thought. 33/314-15

The Bible is unique, "different from all others," in the following ways (plus a multitude more):

Unique in Its Continuity

Here is a book . . .

1. written over a 1,500 year span;
2. written over 40 generations;
3. written by more than 40 authors, from every walk of life—including kings, peasants, philosophers, fishermen, poets, statesmen, scholars, etc.:
   - Moses, a political leader, trained in the universities of Egypt
   - Peter, a fisherman
   - Amos, a herdsman
   - Joshua, a military general
   - Nehemiah, a cupbearer
   - Daniel, a prime minister
   - Luke, a doctor
   - Solomon, a king
   - Matthew, a tax collector
   - Paul, a rabbi
4. written in different places:
   - Moses in the wilderness
   - Jeremiah in a dungeon
   - Daniel on a hillside and in a palace
   - Paul inside prison walls
   - Luke while traveling
   - John on the isle of Patmos
   - others in the rigors of a military campaign
5. written at different times:

David in times of war

Solomon in times of peace

6. written during different moods:

   some writing from the heights of joy and others from the depths of sorrow and despair

7. written on three continents:

   Asia, Africa and Europe

8. written in three languages:

   Hebrew, the language of the Old Testament (in 2 Kings 18:26-28 called "the language of Judah," in Isaiah 19:18 called "the language of Canaan").

   Aramaic, the "common language" of the Near East until the time of Alexander the Great (6th century B.C.—4th century B.C.). 54/218

   Greek, the New Testament language (the international language at the time of Christ).

9. Finally, its subject matter includes hundreds of controversial topics. Yet, the biblical authors spoke with harmony and continuity from Genesis to Revelation. There is one unfolding story: "God's redemption of man."

   Geisler and Nix put it this way:

   > The "Paradise Lost" of Genesis becomes the "Paradise Regained" of Revelation. Whereas the gate to the tree of life is closed in Genesis, it is opened forevermore in Revelation. 54/24

   F. F. Bruce observes:

   > The writings themselves belong to a great variety of literary types. They include history, law (civil, criminal, ethical, ritual, sanitary), religious poetry, didactic treatises, lyric poetry, parable and allegory, biography, personal correspondence, personal memoirs and diaries, in addition to the distinctively biblical types of prophecy and apocalyptic. . . . For all that, the Bible is not simply an anthology; there is a unity which binds the whole together. An anthology is compiled by an anthologist, but no anthologist compiled the Bible. 28/88

A representative of the *Great Books of the Western World* came to my house recruiting salesmen for their series. He spread out their chart and spent five minutes talking about the series. Then we spent an hour and a half talking to him about the Greatest Book.

I challenged him to pick just ten of the authors, all from one walk of life, one generation, one place, one time, one mood, one continent, one language and just one controversial subject. I asked him: "Would those ten authors agree?"

He paused and then replied, "No!"

"What would you have?"

Immediately he said, "A conglomeration."

Two days later he committed his life to Christ.

Why all this? Very simple! Any person sincerely seeking truth would at least consider a book with the above unique qualifications.

Unique in Its Circulation

The Bible has been read by more people and published in more languages than any other book in history. More copies of its entirety and more portions and selections have been produced than any other book. Some people will argue that in a designated month or year more of a certain other book was sold. However, overall, the circulation of absolutely no other book even begins to compare with that of the Scriptures. In fact, the first major book printed was the Latin Vulgate. It was printed on Gütenberg's press. 61/478-80

Hy Pickering says that about thirty years ago, for the British and Foreign Bible Society to meet its demands, it had to publish "one copy every three seconds day and night; 22 copies every minute day and night; 1,369 copies every hour day and night; 32,876 copies every day in the year."

According to *The Cambridge History of the Bible*, "No other book has known anything approaching this constant circulation." 61/479

The critic is right: "This doesn't prove the Bible is the Word of God!" It does show factually, though, that the Bible is unique.

> **NOTE:** See *Evidence That Demands a Verdict, Vol I,* p. 18, for publication figures up through 1966.

Unique in Its Translation

The Bible was one of the first major books translated (Septuagint: Greek translation of the Hebrew Old Testament, ca 250 B.C.). 126/1147

The Bible has been translated and retranslated, and paraphrased, more than any other book in existence.

Encyclopedia Britannica says that "by 1966 the whole Bible has appeared . . . in 240 languages and dialects . . . one or more whole books of the Bible in 739 additional ones." 42/588

Three thousand Bible translators between 1950 and 1960 were at work translating the Scriptures. 42/588

The Bible factually stands unique (one of a kind) in its translation.

Unique in Its Survival

1. Survival through time

Being written on material that perishes and having to be copied and recopied for hundreds of years before the invention of the printing press did not diminish the style, correctness, or existence of the Bible. Compared with other ancient writings, it has more manuscript evidence than any ten pieces of classical literature combined.

John Warwick Montgomery says:

> To be skeptical of the resultant text of the New Testament books is to allow all of classical antiquity to slip into obscurity, for no documents of the ancient period are as well attested bibliographically as the New Testament. 95/29

Bernard Ramm speaks of the accuracy and the number of biblical manuscripts:

> Jews preserved it as no other manuscript has ever been preserved. With their massora (parva, magna and finalis) [methods of counting] they kept tabs on every letter, syllable, word and paragraph. They had special classes of men within their culture whose sole duty was to preserve and transmit these documents with practically perfect fidelity—scribes, lawyers, massoretes. Who ever counted the letters and syllables and words of Plato or Aristotle? Cicero or Seneca? 108/230-31

2. Survival through persecution

The Bible has withstood vicious attacks of its enemies as no other book has. Many have tried to burn it, ban it, and "outlaw it, from the days of the Roman emperors to present-day Communist-dominated countries." 108/232

Sidney Collett in *All About the Bible* says,

> Voltaire, the noted French infidel who died in 1778, said that in one hundred years from his time Christianity would be swept from existence and passed into history. But what happened? Voltaire has passed into history, while the circulation of the Bible continues to increase in almost all parts of the world, carrying blessing wherever it goes. 33/63

Concerning the boast of Voltaire on the extinction of Christianity and the Bible in a hundred years, Geisler and Nix point out that "only fifty years after [Voltaire's] death the Geneva Bible Society used his press and his house to produce stacks of Bibles." 54/123-24 WHAT AN IRONY OF HISTORY!

The Bible is unique in its survival. This does not prove the Bible is the Word of God—but it does prove it stands alone among books. Anyone seeking truth ought to consider a book that has the above qualifications.

3. Survival through criticism

H. L. Hastings, cited by John W. Lea, has forcibly illustrated the unique way the Bible has withstood the attacks of infidelity and skepticism:

> Infidels for eighteen hundred years have been refuting and overthrowing this book, and yet it stands today as solid as a rock. Its circulation increases, and it is more loved and cherished and read today than ever before. . . . When the French monarch proposed the persecution of the Christians in his dominion, an old statesman and warrior said to him, "Sire, the Church of God is an anvil that has worn out many hammers." So the hammers of the infidels have been pecking away at this book for ages, but the hammers are worn out, and the anvil still endures. If the book had not been the book of God, men would have destroyed it long ago. Emperors and popes, kings and priests, princes and rulers have all tried their hand at it; they die and the book still lives. 83/17-18

Bernard Ramm adds:

> A thousand times over, the death knell of the Bible has been sounded, the funeral procession formed, the inscription cut on the tombstone, and committal read. But somehow the corpse never stays put.
>
> No other book has been so chopped, knived, sifted, scrutinized, and vilified. What book on philosophy or religion or psychology or *belles lettres* of classical or modern times has been subject to such a mass attack as the Bible? with such venom and skepticism? with such thoroughness and erudition? upon every chapter, line and tenet?
>
> The Bible is still loved by millions, read by millions and studied by millions. 108/232-33

The Bible is unique in facing its critics. There is no other book in all of literature like it. Again, a person looking for truth would certainly consider a book that has the above qualifications.

NOTE: For detailed evidence on how the Bible has withstood its critics, see Part II of this section, "Answering the Bible's Critics."

Unique in Its Teaching

1. Prophecy

Wilbur Smith, who compiled a personal library of 25,000 volumes, concludes that the Bible

> is the only volume ever produced by man, or a group of men, in which is to be found a large body of prophecies relating to individual nations, to Israel, to all the peoples of the earth, to certain cities, and to the coming of one who was to be the Messiah. The ancient world had many different devices for determining the future, known as divination, but not in the entire gamut of Greek and Latin literature, even though they use the words prophet and prophecy, can we find any real specific prophecy of a great historic event to come in the distant future, nor any prophecy of a Savior to arise from the human race . . .

> Mohammedanism cannot point to any prophecies of the coming of Mohammed uttered hundreds of years before his birth. Neither can the founders of any cult in this country rightly identify any ancient text specifically foretelling their appearance. 121/9-10

2. History

The distinguished archaeologist, Professor Albright, begins his classic essay, *The Biblical Period*:

> Hebrew national tradition excels all others in its clear picture of tribal and family origins. In Egypt and Babylonia, in Assyria and Phoenicia, in Greece and Rome, we look in vain for anything comparable. There is nothing like it in the tradition of the Germanic peoples. Neither India nor China can produce anything similar, since their earliest historical memories are literary deposits of distorted dynastic tradition, with no trace of the herdsman or peasant behind the demigod or king with whom their records begin. Neither in the oldest Indic historical writings (the Puranas) nor in the earliest Greek historians is there a hint of the fact that both Indo-Aryans and Hellenes were once nomads who immigrated into their later abodes from the north. The Assyrians, to be sure, remembered vaguely that their earliest rulers, whose names they recalled without any details about their deeds, were tent dwellers, but whence they came had long been forgotten. 46/3

"The Table of Nations" in Genesis 10, according to Albright, "remains an astonishingly accurate document." 3/70*ff.*

3. Personalities

The Bible deals very frankly with the sins of its characters. Read the biographies today, and see how they try to cover up, overlook or ignore the shady side of people. Take the great literary geniuses; most are painted as saints. The Bible does not do it that way. It simply tells it like it is.

Unique in Its Influence on Surrounding Literature

Cleland B. McAfee writes in *The Greatest English Classic:*

> If every Bible in any considerable city were destroyed, the Book could be restored in all its essential parts from the quotations on the shelves of the city public library. There are works, covering almost all the great literary writers, devoted especially to showing how much the Bible has influenced them. 86/134

Bernard Ramm adds:

> From the Apostolic Fathers dating from A.D. 95 to modern times is one great literary river inspired by the Bible—Bible dictionaries, Bible encyclopedias, Bible lexicons, Bible atlases, and Bible geographies. These may be taken as a starter. Then at random, we may mention the vast bibliographies around theology, religious education, hymnology, missions, the biblical languages, church history, religious biography, devotional works, commentaries, philosophy of religion, evidences, apologetics, and on and on.

There seems to be an endless number. 108/239

The Obvious Conclusion

The above does not prove that the Bible is the Word of God, but to me it proves that it is unique ("different from all others; having no like or equal").

A professor remarked to me, "If you are an intelligent person, you will read the one book that has drawn more attention than any other, if you are searching for the truth."

CHAPTER 4 *Who Decided What to Accept?*

The Canon (E/29)

The word *canon* comes from the root word *reed* (English word *cane;* Hebrew form *ganeh* and Greek *Kanon*). The reed was used as a measuring rod and eventually meant "standard."

Origen used the word "*canon* to denote what we call the 'rule of faith,' the standard by which we are to measure and evaluate." Later it meant a "list" or "index." 28/95

The word *canon* applied to Scripture means "an officially accepted list of books." 40/31

One thing to keep in mind is that the church did not create the canon or books included in what we call Scripture. Instead, the church recognized the books that were inspired from their inception. They were inspired by God when written.

Old Testament Canon (E/29-33)

The Jewish sacrificial system was ended by the destruction of Jerusalem and the Temple in A.D. 70. Even though the Old Testament canon was settled in the Jewish mind long before that year, there was a need for something more definitive. The Jews were scattered, and they needed to determine which books were the authoritative Word of God because of the many extra-scriptural writings and the decentralization. The Jews became a people of one Book and it was this Book that kept them together.

Christianity started to blossom, and many writings of the Christians were beginning to be circulated. The Jews needed to expose them vividly and exclude them from their writings and use in the synagogues.

The following is the breakdown of the Jewish Old Testament canon:

The Law
(Torah)

1. Genesis
2. Exodus
3. Leviticus
4. Numbers
5. Deuteronomy

The Prophets (Nebhim)

A. Former Prophets

1. Joshua
2. Judges
3. Samuel
4. Kings

B. Latter Prophets

1. Isaiah
2. Jeremiah
3. Ezekiel
4. The Twelve

The Writings
(Kethubhim or Hagiographa [GK])

A. Poetical Books

1. Psalms
2. Proverbs
3. Job

B. Five Rolls *(Megilloth)*

1. Song of Songs
2. Ruth
3. Lamentations
4. Esther
5. Ecclesiastes

C. Historical Books

1. Daniel
2. Ezra-Nehemiah
3. Chronicles

Although the Christian church has the same Old Testament canon, the number of books differs because we divide Samuel, Kings and Chronicles into two books each; the Jews also consider the Minor Prophets as one book.

The order of books also differs. The Protestant Old Testament follows a topical order instead of an official order. 54/22

Christ's Witness to the Old Testament Canon

Luke 24:44: In the upper room Jesus told the disciples that "all things must be fulfilled, which were written in the law of Moses, and the Prophets, and the Psalms concerning Me." With these words, "He indicated the three sections into which the Hebrew Bible was divided—the Law, the Prophets, and the 'Writings' (here called 'the Psalms' probably because the Book of Psalms is the first and longest book in this third section)." **28/96**

Luke 11:51 (also Matthew 23:35): "From the blood of Abel to the blood of Zechariah." Jesus here confirms His witness to the extent of the Old Testament canon. Abel, as everyone knows, was the first martyr (Genesis 4:8). Zechariah is the last martyr to be named (in the Hebrew Old Testament order. See listing above—2C, 1D), having been stoned while prophesying to the people "in the court of the house of the Lord" (2 Chronicles 24:21). Genesis was the first book in the Hebrew canon and Chronicles the last book. Jesus basically said, "From Genesis to Chronicles"; or, according to our order, "From Genesis to Malachi." **28/96**

Extra-Biblical Writers' Testimonies

The earliest record of a three-fold division of the Old Testament is in the prologue of the book *Ecclesiasticus* (ca 130 B.C.). The prologue, written by the author's grandson, calls it: "The Law, and the Prophets and the other books of the fathers." There existed three definite divisions of Scripture. **136/71**

Josephus, the Jewish historian (end of the first century A.D.), writes:

> How firmly we have given credit to those books of our own nation is evident by what we do; for during so many ages as have already passed, no one has been so bold as either to add anything to them, to take anything from them, or to make any change in them; but it becomes natural to all Jews, immediately and from their very birth, to esteem those books to contain divine doctrines, and to persist in them, and, if occasion be, willingly to die for them. For it is no new thing for our captives, many of them in number, and frequently in time, to be seen to endure racks and deaths of all kinds upon the theatres, that they may not be obliged to say one word against our laws, and the records that contain them. **76/609**

Babylonian Talmud, Tractate "Sanhedrin" VII-VIII, 24: "After the latter prophets Haggai, Zechariah, [and] Malachi, the Holy Spirit departed from Israel."

The threefold division of the present Jewish text (with 11 books in the Writings) is from the Mishnah (Baba Bathra tractate, fifth century A.D.). **54/20**

The New Testament Witness to the Old Testament as Sacred Scripture

Matthew 21:42; 22:29; 26:54,56

Luke 24

John 5:39; 7:38; 10:35
Acts 17:2,11; 18:28
Romans 1:2, 4:3; 9:17; 10:11; 11:2; 15:4; 16:26
1 Corinthians 15:3,4
Galatians 3:8; 3:22; 4:30
1 Timothy 5:18
2 Timothy 3:16
2 Peter 1:20,21; 3:16

The Council of Jamnia

Many students remark: "Sure, I know about the canon. The leaders got together in a council and decided which books best helped them and then forced the followers to accept them." This is about as far away from the truth as one can get. (Of course, for some people, distance is no problem in the space age.)

The comments of F. F. Bruce and H. H. Rowley are appropriate here. F. F. Bruce:

> When the destruction of the city and Temple was imminent, a great rabbi belonging to the school of Hillel in the Pharisaic party—Yochanan ben Zakkai by name—obtained permission from the Romans to reconstitute the Sanhedrin on a purely spiritual basis at Jabneh or Jamnia, between Joppa and Azotus (Ashod). Some of the discussions which went on at Jamnia were handed down by oral transmission and ultimately recorded in the rabbinical writings. Among their debates they considered whether canonical recognition should be accorded to the books of Proverbs, Ecclesiastes, the Song of Songs and Esther. Objections have been raised against these books on various grounds; Esther, for example, did not contain the name of God, and Ecclesiastes was none too easy to square with contemporary orthodoxy. But the upshot of the Jamnia debates was the firm acknowledgement of all these books as Holy Scripture. 28/97

H. H. Rowley:

> It is, indeed, doubtful how far it is correct to speak of the Council of Jamnia. We know of discussions that took place there amongst the Rabbis, but we know of no formal or binding decisions that were made, and it is probable that the discussions were informal, though nonetheless helping to crystallize and to fix more firmly the Jewish tradition. 117/170

New Testament Canon (HW/90-92, 104; E/33-36)

Skeptics often charge: How can Christians believe to be the Word of God twenty-seven books designated as Scripture by fallible men at a fourth-century council? But this question presents a distorted view of the New Testament canon. Long before councils were ever convened, Christians, especially local church elders, were constantly collecting, evaluating and deciding which of the many writings of their day carried the authority of the apostles (Cf. Colossians 4:16; 2 Peter 3:15,16). The question asked of any writing to be read in the churches was: To what extent is this book (epistle, narrative, apocalypse, or gospel) an authentic and pure representation of the life and teachings of Jesus and His apostles? Thus, as Donald Guthrie puts it, "The content of the canon was determined by general usage, not by authoritarian pronouncement." 64

F. F. Bruce states that

> when at last a church council—The Synod of Hippo in A.D. 393—listed the twenty-seven books of the New Testament, it did not confer upon them any authority which they did not already possess, but simply recorded their previously established canonicity. (The ruling of the Synod of Hippo was repromulgated four years later by the Third Synod of Carthage.) 28/113

Geisler and Nix conclude, "Canonicity is *determined* or fixed authoritatively by God; it is merely *discovered* by man." 54/221

First century Christians saw in the words of Jesus and the writings of the apostles an authority of divine inspiration equaling that of the Old Testament Scriptures. This was only natural, for if Jesus was the long-awaited Messiah, then His words should be every bit as authoritative as those of Moses and the prophets of old. Thus, the gospel records, which contained the reports of His words and actions, gained credibility over the first century as eyewitnesses could orally verify the truth of what was written. Further, the deaths of the apostles elevated the importance of their writings as Christians saw the need to preserve what the apostles had reported. Prior to this time, in accordance with common Jewish practice, "Oral teaching was regarded more highly than written testimony." 63

As time passed, an increasing circulation of books recognized as either not in accordance with the apostle's teachings (i.e., heretical) or not written by them even though an apostle's name may have been attached to them (i.e., pseudonymous), motivated the believers to become increasingly concerned about identifying the authentic works of the apostles or those entrusted with their teachings (namely Mark for Peter and Luke for Paul). The very fact that many heretical or unauthentic writings falsely attached the names of various apostles as their authors demonstrates how eager the early Christians were to know that the teaching they received from books read in their churches actually did come from the apostles of Jesus.

Christians today can be thankful that the final formation of the New Testament canon was such a long and difficult process. It was so difficult, in fact, that there was heated debate over whether Hebrews, James, 2 and 3 John, 2 Peter, Jude and Revelation were truly canonical. But the close scrutiny to which the New Testament books were subjected before being universally accepted as authentic should give readers today increased confidence in the reliability of these books and the things which they report and teach. 88/92

Tests of a Book for In·lusion in the Canon (E/29)

There were possibly five guiding principles used to determine whether or not a New Testament book was canonical or Scripture. Geisler and Nix record these five principles: 54/141

Is it authoritative—did it come from the hand of God? (Does this book come with a divine "thus saith the Lord"?)

Is it prophetic—was it written by a man of God?

Is it authentic? [The fathers had the policy: "If in doubt, throw it out." This enhanced the "validity of their discernment of canonical books."]

Is it dynamic—did it come with the life-transforming power of God?

Was it received, collected, read and used—was it accepted by the people of God?

Peter acknowledged Paul's work as Scripture that was parallel to Old Testament Scripture (2 Peter 3:16).

The "Apocrypha" and "Pseudepigrapha"

Apocrypha: The term, from the Greek word *apokruphos,* means "hidden or concealed."

In the fourth century Jerome was the first to call these writings "Apocrypha." The Apocrypha consists of the books that were added to the Old Testament by the Roman Catholic church but that Protestants say are not canonical. 87/33

There is also another group of writings often called the New Testament Apocrypha. The term *apocrypha* is appropriate for many of these works for they often purport to tell of secret or hidden details of the lives and teachings of Jesus and His disciples.

Pseudepigrapha: The name comes from a Greek word meaning "false writings." It normally applies to books related to the Old Testament but also has been used to apply to a number of New Testament apocryphal works and other works which falsely attribute their contents to an apostolic author. The term *pseudonymous,* meaning "false name," is used also for these works since they falsely claim to be written by true prophets or apostles. 89/90-91

Why Not Canonical?

Unger's Bible Dictionary gives reasons for the exclusion of these writings:

"They abound in historical and geographical inaccuracies and anachronisms.

"They teach doctrines which are false and foster practices which are at variance with inspired Scripture.

"They resort to literary types and display an artificiality of subject matter and styling out of keeping with inspired Scripture.

"They lack the distinctive elements which give genuine Scripture their divine character, such as prophetic power and poetic and religious feeling." 126/70

Historical Testimony of Their Exclusion

Geisler and Nix give a succession of ten testimonies of antiquity against accepting the Apocrypha:

1. Philo, Alexandrian Jewish philosopher (20 B.C.–A.D. 40), quoted the Old Testament prolifically and even recognized the threefold division, but he never quoted from the Apocrypha as inspired.
2. Josephus (A.D. 30–100), Jewish historian, explicitly excludes the Apocrypha, numbering the books of the Old Testament as 22. Neither does he quote these books as Scripture.
3. Jesus and the New Testament writers never once quote the Apocrypha although there are hundreds of quotes and references to almost all of the canonical books of the Old Testament.
4. The Jewish scholars of Jamnia (A.D. 90) did not recognize the Apocrypha.
5. No canon or council of the Christian church for the first four centuries recognized the Apocrypha as inspired.
6. Many of the great fathers of the early church spoke out against the Apocrypha, for example, Origen, Cyril of Jerusalem, Athanasius.
7. Jerome (340–420), the great scholar and translator of the Vulgate, rejected the Apocrypha as part of the canon. He disputed across the Mediterranean with Augustine on this point. He at first refused even to translate the Apocryphal books into Latin, but later he made a hurried translation of a few of them. After his death, and literally "over his dead body," the Apocryphal books were brought into his Latin Vulgate directly from the Old Latin Version.
8. Many Roman Catholic scholars through the Reformation period rejected the Apocrypha.
9. Luther and the Reformers rejected the canonicity of the Apocrypha.
10. Not until A.D. 1546, in a polemical action at the Counter Reformation Council of Trent, did the Apocryphal books receive full canonical status by the Roman Catholic Church. 54/173

You probably have asked or have been asked, "How can we trust gospel accounts written years after Jesus' death? After all, everyone knows what happens to a message when you whisper it around in a circle." The New

Testament apocryphal and pseudepigraphal writings demonstrate that much was being said and written about Jesus in the first four centuries, some of it true, some not. It is as though a handful of people in an auditorium are given the same message to spread to everyone else in the auditorium. Each person has the freedom to verify with others what the true, original message was. Under these circumstances, one would expect that those who wanted to get the message right certainly could. 89/104

CHAPTER 5 *Is the Bible Reliable?*

(E/39)

What we are establishing here is the historical reliability of the Scripture, not its inspiration.

Often when I talk with someone about the Bible they sarcastically reply that "you can't trust what the Bible says. Why, it was written almost two thousand years ago. It's full of errors and discrepancies."

I reply that I believe I **can** trust the Scriptures. Then I describe an incident that took place during a lecture in a history class. I stated that I believed there was more evidence for the reliability of the New Testament than for almost any ten pieces of classical literature put together.

The professor sat over in the corner snickering, as if to say, "Oh, gee—come on."

I said, "What are you snickering about?"

He said, "The audacity to make the statement in a history class that the New Testament is reliable. That's ridiculous."

Well, I appreciate it when somebody says something like that because I always like to ask this one question (and I've never had a positive response), "Tell me, sir, as a historian, where are the tests that you apply to any piece of literature of history to determine if it's accurate or reliable?"

The amazing thing was he didn't have any tests to apply.

I answered, "I have some tests."

I believe that the historical reliability of the Scripture should be tested by the same criteria used on all historical documents. Military historian C. Sanders lists and explains the basic principles of historiography: (1) the bibliographical test; (2) the internal evidence test; and (3) the external evidence test. 118/143*ff.*

NOTE: The bibliographical test for the New and Old Testaments is given below, followed by some brief comments on the internal evidence test. The remaining topics of part I: "The Bible—I Trust It" may be classified under the external evidence test. Finally, almost all of the topics of part II: "Answering the Bible's Critics" may be applied toward the internal evidence test.

Bibliographical Test for the Reliability of the New Testament (E/39-51)

The bibliographical test is an examination of the textual transmission by which documents reach us. In other words, since we do not have the original documents, how reliable are the copies we have in regard to the number of manuscripts (MSS) and the time interval between the original and existing copies? 96/26

F. E. Peters points out that "on the basis of manuscript tradition alone, the works that made up the Christians' New Testament were the most frequently copied and widely circulated books of antiquity." 102/50

Manuscript Evidence of the New Testament

There are now more than 5,300 known Greek manuscripts of the New Testament. Add over 10,000 Latin Vulgate and at least 9,300 other early versions and we have more than 24,000 manuscript copies of portions of the New Testament in existence.

No other document of antiquity even begins to approach such numbers and attestation. In comparison, the *Iliad* by Homer is second with only 643 manuscripts that still survive. The first complete preserved text of Homer dates from the thirteenth century. 84/145

NOTE: For a breakdown of the number of surviving manuscripts and sources to consult, see *Evidence That Demands a Verdict, Vol I,* p. 40.

Sir Frederic G. Kenyon, who was the director and principal librarian of the British Museum, and second to none in authority for issuing statements about MSS, says,

> Besides number, the manuscripts of the New Testament differ from those of the classical authors, and this time the difference is clear gain. In no other case is the interval of time between composition of the book and the date of the earliest extant [existing] manuscripts so short as in that of the New Testament. The books of the New Testament were written in the latter part of the first century; the earliest extant manuscripts (trifling scraps excepted) are of the fourth century—say from 250 to 300 years later.
>
> This may sound a considerable interval, but it is nothing to that which parts most of the great classical authors from their earliest manuscripts. We believe that we have in all essentials an accurate text of the seven extant plays of Sophocles; yet the earliest substantial manuscript upon which it is based was written more than 1400 years after the poet's death. 80/4

Kenyon continues in *The Bible and Archaeology:*

> The interval then between the dates of original composition and the earliest extant evidence becomes so small as to be in fact negligible, and the last foundation for any doubt that the Scriptures have come down to us substantially as they were written has now been removed. Both the authenticity and the general integrity of the books of the New Testament may be regarded as finally established. 79/288

The New Testament Compared With Other Works of Antiquity

The Manuscript Comparison

F. F. Bruce in *The New Testament Documents* vividly pictures the comparison between the New Testament and ancient historical writings:

> Perhaps we can appreciate how wealthy the New Testament is in manuscript attestation if we compare the textual material for other ancient historical works. For Caesar's Gallic Wars (composed between 58 and 50 B.C.) there are several extant MSS, but only nine or ten are good, and the oldest is some 900 years later than Caesar's day. Of the 142 books of the Roman history of Livy (59 B.C.—A.D. 17), only 35 survive; these are known to us from not more than 20 MSS of any consequence, only one of which, and that containing fragments of Books III—VI, is as old as the fourth century. Of the 14 books of the Histories of Tacitus (ca A.D. 100) only four and a half survive; of the 16 books of his Annals, 10 survive in full and two in part. The text of these extant portions of his two great historical works depends entirely on two MSS, one of the ninth century and one of the eleventh. 29/16-17

Bruce also comments, "There is no body of ancient literature in the world which enjoys such a wealth of good textual attestation as the New Testament." 28/178

AUTHOR	When Written	Earliest Copy	Time Span	No. of Copies
Caesar	100–44 B.C.	A.D. 900	1,000 yrs.	10
Livy	59 B.C.–A.D. 17			20
Plato *(Tetralogies)*	427–347 B.C.	A.D. 900	1,200 yrs.	7
Tacitus *(Annals)*	A.D. 100	A.D. 1100	1,000 yrs.	20 (-)
also minor works	A.D. 100	A.D. 1000	900 yrs.	1
Pliny the Younger *(History)*	A.D. 61–113	A.D. 850	750 yrs.	7
Thucydides *(History)*	460–400 B.C.	A.D. 900	1,300 yrs.	8
Suetonius *(De Vita Caesarun)*	A.D. 75–160	A.D. 950	800 yrs.	8
Herodotus *(History)*	480–425 B.C.	A.D. 900	1,300 yrs	8
Horace			900 yrs.	
Sophocles	496–406 B.C.	A.D. 1000	1,400 yrs.	193
Lucretius	Died 55 or 53 B.C.		1,100 yrs.	2
Catullus	54 B.C.	A.D. 1550	1,600 yrs.	3
Euripides	480–406 B.C.	A.D. 1100	1,500 yrs.	9
Demosthenes	383–322 B.C.	A.D. 1100	1,300 yrs.	200 *
Aristotle	384–322 B.C.	A.D. 1100	1,400 yrs.	49 †
Aristophanes	450–385 B.C.	A.D. 900	1,200 yrs.	10

* All from one copy.
† Of any one work.

Greenlee states,

> Since scholars accept as generally trustworthy the writings of the ancient classics even though the earliest MSS were written so long after the original writings and the number of extant MSS is in many instances so small, it is clear that the reliability of the text of the New Testament is likewise assured. 60/16

The Textual Comparison

Bruce Metzger observes:

> In the entire range of ancient Greek and Latin literature, the *Iliad* ranks next to the New Testament in possessing the greatest amount of manuscript testimony. 90/144

WORK	When Written	Earliest Copy	Timespan	No. Of Copies
Homer *(Iliad)*	900 B.C.	400 B.C.	500 yrs.	643
New Testament	A.D. 40–100	A.D. 125	25 yrs.	over 24,000

Geisler and Nix make a comparison of the textual variations between the New Testament documents and ancient works:

> Next to the New Testament, there are more extant manuscripts of the *Iliad* (643) than any other book. Both it and the Bible were considered "sacred," and both underwent textual changes and criticism of their Greek manuscripts. 54/366

They continue:

> Only 40 lines (or 400 words) of the New Testament are in doubt whereas 764 lines of the *Iliad* are questioned. This five percent textual corruption compares with one-half of one percent of similar emendations in the New Testament. 54/367

Geisler and Nix make the following comment about how the textual variations are counted:

> There is an ambiguity in saying there are some 200,000 variants in the existing manuscripts of the New Testament, since these represent only 10,000 places in the New Testament. If one single word is misspelled in 3,000 different manuscripts, this is counted as 3,000 variants or readings. 54/361

That textual variations do not endanger doctrine is emphatically stated by Sir Frederic Kenyon (one of the great authorities in the field of New Testament textual criticism):

> One word of warning already referred to must be emphasized in conclusion. No fundamental doctrine of the Christian faith rests on a disputed reading . . .
>
> It cannot be too strongly asserted that in substance the text of the Bible is certain: Especially is this the case with the New Testament. The number of manuscripts of the New Testament, of early translations from it, and of quotations from it in the oldest writers of the Church, is so large that it is practically certain that the true reading of every doubtful passage is preserved in some one or other of these ancient authorities. *This can be said of no other book in the world.*
>
> Scholars are satisfied that they possess substantially the true text of the principal Greek and Roman writers whose works have come down to us, of Sophocles, of Thucydides, of Cicero, of Virgil; yet our knowledge of their writings depends on a mere handful of manuscripts, whereas the manuscripts of the New Testament are counted by hundreds, and even thousands. 78/23

Gleason Archer, in answering the question about objective evidence, shows that variants or errors in transmission of the text do not affect God's revelation:

> A careful study of the variants [different readings] of the various earliest manuscripts reveals that none of them affects a single doctrine of Scripture. The system of spiritual truth contained in the standard Hebrew

> text of the Old Testament is not in the slightest altered or compromised by any of the variant readings found in the Hebrew manuscripts of earlier date found in the Dead Sea caves or anywhere else. All that is needed to verify this is to check the register of well-attested variants in Rudolf Kittel's edition of the Hebrew Bible. It is very evident that the vast majority of them are so inconsequential as to leave the meaning of each clause doctrinally unaffected. 12/25

Frederic G. Kenyon continues in *The Story of the Bible:*

> It is reassuring at the end to find that the general result of all these discoveries of the authenticity of the Scriptures, [is] our conviction that we have in our hands, in substantial integrity, the veritable Word of God. 77/113

I believe one can logically conclude, from the perspective of literary evidence, that the New Testament's reliability is far greater than any other record of antiquity.

NOTE: For a listing of some of the earliest and most important manuscripts, see *Evidence That Demands a Verdict, Vol I,* pp. 46-48.

Manuscript Reliability Supported by Various Versions

Another strong support for textual evidence and accuracy is the ancient versions. For the most part, "Ancient literature was rarely translated into another language." 60/45

Christianity from its inception has been a missionary faith. "The earliest versions of the New Testament were prepared by missionaries to assist in the propagation of the Christian faith among peoples whose native tongue was Syriac, Latin, or Coptic." 91/67

Syriac and Latin versions (translations) of the New Testament were made around A.D. 150. This brings us back very near to the time of the originals.

There are more than 15,000 existing copies of various versions.

Manuscript Reliability Supported by Early Church Fathers

Sir David Dalrymple was wondering about the preponderance of Scripture in early writing when someone asked him, "Suppose that the New Testament had been destroyed, and every copy of it lost by the end of the third century, could it have been collected together again from the writings of the Fathers of the second and third centuries?"

After a great deal of investigation Dalrymple concluded:

> That question roused my curiosity, and as I possessed all the existing

works of the Fathers of the second and third centuries, I commenced to search, and up to this time I have found the entire New Testament, except eleven verses. 84/35-36

Bibliographical Test for the Reliability of the Old Testament (E/52-58)

In the case of the Old Testament we do not have the abundance of close MS authority as in the New Testament. Until the recent discovery of the Dead Sea Scrolls, the oldest complete extant Hebrew MS was around A.D. 900. This made a time gap of 1,300 years (the Hebrew Old Testament was completed about 400 B.C.). At first sight it would appear that the Old Testament is no more reliable than other ancient literature.

With the discovery of the Dead Sea Scrolls, however, a number of Old Testament manuscripts have been found which scholars date before the time of Christ.

When the facts are known and compared, there is an overwhelming abundance of reasons for believing that the MSS we possess are trustworthy. We shall see, as Sir Frederic Kenyon put it, that "the Christian can take the whole Bible in his hand and say without fear or hesitation that he holds in it the true Word of God, handed down without essential loss from generation to generation throughout the centuries." 78/23

First, in order to see the uniqueness of the Scripture in its reliability, one needs to examine the extreme care with which the copyists transcribed the Old Testament MSS.

The Talmudists (A.D. 100–500)

During this period a great deal of time was spent in cataloging Hebrew civil and canonical law. The Talmudists had quite an intricate system for transcribing synagogue scrolls.

Samuel Davidson describes some of the disciplines of the Talmudists in regard to the Scriptures. These minute regulations (I am going to use the numbering incorporated by Geisler and Nix) are as follows:

> [1] A synagogue roll must be written on the skins of clean animals, [2] prepared for the particular use of the synagogue by a Jew. [3] These must be fastened together with strings taken from clean animals. [4] Every skin must contain a certain number of columns, equal throughout the entire codex. [5] The length of each column must not extend over less than 48 or more than 60 lines; and the breadth must consist of thirty letters. [6] The whole copy must be first lined; and if three words be written without a line, it is worthless. [7] The ink should be black, neither red, green, nor any other colour, and be prepared according to a definite recipe. [8] An authentic copy must be the exemplar, from which the transcriber ought not in the least deviate. [9] No word or letter, not even a yod, must be written from

> memory, the scribe not having looked at the codex before him . . . [10] Between every consonant the space of a hair or thread must intervene; [11] between every new parashah, or section, the breadth of nine consonants; [12] between every book, three lines. [13] The fifth book of Moses must terminate exactly with a line; but the rest need not do so. [14] Besides this, the copyist must sit in full Jewish dress; [15] wash his whole body, [16] not begin to write the name of God with a pen newly dipped in ink, [17] and should a king address him while writing that name, he must take no notice of him. 35/89, 54/241

Davidson adds that "the rolls in which these regulations are not observed are condemned to be buried in the ground or burned; or they are banished to the schools, to be used as reading-books."

Why don't we have more old MSS? The very absence of ancient MSS, when the rules and accuracies of the copyists are considered, confirms the reliability of the copies we have today.

Gleason Archer, in comparing the manuscript variations of the Hebrew text with pre-Christian literature such as the Egyptian Book of the Dead, states that it is amazing that the Hebrew text does not have the phenomenon of discrepancy and MS change of other literature of the same age. He writes:

> Even though the two copies of Isaiah discovered in Qumran Cave 1 near the Dead Sea in 1947 were a thousand years earlier than the oldest dated manuscripts previously known (A.D. 980), they proved to be word for word identical with our standard Hebrew Bible in more than 95 percent of the text. The 5 percent of variation consisted chiefly of obvious slips of the pen and variations in spelling. Even those Dead Sea fragments of Deuteronomy and Samuel which point to a different manuscript family from that which underlies our received Hebrew text do not indicate any differences in doctrine or teaching. They do not affect the message of revelation in the slightest. 12/25

When the Talmudists finished transcribing a MS they were so convinced they had an exact duplicate that they would give the new copy equal authority.

Frederic Kenyon in *Our Bible and the Ancient Manuscripts* expands on the above and on the destruction of older copies:

> The same extreme care which was devoted to the transcription of manuscripts is also at the bottom of the disappearance of the earlier copies. When a manuscript had been copied with the exactitude prescribed by the Talmud, and had been duly verified, it was accepted as authentic and regarded as being of equal value with any other copy. If all were equally correct, *age gave no advantage to a manuscript;* on the contrary, age was a positive disadvantage, since a manuscript was liable to become defaced or damaged in the lapse of time. A damaged or imperfect copy was at once condemned as unfit for use. 78/43

The Massoretic Period (A.D. 500–900)

The Massoretes (from *Massora,* "Tradition") were well disciplined, and they treated the text "with the greatest imaginable reverence, and devised a complicated system of safeguards against scribal slips. 28/117

Sir Frederic Kenyon says:

> Besides recording varieties of reading, tradition, or conjecture, the Massoretes undertook a number of calculations which do not enter into the ordinary sphere of textual criticism. They numbered the verses, words, and letters of every book. They calculated the middle word and the middle letter of each. They enumerated verses which contained all the letters of the alphabet, or a certain number of them; and so on. These trivialities, as we may rightly consider them, had yet the effect of securing minute attention to the precise transmission of the text; and they are but an excessive manifestation of a respect for the sacred Scriptures which in itself deserves nothing but praise. The Massoretes were indeed anxious that not one jot nor tittle, not one smallest letter nor one tiny part of a letter of the Law should pass away or be lost. 78/38

The Witness of the Dead Sea Scrolls to the Reliability of the Hebrew Scriptures

The big question was asked first by Sir Frederick Kenyon: "Does this Hebrew text, which we call Massoretic, and which we have shown to descend from a text drawn up about A.D. 100, faithfully represent the Hebrew Text as originally written by the authors of the Old Testament books?" 78/47

The Dead Sea Scrolls give us an explicit and positive answer.

The problem before the discovery of the Dead Sea Scrolls was: How accurate are the copies we have today compared to the text of the first century? Since the text has been copied over many times, can we trust it?

What are the Dead Sea Scrolls?

The Scrolls are made up of some 40,000 inscribed fragments. From these fragments more than 500 books have been reconstructed.

Many extra-biblical books and fragments were discovered that shed light on the religious community of Qumran. Such writings as the "Zadokite documents," a "Rule of the Community" and the "Manual of Discipline" help us to understand the purpose of daily Qumran life. Some very helpful commentaries on the Scriptures also were found in the various caves.

The Value of the Scrolls

The oldest complete Hebrew MSS we possessed were from A.D. 900 on. How could we be sure of their accurate transmission since the time of Christ in A.D. 32? Thanks to archaeology and the Dead Sea Scrolls, we now know. One of the scrolls found was a complete MS of the Hebrew text of Isaiah. It is dated by paleographers around 125 B.C. This MS is more than 1,000 years older than any MS we previously possessed.

The impact of this discovery is in the exactness of the Isaiah scroll (125 B.C.) with the Massoretic text of Isaiah (A.D. 916) 1,000 years later.

> Of the 166 words in Isaiah 53, there are only seventeen letters in question. Ten of these letters are simply a matter of spelling, which does not affect the sense. Four more letters are minor stylistic changes, such as conjunctions. The remaining three letters comprise the word "light" which is added in verse 11, and does not affect the meaning greatly. Furthermore, this word is supported by the LXX [Septuagint] and IQ Is [first cave of Qumran, Isaiah scroll]. Thus, in one chapter of 166 words, there is only one word (three letters) in question after a thousand years of transmission—and this word does not significantly change the meaning of the passage. 54/263

F. F. Bruce says, "An incomplete scroll of Isaiah, found along with the other in the first Qumran cave, and conveniently distinguished as 'Isaiah B,' agrees even more closely with the Massoretic text." 28/123

> **NOTE:** See *Evidence That Demands a Verdict, Vol I,* pp. 58–60, for comments on how the Old Testament Text is further substantiated by the Septuagint, Samaritan Text, Jewish Targums, Mishnah, Gemarahs, Midrash, and other ancient literature.

Internal Evidence Test for the Reliability of the Bible

(C/49-54)

The bibliographical test has determined only that the text we have now is essentially what was originally recorded. One has still to determine whether that written record is credible and to what extent. That is the problem of internal criticism, which is the second test of historicity listed by C. Sanders.

At this point the literary critic continues to follow Aristotle's dictum: "The benefit of the doubt is to be given to the document itself, and not arrogated by the critic to himself." 96/29

In other words, as John W. Montgomery summarizes: "One must listen to the claims of the document under analysis, and not assume fraud or error unless the author disqualified himself by contradictions or known factual inaccuracies." 96/29

Dr. Louis Gottschalk, former professor of history at the University of Chicago, outlines his historical method in a guide used by many for historical investigation. Gottschalk points out that the ability of the writer or the witness to tell the truth is helpful to the historian to determine credibility. 59/161-68

This "ability to tell the truth" is closely related to the witness's nearness both geographically and chronologically to the events recorded. The New Testament accounts of the life and teaching of Jesus were recorded by men who had been either eyewitnesses themselves or who related the accounts of eyewitnesses of the actual events or teachings of Jesus.

> **Luke:** Inasmuch as many have undertaken to compile an account of the things accomplished among us, just as those who from the beginning were eyewitnesses and servants of the Word have handed them down to us, it seemed fitting for me as well, having investigated everything carefully from the beginning, to write it out for you in consecutive order, most excellent Theophilus (1:1-3).
>
> **Peter:** For we did not follow cleverly devised tales when we made known to you the power and coming of our Lord Jesus Christ, but we were eyewitnesses of His majesty (2 Peter 1:16).
>
> **John:** What we have seen and heard we proclaim to you also, that you also may have fellowship with us; and indeed our fellowship is with the Father, and with His Son Jesus Christ (1 John 1:3).
>
> **John:** And he who has seen has borne witness, and his witness is true; and he knows that he is telling the truth, so that you also may believe (19:35).
>
> **Luke:** In the fifteenth year of the reign of Tiberius Caesar, when Pontius Pilate was governor of Judea, and Herod was tetrarch of Galilee, and his brother Philip was tetrach of the region of Ituraea and Trachonitis, and Lysanias was tetrach of Abiline . . . (3:1).

This closeness to the recorded accounts is an extremely effective means of certifying the accuracy of what is retained by a witness. The historian, however, also has to deal with the eyewitness who consciously or unconsciously tells falsehoods even though he is near to the event and is competent to tell the truth.

The New Testament accounts of Jesus began to be circulated within the lifetimes of those alive at the time of His life. These people could certainly confirm or deny the accuracy of the accounts. In advocating their case for the gospel, the apostles had appealed (even when confronting their most severe opponents) to common knowledge concerning Jesus. They not only said, "Look, we saw this"; or "We heard that"; but in addition they turned the tables around and right in front of adverse critics said, "You also know about these things . . . You saw them; you yourselves know about it." One had better be careful when he says to his opposition, "You know this also," because if he isn't right in the details, it will be shoved right back down his throat.

> Men of Israel, listen to these words: Jesus, the Nazarene, a man attested

> to you by God with miracles and wonders and signs which God performed through Him in your midst, just as you yourselves know (Acts 2:22).
>
> And while Paul was saying this in his defense, Festus said in a loud voice, "Paul, you are out of your mind! Your great learning is driving you mad." But Paul said, "I am not out of my mind, most excellent Festus, but I utter words of sober truth. For the king knows about these matters, and I speak to him also with confidence, since I am persuaded that none of these things escape his notice; for this has not been done in a corner" (Acts 26:24-28).

Concerning the primary-source value of the New Testament records, F. F. Bruce, former Rylands Professor of Biblical Criticism and Exegesis at the University of Manchester, says:

> And it was not only friendly eyewitnesses that the early preachers had to reckon with; there were others less well disposed who were also conversant with the main facts of the ministry and death of Jesus. The disciples could not afford to risk inaccuracies (not to speak of willful manipulation of the facts), which would at once be exposed by those who would be only too glad to do so. On the contrary, one of the strong points in the original apostolic preaching is the confident appeal to the knowledge of the hearers; they not only said, "We are witnesses of these things"; but also, "As you yourselves know" (Acts 2:22). Had there been any tendency to depart from the facts in any material respect, the possible presence of hostile witnesses in the audience would have served as a further corrective. 30/16*ff.*,33

Historian Will Durant, who has spent his life analyzing records of antiquity, says the literary evidence indicates historical authenticity regarding the New Testament:

> Despite the prejudices and theological preconceptions of the evangelists, they record many incidents that mere inventors would have concealed—the competition of the apostles for high places in the kingdom, their flight after Jesus' arrest, Peter's denial, the failure of Christ to work miracles in Galilee, the references of some auditors to His possible insanity, His early uncertainty as to His mission, His confessions of ignorance as to the future, His moments of bitterness, His despairing cry on the cross; no one reading these scenes can doubt the reality of the figure behind them. That a few simple men should in one generation have invented so powerful and appealing a personality, so lofty an ethic, and so inspiring a vision of human brotherhood, would be a miracle far more incredible than any recorded in the gospels. After two centuries of higher criticism the outlines of the life, character, and teaching of Christ remain reasonably clear, and constitute the most fascinating feature in the history of Western man. 39/3:557

NOTE: See part II, "Answering the Bible's Critics," where almost all of the topics may be applied toward the internal evidence test.

External Evidence Test for the Reliability of the Bible (C/54-57)

The third test of historicity is that of external evidence – whether other historical material confirms or denies the internal testimony of the documents themselves. In other words, what sources are there, apart from the literature under analysis, that substantiate its accuracy, reliability, and authenticity?

Gottschalk argues that "conformity or agreement with other known historical or scientific facts is often the decisive test of evidence, whether of one or more witnesses." 59/168

Two friends of the apostle John confirm the internal evidence from John's accounts. The historian Eusebius preserves writings of Papias, bishop of Hierapolis (A.D. 130):

> The Elder [apostle John] used to say this also: "Mark, having been the interpreter of Peter, wrote down accurately all that he [Peter] mentioned, whether sayings or doings of Christ, not, however, in order. For he was neither a hearer nor a companion of the Lord; but afterwards, as I said, he accompanied Peter, who adapted his teachings as necessity required, not as though he were making compilation of the sayings of the Lord. So then Mark made no mistake, writing down in this way some things as he mentioned them; for he paid attention to this one thing, not to omit anything that he had heard, nor to include any false statement among them. 44/3.39

Iraneus, Bishop of Lyons in A.D. 180, who was a student of Polycarp, Bishop of Smyrna (who had been a Christian for eighty-six years and was a disciple of John the Apostle), wrote:

> Matthew published his gospel among the Hebrews [i.e., Jews] in their own tongue, when Peter and Paul were preaching the gospel in Rome and founding the church there. After their departure [i.e., death, which strong tradition places at the time of the Neronian persecution in 64], Mark, the disciple and interpreter of Peter, himself handed down to us in writing the substance of Peter's preaching. Luke, the follower of Paul, set down in a book the gospel preached by his teacher. Then John, the disciple of the Lord, who also leaned on His breast [this is a reference to John 13:25 and 21:20], himself produced his gospel, while he was living at Ephesus in Asia. 72/3. 1. 1.

Archaeology often provides some extremely powerful external evidence. It contributes to biblical criticism, not in the area of inspiration and revelation, but by providing evidence of accuracy about events that are recorded. Archaeologist Joseph Free writes: "Archaeology has confirmed countless passages which have been rejected by critics as unhistorical or contradictory to known facts." 51/331

A. N. Sherwin-White, a classical historian, writes that "for Acts the confirmation of historicity is overwhelming." He continues by saying that "any attempt to reject its basic historicity even in matters of detail must now appear absurd. Roman historians have long taken it for granted." 120/189

After personally trying, as a skeptic myself, to shatter the historicity and validity of the Scriptures, I had to conclude that they actually are historically trustworthy. If a person discards the Bible as unreliable in this sense, then he or she must discard almost all the literature of antiquity.

One problem I constantly face is the desire on the part of many to apply one standard or test to secular literature and another to the Bible. We need to apply the same test, whether the literature under investigation is secular or religious. Having done this, I believe we can say, "The Bible is trustworthy and historically reliable in its witness about Jesus."

Dr. Clark H. Pinnock states:

> There exists no document from the ancient world witnessed by so excellent a set of textual and historical testimonies and offering so superb an array of historical data on which an intelligent decision may be made. An honest [person] cannot dismiss a source of this kind. Skepticism regarding the historical credentials of Christianity is based upon an irrational [i.e., antisupernatural] bias. 103/58

NOTE: The remaining material in part I, "The Bible–Can It Be Trusted?" can be applied to the external evidence test. Also, some of the material in part II, "Answering the Bible's Critics," may be applied to the external evidence test.

CHAPTER 6 *Old Testament Prophecy Fulfilled in History*

One of the unique and fascinating aspects of the Bible is that in no other religious literature do we find the accuracy of fulfilled prophecy. Biblical predictions recorded sometimes hundreds of years in advance of their happening are fulfilled in minute detail. Following are a few of those predictions and fulfillments.

Cyrus (A/35)

The prophet Isaiah, writing about 700 B.C., names Cyrus as the king who will say to Jerusalem that it shall be built and that the Temple foundation shall be laid (Isaiah 44:28; 54:1).

At the time of Isaiah's writing, the city of Jerusalem was fully built and the entire temple was standing. Not until more than 100 years later, in 586 B.C., would the city and Temple be destroyed by King Nebuchadnezzar.

After Jerusalem was taken by the Babylonians, it was conquered by the Persians in about 539 B.C. Shortly after that, a Persian king named Cyrus gave the decree to rebuild the Temple in Jerusalem. This was around

160 years after the prophecy of Isaiah!

Thus Isaiah predicted that a man named Cyrus, who would not be born for about a hundred years, would give the command to rebuild the Temple, which was still standing in Isaiah's day and would not be destroyed for more than a hundred years. This prophecy is truly amazing, but it is not isolated. There are, in fact, hundreds of prophecies which predict future events.

Daniel's Seventy Weeks (D/15-16, 18-21)

In Daniel 9:24-27, a prophecy concerning the Messiah is given in three specific parts. The first part states that at the end of 69 weeks, the Messiah will come to Jerusalem. (Actually the 7 and 62 weeks are understood as 69 seven-year periods. For the explanation see Hoehner 69/117*ff.*) The starting point of the 69 weeks is the decree to restore and rebuild Jerusalem.

Concerning the first part of the prophecy (the coming of the Messiah), Wilson explains:

> Included in the prophecy of the seventy weeks is the specific prediction that from the going forth of a commandment to restore and build Jerusalem unto Messiah the Prince, there would be sixty-nine weeks. Those weeks are weeks of years. After four hundred and eighty-three years Messiah was to come. 133/139

Daniel 9:24-27:

> Seventy weeks have been decreed for your people and your holy city, to finish the transgression, to make an end of sin, to make atonement for iniquity, to bring in everlasting righteousness, to seal up vision and prophecy, and to anoint the most holy place.
>
> So you are to know and discern that from the issuing of a decree to restore and rebuild Jerusalem until Messiah the Prince there will be seven weeks and sixty two weeks; it will be built again, with plaza and moat, even in times of distress. Then after the sixty-two weeks the Messiah will be cut off and have nothing, and the people of the prince who is to come will destroy the city and the sanctuary. And its end will come with a flood; even to the end there will be war; desolations are determined. And he will make a firm covenant with the many for one week, but in the middle of the week he will put a stop to sacrifice and grain offering; and on the wing of abominations will come one who makes desolate, even until a complete destruction, one that is decreed, is poured out on the one who makes desolate.

Beginning of Seventy Weeks

Several commandments, or decrees, in Israel's history have been suggested as the *terminus a quo* of the 483 years. These are:

1. The decree of Cyrus, 539 B.C. (Ezra 1:1-4)

2. The decree of Darius, 519–518 B.C. (Ezra 5:3-7)
3. The decree of Artaxerxes to Ezra, 457 B.C. (Ezra 7:11-16)
4. The decree of Artaxerxes to Nehemiah, 444 B.C. (Nehemiah 2:1-8) 68/121*ff.*

J. D. Wilson comments on the starting point of this prophecy:

> The next decree is referred to in Nehemiah 2. It was in the twentieth year of Artaxerxes. The words of the decree are not given, but its subject matter can easily be determined. Nehemiah hears of the desolate condition of Jerusalem. He is deeply grieved. The King asks the reason. Nehemiah replies, "The city, the place of my fathers' sepulchers, lieth in waste and the gates thereof are consumed with fire." The king bids him make request. He does so promptly, asking an order from the King that "I be sent to the city that I may build it." And as we read, he was sent, and he rebuilt Jerusalem.
>
> This decree then is the "commandment to restore and rebuild Jerusalem." There is no other decree authorizing the restoration of the city. This decree authorizes the restoration and the book of Nehemiah tells how the work was carried on. The exigencies of their various theories have led men to take some other decree for the *terminus a quo* of their calculations, but it is not apparent how any could have done so without misgivings. This decree of Nehemiah 2 is the commandment to restore and rebuild Jerusalem; no other decree gives any permission to restore the city. All other decrees refer to the building of the Temple and the Temple only. 133/141-42

Wilson then gives the length of the year used in the calculation of the 483 years:

> The only years whose length is given in the Bible are of 360 days—twelve months of 30 days each. Gen. vii, 11, vii, 3-4; Rev. xi, 2-3, xii, 6, xiii, 5. It seems not unreasonable to take the period designed as 360 days. In that case the 483rd year from [444] B.C. is A.D. [33], the date of the Crucifixion. 133/143

NOTE: The dates I have used in this work are from the most recent scholarship. When older sources with unlikely dates are quoted, the correct dates are set in to avoid confusion. The dates quoted in this work are from H. W. Hoehner's *Chronological Aspects of the Life of Christ.* Hoehner has researched this issue thoroughly, and has included careful scrutiny of Robert Anderson's *The Coming Prince.* Therefore, for a complete explanation of the dating, see Hoehner's work.

If Daniel is correct, the time from the edict to restore and rebuild Jerusalem (Nisan 1, 444 B.C.) to the coming of the Messiah to Jerusalem is 483 years, each year equaling the 360-day year (173,880 days). Will these calculations match with history and time?

Day of Christ's Crucifixion

Hoehner demonstrates that the only logical day for Christ's crucifixion is Nisan 14, A.D. 33, or according to our calendar, April 3, A.D. 33. See chapters IV and V of Hoehner's *Chronological Aspects of the Life of Christ.*

Calculation of 69 Weeks

Using the 360-day year, Hoehner calculates the terminal day of the 69 weeks of Daniel's prophecy as follows:

> Multiplying the sixty-nine weeks by seven years for each week by 360 days gives a total of 173,880 days. The difference between 444 B.C. and A.D. 33 then is 476 solar years. By multiplying 476 by 365.24219879, or by 365 days, 5 hours, 48 minutes, 45.975 seconds, one comes to 173,855 days. This leaves only 25 days to be accounted for between 444 B.C. and A.D. 33. By adding the 25 days to March 5 (of 444 B.C.), one comes to March 30 (of A.D. 33) which was Nisan 10 in A.D. 33. This is the triumphal entry of Jesus into Jerusalem. 69/138

The terminal event of the 69 weeks is the presentation of Christ Himself to Israel as the Messiah as predicted in Zechariah 9:9. This materialized on Monday, Nisan 10 (March 30), A.D. 33. On the following Friday, April 3, A.D. 33, Christ was crucified or "cut off" (Daniel 9:26).

After the termination of the 69 weeks and before the commencement of the 70th week, two events had to occur:

(1) The "cutting off" of the Messiah.

(2) The destruction of the city and the Temple.

The Temple was destroyed in A.D. 70 by Titus the Roman. Therefore, according to Daniel's prophecy, the Messiah had to come and be crucified between March 30, A.D. 33 and A.D. 70. Christ was crucified April 3, A.D. 33.

Verification of the prophetic calculations using our calendar (Julian):

a. 444 B.C. to A.D. 33 is 476 years.
(444 plus 33 is 477, but 1 B.C.
to A.D. 1 is 1 year not two.
One must subtract 1 year from 477.)

b. 476 years x 365.24219879 days = ...173,855 days
c. March 5 to March 30 = ... 25 days
173,880 days

Historical Cities

1. Tyre (E/274-80)

Ezekiel 26 (592–570 B.C.)

Therefore, thus says the Lord GOD, "Behold, I am against you, O Tyre, and

I will bring up many nations against you, as the sea brings up its waves. "And they will destroy the walls of Tyre and break down her towers; and I will scrape her debris from her and make her a bare rock" (verses 3,4).

For thus says the Lord GOD, "Behold, I will bring upon Tyre from the north Nebuchadnezzar king of Babylon, king of kings, with horses, chariots, cavalry, and a great army. He will slay your daughters on the mainland with the sword; and he will make siege walls against you, cast up a mound against you, and raise up a large shield against you (verses 7,8).

"Also they will make a spoil of your riches and a prey of your merchandise, break down your walls and destroy your pleasant houses, and throw your stones and your timbers and your debris into the water (verse 12).

"And I will make you a bare rock; you will be a place for the spreading of nets. You will be built no more, for I the LORD have spoken," declares the Lord GOD (verse 14).

"I shall bring terrors on you, and you will be no more; though you will be sought, you will never be found again," declares the Lord GOD (verse 21).

Predictions

1. Nebuchadnezzar will destroy the mainland city of Tyre (26:8).
2. Many nations will come against Tyre (26:3).
3. She will be made a bare rock; flat like the top of a rock (26:4).
4. Fishermen will spread nets over the site (26:5).
5. The debris will be thrown into the water (26:12).
6. She will never be rebuilt (26:14).
7. She will never be found again (26:21).

NEBUCHADNEZZAR

Nebuchadnezzar laid siege to mainland Tyre three years after the prophecy. The *Encyclopedia Britannica* says: "After a 13-year siege (585–573 B.C.) by Nebuchadnezzar II, Tyre made terms and acknowledged Babylonian suzerainty." 43/xxii 452

When Nebuchadnezzar broke the gates down, he found the city almost empty. The majority of the people had moved by ship to an island about one-half mile off the coast and fortified a city there. The mainland city was destroyed in 573 (prediction #1), but the city of Tyre on the island remained a powerful city for several hundred years.

ALEXANDER THE GREAT

The next incident was with Alexander the Great.

"In his war on the Persians," writes the *Encyclopaedia Britannica*, "Alexander III, after defeating Darius III at the Battle of Issus (333), marched southward toward Egypt, calling upon the Phoenician cities to open their gates, as it was part of his general plan to deny their use to the Persian fleet. The citizens of Tyre refused to do so, and Alexander laid siege to the city. Possessing no fleet, he demolished old Tyre, on the mainland, and with the debris built a mole 200 ft. (60m.) wide across the straits separating the old and new towns, erecting towers and war engines at the farther end. 43/xxii 452 (Prediction #5.)

The Tyrians countered here with a full-scale raid on the whole operation, which was very successful; they made use of fireships to start the towers burning and then swarmed over the mole after the Greeks were routed. General destruction of the mole was made to as great an extent as the raiding party was capable. Arrian progressed to the sea struggle. Alexander realized he needed ships. He began pressuring and mustering conquered subjects to make ships available for this operation. Alexander's navy grew from cities and areas as follows: Sidon, Aradus, Byblus (these contributed about 80 sails), 10 from Rhodes, 3 from Soli and Mallos, 10 from Lycia, a big one from Macedon, and 120 from Cyprus. (Prediction #2.)

With this now superior naval force at Alexander's disposal, the conquest of Tyre through completion of the land bridge was simply a question of time. How long would this take? Darius III, Alexander's Persian enemy, was not standing idle at this time, but finally the causeway was completed, the walls were battered down, and mop-up operations began.

"The causeway still remains," writes Philip Myers, "uniting the rock with the mainland. When at last the city was taken after a siege of seven months, eight thousand of the inhabitants were slain and thirty thousand sold into slavery." 99/153

Philip Myers made an interesting observation here; he is a secular historian (not a theologian), and this is found in a history textbook:

> Alexander the Great . . . reduced [Tyre] to ruins (332 B.C.). She recovered in a measure from this blow, but never regained the place she had previously held in the world. The larger part of the site of the once great city is now bare as the top of a rock [prediction #3]—a place where the fishermen that still frequent the spot spread their nets to dry. 99/55 (Prediction #4.)

John C. Beck keeps the history of the island city of Tyre in the proper perspective:

> The history of Tyre does not stop after the conquest of Alexander. Men continue to rebuild her and armies continue to besiege her walls until finally, after sixteen hundred years, she falls never to be rebuilt again. 21/41

Specific Fulfillment

1. Nebuchadnezzar did destroy the old (mainland) city of Tyre.
2. Many nations were against Tyre.

   This fact can be seen even in this very brief history by Beck:

Because a characteristic of waves is that they come in succession with their destructive force due to their repetition and continuous pounding, this author understands Ezekiel to be referring to a succession of invaders extending over a prolonged period of time.

With this understanding, this summary of Ezekiel (verses 3-6) unfolds. First, "They will destroy the walls of Tyre and break down her towers" (Nebuchadnezzar's siege). Next, "I will also scrape her dust from her and make her a bare rock" (Alexander's siege). And finally, "She shall become a spoil to the nations" (history following the siege of Alexander). 21/11-12

3. Alexander scraped the old site of Tyre clean when he made the causeway out to the island and left a "bare rock."
4. Numerous references have been previously made (some by secular observers) to the spreading of nets. Nina Nelson observes during a visit: "Pale turquoise fishing nets were drying on the shore." 100/220

   Hans-Wolf Rackl, describing the present situation of the site of ancient Tyre, writes: "Today hardly a single stone of old Tyre remains intact. . . . Tyre has become a place 'to dry fish nets,' as the prophet predicted." 105/179
5. Alexander threw the debris into the water in order to make the causeway.

   "Ezekiel's prophecy," writes Joseph Free, "concerning the laying of the stones, the timber, and the dust in 'the midst of the water' (Ezek. 26:12*b*) was specifically fulfilled when Alexander's engineers built the mole, and used the remains of the ancient land city of Tyre, laying them in the midst of the water." 51/263-64
6. The city was never to be rebuilt.

   Floyd Hamilton in *The Basis of the Christian Faith* states:

> It is also written, "Thou shalt be built no more" (XXVI:14). Other cities destroyed by enemies had been rebuilt; Jerusalem was destroyed many times, but always has risen again from the ruins; what reason was there for saying that Old Tyre might not be rebuilt? But twenty-five centuries ago a Jew in exile over in Babylonia looked into the future at the command of God and wrote the words, "Thou shalt be built no more!" The voice of God has spoken and Old Tyre today stands as it has for twenty-five centuries, a bare rock, uninhabited by man! Today anyone who wants to see the site of the old city can have it pointed out to him along the shore, but there is not a ruin to mark the spot. It has been scraped clean and has never been rebuilt. 65/229

The great freshwater springs of Reselain are at the site of the mainland city of Tyre, and no doubt supplied the city with an abundance of fresh water. These springs are still there and still flow, but their water runs into the sea. The flow of these springs was measured by an engineer, and found to be about 10,000,000 gallons daily. It is still an excellent site for a city and would have free water enough for a large modern city, yet it has never been rebuilt. 124/76-77

7. The city was never to be found again.

   Most commentators say that the actual site of the ancient city would be forgotten or lost because of destruction. A better interpretation of this verse is that the seeking by men would be for the purpose of elevating Tyre to her former position of wealth and splendor. It is difficult to believe that the actual location of the city could be lost when it formerly occupied completely the island with walls built to the water's edge.

CONCLUSION

Peter Stoner's seven predictions regarding this miracle were like the ones here—except for my last one, which he did not use, and one of his which is omitted. Stoner evaluated the miracle in the following manner:

> If Ezekiel had looked at Tyre in his day and had made these seven predictions in human wisdom, these estimates mean that there would have been only one chance in 75,000,000 of their all coming true. They all came true in the minutest detail. 124/80

2. Sidon (E/280-81)

Ezekiel 28:22,23 (592–570 B.C.) And say, "Thus says the Lord GOD,

'Behold, I am against you, O Sidon,
And I shall be glorified in your midst.
Then they will know that I am the LORD,
when I execute judgments in her.
And I shall manifest My holiness in her.
'For I shall send pestilence to her
And blood to her streets,
And the wounded will fall in her midst
By the sword upon her on every side;
Then they will know that I am the LORD.' "

Predictions

1. There is no mention of her destruction.
2. Blood will be in the streets (28:23).
3. A sword will be on every side (28:23).

George Davis strikes a good contrast between Tyre and Sidon in his book, *Fulfilled Prophecies That Prove the Bible.* He says:

> The prophecy against Sidon is very different from that concerning

Tyre. It was foretold that Tyre would be destroyed, made bare like a rock, and built no more. The prediction against Sidon is that blood will be in her streets, her wounded shall fall in the midst of her, and the sword is to be on her every side. But there is no doom of extinction pronounced against her as was the case of Tyre. 36/16,18

Fulfillment

Floyd Hamilton explains what happened in the fourth century B.C.:

> In 351 B.C. the Sidonians, who had been vassals of the Persian king, rebelled, and successfully defended their city against his attacks. At last their own king, in order to save his own life, betrayed the city to the enemy. Well knowing what the vengeance of the Persian king would be, 40,000 of the citizens shut themselves up in their homes, set fire to their own houses and perished in the flames rather than submit to the torture of their enemies! Blood indeed was sent into the streets. 65/300 (Prediction #2.)

Mr. Davis explains that "not once but many times blood has been in [Sidon's] streets, her wounded have fallen in the midst of her and the sword has been 'upon every side.' " 36/19 (Predictions #2 and 3.)

In *The Basis of the Christian Faith,* Floyd Hamilton cites another time Sidon was destroyed, writing that Sidon

> was soon rebuilt, however, and though it has been captured over and over again, its citizens butchered and houses razed time after time, the city has always been rebuilt, and is today [1927] a town of over 15,000 inhabitants. Blood has flowed in the streets again and again, but the city stayed in existence and stands today, a monument to fulfilled prophecy. 65/300

George Davis records: "In the days of the Crusades [Sidon] was taken and retaken, again and again, by opposing forces. Three times it was captured by the Crusaders, and three times it fell before the Moslem armies." 34/18-19

And he further notes that

> even in modern times tribulation has continued to be meted out to the city. It has been the scene of conflicts between the Druses and the Turks, and between the Turks and the French. In 1840 Sidon "was bombarded by the combined fleets of England, France and Turkey." 36/19

Morris explains: "No fate of extinction was foretold for Sidon and even today it is a city of about 20,000 [1956]. However, it has had one of the bloodiest histories any city ever had." 97/113 (Predictions #1 and 2.)

CONCLUSION

George Davis concludes with a chilling claim:

> No human mind could have foretold 2,500 years ago that Tyre would be extinct, and Sidon would continue, but suffer tribulation during the succeeding centuries, instead of Tyre enduring sorrows, and Sidon being desolate and deserted during the long period. 36/19-20

3. Samaria (E/282-83)

Hosea 13:16:

Samaria will be held guilty,
for she has rebelled against her God.
They will fall by the sword,
Their little ones will be dashed in pieces,
And their pregnant women will be ripped open.

Micah 1:6:

For I will make Samaria a heap of ruins
in the open country,
Planting places for a vineyard.
I will pour her stones down into the valley,
And will lay bare her foundations.

Predictions

1. The city will fall violently (Hosea).
2. It will become "as a heap in the field" (Micah).
3. Vineyards will be planted there (Micah).
4. Samaria's stones will be poured down into the valley (Micah).
5. The foundations shall be "discovered" (Micah).

Fulfillment

According to the *International Standard Bible Encyclopedia,* Sargon took Samaria in 722 B.C. Not only did Samaria fall by the sword in 722, but also in 331 B.C. by Alexander and a third time in 120 B.C. by John Hyrcanus, all conquerors causing great damage and death to the citizens of Samaria. Even the skeptic who would contend that the destruction of Samaria came after the event will not be able to disagree about the rest of the ramifications. 101/2672

John Urquhart records Henry Maundrell's reaction in 1697 to what he witnessed:

> Sabaste is the ancient Samaria, the imperial city of the ten tribes after their revolt from the house of David. . . . This great city is now wholly converted into gardens, and all the tokens that remain to testify that there has ever been such a place, are only on the north side, a large square piazza encompassed with pillars, and on the east some poor remains of a great church. 128/128 (Predictions #2 and 3.)

Predictions #4 and #5 find fulfillment through Van de Velde, who calls Samaria

> a pitiable hamlet, consisting of a few squalid houses, inhabited by a band of

plunderers. . . . The shafts of a few pillars only remain standing to indicate the sites of the colonnades. . . . Samaria, a huge heap of stones! Her foundations discovered, her streets ploughed up, and covered with corn fields and olive gardens. . . . Samaria has been destroyed, but her rubbish has been thrown down into the valley; her foundation stones, those ancient quadrangular stones of the time of Omri and Ahab, are discovered, and lie scattered about on the slope of the hill. 128/128 (Predictions #4 and 5.)

4. Gaza-Ashkelon (E/283-87)

There are two cities on the Mediterranean coast west of the Dead Sea, Gaza and Ashkelon, which have been mentioned in prophecy.

Amos 1:8 (775 – 750 B.C.)

"I will also cut off the inhabitant from Ashdod,
And him who holds the scepter, from Ashkelon;
I will even unleash My power upon Ekron,
And the remnant of the Philistines will perish,"
says the Lord GOD.

Jeremiah 47:5 (626 – 586 B.C.)

Baldness has come upon Gaza;
Ashkelon has been ruined.
O remnant of their valley,
How long will you gash yourself?

Zephaniah 2:4,6 (640 – 621 B.C.)

For Gaza will be abandoned,
And Ashkelon a desolation;
Ashdod will be driven out at noon,
And Ekron will be uprooted. . .

So the seacoast will be pastures,
With caves for shepherds and folds for flocks. . . .

And the coast will be
For the remnant of the house of Judah,
They will pasture on it.
In the houses of Ashkelon they will
lie down at evening;
For the LORD their God will care for them
And restore their fortune.

Predictions

1. The Philistines will not continue (Amos 1:8)
2. Baldness shall come upon Gaza (Jeremiah 47:5).
3. Desolation shall come on Ashkelon (Zephaniah 2:4).
4. Shepherds and sheep will dwell in the area around Ashkelon

(Zephaniah 2:6).

5. Remnant of the house of Judah will reinhabit Ashkelon (Zephaniah 2:7).

Fulfillment

George Davis comments:

> And not only was Ashkelon destroyed but the entire nation of the Philistines was "cut off" precisely as predicted by the prophet Ezekiel 2,500 years ago. The Philistines have been destroyed so completely that there is not a single Philistine living anywhere in the world today. 37/46 (Prediction #1.)

Davis gives a good picture of present-day Ashkelon:

> Following the establishment of the State of Israel the Jews recognized the splendid location of the old city of Ashkelon on the seacoast of their country. They decided to make it a beautiful city of Israel's new State. The *Jerusalem Post* says the new city of Ashkelon has been "designed on the lines of a Garden City." 37/48

Davis adds that today, "after long centuries of mighty Ashkelon lying waste and desolate, it is now being transformed into a garden city. The coast of the Mediterranean is indeed for 'the house of Judah,' and 'in the house of Ashkelon shall lie down in the evening.' " 37/48 (Prediction #5.)

Davis presents a good conclusion:

> Ashkelon was destroyed exactly as foretold! The Philistines were "cut off" from the face of the earth till not one Philistine remains in all the world! [Prediction #1.] And lastly, long desolate Ashkelon [prediction #3] has been revived from its ruins of centuries, and is becoming a Garden City. 37/49

Of Gaza, Peter Stoner writes,

> A city of Gaza still exists, so for a long time, the prophecy with respect to Gaza was thought to be in error. Finally a careful study was made of the location of Gaza, as described in the Bible, and it was found that the new city of Gaza was in the wrong location. A search was made for the old city and it was found buried under the sand dunes. It had indeed become bald. What better description could you give of a city buried under sand dunes than to say that it had become bald? 124/83 (Prediction #2.)

John Urquhart expands on Gaza's total disappearance: "It is so forsaken that there is not a single hut resting on its site. It is so bald that neither pillar nor standing stone marks the place where the city stood, nor is there a single blade of grass on which the weary eye can rest." 128/105

5. Petra and Edom (E/287-93)

"In all, six prophets heap condemnation upon this nation Edom:

Isaiah, Jeremiah, Ezekiel, Joel, Amos, and Obadiah." 131/173

"Their prophecies on Edom," writes George Smith, "number so great, they are so exuberant in language, so various, grand, and minute, that many pages might be filled in reciting them, and many more employed in showing their exact and complete fulfillment." 122/217-18

Predictions

1. Edom will become a desolation (Isaiah 34:13).
2. It will never be populated again (Jeremiah 49:18).
3. It will be conquered by heathen (Ezekiel 25:14).
4. It will be conquered by Israel (Ezekiel 25:14).
5. It shall have a bloody history (Ezekiel 35:5,6; Isaiah 34:6,7).
6. Edom will be made desolate as far as the city of Teman (Ezekiel 25:13).
7. Wild animals will inhabit the area (Isaiah 34:13-15).
8. Trade will cease (Isaiah 34:10; Ezekiel 35:7).
9. Spectators will be astonished (Jeremiah 49:17).

History of Edom After Prophecies

The fall of Assyria marked the approximate period of completion of the prophecies against Edom. What follows is the history after the prophecies were completed. "The Nabeans are probably 'the children of the east' mentioned in Ezekiel 25:4. Some time during the sixth century B.C. [they] succeeded in expelling Edom from their rock fortresses and taking the city of Petra." 68/40 (Prediction #3.)

Discussing the fulfillment of prediction #4, Bernard Ramm explains the Jewish conquest of Petra and Edom:

> That the Jews conquered them [Edomites] is proved by reference to I Maccabees 5:3 and to Josephus' *Antiquities* (XII, 18, 1). They were attacked successively by John Hyrcanus and Simon of Gerasa. Therefore, the prediction that the Jews too would conquer them has been fulfilled. 108/103

Around the time of the birth of Christ, Petra was prosperous. Citing Strabo, who lived about that time, George Davis explains, "Petra was also a city of great prosperity. Strabo tells that it was the terminus of one of the great commercial routes of Asia. It was the market of the Arabians for their spice and frankincense." 37/52

Unger's Bible Dictionary, concerning Edom during Roman times, records:

> The Edomites were now incorporated with the Jewish nation, and the whole province was often termed by Greek and Roman writers *Idumaea.* Immediately before the siege of Jerusalem by Titus, 20,000 Idumaeans

were admitted to the Holy City, which they filled with robbery and bloodshed. From this time, the Edomites, as a separate people, disappear from the pages of history. 126/286

When the Jews needed help the most, during the Roman siege (A.D. 70), was when the Edomites hurt the worst. "After the massacre of the Jews," writes David Higgins, "the Idumeans returned home. But with the fall of Jerusalem in A.D. 70 the children of Esau disappear as a separate people from the stage of recorded history." 68/44-45 (Prediction #5.)

To the above, Davis adds:

> Petra, the capital of the land of Edom, was one of the wonders of the ancient world. It was built out of a mountain of rock. Many of its buildings were hewn out of the solid rock. Petra presents a stupendous sight with its rock-hewn buildings, carved out of the very mountainside itself, of beautiful rose-red stone. It was practically impregnable from the assault of enemies. There was just one long narrow canyon-like entrance, where a small force of soldiers could protect the city from being taken by a large army. 37/50-52

But what does Petra look like today? The description is like something from Edgar Allen Poe's scariest stories, yet it is completely true. George Smith vividly describes Edom by referring to various authors:

> The fulfillment of these prophecies is equally complete, and as minutely exact as the preceding. Captain Mangles, who visited these ruins, says that when surveying the scenery of Petra, "the screaming of the eagles, hawks, and owls, who were soaring over our heads in considerable numbers, seemingly annoyed at anyone approaching their lonely habitation, added much to the singularity of the scene." It was also declared, "It shall be a habitation for dragons (or serpents). I laid his heritage waste for the dragons of the wilderness." Dr. Shaw represented the land of Edom, and the desert of which it now forms a part, "as abounding with a variety of lizards and vipers, which are very numerous and troublesome." And Volney relates that "the Arabs, in general, avoid the ruins of the cities of Idumea, on account of the enormous scorpions with which they swarm." So plentiful, as observed by Mr. Cory, "are the scorpions in Petra, that, though it was cold and snowy, we found them under the stones, sometimes two under one stone!" The sheik, and his brother, who accompanied Mr. Cory, assured him that "both lions and leopards are often seen in Petra, and on the hills immediately beyond it, but that they never descend into the plain beneath." As the term "satyr" is known to be usually applied to a fabulous animal, the use of the name in the Scriptures has occasioned some surprise and inquiry. The word signifies "a rough hairy one," and may well have been used to designate the wild goat, large herds of which are found on these mountains. 122/221-22 (Predictions #1, #2, #7 and #9.)

Higgins ties up the prophecy with the fulfillments:

> Again and again the desolation of Edom is foretold. In the time of the prophets such a prediction seemed most unlikely of fulfillment. Even after the Edomites had been pushed out, the [Nabeans] developed a flourishing

civilization that lasted for centuries. But God had said, "I will lay thy cities waste." Today the land stands deserted, a mute testimony to the sure Word of the Lord. Petra is a remarkable example of the literal fulfillment of this prophecy. This great ancient capital with its theatre seating 4000, its temples, its altars and its monuments, is now silent and alone, decaying with the passage of time. 68/55 (Predictions #1, #2 and #8.)

Herbert Stewart gives a further description:

The ground is covered with broken pillars and pavements, heaps of hewn stone, and many other ruins. Scorpions and owls abound among its ruins. Burchardt, one of the boldest and most daring of travelers, says he never knew what fear was until he came near Petra. At nightfall the jackal howl is heard from the top of the rocks, answered by another far up the Wadi. The stone on which the traveler may sit is surrounded by nettles and thistles in what had been in the precincts of noble temples or palaces of beauty, and everything mentioned in the passages quoted [Isaiah 34:10-14; Jeremiah 49:16] during the past centuries have found resting places within the deserted city. 123/71-72 (Predictions #1, #7 and #8.)

George L. Robinson elucidates the feelings of standing in Petra today:

Petra is a place which astonishes and baffles, but above all fascinates. Your first visit is an event in your life. Elemental feelings stir; again you know what awe is and humility. You have a sense of God's work through man and without man. If you have never experienced the sensation before, here at last you come under the spell of mystery. The place seems so remote, so unrelated to its surroundings . . . so undiscovered and so undiscoverable. What other city has been lost for a thousand years and at last, when stumbled upon by accident, has had still so much of its glory left with which to astonish the amazed traveler? 116/9 (Prediction #9.)

Specific Fulfillments

Individual predictions will now be expounded. The first has been dealt with very effectively: Edom is clearly a desolate place. The second has been established equally. The Moslem takeover of Edom, in the sixth century A.D., can surely qualify as the "heathen" conquering of the third prediction. The fourth prediction, conquered by Israel:

It was predicted in Ezekiel 25:14 that Israel would be used by God to take vengeance on Edom. Considering the fact that Israel was then in the Babylonian captivity, such a prophecy probably seemed ludicrous. Yet, some four centuries later the prediction finds its fulfillment in Judas Maccabeus and John Hyrcanus. Thousands of Edomites were slain and the nation was forced to submit to Jewish circumcision, and for all practical purposes they became Jews. 68/58-59

The fifth prediction, that of a bloody history, follows:

A study of Edom's history has already borne this out. Assyria invaded the land and reduced Edom to servitude. The coming of Nebuchadnezzar took its toll. The migration of the Nabateans reduced their numbers. Forty thousand Edomites died at the hand of Judas Maccabeus. 68/55

The fulfillment of the sixth prediction, concerning Teman, or Maan, is described by Floyd Hamilton:

> And strange as it may seem, Teman, or Maan, as it is called today, is still a prosperous town, on the eastern border of the land of Edom, and the only city in all that land that is not deserted! Could any more marvelous fulfillment of prophecy be found than this? Think what small chance there would be of a mere man picking out only one city in the whole land as the one city that should live down the centuries, while all the other cities shared in the general fate of destruction and desolation! God alone could foretell such a result, and the book which contains such prophecies must be His Book! 65/312-13

The seventh prediction, concerning wild animals, has been borne out previously.

Of the eighth prediction, the cessation of trade, D. Higgins says,

> Isaiah said that "none shall pass through it forever and ever" (34:10); to which Ezekiel adds: "I will cut off from it him that passeth through" (35:7). That the commerce of Edom should cease was unthinkable, for the land was the crossroads of the trade routes. But the prophecy has been literally fulfilled. 68/56

From William G. Blaikie's *A Manual of Bible History*, regarding the prophecy that "none shall pass through it," we see

> the objection that the prophecy . . . has not been literally fulfilled, inasmuch as travelers have passed through Edom, is evidently frivolous. When the vast streams of traffic that used to pass through Edom have been so withdrawn that not a single caravan is ever seen on the route, the prophecy has surely been abundantly verified. 22/141

The ninth prediction, that of the astonishment of spectators, has also been fully explored. Higgins makes a good summation: "Jeremiah indicated that those who passed through Edom would be astonished at her desolation. . . . The magnificent cities of Edom have been laid waste and curious travelers never cease to wonder at the abandoned fortresses in the mountains." 68/59

PROBABILITY AND CONCLUSION

Many people probably realize that this estimate of prophecy is difficult to grasp; the best course of action is to bring it closer to home. Edom was about 60 miles wide and 110 miles long; this rectangular-shaped kingdom was roughly 6,600 square miles. The "kingdom" of New Jersey is about 7,500 square miles. Consider a hypothetical prediction: (1) New Jersey will become desolate. (2) It will never be reinhabited after it is conquered. (3) It will be invaded by men of the East, from across the sea. (4) It will also be conquered by men of the North. (5) It will have a bloodier and more corrupt future than any other nation in the United Kingdom of America.

(6) It will be totally destroyed up to Philadelphia. (7) The site of the old kingdom will be infested with wild animals and beasts.

If one were to predict this seriously today, he would either be mocked, ignored, or locked up. It sounds ridiculous. Three hundred million to one odds would be conservative, yet that is roughly what happened in real life to Edom. Edom was populous and powerful; Israel was broken and captive in Babylon, and it was Ezekiel who made prophecies too fantastic to be true—yet they *have* come true. The grim reality is staring us in the face. The prophecy was real. God's wrath is real. Ezekiel was real. The ruins of Petra are very real.

The Jewish People (A/31-33)

If anyone wishes to know whether or not the God of the Bible exists, one of the strongest reasons he can examine is the Jewish people. An honest inquiry into this question will provide more than an adequate answer to the truthfulness of the Christian faith.

About 4,000 years ago, God called a man named Abram out of the country where he was living and gave him these promises:

> I will make you a great nation, and I will bless you and make your name great; so you shall be a blessing: And I will bless those that bless you and the one who curses you I will curse: and in you all the families of the earth shall be blessed (Genesis 12:2,3).

> And the LORD said to Abram . . . Now lift up your eyes, and look from the place where you are, northward and southward and eastward and westward; for all the land which you see, I will give it to you and to your descendants forever (Genesis 13:14,15).

In other words, God promised to Abram (1) a great nation; (2) a great name; (3) being a blessing to all nations; and (4) a land which shall forever belong to his descendants.

Several hundred years after God made these promises to Abram, the great nation had indeed appeared, numbering in the millions. They were about to enter the land of promise when God, through their leader, Moses, gave them some warnings as recorded in Deuteronomy chapters 28—33.

God warned them against disobedience and promised that He would use other nations to remove them from that land if they were unfaithful to Him. He predicted that they would eventually be scattered across the whole earth as strangers in unfamiliar lands and that they would find no rest from their wanderings. However, God in His faithfulness did promise to bring them back into their land.

What has been the verdict of history? The children of Israel, even though they were warned, fell into idolatry and were removed from their homeland. In 606 B.C. King Nebuchadnezzar took the people captive to

Babylon and returned in 588–586 B.C., at which time, after a long siege, he burned the city and the Temple.

However, as God promised, He allowed those who desired to return to the land in 537–536 B.C., or after 70 years (Ezra, chapter 1). The removal from their homeland occurred a second time in A.D. 70 when Titus the Roman destroyed the city of Jerusalem and scattered the people.

For almost 1,900 years, the Jews wandered about the earth as strangers who were persecuted from every side. This culminated in the holocaust of World War II, when six million Jews were put to death in the concentration camps.

Yet, against all odds, the state of Israel was reborn on May 14, 1948, and the Jews began to return to their homeland from all points of the compass. This was the second time in their history since becoming a nation that they have come back into their land. Since 1948 they have survived some terrible conflicts, including the 1967 Six-Day War and the 1973 Holy Day War.

Through all this, the nation neither perished nor lost its national identity. History has demonstrated that any people who leave their homeland will, after about five generations, lose their national identity by being absorbed into the new culture, but the Jews remained a distinct entity.

Not only have they survived, but also the nations that persecuted them–Moab, Ammon, Edom, Philistia and many others–have either been destroyed or have completely lost their individual identity.

Have you ever heard of a Swedish Moabite? A Russian Philistine? A German Edomite? An American Ammonite? No! These people have been totally absorbed into other cultures and races.

However, have you ever heard of a Swedish Jew? A Russian Jew? A German Jew? An American Jew? Yes! As prophesied, they have not lost their identity.

The God of the Bible is faithful. By His dealings with the nation Israel, He has aobjectively demonstrated to the world both His faithfulness and His existence and He has verified His promises.

Conclusion (E/320)

In Isaiah 41:23 the prophet hurled out the challenge to heathen gods: "Show the things that are to come hereafter, that we may know that ye are gods."

God has accepted this challenge. He has predicted multitudes of events to happen in the future. They have come true exactly as predicted, even though in some cases thousands of years were involved for the fulfillment. God has proven that He is our supernatural God with all wisdom. We have no alternative but to believe.

CHAPTER 7 Is the New Testament Historically Reliable?

How did the Gospels come into being?

The Gospel Before the Gospels (HW/152-54)

Originally, there were not four Gospels, only the one gospel or good news about Jesus Christ. As the four Gospel accounts came to be seen as distinctively authoritative, Christians still recognized only one gospel, stated by four separate evangelists. The French scholar, Henri Daniel-Rops, comments:

> St. Irenaeus spoke very accurately of the tetramorphic gospel, the gospel, that is, which is under four forms. And from the middle of the second century, with Clement of Alexandria and the Muratorian Canon, it was the practice—and the only right practice—to say, the Gospel according to St. Matthew, according to St. Mark, according to St. Luke, according to St. John, to make it clear that here is a body of truth, substantially one and unique, communicated to men in different modes. 11/39

For centuries, scholars have struggled to explain how the various Gospel accounts came into existence. In his excellent book, *The Roots of the Synoptic Gospels,* Bo Reicke, the late professor of New Testament at the University of Basel, summarizes the various theories which have been proposed up to the present day:

> First, since the middle of the nineteenth century, most scholars have based their synoptic investigations on the assumption that texts were used by the evangelist as *literary* sources.
>
> (1) Widely dominant today is the two-source theory, according to which Mark and a presumed document called *Q* were the common sources of Matthew and Luke.
>
> (2) Some contemporary scholars, however, reject this position and return to an older tradition which reserved a priority for Matthew.
>
> (3) Others prefer to reconstruct a number of different sources behind the Gospels by separating a proto-Luke from Luke, a pre-Mark from Mark, or by dividing the so-called *Q* into various documents.
>
> These literary approaches contradict each other, and their advocates have not yet been able to convince the adherents of the other theories. 112/preface

The culture into which Jesus was born did use literary documents, but it was primarily an oral-tradition-based culture. "To understand this," says Daniel-Rops,

> we must rid ourselves for the moment of our habits as modern men, men of a paper civilization. For us, reading and writing are two such automatic operations that we can scarcely imagine how some societies have almost managed to do without them. Our memories, in consequence, have become anemic and stiff, but it is not so among many Eastern peoples who make more demands on it; it was not so in the time of Christ. To learn by heart and recite were the two normal operations for the transmission of a text. The great writers of Israel were no doubt, quite literally, great speakers; thus the prophecies of Jeremias were spoken over a period of twenty-two years before being written down.
>
> Later, in the same way, the Mishna, the most essential part of the *Talmud,* was only written down after centuries of oral transmission. "A good disciple," said the rabbis, "is like a well-built cistern: He does not let fall one drop of water from his master's teaching." We must imagine the first instruction in the gospel in the same fashion; what the apostles stored up in their memory, they taught infallibly to their own disciples, who in their turn would repeat it to their hearts. 11/35

The Accuracy of the Oral Gospel (HW/153-65)

Was this dependence on oral tradition a hindrance to those who lived in Jesus' day? They didn't seem to think so. We have already noted how Papias valued the "living and permanent voice" of the apostles and their disciples more than books. The *Mishnah* upheld oral tradition, warning that written documents could be falsified and thus forever preserve error. Daniel-Rops adds:

> In the same way, St. Irenaeus, bishop of Lyons, recalls the time when he heard St. Polycarp, the great bishop of Smyrna, telling what he had himself remembered of St. John. Here we can feel the human warmth, the very truth of life; when, much later, the written text was definitely imposed, after being long concurrent with the spoken word, can we imagine that in these conditions the two could have differed? The written text preserves, for all who can hear, the moving accent of those living testimonies. 11/37

The dissemination of material about Jesus, however, was not haphazardly entrusted to unknowledgeable Christians who could distort the message. When a successor was needed for Judas Iscariot, the one qualification accepted by the apostles was that the successor be an eyewitness of the entire ministry of Jesus:

> It is therefore necessary that of the men who have accompanied us all the time that the Lord Jesus went in and out among us—beginning with the baptism of John, until the day that He was taken up from us—one of these should become a witness with us of His resurrection (Acts 1:21,22).

Harold Riesenfeld, the respected Swedish New Testament scholar, concludes that for the disciples, "The words and deeds of Jesus are a holy word, comparable with that of the Old Testament, and the handing down of this precious material is entrusted to special persons." 114/19

Thus, the disciples followed the practice of their Jewish communities in choosing special people, comparable in many respects to the rabbis, to be responsible for preserving and passing along the "holy" tradition. The task consumed enough time that these people were relieved of other household duties that they might devote full time "to prayer and to the ministry of the word" (Acts 6:4).

The Swedish scholar, Birger Gerhardsson, in the first half of his *Memory and Manuscript,* explains the procedures Jewish authorities used to receive and transmit accurately their oral tradition. In the second half of the book he reveals the evidence for the early church's use of similar practices for passing on the oral tradition about Jesus.

Gerhardsson cites a number of rabbinic quotations to demonstrate how important it was in Jewish culture to receive and transmit its oral tradition accurately. For example, in the *Babylonian Talmud,* tractate Sotah 22*a* reveals that the Jews were intent to memorize even what they didn't understand: "The magician mumbles and does not understand what he is saying. In the same way the tanna recites and does not understand what he is saying." In the same *Talmud,* tractate Abodah Zarah 19*a* says, "One should always recite, (although one forgets and) although one does not understand what one is saying." In several different texts, a pupil is described as having learned a particular doctrine by the words, "He learned it from him 'forty times,' and it became for him as though it lay in his purse." 16

In several places, the rabbis give their students mnemonic devices to help them memorize certain passages.

Those who have discovered the helpful technique of memorizing by repeating aloud will recognize the soundness of this advice: "Let your ears hear what you allow to cross your lips." 15 R. Akiba emphasized daily study of the Torah by saying, "Sing every day, sing every day." 18

Strong admonitions against forgetting included this one from R. Meir, "Every man who forgets a single word of his *Mishnah* (i.e., what he has learned), Scripture accounts it unto him as if he had forfeited his soul!" 93 If a teacher forgot what he once knew, for example because of bad health, he had to return to his own pupils to relearn what he had forgotten. 55/169

Is it any wonder that for hundreds of years the Jews were able to preserve volumes of oral tradition? They finally recorded the *Mishnah* circa A.D. 200, the *Jerusalem* or *Palestinian Talmud* in A.D. 350-425, and the *Babylonian Talmud* in A.D. 500. When you think for a moment that every one of the eyewitnesses to Jesus' life had at least some of the childhood training illustrated above, it is almost ludicrous to think that they would have allowed error to creep into the words of Jesus which they wanted to preserve. One almost wonders why Jesus needed to send the Holy Spirit to "bring to your remembrance all that I said to you" (John 14:26).

It is clear from the Gospels that Jesus phrased His teaching in easy-to-remember segments. The parables are generally concise and easily recalled. Certain sayings such as Matthew 11:17 indicate Jesus' teaching skill within an oral culture: "We played the flute for you, and you did not dance; we sang a dirge, and you did not mourn." The story of the two who built their houses, one on sand and one upon the rock, contains parallels and contrasts in phraseology which stick with the listener (Matthew 7:24-27).

From the very beginning, though the disciples misunderstood what Jesus' messiahship meant, they did not doubt that He was the Messiah. John probably noticed that the other gospel writers failed to record some crucial events concerning the time prior to when they left their nets to follow Jesus. So he tells of Andrew finding Peter and announcing, "We have found the Messiah" (John 1:41).

When Philip told Nathanael about Jesus, Philip used clearly understood Jewish terms to refer to Jesus as the Messiah: "We have found Him of whom Moses in the Law and also the Prophets wrote" (John 1:45).

Using the Greek word for Messiah, Matthew 23:10 recalls Jesus' teaching: "And do not be called leaders; for one is your Leader, that is, Christ." Gerhardsson concludes:

> All historical probability is in favor of Jesus' disciples, and the whole of

early Christianity, having accorded the sayings of the one whom they believed to be the Messiah at least the same degree of respect as the pupils of a rabbi accorded the words of their master! 55/332

Similarities and Differences in the Gospels (HW/159-63)

In addition to the Gospel According to Mark, scholars today commonly refer to the *Q* document which is held to be the other document from which Matthew and Luke obtained much of their material. The existence of this *literary* document is presumed so strongly by some, that you would think we possess it in hand. In fact, all that we really possess is a collection of various verses from Matthew and Luke which are said to make up the *Q* document based on present literary criticism. After presenting strong technical arguments against the existence of a literary *Q* document, professor Reicke states:

> These specific Matthean and Lukan traditions have in no way proven themselves as deriving from a document or text collection. Mainly comprised of sayings, or logia, they oftentimes contain narratives too. The peculiar dispersion of the relevant 35 or 31 plus 4 units, among which there are only 2 really contextual parallels, shows that any supposition of a written source behind the Matthean-Lukan double traditions, such as the Logia source or the presumed document *Q*, is an illusion. 112/27

In order to explain how large blocks of material within each of the Gospels (in particular, Matthew and Luke) describe similar events but occur in different contexts, Reicke states:

> The explanation lies in the principle of supply and demand, that is, each synoptic writer had a certain material at his disposal which had been transmitted and formulated in various ways among the Christians and which he took up, eventually rearranged, broadened, or limited according to his interests. 112/29

Reicke is not saying here that the gospel writers used some basic material to make up their own stories, but rather that they fit together oral traditions in a manner that highlighted the particular facets of Jesus' life that they wanted to emphasize. Therefore, whereas we find no contradiction of historical details within the Gospel accounts, we will find various rearrangements of the material which helped each gospel writer communicate the life of Christ to the particular audience which he had targeted.

One additional cause for differences between Gospel narratives: The events of Pentecost, fifty days after Jesus' resurrection, indicate that very early in the life of the church the tradition about Jesus had to be translated into other languages. Even the single step of translating from Aramaic or Hebrew into Greek would account for some of the dissimilarities between the various Gospel accounts.

The Formative Period and Dating of the Gospels

(HW/154-56; RF/24-27)

The formative period has been designated as that period of time between the crucifixion and the writing of the Gospels. During the heyday of the German Tübingen school, it was popular to date the Gospel accounts to a hundred or more years after Jesus' crucifixion.

F. C. Bauer, along with other critics, assumed that the New Testament Scriptures were not written until late in the second century A.D. He concluded that these writings came mainly from myths or legends that had developed during the lengthy interval between the lifetime of Jesus and the time these accounts were set down in writing.

By the end of the nineteenth century, however, archaeological discoveries had confirmed the accuracy of the New Testament manuscripts. Discoveries of early *papyri* manuscripts bridged the gap between the time of Christ and existing manuscripts from a later date. In 1955, Dr. William F. Albright, recognized as one of the world's outstanding biblical archaeologists, wrote:

> We can already say emphatically that there is no longer any solid basis for dating any book of the New Testament after circa A.D. 80, two full generations before the date between 130 and 150 given by the more radical New Testament critics of today. 37/136

Eight years later he stated in an interview that the completion date for all the books in the New Testament was "probably sometime between circa A.D. 50 and 75." 9/3

Dr. John A. T. Robinson, lecturer at Trinity College, Cambridge, has been for years one of England's more distinguished critics. Robinson accepted the consensus typified by German criticism that the New Testament was written years after the time of Christ, at the end of the first century. But, as "little more than a theological joke," he decided to investigate the arguments on the late dating of all the New Testament books, a field largely dormant since the turn of the century.

The results stunned him. He said that owing to scholarly "sloth," the "tyranny of unexamined assumptions" and "almost willful blindness" by previous authors, much of the past reasoning was untenable. He concluded that the New Testament is the work of the apostles themselves or of contemporaries who worked with them and that all the New Testament books, including John, had to have been written before A.D. 64.

Robinson challenges his colleagues to try to prove him wrong. If scholars reopen the question, he is convinced, the results will force "the rewriting of many introductions to—and ultimately, theologies of—the

New Testament." 115/95

With the arrival of Robinson's *Redating the New Testament* (1976) which pays greater attention to historical evidence than did the form critics, the date has been pushed back to as early as circa A.D. 40 for a possible first draft of Matthew. Most scholars who do not presuppose an antisupernatural bias date the synoptic Gospels generally in the 60s, some a little earlier. Those who accept the existence of a *Q* source document behind Matthew and Mark usually date it from before A.D. 50. There is, then, strong evidence that the formative period was no more than seventeen to twenty years in length, possibly as little as seven to ten years for an Aramaic or Hebrew version of Matthew spoken of by Papias.

This conclusion is corroborated by several pieces of converging evidence. First, it is evident that the Book of Acts was written in approximately A.D. 62. It does not mention the fall of Jerusalem in A.D. 70, an event which would have been impossible to omit since Jerusalem is central to much of Acts. Nothing is mentioned of Nero's persecution of A.D. 64. The book ends with Paul in Rome under the confinement of Nero. Neither does Acts mention the martyrdoms of three central figures of the book: James (A.D. 62), Paul (A.D. 64), and Peter (A.D. 65). Why aren't their deaths mentioned when Acts does record the deaths of Stephen and James, the brother of John?

If the book of Acts was written by Luke in A.D. 62, then the Gospel of Luke must be dated earlier, probably in the late 50s.

The early church fathers affirm that Matthew wrote his account first. Many modern critics say Mark wrote his first. In either case almost everyone agrees that they both wrote before Luke, which puts their dates of composition no later than the late 50s. Earlier drafts, partial written drafts or collections of things Jesus said or did were likely in circulation for years prior to being used in the Gospel accounts as we know them. These reports probably circulated in the 40s and 50s. Thus again, the formative period could have been no longer than seventeen to twenty years.

The formative period should not be construed as that period of time in which the content of the Gospels was being formed by some "creative community." It is rather that period of time when the form of the material was in transition from an oral to a written medium.

Analyzing the critics' conclusions of late authorship, Albright wrote: "Only modern scholars who lack both historical method and perspective can spin such a web of speculation as that with which critics have surrounded the Gospel tradition."

He added that the period is "too slight to permit any appreciable corruption of the essential center and even of the specific wording of the sayings of Jesus." 2/297-98

Howard Vos, researcher, declares, "From the standpoint of literary evidence the only logical conclusion is that the case for the reliability of the New Testament is infinitely stronger than that for any other record of antiquity." 130/176

Evidence for Reliability From Historical Geography

(HW/198-209)

Unlike the mythical accounts of various alleged gods of pagan mystery religions, the Gospel narratives describe Jesus as a man of flesh and blood who traveled to actual geographic locations and interacted with known historical persons. That He occupied a specific place in time and space becomes clearer as one studies the historical geography of Jesus' day. The details of history and geography in the Gospel accounts yield clear evidence that the writers were not making up their story.

Rudolf Bultmann, who viewed the New Testament as an historically flawed document, had never visited the sites in Israel and had never considered the influence of Jewish culture on Jesus. Martin Hengel of the University of Tübingen in West Germany said of the lack of considering the cultural element that it was a "bad old German tradition with dangerous results." 66/38

Historical geography seeks to relate events in history to geographic locations. Knowing what has happened in a certain location in the past reveals why Jesus would do something at that location when He was there. Since it would be practically impossible for a later Gentile writer to have knowledge of the historical-geographical context surrounding an event in Jesus' life, these incidents provide good evidence that what the Gospel writers describe actually happened. A few examples:

In the city of Nain, Jesus raised the widow's dead son. Nain sits on the north side of a hill in southern Galilee. Just over the hill, on the south side, is the place where Elisha resuscitated the dead son of the Shunemite woman. Because the people of this locality were especially attuned to that miracle, Jesus was able to establish His authority by performing a similar miracle in the nearby town. The people of Nain responded, "A great prophet has arisen among us!" and, "God has visited His people!"

Mary and Joseph's flight to Egypt with the infant Jesus was not an odd move. Eighty-five percent of all Jews lived outside Israel, and Alexandria, Egypt, contained a large and old Jewish population. Joseph and Mary may have had friends or relatives there.

Jesus' home town of Nazareth is significant for several reasons. **First,** it was an obscure village "out in the sticks" with perhaps only 20 to 30 families living there. This is confirmed by the discovery of 23 tombs, believed to be the first-century cemetery for the entire town. Nazareth does not appear in any of the lists of cities found in Josephus, in the Old Testament, or in the *Talmud*. No wonder Nathanael, when Philip first told him about Jesus, responded, "Can any good thing come out of Nazareth?" (John 1:46)

Second, Nazareth sits on the side of a high ridge overlooking the Jezreel Valley. The geography fits well with Luke's description of the city when he reports, "They rose up and cast Him out of the city, and led Him to the brow of the hill on which their city had been built, in order to throw Him down the cliff" (Luke 4:29).

Third, the Jezreel valley, also called the Plain of Megiddo or Armageddon, was literally the front yard of Nazareth. More than 250 battles in history have been fought at this location, and the prophets predict the final battle will be waged here as well. Armies can enter the valley through seven major passes, making it an ideal battleground. As Jesus was growing up, He must have walked across this valley many times and perhaps here reflected often that "all those who take up the sword shall perish by the sword" (Matthew 26:25). It is ironic and yet typical of the way God often works, that the one called "the Prince of Peace" should grow up looking out over "the battleground of history."

The Gospel writers often casually refer to geographical features which indicate how familiar they are with the land. More important, Jesus seems to have done and said certain things in relationship to His surroundings with the purpose of leaving behind unforgettable messages vividly imprinted on the minds of the disciples. For example, at the base of the 9,000-foot high "rock" of Mt. Hermon, Jesus says to Peter, "You are Peter [Greek *Petros,* a stone], and upon this rock [Greek *petra,* large rock, bedrock] I will build My church; and the gates of Hades shall not overpower it" (Matthew 16:18). "Gates of Hades" was a rabbinic term referring to Gentile cities. Jesus was predicting that the mission entrusted to His apostles would one day overpower the Gentiles. Again, Jesus made His prediction in an appropriate place as the base of Mount Hermon at Caesarea-Philippi contains numerous large niches, carved into the cliff, which housed statues of the Greco-Roman pantheon of gods.

Later, in Jerusalem, the disciples would be reminded again of Mt. Hermon when Jesus cried out, "He who believes in Me, as the Scripture said, 'From his innermost being shall flow rivers of living water' " (John 7:38). Most rivers begin with a trickle . . . but not the river Jordan. When the snows on Mount Hermon melt, the water seeps down through the mountain and then gushes full force from the base of the mountain. From personal observation, we can verify that some of these springs are more than ten feet across at the point where they flow out from under Mount Hermon.

The countryside around the Sea of Galilee, made Jesus' teaching even more vivid by the way He incorporated the surroundings into that teaching. For example, from Capernaum on the northwest shore of the sea, one could see several cities on top of hills all around the sea. Directly opposite, on the southeast shore lay Hippus, the largest city visible to those in Capernaum. Its primary location was not down by the water but high on a hill overlooking the sea. Several other cities and villages perched on hilltops around the Sea of Galilee. For example, Gamala was the zealot stronghold to the east. The lights of these cities would often remind the apostles of the time Jesus gestured toward them as He said, "You are the light of the world. A city set on a hill cannot be hidden" (Matthew 5:14).

John states that Jesus "came to His own, and those who were His own did not receive Him" (John 1:11). This statement is certainly borne out by a list of towns Jesus did and did not visit. The towns He did visit consisted mainly of religious Jews: Capernaum, Chorazin, Bethsaida, Gennesaret, Cana and Nazareth. By curious contrast, there is no record of Jesus having entered the larger cities where Hellenized Jews mingled with Gentiles: Hippus, Gadara, Julias (next to Bethsaida), Sepphoris (less than five miles from Nazareth), Tiberias, Scythopolis, and Caesarea Philippi (though He did visit the countryside around Caesarea Philippi). Jesus indicated on various occasions that His mission went beyond the Jews, yet He carried out His ministry almost exclusively among the religious or orthodox Jews.

Even some of Jesus' strangest miracles are at home in the setting around the Sea of Galilee. One kind of fish dwelling in this sea belongs to the Cichlidae family and is sometimes called the "mouth breeder." It is found only in Lake Victoria (Uganda), along the Nile River, and in the Sea of Galilee. Cartographer Dr. Jim Fleming, who teaches classes in archaeology and historical geography at Hebrew University in Jerusalem, explains its significance:

> The female keeps the eggs in her mouth until they hatch. As the brood begins to grow she lets them out from time to time on an "outing," but quickly scoops them up when danger is near. The mother will fast until near starvation in order not to swallow her young. These strong instincts have given the Hebrew name of the fish "The Mother-Fish." After the young are off on their own the mother often keeps a substitute in her mouth. They are sometimes caught today with pebbles or coke bottle caps in their mouths! The popular name for the fish is "St. Peter's fish" because of the gospel story in Matthew 17:24-27 about Peter catching a fish with a shekel coin in its mouth. 48/6

Galilee is a volcanic area. Volcanic rock is everywhere, and thorns grow there rapidly during the summer months. When Jesus told His parable of the four soils, His listeners would have related well to what He said. Later, His disciples would recall the parable easily whenever they visited the area.

The things Jesus did and said in and around Jerusalem likewise fit well with what is known of the local geography. The small town of Bethphage sits on the side of the Mount of Olives facing away from Jerusalem. It takes its name from a preseason fruit which grows on the fig trees of the area. The fruit is called *phage* (fah-gay) in Hebrew, and appears in the early spring with the first leaves. Did you ever wonder why Jesus was looking for figs on the fig tree when the text specifically says, "It was not the season for figs"? The answer is that even though it was not the season for figs (Gr. *sukon* meaning ripe figs), the fact that the tree had leaves indicated that it also should have had the preseason figs (*phage*), which were edible. Since the tree contained no fruit, Jesus seems to have used it as an object lesson to warn against professing something by our appearance but having no fruit to back it up. (See Mark 11:12-14 and Matthew 21:18,19.)

From this same area one can look off to the south and see the Herodium with the Dead Sea shimmering in the distance behind it. Herod had this palatial fortress built between 24 and 15 B.C. The small mountain on which it sits was heightened by using part of another nearby mountain. Immediately after cursing the fig tree at Bethphage, Jesus commented, "Truly I say to you, whoever says to this mountain, 'Be taken up and cast into the sea,' and does not doubt in his heart, but believes that what he says is going to happen; it shall be granted him" (Mark 11:23). Jesus was probably pointing at the Herodium and the Dead Sea as He spoke, indicating that not even the power of Herod (or other kings and authorities) could prevent the establishment of His kingdom.

Mustard trees still grow in Israel, and one can readily see that their minute seeds (hundreds can fit on the tip of a finger) and 15-foot height fit precisely with Jesus' parable:

> The kingdom of heaven is like a mustard seed . . . and this is smaller than all other seeds; but when it is full grown, it is larger than the garden plants, and becomes a tree, so that the birds of the air come and nest in its branches (Matthew 13:31,32).

In Jerusalem, from the steps on the southern side of the Temple where rabbis often addressed their pupils, the chalk-white tombstones that cover the Mount of Olives are clearly visible. Jesus probably looked in that direction as He proclaimed:

> Woe to you, scribes and Pharisees, hypocrites! For you are like whitewashed tombs which on the outside appear beautiful, but inside they are full of dead men's bones and all uncleanness. Even so you too outwardly appear righteous to men, but inwardly you are full of hypocrisy and lawlessness (Matthew 23:27,28).

Fulfilled Prophecy in the New Testament (E/309-11)

Most readers are familiar with Jesus' pronouncements against Jerusalem:

> For the days shall come upon you when your enemies will throw up a bank

> before you, and surround you, and hem you in on every side, and will level you to the ground and your children within you, and they will not leave in you one stone upon another, because you did not recognize the time of your visitation (Luke 20:43,44).

This prophecy was fulfilled literally in A.D. 70 when the Romans decimated Jerusalem. Nothing was left of the Temple except its foundation.

Lesser known is the fulfillment of Jesus' predictions concerning Chorazin, Bethsaida and Capernaum. George Davis comments:

> We read in the New Testament of four ancient cities which were beautifully situated near or in the shores of the Sea of Galilee. These four cities were Capernaum, Chorazin, Bethsaida, and Tiberias. Three of these cities have perished. Only the last named is standing today. 37/33

In Matthew 11:20-24, Jesus predicts that Chorazin and Bethsaida will incur a greater judgment than Tyre and Sidon, and that Capernaum will suffer a worse fate than the city of Sodom.

Though there is recorded no specific prophecy on how the cities were to be destroyed, the unmistakable mark of God's judgment and displeasure is on the brow of the three cities. History records a distinct story for these cities.

George Davis in his *Bible Prophecies Fulfilled Today* records that "an earthquake destroyed Capernaum about A.D. 400 and doubtless Chorazin and Bethsaida perished at the same time." 37/36

Davis expands:

> Ancient Bethsaida's situation on the shore of the Sea of Galilee had been so beautiful that about A.D. 700, King Albalid I of Damascus decided to build a magnificent winter palace on the site of the ruined city. For fifteen years his workmen labored erecting the palace. Then King Albalid died, and the great palace was never completed. As the centuries rolled by, the palace became mere ruins. Today about all that remains of its former grandeur are some foundation stones and some unfinished mosaic flooring. Archaeologists have covered up this mosaic with sand, lest it too should be carried away by vandals, and thus all traces of the palace should be lost. 37/36-37

Davis explains the situation of Capernaum:

> For long centuries the synagogue lay buried under the earth like the rest of the destroyed city. . . . A man conceived the idea of restoring the ancient synagogue from its ruins. At length part of the walls of the building were re-erected, and a number of the pillars were put in their places.
>
> Then the unexpected happened. The architect of the partly restored synagogue suddenly died—just as King Albalid had died centuries ago before his palace in Bethsaida was completed. 37/38

Unger's Bible Dictionary sums up the plight of the three doomed cities:

> The doom pronounced against Capernaum and the other unbelieving

cities (Matthew 11:23) has been remarkably fulfilled. Tell Hum, its now generally accepted site, is a mass of ruins adjacent to Bethsaida and Tabgha, and yielded a third century A.D. synagogue when excavated. 126/180

Davis concludes the prophecy with these comments: "Not one word of judgment was pronounced on the city of Tiberias by our Lord. It has been partly destroyed several times but it has always been rebuilt." 37/40

Davis adds:

> Each time we have visited Tiberias and the area around the Sea of Galilee we have been impressed anew with the truthfulness and the supernatural inspiration of the Word of God. There are the ruins of three cities, destroyed exactly as foretold by our Lord, and one city, Tiberias, upon which no word of judgment was uttered, still standing and flourishing after nineteen long centuries. 37/41

Jewish Cultural Evidence for Reliability of the Gospels (HW/243-45)

The setting of all four Gospel accounts is unmistakably first-century Hebrew. Some events seem strange to us but are perfectly natural in the Jewish culture of Jesus' day. For example, Luke 7:38 speaks of a woman weeping and wetting Jesus' feet with her tears. Weeping was an important part of Jewish culture. Professional mourners were hired for funerals, and many Jews had "tear vases" where they collected the tears of their grief. The woman described by Luke may have been literally pouring out the tears from her tear vase to indicate to Jesus her sorrow for her sins. The present day visitor to Israel may observe many of these ancient tear vases in museums there.

Luke 2:24 speaks of another of many cultural practices mentioned in the Gospel narratives. In obedience to Leviticus 12:2,6,8, Joseph and Mary brought the sacrifice required after the birth of a child. Their offering of two turtledoves or pigeons indicates that they were among the poor of the land.

Hebrew marriage customs help to explain what otherwise appears to be a contradiction in Matthew 1:18,19. In verse 18, Mary is only betrothed to Joseph, whereas in verse 19, Joseph is called her "husband." The Reverend James Freeman, who compiled a vast collection of Bible customs, explains:

> Espousal among the Hebrews was something more than what a mere marriage engagement is with us. It was considered the beginning of marriage, was as legally binding as marriage itself, and could not be broken off save by a bill of divorce. Hence we find that Joseph is called the "husband" of Mary. 53/330

Jesus' confrontation with the Sadducees in Mark 12 accords with what we know about the Sadducees' attitude toward Levirate marriage. In Yebamoth 4.6*b* of the *Palestinian Talmud,* the Sadducees again use Levirate marriage, this time to mock the Pharisees. They pose the hypothetical problem of one of thirteen brothers who is required to be joined in Levirate marriage with the widows of his twelve deceased brothers.

The account of the woman with the hemorrhage becomes much more meaningful and realistic in light of the Jewish laws of purity (Matthew 9:20-22; Mark 5:25-34; Luke 8:43-48). The woman's condition meant that she had been continuously ceremonially impure for twelve years, and that by the law, her touching Jesus' garments would defile Him. She is understandably frightened when she learns that Jesus detected her act. And can you imagine the rare sense of compassion she must have felt when Jesus said to her, "Daughter, your faith has made you well; go in peace"? (Luke 8:48).

The synoptic Gospels speak of Jesus cleansing the Temple at the beginning of His last week in Jerusalem. John indicates that He had previously performed the same operation at the beginning of His ministry. It was not that Jesus objected to the exchanging of money. Roman coins, which most of the people carried and which were stamped with the image of Caesar, could not be used in the Temple under the Mosaic prescription against graven images. Therefore there was a legitimate need for money-changers—the people needed the Jewish coins because they contained only geometric, floral, or ceremonial decorations. Jewish sources suggest that some of the priestly families probably made personal profits on those money-changing dealings. (See top of page 89 for one such source.) What incensed Jesus was the corruption and commotion going on in a place that represented God's majesty and purity, a place that was to be used for prayer.

One striking feature of the Gospel narratives is that they speak of Jesus going almost exclusively to Jewish towns in order to carry out his ministry. The accounts record that Jesus entered only two cities which were not primarily orthodox Jewish: the Gentile city of Sidon and the Samaritan city of Sychar. Since we are told of no incident occurring in Sidon, we have no report of any ministry performed by Jesus inside a Gentile city. It is striking that the Gospels report Jesus going into Bethsaida, but not Julius, probably 100 yards away. He goes into obscure Nazareth, but not the major city of Sepphoris approximately three miles away. He goes into the country or regions of Decapolis, Caesarea Philippi and Tyre, but not into the Gentile cities themselves. Everything in the historical geographical situation is thoroughly Jewish—orthodox Jewish.

The Gospels make comments in a number of places which show that Jesus was very pro-Semitic; some even sound strongly anti-Gentile. In Matthew 15:26 and Mark 7:27, Jesus refers to Gentiles as "dogs" after stating, "I was sent only to the lost sheep of the house of Israel." In

Matthew 10:5,6, Jesus instructs His disciples not to go "in the way of the Gentiles, and do not enter any city of the Samaritans." In John 4:22, Jesus, speaking as a Jew to a Samaritan, says, "You worship that which you do not know; we worship that which we know; for salvation is of the Jews."

Are Accounts of the Trial of Jesus Anti-Semitic? (HW/259-61)

While we're on the subject of the Jewish flavor of the Gospel accounts, we need to answer one objection. The charge is repeatedly made that the accounts represent the anti-Semitic attitude of later Gentile Christians who redacted the writings. Maurice Goguel, for example, believes that the Romans collaborated with the Jews in order to arrest Jesus, and concludes: "The Gospel narrative which attributes this initiative wholly to the Jews is a biased perversion of the primitive tradition." 56/469

It is important, whenever someone claims a particular statement is anti-Semitic, to know whether the person making the statement is Jewish or non-Jewish. In teaching his class on New Testament to Jewish students at Hebrew University in Jerusalem, Professor Fleming says he begins

> by saying "I don't know why some Jews are so sensitive about the *supposed* anti-Semitism of the New Testament. How can anyone say, 'I will vomit you out of the land' is anti-Semitic? How can anyone say, 'Your prayers are a stench to the nostrils of God' is anti-Semitic?" And of course they all get upset. "How could you say that isn't anti-Semitic?" Then I remind them it's Isaiah and Jeremiah that I am quoting. 47

If the Gospel writers wanted to whitewash the Romans and defame the Jews, it is impossible to explain many statements in their narratives. Why would they have Pontius Pilate scourging Jesus? Why wouldn't they have Pilate taking responsibility and putting an end to the whole thing? Certainly he had the authority to do so.

And what about all the pro-Jewish statements in the Gospel accounts? John, for example, supposedly the most anti-Semitic of the Gospel writers, has Jesus saying, "Salvation is of the Jews" (John 4:22). Or why does Luke have Jesus saying regarding those who crucified Him, "Father, forgive them; for they do not know what they are doing" (Luke 23:34). That doesn't sound like someone trying to heap condemnation on the Jews.

When the gospel writers (remember, they are Jewish too) say negative things about the Jewish leaders, they are saying nothing that other Jews were not already saying. Excavations in the upper city of old Jerusalem, which uncovered the large homes of the more wealthy and aristocratic Jews, discovered dishes with the family name "Kathros" on them. The name also appears in a Baraita which reveals the character of the ruling priestly families of Jesus' day:

> Woe to me because of the house of Hannan [Annas] because of their whispers! Woe to me because of the house of Kathros, because of their pens! [a probable reference to the forging of illegal documents] . . . For they are high priests and their sons are treasurers, and their sons-in-law [Caiaphas was the son-in-law of Annas] are overseers, and their servants beat the people with rods. 17

Are the Gospel reports anti-Semitic? Judging by the rabbinic reflection above, it appears that more than just the Gospel writers were concerned about corruption in the high court. It is known that Sanhedrin members in the Herodian period were appointed for political favors, and it is not likely that such a Sanhedrin would act in the most just and pious manner. The Gospel writers were not anti-Semitic. They simply reported what others of their fellow Jews had already observed.

New Testament writers often use the term "the Jews." It is a general term referring to a group of Jewish people, most often Jewish leaders and their employees or servants, who are involved in a particular action. When a New Testament writer states that "the Jews" did such and such, he does not mean the entire race of Jews. He means simply the Jews who were there. Was it, for example, all the Jews in Jerusalem who called for Jesus to be crucified? Of course not. Jesus' own disciples were Jews. It was simply the crowd of Jews who were there. And as Ian Wilson brings out, "With twenty thousand Temple servants and eighteen thousand workmen on their payroll, the Temple's controllers would scarcely have had any difficulty in finding a mob to perform to whatever tune they called." 129/126 In fact, the gospel writers never once say "the Jews" crucified Jesus. They refer to the mob simply as "they." Further, Luke, writing in Acts, demonstrates conclusively that the very earliest church did not see the Jews as "Christ-killers." When Peter and John return to their friends after being jailed and interrogated, they all agree in prayer:

> O Lord, it is Thou who didst make the heaven and the earth and the sea, and all that is in them, who by the Holy Spirit, through the mouth of our father David Thy servant, didst say,
>
> > Why did the Gentiles rage, and the peoples devise futile things? The kings of the earth took their stand, and the rulers were gathered together, against the LORD, and against His Christ.
>
> For truly in this city there were gathered together against Thy holy Servant Jesus, whom Thou didst anoint, both Herod and Pontius Pilate, along with the Gentiles and the peoples of Israel, to do whatever Thy hand and Thy purpose predestined to occur (Acts 4:24-28).

The point of the Gospel accounts is not to assign blame. The message the New Testament wants its readers to get is simply: "It was people like me who killed Jesus; it was my sin that put Him on the cross." Thus Paul would write, "For I delivered to you as of first importance what I also received, that Christ died for *our* sins" (1 Corinthians 1:3, emphasis ours).

Likewise, Peter recorded, "And He Himself bore *our* sins in His body on the cross" (1 Peter 2:24, emphasis ours).

Evidence for Reliability From the Apostle Paul

(HW/168-70)

When we come to the apostle Paul, we find what some would say is the greatest evidence for the truth of the Christian faith. Here is a man cut completely from the cloth of Jewish culture. Fashioned by it and steeped in it, he was probably one of the most intense protagonists of the day for rabbinic Judaism. In his own words, "I was advancing in Judaism beyond many of my contemporaries among my countrymen, being more extremely zealous for my ancestral traditions" (Galatians 1:14). Paul's sudden conversion from persecutor of the church to its foremost early missionary is one of the most difficult challenges to a skeptic of biblical Christianity. Phillip Schaff remarks that even "Dr. Baur, the master-spirit of skeptical criticism and the founder of the 'Tübingen School,' " felt constrained to admit that in " 'the sudden transformation of Paul from the most violent adversary of Christianity into its most determined herald' he could see 'nothing short of a miracle.' " 119/315 quoting 20/1:47

One of the main reasons the evidence from Paul is so strong is that he produced his letters so early. The chart on the next page compares the dates given by three recognized scholars in the field (representing both liberal and moderate views) and helps set the works of Paul in their historical time frame.

As you can see in the chart, even though different scholars vary on specific dates, it is usually by not more than two or three years. (Obviously Kümmel does not accept Pauline authorship on some of the New Testament books attributed to Paul.) 70

The dates of Paul's letters become particularly significant in view of objections critics raise against the Gospel accounts. For example, critics are fond of dating the Gospels fairly late because the Gospels supposedly indicate a more sophisticated view of Christ ("high Christology") which would not have existed in earliest Christianity. But one of the chief indicators for a high Christology is the use of the word *Christ* as a name (as in "Jesus Christ") rather than as a title (as in "Jesus the Christ"). It is odd then that Paul, supposedly writing earlier than the gospel writers, exhibits this high Christology.

Matthew, Mark, Luke and John combined use the name "Jesus Christ"

Book	Kümmel 81/n.p.	Guthrie 61/n.p.	Robinson
1 Thessolians	50	51	Early 50
2 Thessalonians	50-51	51	50-51
1 Corinthians	54-55	57	Spring 55
1 Timothy	100+	61-64	Autumn 55
2 Corinthians	55-56	57	Early 56
Galatians	54-55	49-50	Late 56
Romans	55-56	57-58	Early 57
Titus	100+	61-64	Late spring 57
Philippians	53-58	59-61	Spring 58
Philemon	56-60	59-61	Summer 58
Colossians	56-60	59-61	Late summer 58
Ephesians	80-100	59-61	Late summer 58
2 Timothy	100+	61-64	Autumn 58

only five times. Paul uses it approximately 125 times. Whereas the gospel writers almost always refer to Jesus by the name "Jesus" alone, Paul almost always uses a term such as "Christ Jesus," "Lord Jesus," "Jesus Christ" or "our Lord Jesus Christ." The Gospel writers only occasionally call Jesus "Christ" as though it were a name.

Why?

There is only one good answer. The Gospel accounts originated earlier than Paul's letters (early as they were) and preserved the wording of the earliest oral traditions through their formative stages to the completed written accounts.

CHAPTER 8 *Archaeological Evidence for the Reliability of the Old Testament*

The Testimony of Archaeologists and Classical Scholars (E/65-68; ME/18-19)

William F. Albright, known for his reputation as one of the great archaeologists, states: "There can be no doubt that archaeology has confirmed the substantial historicity of Old Testament tradition." 1/176

Albright adds:

> The excessive skepticism shown toward the Bible by important historical schools of the eighteenth and nineteenth centuries, certain phases of which still appear periodically, has been progressively discredited. Discovery after discovery has established the accuracy of innumerable details, and has brought increased recognition to the value of the Bible as a source of history. 5/127-28

Millar Burrows of Yale observes: "Archaeology has in many cases refuted the views of modern critics. It has shown in a number of instances that these views rest on false assumptions and unreal, artificial schemes of historical development." 32/291

F. F. Bruce notes: "Where Luke has been suspected of inaccuracy, and accuracy has been vindicated by some inscriptional evidence, it may be legitimate to say that archaeology has confirmed the New Testament record." 27/331

Merrill Unger summarizes: "Old Testament archaeology has rediscovered whole nations, resurrected important peoples, and in a most astonishing manner filled in historical gaps, adding immeasurably to the knowledge of biblical backgrounds." 127/15

William Albright continues:

> As critical study of the Bible is more and more influenced by the rich new material from the ancient Near East we shall see a steady rise in respect for the historical significance of now neglected or despised passages and details in the Old and New Testament. 2/81

Burrows exposes the cause of much unbelief: "The excessive skepticism of many liberal theologians stems not from a careful evaluation of the available data, but from an enormous predisposition against the supernatural." 130/176

The Yale archaeologist adds to his above statement:

> On the whole, however, archaeological work has unquestionably strengthened confidence in the reliability of the scriptural record. More than one archaeologist has found his respect for the Bible increased by the experience of excavation in Palestine. 32/1
>
> Such evidence as archaeology has afforded thus far, especially by providing additional and older manuscripts of the books of the Bible, strengthens our confidence in the accuracy with which the text has been transmitted through the centuries. 32/42

Sir Frederic Kenyon says:

> It is therefore legitimate to say that, in respect of that part of the Old Testament against which the disintegrating criticism of the last half of the nineteenth century was chiefly directed, the evidence of archaeology has been to re-establish its authority, and likewise to augment its value by rendering it more intelligible through a fuller knowledge of its background and setting. Archaeology has not yet said its last word; but the results already achieved confirm what faith would suggest, that the Bible can do nothing but gain from an increase of knowledge. 79/279

Reformed Jewish scholar, Nelson Glueck, has affirmed: "It is worth emphasizing that in all this work no archaeological discovery has ever controverted a single, properly understood biblical statement." 94/6

A WORD OF CAUTION (ME/20)

All too often we hear the phrase, "Archaeology proves the Bible." There needs to be a word of caution. Archaeology cannot "prove" the Bible, if by that you mean "prove it to be inspired and revealed by God." If by prove, one means "showing some biblical event or passage to be historical," then it would be a correct usage.

I believe archaeology contributes to biblical criticism, not in the area of inspiration or revelation, but in historical accuracy and trustworthiness about the events that are recorded. Let's say the rocks on which the Ten Commandments were written are found. Archaeology could confirm that they were rocks, that the Ten Commandments were written on them, and that they came from the period of Moses; it could not prove that God had written them.

Selected Archaeological Evidence Supporting the Old Testament

The "Black Stele" (E/21)

The phrase used to be "the assured results of higher criticism," but now the higher critics are falling by the wayside. Take, for example, the Documentary Hypothesis. One of the reasons for its development, apart from the different names used for God in Genesis, was that the Pentateuch could not have been written by Moses because the "assured results of higher criticism" had proved that writing was not in existence at the time of Moses, or, if it was in existence at that time, it was used sparingly. Therefore, it was obvious that the Pentateuch had to be of later authorship.

But then, some fellows discovered the "black stele." It had wedge-shaped characters on it and contained the detailed laws of Hammurabi. Was it post-Moses? No! Moses was supposed to be a primitive man without an alphabet, but this was pre-Mosaic by at least three centuries. 126/444

Hittites (E/22)

The "assured results of higher criticism" said there were no Hittites at the time of Abraham, for there were no other records of them apart from the Old Testament. They must be myth. Well, wrong again. As the result of archaeological finds, there are now hundreds of references overlapping more than 1,200 years of Hittite civilization. (For further details on the Hittites, see *Evidence That Demands a Verdict, Vol. II,* pp. 339-41.)

David's Conquest of Jerusalem (ME/19,20)

S. H. Horn, an archaeologist, gives an excellent example of how archaeological evidence helps in biblical study:

Archaeological explorations have shed some interesting light on the capture of Jerusalem by David. The biblical accounts of that capture (2 Samuel 5:6-8 and 1 Chronicles 11:6) are rather obscure without the help obtained from archaeological evidence. Take for example 2 Samuel 5:8, which in the King James Version reads: "And David said on that day, Whosoever getteth up to the gutter, and smiteth the Jebusites, and the lame and the blind, that are hated of David's soul, so shall be chief and captain." Add to this statement 1 Chronicles 11:6—"So Joab the son of Zeruiah went first up and was chief."

Some years ago I saw a painting of the conquest of Jerusalem in which the artist showed a man climbing up a metal downspout, running on the outside face of the city wall. This picture was absurd, because ancient city walls had neither gutters nor downspouts, although they had weeping holes in the walls to drain water off. The Revised Standard Version, produced after the situation had become clear through archaeological discoveries made on the spot, translates the pertinent passages: "And David said on that day, 'Whoever would smite the Jebusites, let him get up the water shaft to attack the lame and the blind, who are hated by David's soul.' " "And Joab the Son of Zeruiah went up first, so he became chief." What was this water shaft that Joab climbed?

Jerusalem in those days was a small city lying on a single spur of the hills on which the large city eventually stood. Its position was one of great natural strength, because it was surrounded on three sides by deep valleys. This was why the Jebusites boastfully declared that even blind and lame could hold their city against a powerful attacking army. But the water supply of the city was poor; the population was entirely dependent on a spring that lay outside the city on the eastern slope of the hill.

So that they could obtain water without having to go down to where the spring was located, the Jebusites had constructed an elaborate system of tunnels through the rock. First they had dug a horizontal tunnel, beginning at the spring and proceeding toward the center of the city. After digging for ninety feet they hit a natural cave. From the cave they dug a vertical shaft forty-five feet high, and from the end of the shaft a sloping tunnel 135 feet long and a staircase that ended at the surface of their city, 110 feet above the water level of the spring. The spring was then concealed from the outside so that no enemy could detect it. To get water the Jebusite women went down through the upper tunnel and let their water skins down the shaft to draw water from the cave, to which it was brought by natural flow through the horizontal tunnel that connected the cave with the spring.

However, one question remained unanswered. The excavations of R. A. S. Macalister and J. G. Duncan some forty years ago had uncovered a wall and a tower that were thought to be of Jebusite and Davidic origin respectively. This tract of wall ran along the rim of the hill of Ophel, west of the tunnel entrance. Thus the entrance was left outside the protective city wall, exposed to the attacks and interference of enemies. Why hadn't the tunnel been built to end inside the city? This puzzle has now been solved by the recent excavations of Kathleen Kenyon on Ophel. She found that

Macalister and Duncan had given the wall and tower they discovered wrong dates; these things actually originated in the Hellenistic period. She uncovered the real Jebusite wall a little farther down the slope of the hill, east of the tunnel entrance, which now put the entrance safely in the old city area.

David, a native of Bethlehem, four miles south of Jerusalem, may have found out about the spring and its tunnel system in the days when as a youth he roamed through the countryside. Later, as king, he based his surprise attack on this knowledge and made the promise that the first man who entered the city through the water shaft would become his commander-in-chief. Joab, who was already general of the army, did not want to lose that position and therefore led the attack himself. The Israelites apparently went through the tunnel, climbed up the shaft, and were in the city before any of the besieged citizens had any idea that so bold a plan had been conceived.

This water system, constructed more than three thousand years ago, is still in existence and can be examined by any tourist. Some good climbers have even climbed the shaft in modern times. 71/15-16

Authenticity of the Book of Daniel (D/11-14)

The historical accuracy of the author regarding Babylonian history makes it difficult to believe the book of Daniel was written some four hundred years after its historical setting. As Raven asserts, Daniel's accurate representation of history in Babylon shows that it must have been written there. 111/331

Ira Price, a liberal critic, admits that Daniel 4:30 gives a true picture of Nebuchadnezzar's building activities. 104/302-3

Another example of historical detail is the story of Darius ordering Daniel thrown into the lions' den. If the book were written in 168 B.C., how did the author know that Darius the Mede was a fire worshiper and would not have thrown Daniel into the fire, as did Nebuchadnezzar with Daniel's friends? It is remarkable that in all the details of the book no historical error has ever been proven. 113/436-50

Nebuchadnezzar's vision is given in Daniel 4 and ends with, "The matter is by the decree of the watchers, and the demand by the word of the holy ones: to the intent that the living may know that the most High ruleth in the kingdom of men, and giveth it to whomsoever He will, and setteth up over it the basest of men" (4:17, KJV). These last words are a remarkable reference to Nebuchadnezzar's humble family origin. This lowly origin was otherwise unknown until the discovery of an inscription made by his father, Nabopolassar. (See *Daniel in the Critic's Den,* p. 12, for this inscription.) 26/89-91

In this inscription Nabopolassar reveals that he was not of royal birth, "the son of a nobody" (an expression found in Assyrian inscriptions to signify non-royal birth). He also indicated that he was not important in social circles by describing himself as "the insignificant," "not visible," "the weak" and "the feeble." This is the kind of knowledge—the lowly origin of Babylon's greatest king—which succeeding generations soon must have forgotten, and therefore it constitutes strong evidence for the historical accuracy of Daniel. 26/89-91

Boutflower writes:

> Such resemblances of style between the utterances of Nebuchadnezzar of the monuments and the Nebuchadnezzar of Holy Scripture form part of the cumulative evidence in favor of the authenticity of the Book of Daniel. For we may well question whether a Jewish writer of the age of the Maccabees would be acquainted with the literary style of the scribes of the New Babylonian empire, or with the strong poetic tendencies of the real Nebuchadnezzar. 26/104

Corresponding to Nebuchadnezzar's boast (Daniel 4:30) of building Babylon, Free states:

The East India House inscription, now in London, has six columns of Babylonian writing telling of the stupendous building operations which the king carried on in enlarging and beautifying Babylon. 51/228

Barton quotes an inscription of Nebuchadnezzar's which bears an amazing correspondence to Daniel 4:30: "The fortifications of Esagila and Babylon I strengthened and established the name of my reign forever." 19/479

Knowledge of Belshazzar seems to have disappeared by the time of Herodotus (ca 450 B.C.). This indicates that the author of Daniel knew more about the sixth century B.C. than would have been possible for a second century writer. 13/371; cf. 38/200

J. D. Wilson quotes Keunen:

> I am certain, after much examination, that the writer of the Book of Daniel shows a most intimate personal acquaintance with the palace of Nebuchadnezzar and the affairs of the Babylonian Court and Empire, and that the book was written during the exile. 133/88-89

Wilson also quotes Lenormant:

> The more I read and reread [Daniel], the more I am struck with the truth of the tableaux of the Babylonian Court traced in the first six chapters. Whoever is not the slave of preconceived opinions must confess when comparing these with the cuneiform monuments that they are really ancient and written but a short distance from the Courts themselves. 133/89

Wilson himself asserts: "No Jew whose people had been living for centuries under Persian and Grecian rule could relate with such unconscious simplicity the actual condition of affairs in Babylon 370 years before his own time." 133/91

Evidence From Ebla (E/68)

An archaeological find that relates to biblical criticism is the recently discovered Ebla tablets. The discovery was made in northern Syria by two professors from the University of Rome, Dr. Paolo Matthiae, an archaeologist; and Dr. Giovanni Petinato, an epigrapher. The excavation of the site, Tell Mardikh, began in 1964; in 1968 they uncovered a statue of King Ibbit-Lim. The inscription made a reference to Ishtar, the goddess who "shines brightly in Ebla." Ebla, at its height of power in 2300 B.C., had a population of 260,000 people. It was destroyed in 2250 B.C. by Naram-Sin, grandson of Sargan the Great.

Since 1974, 17,000 tablets have been unearthed from the era of the Ebla Kingdom.

It will be quite a while before there can be any significant research done to determine the relationship of Ebla to the biblical world. However, valuable contributions have already been made to biblical criticism.

The proponents of the Documentary Hypothesis have taught in the past that the period described in the Mosaic narrative (1400 B.C., a thousand years after the Ebla Kingdom) was a time prior to all knowledge of writing. 88/63 But Ebla shows that a thousand years before Moses, laws, customs and events were recorded in writing in the same area of the world in which Moses and the patriarchs lived.

The higher critics have not only taught that it was a time prior to writing but also that the priestly code and legislation recorded in the Pentateuch were too far developed to have been written by Moses. It was alleged that the Israelites were too primitive at that time to have written them and it wasn't until about the first half of the Persian period (538–331 B.C.) that such detailed legislation was recorded.

However, the tablets containing the law codes of Ebla have demonstrated elaborate judicial proceedings and case law. Many are very similar to the Deuteronomy law code (example: Deuteronomy 22:22-30) which critics have claimed has a very late date.

An additional example of the contribution of the Ebla discovery is in relation to Genesis 14, which for years has been considered to be historically unreliable. The victory of Abraham over Chedorlaomer and the Mesopotamian kings has been described as fictitious and the five Cities of the Plain (Sodom, Gomorrah, Admah, Zeboiim and Zoar) as legendary. 88/79-83

Yet the Ebla archives refer to all five Cities of the Plain and on one table the cities are listed in the exact same sequence as Genesis 14. The milieu of the tablets reflect the culture of the patriarchal period and depict that, before the catastrophe recorded in Genesis 14, the area was a flourishing region experiencing prosperity and success, as recorded in Genesis.

The Mari Tablets (ME/74-75)

In his article, "The Bible After Twenty Years of Archaeology," William F. Albright comments:

> The excavation of Mari began in 1933, under the direction of Andre Parrot. Situated on the Middle Euphrates, Mari was one of the most important centers of the Northwest Semitic life of patriarchal times. In 1936, M. Parrot unearthed many thousands of cuneiform tablets dating mostly from about 1700 B.C., which are now in course of being studied and published. These tablets throw direct light on the background of the patriarchal traditions of Genesis. 6/538

He goes on to explain further the impact of the Mari Tablets:

> Now we can speak even more emphatically, and with a wealth of additional detail. For example, the "city of Nahor" which plays a role next to Harran in the Patriarchal stories (Genesis 24:10) turns up frequently along with Harran in the Mari documents about 1700 B.C. The name of a prince of Mari, Arriyuk, is evidently the same as the Arioch of Genesis 14. "Benjamin" often appears as a tribal name at Mari. 6/541-42

Henry T. Frank in *Bible, Archaeology, and Faith* elucidates an Abrahamic episode:

> A number of once puzzling incidents associated with the patriarchs are also shown by archaeological discoveries to have been commonplace in the early second millennium. We have already seen that Abraham's haggling with Ephron concerning the purchase of the Cave of Machpelah was in accordance with common ancient practice. Apparently Abraham wished to purchase only the cave itself in which to bury his wife Sarah. Yet governed by Hittite practice he had to buy not only the cave but the land and the arbors associated with it. This assumption of feudal obligation described in Genesis 23:1-20 is exactly in accord with the recovered Hittite documents from Boghazköy in which such details are stressed. 50/74

The Nuzi Tablets (ME/75-76)

S. H. Horn in his *Christianity Today* article, "Recent Illumination of the Old Testament," introduced the Nuzi Tablets:

> The discovery of a whole archive of legal and social texts at Nuzi, a small place in northeastern Iraq, has revealed that the social and legal background of the patriarchal age is reflected accurately and in great detail in the Old Testament patriarchal narratives. 71/14

Wright points out that the "Nuzi tablets elucidate many a custom typical of the patriarchal age in the second millennium, but not of Israelite life in the first." 135/87

Cyrus Gordon contends: "Thanks to the Nuzi texts we may feel confident that the social institutions have come down to us authentically." 57/9

What are some specific instances in which the Nuzi tablets help us to understand Genesis? Horn answers:

> First, in the patriarchal stories we find several strange accounts of a barren wife who asked her husband to produce a child for her by her maid servant. Sarah did this, and later also Jacob's two wives, Rachel and Leah. Today we know that this practice was not unusual during the patriarchal age. The laws of that period as well as ancient marriage contracts mention it. For example, in a marriage contract from Nuzi, the bride Kelim-ninu promises in written form to procure for her husband Shennima a slave girl as a second wife, if she fails to bear him children. She also promises that she will not drive out the offspring of such a union. In no other period besides the patriarchal age do we find this strange custom. 71/14

Gordon in another article refers to the Documentary Hypothesis: "The cuneiform contracts from Nuzi have demonstrated that the social institutions of the patriarchs are genuine and pre-Mosaic. They cannot have been invented by any post-Mosaic *J, E, D* or *P.*" 58/241

Laban's Stolen Images (ME/329-30)

The following, from J. P. Free's "Archaeology and the Bible" *(His* magazine), gives a good explanation of not only the episode, but also the background of the Nuzi tablets:

> Over 1000 clay tablets were found in 1925 in the excavation of a Mesopotamian site known today as Yorgan Tepe. Subsequent work brought forth another 3000 tablets and revealed the ancient site as "Nuzi." The tablets, written about 1500 B.C., illuminate the background of the biblical patriarchs, Abraham, Isaac, and Jacob. One instance will be cited: When Jacob and Rachel left the home of Laban, Rachel stole Laban's family images or "teraphim." When Laban discovered the theft, he pursued his daughter and son-in-law, and after a long journey overtook them (Genesis 31:19-23). Commentators have long wondered why he would go to such pains to recover images he could have replaced easily in the local shops. The Nuzi tablets record one instance of a son-in-law who possessed the family images having the right to lay legal claim to his father-in-law's property, a fact which explains Laban's anxiety. 52/20

Doors in Sodom (ME/78)

Joseph P. Free even mentions the custom of heavy doors during Lot's time. He mentions Genesis 19:9 where the evil men of Sodom could not get through Lot's doorway. Keil and Albright studied Tell Beit Mirsim which is Kirjath-Sepher of the Bible and found walls and doors of 2200–1600 B.C. to be heavy and strong. At the 900–600 B.C. level, homes most likely had used archways or curtains, but no doors were found. In Lot's day, the police force was not so strong and forbidding doors were needed. But with stronger law and order, doors were no longer needed for protection. 51/62

Free then took the offensive: "Lot's heavy door fits precisely in this period. The critics, however, date the writing of the accounts of Abraham in the ninth and eighth centuries B.C. How did the writer know the conditions a thousand years or more before his time?" 51/63

The Five Cities of the Plain (ME/78)

Unger notes:

> The five cities of the plain (circle) of the Jordan, Sodom, Gomorrah, Admah, Zeboiim and Zoar, also belong to the early patriarchal age. The biblical notices that the district of the Jordan, where these cities were located, was exceedingly fertile and well-peopled around 2065 B.C. but that not long afterward was abandoned, are in full accord with the archaeological facts. 127/114

Earlier scholars maintained that the Jordan Valley was hardly populated in Abraham's day. Archer, however, shows that "Nelson Glueck has in recent decades uncovered more than seventy sites in the Jordan Valley, some of them as ancient as 3000 B.C." 13/159

An Extra-Biblical Tenth-Century B.C. Reference to Abraham (ME/80-81)

G. E. Wright gives the story behind an extra-biblical reference to Abraham, which is most rare:

> The first great disaster since the reign of Saul descended upon the two kingdoms about 918 B.C. Our books of Kings give us scant information about it:
>
> And it came to pass in the fifth year of King Rehoboam that Shishak, king of Egypt, came up against Jerusalem. And he took away the treasures of the house (Temple) of the Lord, and the treasures of the king's house. . . And he took away all the shields of gold which Solomon had made (1 Kings 14:25,26).
>
> This king of Egypt thought more highly of his campaign, however, and on the walls of the great temple of Karnak in Upper Egypt he had his artists carve a picture of himself smiting the Asiatics in the presence of the god Amon, who with a goddess is depicted as presenting to him ten lines of captives. Each captive symbolized a town or locality, the name of which was inscribed below. From these names we can gather the extent of his campaign. The biblical account implies that only Judah was affected, but all of Palestine apparently suffered, for the list includes cities in the Esdraelon, Transjordan, the hill country of both Israel and Judah, and even Edom. There is an interesting reference to the Field of Abram, presumably the Hebron area, and this is the first time that a source outside the Bible confirms that patriarch's connection with a locality in Palestine. 135/148

The Historicity of Joseph (ME/330-32)

Sold as a slave:

K. A. Kitchen brings out in his book, *Ancient Orient and Old Testament,* that Genesis 37:28 gives the correct price for a slave in the 18th century B.C.:

> Finally, the price of twenty shekels of silver paid for Joseph in Genesis 37:28 is the correct average price for a slave in about the eighteenth century B.C.: earlier than this, slaves were cheaper (average, ten to fifteen shekels), and later they became steadily dearer. This is one more little detail true to its period in cultural history. 81/52-53

The visit to Egypt:

The possibility of Joseph's family visiting Egypt has been questioned by some. Millar Burrows *(What Mean These Stones?)* points out:

> Accounts of going down to Egypt in times of famine (12:10; 42:1,2) bring to mind Egyptian references to Asiatics who came to Egypt for this purpose. A picture of visiting Semites may be seen on the wall of a tomb at Beni Hasan which comes from a time not far from that of Abraham. 32/266-67

Joseph's promotions:

Joseph's being lifted from slavery to prime minister of Egypt has caused some critical eyebrows to rise, but we have some archaeological accounts of similar things happening in the Land of the Nile. The following, a summary of Howard Vos's discussion of the question of Joseph's admittedly unique rise, is found in his *Genesis and Archaeology*:

> A Canaanite, Meri-Ra, became armor bearer to Pharaoh; another Canaanite, Ben-Mat-Ana, was appointed to the high position of interpreter; and a Semite, Yanhamu or Jauhamu, became deputy to Amenhotep III, with charge over the granaries of the delta, a responsibility similar to that of Joseph before and during the famine. 129

When Pharaoh appointed Joseph prime minister, Joseph was given a ring and a gold chain or collar which is normal procedure for Egyptian office promotions. 129/106

Joseph's tomb:

John Elder in his *Prophets, Idols and Diggers* made an interesting comment:

> In the last verses of Genesis it is told how Joseph adjured his relatives to take his bones back to Canaan whenever God should restore them to their original home, and in Joshua 24:32 it is told how his body was indeed brought to Palestine and buried at Shechem. For centuries there was a tomb at Shechem reverenced as the tomb of Joseph. A few years ago the tomb was opened. It was found to contain a body mummified according to the Egyptian custom, and in the tomb, among other things, was a sword of the kind worn by Egyptian officials. 41/54

General Customs of the Patriarchs (ME/332)

S. H. Horn lists six areas of influence which the Nuzi texts have exercised:

> Other texts show that a bride was ordinarily chosen for a son by his father, as the patriarchs did; that a man had to pay a dowry to his father-in-law, or to work for his father-in-law if he could not afford the dowry, as poor Jacob had to do; that the orally expressed will of a father could not be changed after it had been pronounced, as in Isaac's refusal to change the blessings pronounced over Jacob even though they had been obtained by deception; that a bride ordinarily received from her father a slave girl as a personal maid, as Leah and Rachel did when they were married to Jacob; that the theft of cult objects or of a god was punishable by death, which was why Jacob consented to the death of the one with whom the stolen gods of his father-in-law were found; that the strange relationship between Judah and his daughter-in-law Tamar is vividly illustrated by the laws of the ancient Assyrians and Hittites. 71/14

Use of Camels (ME/333)

Kenneth Kitchen remarks:

> It is often asserted that the mention of camels and of their use is an anachronism in Genesis. This charge is simply not true, as there is both philological and archaeological evidence for knowledge and use of this animal in the early second millennium B.C. and even earlier. 81/79

He further explains:

> While a possible reference to camels in a fodder-list from Alalakh (ca eighteenth century B.C.) has been disputed, the great Mesopotamian lexical lists that originated in the Old Babylonian period show a knowledge of the camel ca 2000/1700 B.C. including its domestication. Furthermore, a Sumerian text from Nippur from the same early period gives clear evidence of domestication of the camel by then, by its allusions to camel's milk. Camel bones were found in house-ruins at Mari of the pre-Sargonic age (twenty-fifth to twenty-fourth centuries B.C.), and also in various Palestinian sites from 2000 to 1200 B.C. From Byblos comes an incomplete camel figurine of the nineteenth/eighteenth centuries B.C. 81/79-80

The Amarna Tablets (ME/336-37)

Archer explains how this discovery has helped clarify the historical picture. The Tell el-Amarna Tablets, Archer says, came to light from the Egyptian site of el-Amarna (1887), ancient capital of Egypt (called Akhetaten then). They are from officials of Palestine and Syria who were upset about attacking Habiru (or 'Apiru). They describe a disorganized turmoil among the states there, speak of how many are deserting their allegiance to Egypt and ask for military aid to stop the onslaught. One letter from Megiddo lists some of the fallen cities, all of which are in the south (region of Arad). This conforms with the Israel conquest pattern. Cities like Gezer, Ashkelon and Lachish are reported as fallen. 12/164

Unger quotes one of the tablets:

> Abdi-Hiba, governor of Jerusalem, wrote numerous letters to the Pharaoh Akhnaton (1387–1366 B.C.) beseeching Egyptian aid against the encroaching Habiru, if the country were to be saved for Egypt:
>
> "The Habiru plunder all lands of the king.
> If archers are here
> this year, then the lands of the king,
> the Lord, will remain; but if the archers are not here,
> then the lands of the king, my lord, are lost."
>
> Taken from Samuel Mercer, the *Tell el-Amarna Tablets* (Toronto 1939), vol. II, no. 287, lines 56-60. 127/146

Concerning the identification of the Habiru with the Hebrews, W. F. Albright states:

> During the past fifteen years [1947–1962] it has become possible to pinpoint the background of the stories of Abraham (Genesis 12–24) with a precision wholly undreamed of when the first edition of this survey was written. The meaning of the term *'Apiru-'Abiru,* later 'Ibri, "Hebrew," has now been established; it meant something like "donkey-man, donkey driver, huckster, caravaneer." Originally it may have meant "dusty," with obvious reference to the dust raised by donkeys on a much-travelled road. 7/5

Unger also maintains a connection:

> In the light of the interesting fact that Abraham is the first person in the Bible to bear the name of the Hebrew, *'Ibri,* (Genesis 14:13), the occurrence of the term "Habiru" in the Mari letters (eighteenth century B.C.) and earlier in the Cappadocian texts (nineteenth century B.C.) as well as in the later Nuzian, Hittite, Amarna and Ugaritic texts (fifteenth–fourteenth centuries B.C.) is significant, since the philological equation Hebrew-Habiru seems assured. 127/124-25

The Lachish Letters (ME/342-344)

Jeremiah 34:6,7 reads as follows:

> Then Jeremiah the prophet spoke all these words to Zedekiah king of Judah in Jerusalem when the army of the king of Babylon was fighting against Jerusalem and against all the remaining cities of Judah, that is, Lachish and Azekah, for they alone remained as fortified cities among the cities of Judah.

Israel had been in a futile rebellion against Nebuchadnezzar. Judah was not united in this revolt. Jeremiah preached submission while the Jewish leaders could only speak of resistance, and resist they did, though they were soundly defeated by the powers of Nebuchadnezzar. In the final days of the rebellion, the last vestiges of Hebrew independence were embodied in a pair of outposts, Lachish and Azekah, 35 miles southwest of Jerusalem. From Lachish came a series of letters giving a graphic picture of what it was like to be in such a situation. These add greatly to our knowledge of Old Testament background. This discovery is known as the Lachish Letters (or Ostraca).

Albright wrote a special article on this find, "The Oldest Hebrew Letters: Lachish Ostraca," in the *Bulletin of the American Schools of Oriental Research,* and he deals with the setting of the Letters:

> In the course of this sketch it will have become increasingly evident to the attentive reader that the language of the Lachish documents is perfect classical Hebrew. The divergences from biblical usage are much fewer and less significant than supposed by Torczner. In these letters we find ourselves in exactly the age of Jeremiah, with social and political conditions agreeing perfectly with the picture drawn in the book that bears his name. 8/17

Albright sums up the question of the dating of the finds:

> Starkey has contributed a useful sketch of the discovery, explaining the archaeological situation in which the Ostraca were found and fixing their date just before the final destruction of Lachish at the end of Zedekiah's reign. The facts are so clear that Torczner has surrendered his objections to this date, which is now accepted by all students. 8/11-12

Haupert speaks of the content of the first letter:

> Letter I . . . though only a list of names, is of striking significance since three of the nine names which occur—Gemariah, Jaazanian, and Neriah—appear in the Old Testament only in the time of Jeremiah. A fourth name is Jeremiah, which, however, is not limited in the Old Testament to the prophet Jeremiah, and need not refer to him. A fifth name, likewise not limited to this period, is Mattaniah, which biblical students will recognize as the pre-throne name of King Zedekiah. 67/31

The Gedaliah Seal (ME/344)

John Elder points out yet another find in addition to Ostraca, which adds even more weight to the biblical story of Lachish:

> The nearby city fortress of Lachish provides clear proof that it had been twice burned over a short period of time, coinciding with the two captures of Jersusalem. In Lachish the imprint of a clay seal was found, its back still shows the fibers of the papyrus to which it had been attached. It reads: "The property of Gedaliah who is over the house." We meet this distinguished individual in 2 Kings 25:22, where we are told: "And as for the people that remained in the land of Judah, whom Nebuchadnezzar king of Babylon had left, even over them he made Gedaliah . . . ruler." 41/108-9

The Cyrus Cylinder (ME/347)

Finegan remarks: "The spirit of Cyrus's decree of release which is quoted in the Old Testment (2 Chronicles 36:23; Ezra 1:2-4) is confirmed by the Cyrus cylinder, where the king related that he allowed the captives to return to their various countries and rebuild their temples." 45/191

Babylonian Reference to Jehoiachin and Sons (ME/348)

Albright reports:

> In recently published tablets from a royal archive of Nebuchadnezzar, dating in and about the year 592 B.C., Jehoiachin and five of his sons, as well as at least five other Jews, are mentioned among recipients of rations from the royal court. It is significant that Jehoiachin was still called "king of Judah" in official Babylonian documents. 7/85

The Dead Sea Scrolls (A/25-26; HW/227-32)

Until 1947, scholars had only the clay tablets of Babylon and the Egyptian papyri to help them understand background information on the Bible, since no ancient Old Testament manuscripts were known to have survived.

However, all that changed with the discovery of some scrolls in caves along the northwest corner of the Dead Sea. These scrolls brought to the world manuscripts of Old Testament books 1,000 years older than any previously in existence.

There was immediate excitement over the find. Dr. William F. Albright, in a telegram to John Trever who had an integral part in revealing the find, said:

> My heartiest congratulations on the greatest manuscript discovery of modern times! There is no doubt in my mind that the script is more archaic than that of the Nash papyrus [a very small portion of the Old Testament dated between the second century B.C. and the first century A.D.] . . . I would prefer a date around 100 B.C. . . .
>
> What an absolutely incredible find! And there can be happily not the slightest doubt in the world about the genuineness of the manuscript.

Before the discovery of these scrolls, the oldest complete copy of the Old Testament in Hebrew was Codex Babylonicus Petropalitanus from A.D. 1008, more than 1,400 years after the Old Testament was completed. Fragments from the Dead Sea Scrolls now closed the gap by a thousand years and left the world waiting to see if the text had been transmitted accurately. The answer was a resounding *yes*.

The Dead Sea Scrolls demonstrated unequivocally the fact that the Jews were faithful in their transcription of biblical manuscripts. This reverence for the Scriptures was summed up long ago by the first century Jewish historian, Flavius Josephus:

> We have given practical proof of our reverence for our own Scriptures. For, although such long ages have now passed, no one has ventured either to add, or to remove, or to alter a syllable; and it is an instinct with every Jew from the day of his birth to regard them as the decrees of God, to abide by them, and, if need be, cheerfully to die for them.
>
> Time and again ere now, the sight has been witnessed of prisoners enduring tortures and death in every form in the theaters, rather than utter a single word against the Laws and the allied documents. 76/179-80

Confirmation of Accuracy

What have we learned from the Dead Sea Scrolls? First, they confirm that between the first and ninth centuries A.D., the Jewish scribal copying of the Old Testament Scriptures was accomplished with remarkably few errors. With the exception of minute copying errors here and there, the Dead Sea manuscripts exhibited virtually identical readings to their counterparts of the ninth century. What this means is that many scholars' doubts concerning the accuracy of the Massoretic text (MT) as a reflection of the first-century text were unfounded. John Allegro, not a Christian sympathizer, reports:

> Excitement had run high among scholars when it became known in 1948 that a cave near the Dead Sea had produced pre-Massoretic texts of the Bible. Was it possible that we were at last going to see traditions differing seriously from the standard text, which would throw some important light on this hazy period of variant traditions? In some quarters the question was raised with some apprehension, especially when news-hungry journalists began to talk about changing the whole Bible in view of the latest discoveries, but closer examination showed that, on the whole, the differences shown by the first Isaiah scroll were of little account, and could often be explained on the basis of scribal errors, or differing orthography, syntax, or grammatical form. 10/65

Millar Burrows, a scholar of exceptional stature reveals his attitude toward the Dead Sea Scrolls:

> It is quite true that as a liberal Protestant I do not share all the beliefs of my more conservative brethren. It is my considered conclusion, however, that if one will go through any of the historic statements of the Christian faith he will find nothing that has been or can be disproved by the Dead Sea Scrolls. 31/39

CHAPTER 9 Archaeological Evidence for the Reliability of the New Testament

Luke (He Changes a Critic's Mind) (E/70-73; RF/35)

Sir William Ramsay is regarded as one of the greatest archaeologists ever to have lived. He was a student in the German historical school of the mid-nineteenth century. As a result, he believed that the Book of Acts was a product of the mid-second century A.D. He was firmly convinced of this belief. In his research to make a topographical study of Asia Minor he was compelled to consider the writings of Luke. As a result he was forced to do a complete reversal of his beliefs due to the overwhelming evidence uncovered in his research. He spoke of this when he said:

> I may fairly claim to have entered on this investigation without prejudice in favor of the conclusion which I shall now seek to justify to the reader. On the contrary, I began with a mind unfavorable to it, for the ingenuity and apparent completeness of the Tübingen theory had at one time quite convinced me. It did not then lie in my line of life to investigate the

> subject minutely; but more recently I found myself brought into contact with the Book of Acts as an authority for the topography, antiquities and society of Asia Minor. It was gradually borne upon me that in various details the narrative showed marvelous truth. In fact, beginning with a fixed idea that the work was essentially a second century composition, and never relying on its evidence as trustworthy for first century conditions, I gradually came to find it a useful ally in some obscure and difficult investigations. 25/36

Concerning Luke's ability as a historian, Ramsay concluded after 30 years of study that "Luke is a historian of the first rank; not merely are his statements of fact trustworthy . . . *this author should be placed along with the very greatest of historians.*" 110/222

Ramsay also says: "Luke's history is unsurpassed in respect of its trustworthiness." 109/81

It was at one time conceded that Luke had entirely missed the boat in the events he portrayed as surrounding the birth of Jesus (Luke 2:1-3). Critics argued that there was no census, that Quirinius was not governor of Syria at that time and that everyone did not have to return to his ancestral home. 41/159-60; 51/285

First of all, archaeological discoveries show that the Romans had a regular enrollment of taxpayers and also held censuses every 14 years. This procedure was indeed begun under Augustus and the first took place in either 23–22 B.C. or in 9–8 B.C. The latter would be the one to which Luke refers.

Second, we find evidence that Quirinius was governor of Syria around 7 B.C. This assumption is based on an inscription found in Antioch ascribing to Quirinius this post. As a result of this finding, it is now supposed that he was governor twice—once in 7 B.C. and the other time in 6 A.D. (the date ascribed by Josephus). 41/160

Last in regard to the practices of enrollment, a papyrus found in Egypt gives directions for the conducting of a census. It reads:

> Because of the approaching census it is necessary that all those residing for any cause away from their homes should at once prepare to return to their own governments in order that they may complete the family registration of the enrollment and that the tilled lands may retain those belonging to them. 41/159-60; 51/285

Archaeologists at first believed Luke's implication wrong that Lystra and Derbe were in Lycaonia and Iconium was not (Acts 14:6). They based their belief on the writings of Romans such as Cicero who indicated Iconium was in Lycaonia. Thus, archaeologists said the Book of Acts was unreliable. However, in 1910, Sir William Ramsay found a monument that showed Iconium as a Phrygian city. Later discoveries confirm this. 51/317

Among other historical references of Luke is that of Lysanias the

Tetrarch of Abilene (Luke 3:1) at the beginning of John the Baptist's ministry in 27 A.D. The only Lysanias known to ancient historians was one who was killed in 36 B.C. However, an inscription found near Damascus speaks of "Freedman of Lysanias the Tetrarch" and is dated between 14 and 29 A.D. 27/321

In his Epistle to the Romans written from Corinth, Paul makes mention of the city treasurer, Erastus (Romans 16:23). During the excavations of Corinth in 1929, a pavement was found inscribed:

ERASTVS PRO:AED:S:P:STRAVIT

("Erastus, curator of public buildings, laid this pavement at his own expense"). According to Bruce, the pavement quite likely existed in the first century A.D. and the donor and the man Paul mentions are probably one and the same. 29/95; 130/185

Luke writes of the riot of Ephesus and represents a civic asembly (*Ecclesia*) taking place in a theater (Acts 19:23*ff.*). The facts are that it did meet there as borne out by an inscription which speaks of silver statues of Artemis (Diana in KJV) to be placed in the "theater during a full session of the *Ecclesia.*" The theater, when excavated, proved to have room for 25,000 people. 27/326

Luke's accuracy is attested by another discovery associated with the Temple. In Acts 21 he speaks of Paul going through the Temple purification process. When some Jews from Asia saw him there, they descended on him seeking to kill him and shouting out, "This is the man who preaches to all men everywhere against our people, and the Law, and this place; and besides he has even brought Greeks into the temple and has defiled this holy place." They had previously seen Paul with a Gentile, Trophimus, and "supposed that Paul had brought him into the Temple." Speaking of the Jewish law prohibiting Gentiles from entering the inner courts of the Temple, Bruce relates the following discovery:

> That none might plead ignorance of the rule, notices in Greek and Latin were fastened to the barricade separating the outer from the inner courts, warning Gentiles that death was the penalty for trespass. One of these Greek inscriptions, found at Jerusalem in 1871 by C. S. Clermont-Ganneau, is now housed in Istanbul, and reads as follows:
>
> NO FOREIGNER MAY ENTER WITHIN THE BARRICADE
> WHICH SURROUNDS THE TEMPLE AND ENCLOSURE.
> ANYONE WHO IS CAUGHT DOING SO WILL HAVE HIMSELF TO THANK
> FOR HIS ENSUING DEATH. 29/93

Also in doubt were Luke's usages of certain words. Luke refers to Philippi as a "part" or "district" of Macedonia. He uses the Greek word *meris* which is translated "part" or "district." F. J. A. Hort believed Luke wrong in this usage. He said that *meris* referred to a "portion" not a "district," thus, his grounds for disagreement. Archaeological excavations, however, have shown that this very word, *meris,* was used to describe the divisions of the district. Thus, archaeology has again shown the accuracy of Luke. 51/320

Other poor word usages were attached to Luke. He was considered not technically correct in referring to the Philippian rulers as *praetors*. According to the "scholars" two *duumvirs* would have ruled the town. However, as usual, Luke was right. Findings have shown that the title of *praetor* was employed by the magistrates of a Roman colony. 51/321

His choice of the word *proconsul* as the title for Gallio (Acts 18:12) is correct as evidenced by the Delphi inscription which states in part, "As Lucius Junius Gallio, my friend, and the Proconsul of Achaia . . . " 130/180

Luke gives to Publius, the chief man in Malta, the title "first man of the island" (Acts 28:7). Inscriptions have been unearthed which do give him the title of "first man." 27/325

Still another case is his usage of *politarchs* to denote the civil authorities of Thessalonica (Acts 17:6). Since *politarch* is not found in the classical literature, Luke was again assumed to be wrong. However, some nineteen inscriptions have been found that make use of the title. Interestingly enough, five of these are in reference to Thessalonica. 27/325

It is no wonder that E. M. Blaiklock, professor of Classics in Auckland University, concludes that "Luke is a consummate historian, to be ranked in his own right with the great writers of the Greeks." 23/89

F. F. Bruce, of the University of Manchester, notes: "Where Luke has been suspected of inaccuracy, and accuracy has been vindicated by some inscriptional evidence, it may be legitimate to say that archaeology has confirmed the New Testament record." 27/331

Bruce comments on the historical accuracy of Luke:

> A man whose accuracy can be demonstrated in matters where we are able to test it is likely to be accurate where the means for testing him are not available. Accuracy is a habit of mind, and we know from happy (or unhappy) experience that some people are habitually accurate just as others can be depended upon to be inaccurate. Luke's record entitles him to be regarded as a writer of habitual accuracy. 30/90

Pilate (HW/215)

Until 1961 the only historical references to Pontius Pilate were secondary. That is, they referred to Pontius Pilate, it was thought, only because the Gospels referred to him. Then two Italian archaeologists excavated the Mediterranean port city of Caesarea that served as the Roman capital of Palestine. During the dig they uncovered a two-by-three-foot inscription in Latin. Antonio Frova was able to reconstruct the inscription. To his surprise it read: "Pontius Pilate, Prefect of Judea, has presented the

Tiberium to the Caesareans." This was the first archaeological discovery of a historical reference to the existence of Pilate.

Nazareth (HW/216-217)

Joshua 19:10-15 lists the towns of the tribe of Zebulun. The city of Nazareth does not appear among them. Josephus gives the names of forty-five towns and villages in Galilee, but Nazareth is not among them. The *Talmud* names sixty-three towns and villages. Again, the name of Nazareth does not appear. You can understand why some critical scholars questioned the existence of a "city called Nazareth" in New Testament times.

In 1962, during Michael Avi-Yonah's excavations at Caesarea, the last two fragments of a three fragment inscription were found. It is known as the Nazareth inscription since it is the first known inscription citing the name "Nazareth." It provides incontestable evidence of the existence of the town of Nazareth in the first century A.D.

Excavations at modern-day Nazareth show that it had been inhabited long before Roman times, but was, as we indicated earlier, an insignificant and very small village. Queen Helena, the mother of Constantine, had a church built over the site that had been indicated as the dwelling of Jesus' family. It was her practice to erect churches over sites mentioned in the Gospels in order to preserve their memory. Through the ages, the Roman Catholic Church has continued the tradition, whenever a church is destroyed, by building a succeeding church where the previous one stood.

Excavations under the present Church of Annunciation gave further indication of the site's authenticity. A pedestal of the earliest church bore the words "Hail Mary," the greeting of Gabriel to Mary, the mother of Jesus. Remains of a ritual bath or *mikveh* indicate the early presence of orthodox Jews, possibly Jewish Christians who built their own synagogue. This should not be surprising as James 2:2 says, "If a man comes into your synagogue . . . " referring to a gathering of Christians.

It is a common rule of thumb that traditions from before Constantine's Edict of Milan (A.D. 313) are considered reliable since official nontoleration of Christians before 313 removed all material motivation for preservation of Christian sites. The findings at Nazareth definitely place the traditions associated with it in the "reliable" category.

A mosaic inscription reading "Offering of Conon, Deacon of Jerusalem" preserves the memory of the famous martyr of Nazareth killed under Decius (249-51). Conon is reported to have claimed that he was a direct descendant of the family of Joseph and Mary. 92/131 A third-century plaster with an inscription petitioning "Christ Lord" indicates Christian veneration of the site prior to Queen Helena's visit to it. Though tourists to the present city of Nazareth may feel it has been commercialized, the archaeological evidence strongly supports the authenticity of the site.

Capernaum (HW/217-18)

Mark tells us that when Jesus "had come back to Capernaum several days afterward, it was heard that He was at home." Then Jesus healed the paralytic lowered through the roof. From Mark 1:29-34, it seems most likely that Jesus' "home" was the insulus (a complex of many rooms, often used for extended families) of Peter's mother-in-law. We would expect it to be larger than normal by the inferences of Peter's prosperous fishing business and the number of people who apparently stayed there.

Just such an insulus has been preserved and excavated in Capernaum. It was customary in the Byzantine period for Christians to build an octagon-shaped church over a *loca sancta*, a holy place. The remains of such a church from the fourth and fifth century have been excavated at Capernaum. Directly beneath the church are the remains of an insulus which revealed continuous occupation from the time of Jesus to the time the church was built. (Eleven levels of floors were revealed.) Additional walls and rooms were added to the first insulus to form what apparently was a house-church. Excavation of the Byzantine church foundation revealed a reverence for the earliest structure in that its walls sometimes arched over those of the early insulus so as not to destroy them. The careful scholars of archaeology, Drs. Eric Meyers and James Strange, report:

> The church in question was centered on one room of the block beneath. This room is 7.0 by 6.5 meters, large for an ancient house. (The synagogue at Magdala measures 8.17 by 7.25 meters.) The lowest floors of this room had early Roman pottery and coins sealed between them, which must mean that the founding and earliest use of this room, and therefore of the entire block of houses, was in the first century B.C.E. Either late in the first century or early in the second century C.E. this room received extensive interior remodeling: The floors were renewed several times and plastered, as were the walls. 92/60

They continue:

> The excavators conclude that the house was founded circa 100 B.C.E. Sometime near the end of the first century C.E., someone plastered it three times, which may suggest conversion to a public building rather than merely the remodeling of a house. . . . Furthermore, the absence of plain pottery correlates with a public rather than a private use for this part of the building. 92/129

During the second and third centuries, Christian pilgrims incised graffiti into the plaster walls of the house-church. Writing, including the name of Peter and invocations to Jesus, was found on 134 fragments of plaster recovered from these walls. The expanded house church was apparently the one Egeria saw in approximately A.D. 380 when he reported, "At Capernaum the house of [the prince of the apostles] has been made into a church, with its original walls still standing." 48/18

The Pool of Bethesda (HW/219)

The northeast quarter of the old city of Jerusalem was called Bezetha ("New Town") in the first century A.D. Some significant excavations near St. Anne's Church in that quarter were conducted a hundred years ago. These excavations uncovered the remains of an ancient church which marked the site of Bethesda.

F. F. Bruce describes later excavations which

> identified the pool itself, or rather twin pools, lying north and south, with a rock partition between them. Porticoes evidently occupied the four sides and the partition. One of the first visitors to Jerusalem after it came under Christian control, the "Bordeau pilgrim" (A.D. 333), saw and described the twin pools. The "Copper Scroll" from Qumran gives the name in the Hebrew dual number, Beth-esh-dathain, "the place of the two outpourings." There are few sites in Jerusalem, mentioned in the gospels, which can be identified so confidently. 30/94

Millstones (HW/219)

The excavations at Capernaum also unearthed a significant number of first-century millstones. In fact, so many were recovered that it appears the inhabitants took advantage of the plentiful volcanic rock to make and export mills to other areas. Handmills could be turned by two women. Jesus referred to these smaller mills in Luke 17:35, "There will be two women grinding at the same place; one will be taken, and the other will be left." Earlier here, He said, "Whoever causes one of these little ones who believes in Me to stumble," and here he probably gestured toward a larger mill turned by a donkey when he warned, "it is better for him that a heavy millstone [literally, 'millstone turned by a donkey'] be hung around his neck, and that he be drowned in the depth of the sea" (Luke 17:2).

Galilean Boat (HW/220)

Moshe and Yuval Lufan, brothers from Kibbutz Ginosar, "lovers of archaeology" but not professional archaeologists, have a feel for the land that has led them to some important discoveries. In January 1986, on the shores of the Sea of Galilee, between Kibbutz Ginosar and Moshava Migdal, they discovered an early Galilean boat dating from the first century B.C. to the first century A.D. It was apparently used for fishing, transporting goods, and ferrying people.

The boat measures almost 27 feet in length and about 7-1/2 feet in width, certainly large enough for a crew of thirteen. Its discovery was made possible by the low level of the lake due to the lack of rain.

Seat of Moses (HW/220-21)

The seat of Moses was not just a figurative term referring to the authority of Moses. At Chorazin, En-Gedi and Delos, carved stone seats of Moses have been found. The teacher in a synagogue would teach from this chair. The seat at Chorazin has an Aramaic inscription on its facade indicating the most common language of the town during the second and third centuries A.D.

The Temple (HW/221-22)

> And as He was going out of the temple, one of His disciples said to Him, "Teacher, behold what wonderful stones and what wonderful buildings!" (Mark 13:1)

Jesus' disciples were not the only ones who were in awe of the Temple. One rabbi, as recorded in the *Talmud,* remembered, "It used to be said: He who has not seen the temple of Herod has never seen a beautiful building." 14

The Temple Mount is the largest site of its kind in the ancient world, covering an area about the size of 25 to 30 football fields. The retaining walls rose approximately the height of a ten-story building above the outside street level. The smallest stone blocks used for constructing the walls weighed from two to five tons. Some of the largest stones are without equal anywhere in the ancient world. One measures 40 feet in length, 13 feet in width, 10 feet in height, and weighs close to 400 tons! Josephus speaks of the magnificence of the Temple in the fifteenth book of *Antiquities.* He tells, for example, of 162 columns in four rows, each column 27 feet high and "the thickness of each pillar was such that three men might, with their arms extended, fathom it round." 75

The Empty Tomb (HW/224-25)

Matthew writes that some of the guards around Jesus' tomb came into the city to tell the chief priests all that had happened. After counseling together, the chief priests and the elders

> gave a large sum of money to the soldiers and said, "You are to say, 'His disciples came by night and stole Him away while we were asleep.' And if this should come to the governor's ears, we will win him over and keep you out of trouble." And they took the money and did as they had been instructed; and this story was widely spread among the Jews, and is to this day (Matthew 28:11-15).

Apparently word did reach the governor's ears, or by some other means, reached all the way to Rome. The emperor, probably Claudius, sent word back to Palestine. His "decree," originally written in Latin and translated into Greek, was posted in, of all places, the obscure village of

Nazareth, home of "the Nazarene." In 1878, a white marble slab, inscribed with the following words, was found in Nazareth:

> ORDINANCE OF CAESAR. IT IS MY PLEASURE THAT GRAVES AND TOMBS REMAIN PERPETUALLY UNDISTURBED FOR THOSE WHO HAVE MADE THEM FOR THE CULT OF THEIR ANCESTORS OR CHILDREN OR MEMBERS OF THEIR HOUSE. IF, HOWEVER, ANYONE CHARGES THAT ANOTHER HAS EITHER DEMOLISHED THEM, OR HAS IN ANY OTHER WAY EXTRACTED THE BURIED, OR HAS MALICIOUSLY TRANSFERRED THEM TO OTHER PLACES IN ORDER TO WRONG THEM, OR HAS DISPLACED THE SEALING ON OTHER STONES, AGAINST SUCH A ONE I ORDER THAT A TRIAL BE INSTITUTED, AS IN RESPECT OF THE GODS, SO IN REGARD TO THE CULT OF MORTALS. FOR IT SHALL BE MUCH MORE OBLIGATORY TO HONOR THE BURIED. LET IT BE ABSOLUTELY FORBIDDEN FOR ANYONE TO DISTURB THEM. IN CASE OF VIOLATION I DESIRE THAT THE OFFENDER BE SENTENCED TO CAPITAL PUNISHMENT ON CHARGE OF VIOLATION OF SEPULCHRE. 85/119

Because the inscription contains lettering belonging to the first half of the first century, scholars place the date of its composition before A.D. 50. And since the central Roman government did not assume the administration of Galilee until after the death of Agrippa, the inscription must date from some time after A.D. 44. Claudius was emperor from A.D. 41-54 and is therefore the only candidate for the inscription's originator. In A.D. 49, Claudius expelled all Jews (and Jewish Christians) from Rome. He appears to have studied the Jewish situation, at least to a certain degree, and found it displeasing. In one of his extant letters of A.D. 41, he

> expressly forbids the Alexandrian Jews "to bring or invite other Jews to come by sea from Syria. If they do not abstain from this conduct," Claudius threatens, "I shall proceed against them for fomenting a malady common to the world." 24/81

Many scholars believe Claudius' phrase, "a malady common to the world," is a specific reference to the growing Christian community across the empire.

The evidence, given in more detail by Blaiklock, therefore suggests that Claudius must have received a letter from the Procurator of Judea or Syria regarding the expansion of the Christian religion. The Jewish authorities had contended it all began when the disciples stole the body of Jesus the Nazarene from its grave. Irritated, Claudius issued his directive with instructions that it be posted in the town of Nazareth. His irritation can especially be seen in the fact that this type of offense did not previously carry anything near the extreme penalty of capital punishment.

John, Greek Gnosticism and the Scrolls

The Gospel account most criticized as being least reflective of the true historical Jesus has been the Gospel of John. Critics have often charged that the Gospel and Epistles of John draw heavily on Greek thought. A recent article in the *Atlantic Monthly,* for example, speaks of "its modest biographical content and its overlay of seemingly Hellenistic philosophy." 98/42 The Dead Sea Scrolls, however, shed a different light on this issue. Allegro states:

> It is a fact that the Qumran library has profoundly affected the study of the Johannine writings and many long-held conceptions have had to be radically revised. No longer can John be regarded as the most Hellenistic of the evangelists; his "gnosticism" and the whole framework of his thought is seen now to spring directly from a Jewish sectarianism rooted in Palestinian soil, and his material recognized as founded in the earliest layers of gospel traditions. 10/142-43

Thus scholars were forced to recognize that John's imagery arose out of Jewish, not Greek (Hellenistic) or gnostic roots. In addition, scholars had to reckon with John's "detailed and accurate references to geographical features of Jerusalem and its environs before the city and its Temple were destroyed in 70 A.D." 134/44 It is John, for example, who pinpoints the location of John the Baptist as being in Aenon (meaning "spring," the one near Salim), approximately a mile away (3:23). John distinguishes Cana as the one in Galilee as opposed to the Cana near Sidon (2:1). John not only says that Jesus took His disciples through Samaria, but also specifies the city of Sychar, and even more specifically, "the parcel of ground that Jacob gave his son Joseph; and Jacob's well was there," as it still is today (4:5,6). Only John mentions the Pool of Siloam (9:7) and the Pool of Bethesda with its five porches (5:2). Remains of both pools have been uncovered in Jerusalem. Also, only John distinguishes "Bethany beyond the Jordan" (1:28) from Bethany near Jerusalem, "about two miles off" (11:18). There is no doubt that John, like the other gospel writers, had definite theological purposes for his writing. Yet recognizing this point, Myers and Strange conclude:

> These examples could be multiplied many times and supplemented with examples of lore, customs, and other bits of information known to the author of this Gospel. The point we wish to make, however, is simply that an unprejudiced reading of the Gospel of John seems to suggest that it is in fact based on a historical and geographical tradition, though not one that simply repeats information from the synoptics. In other words, this Gospel, as well as Matthew, Mark and Luke, firmly anchors its tradition in the land, not in an ideal, heavenly Israel. 92/161

All of this evidence affirms what John himself claimed: "This is the disciple who bears witness of these things, and wrote these things; and we know that his witness is true" (John 1:24).

1 THE BIBLE

Part One: Bibliography

1. Albright, William F. *Archaeology and the Religions of Israel.* Baltimore: Johns Hopkins University Press, 1956.
2. Albright, William F. *From Stone Age to Christianity.* 2nd ed. Baltimore: Johns Hopkins Press, 1946.
3. Albright, William F. *Recent Discoveries in Bible Lands.* New York: Funk & Wagnalls, 1955.
4. Albright, William F. "Retrospect and Prospect in New Testament Archaeology." *The Teacher's Yoke.* Ed. E. Jerry Vardaman. N.d.
5. Albright, William F. *The Archaeology of Palestine.* Rev. ed. Harmondsworth, Middlesex: Pelican Books, 1960.
6. Albright, William F. "The Bible After Twenty Years of Archaeology." *Religion in Life* 21 (1952).
7. Albright, William F. *The Biblical Period from Abraham to Ezra.* New York: Harper, 1960.
8. Albright, William F. "The Oldest Hebrew Letters: Lachish Ostraca." *Bulletin of the American Schools of Oriental Research* 70 (April 1938).
9. Albright, William F. "Toward a More Conservative View." *Christianity Today.* January 18, 1963.
10. Allegro, John. *The Dead Sea Scrolls: A Reappraisal.* New York: Penguin Books, 1964.
11. Amiot, Francois; Brunot, Amedee; Danielou, Jean; and Daniel-Rops, Henri. *The Sources for the Life of Christ.* Translated by P. J. Hepburne-Scott. New York: Hawthorn Books, 1962.
12. Archer, Gleason L. *A Survey of the Old Testament.* Chicago: Moody Press, 1964.
13. Archer, Gleason L. *A Survey of Old Testament Introduction.* Chicago: Moody Press, 1973.
14. *Babylonian Talmud.* Baba Bathra 4*a*.
15. *Babylonian Talmud.* Berakhoth 13*a*.
16. *Babylonian Talmud.* Megillah 7*b*, Ketuboth 50*a*, and elsewhere.
17. *Babylonian Talmud.* Pesahim 57*a*.
18. *Babylonian Talmud.* Sanhedrin 99*b*.
19. Barton, G. A. *Archaeology and the Bible.* 7th ed. Philadelphia: American Sunday School Union, 1937.
20. Baur, Ferdinand C. *Church History of the First Three Centuries.* 2nd ed. Tübingen. English translation by Allan Menzies. London, 1878.
21. Beck, John Clark, Jr. *The Fall of Tyre According to Ezekiel's Prophecy.* Unpublished master's thesis, Dallas Theological Seminary, 1971.
22. Blaikie, William G. *A Manual of Bible History.* London: Thomas Nelson and Sons, 1904.
23. Blaiklock, Edward Musgrave. *The Acts of the Apostles.* Grand Rapids: William B. Eerdmans Publishing Co., 1959.
24. Blaiklock, Edward Musgrave. *The Archaeology of the New Testament.* Grand Rapids: Zondervan Publishing House, 1970.

25. Blaiklock, Edward Musgrave. *Layman's Answer: An Examination of the New Theology*. London: Hodder and Stoughton, 1968.

26. Boutflower, Charles. *In and Around the Book of Daniel*. London: Society for Promoting Christian Knowledge, 1923.

27. Bruce, F. F. "Archaeological Confirmation of the New Testament." *Revelation and the Bible*. Edited by Carl Henry. Grand Rapids: Baker Book House, 1969.

28. Bruce, F. F. *The Books and the Parchments*. Rev. ed. Westwood: Fleming H. Revell Co., 1963.

29. Bruce, F. F. *The New Testament Documents: Are They Reliable?* Downer's Grove, IL: InterVarsity Press, 1964.

30. Bruce, F. F. *The New Testament Documents: Are They Reliable?* 5th rev. ed. Grand Rapids: Wm. B. Eerdmans Publishing Co., 1985.

31. Burrows, Millar. *More Light on the Dead Sea Scrolls*. New York: Viking, 1958.

32. Burrows, Millar. *What Mean These Stones?* New York: Meridian Books, 1956.

33. Collett, Sidney. *All About the Bible*. Old Tappan, NJ: Revell, n.d.

34. Curtius, Quintus. *History of Alexander*, 2 vol. Translated by John C. Rolfe (from the Loeb Classical Library, edited by T. E. Page). Cambridge: Harvard University Press, 1946.

35. Davidson, Samuel. *Hebrew Text of the Old Testament*. 2nd ed. London: Samuel Bagster & Sons, 1859.

36. Davis, George T. B. *Fulfilled Prophecies That Prove the Bible*. Philadelphia: The Million Testaments Campaigns, Inc., 1931.

37. Davis, George T. B. *Bible Prophecies Fulfilled Today*. Philadelphia: The Million Testaments Campaigns, Inc., 1955.

38. Dougherty, Raymond P. *Nabonidus and Belshazzar*. New Haven: Yale University Press, 1929.

39. Durant, Will. *Caesar and Christ*. In *The Story of Civilization* series, vol. 3. New York: Simon & Schuster, 1944.

40. Earle, Ralph. *How We Got Our Bible*. Grand Rapids: Baker Book House, 1971.

41. Elder, John. *Prophets, Idols and Diggers*. New York: Bobbs-Merrill Co., 1960.

42. *Encyclopedia Britannica* 3 (1970).

43. *Encyclopedia Britannica*. 1970.

44. Eusebius. *The History of the Church*.

45. Finegan, Jack. *Light From the Ancient Past*. London: Oxford Press. Distributed in the U.S. by Princeton University Press, 1946.

46. Finkelstein, Louis, ed. *The Jews, Their History, Culture, and Religion* 1. 3rd ed. New York: Harper and Brothers, 1960.

47. Fleming, Jim. Lecture at the Jerusalem Center for Biblical Studies, Jerusalem, Israel, January, 1987.

48. Fleming, Jim. Lecture on cassette tape and booklet entitled, "Jesus Around the Sea." P.O. Box 71055, Jerusalem, Israel.

49. Fodor, Eugene. *Fodor's Israel*. New York: David McKay Co., Inc., 1974.

50. Frank, Henry Thomas. *Bible, Archaeology and Faith*. Nashville: Abingdon Press, 1971.

51. Free, Joseph P. *Archaeology and Bible History*. Wheaton, IL: Scripture Press Publications, 1950, 1969.

52. Free, Joseph P. "Archaeology and the Bible." *HIS* magazine 9 (May 1949).

53. Freeman, James M. *Manners and Customs of the Bible.* Reprint ed. Plainfield, IL: Logos International, 1972.

54. Geisler, Norman L. and Nix, William E. *A General Introduction to the Bible.* Chicago: Moody Press, 1968.

55. Gerhardsson, Birger. *Memory and Manuscript.* Translated by Eric J. Sharpe. Copenhagen: Villadsen og Christensen, 1964.

56. Goguel, Maurice. *The Life of Jesus.* New York: Macmillan Publishing Co., 1944.

57. Gordon, C. H. "Biblical Customs and the Nuzi Tablets." *The Biblical Archaeologist* 3 (February 1940).

58. Gordon, Cyrus. "The Patriarchal Age." *Journal of Bible and Religion* 21, no. 4 (October 1955).

59. Gottschalk, Louis R. *Understanding History.* New York: Alfred A. Knopf, 1950.

60. Greenlee, J. Harold. *Introduction to New Testament Textual Criticism.* Grand Rapids: Wm. B. Eerdmans Publishing Co., 1964.

61. Greenslade, Stanley Lawrence, ed. *Cambridge History of the Bible.* New York: Cambridge University Press, 1963.

62. Guthrie, Donald. *New Testament Introduction.* 3rd ed. Downers Grove, IL: InterVarsity, 1970.

63. Guthrie, Donald. "Canon of the New Testament." In *The Zondervan Pictorial Encyclopedia of the Bible.* Merrill C. Tenny, gen. ed. Grand Rapids: Zondervan Publishing House, 1975.

64. Guthrie, Donald. "Canon of Scripture." In *The New International Dictionary of the Christian Church.* Rev. ed. J. D. Douglas, ed. Grand Rapids: Zondervan Publishing House, 1974.

65. Hamilton, Floyd E. *The Basis of Christian Faith.* New York: George H. Doran Company, 1927.

66. Harris, Michael P.; Levin, Marlin; and Wilwerth, James. "Who Was Jesus?" *Time,* August 15, 1988.

67. Haupert, R. S. "Lachish—Frontier Fortress of Judah." *Biblical Archaeologist* vol. 1, no. 4 (December 1938).

68. Higgins, David C. *The Edomites Considered Historically and Prophetically.* Unpublished master's thesis. Dallas Theological Seminary, 1960.

69. Hoehner, H. W. *Chronological Aspects of the Life of Christ.* Grand Rapids: Zondervan Publishing House, 1977.

70. Hoehner, Harold W. Class notes.

71. Horn, S. H. "Recent Illumination of the Old Testament." *Christianity Today* 12 (June 21, 1968).

72. Irenaeus. *Against Heresies.*

73. Jamieson, Robert; Faussett, A. R.; and Brown, David. *A Commentary: Critical Experiential and Practical on the Old and New Testaments.* Grand Rapids: Wm. B. Eerdmans Publishing Co., 1961.

74. Jidejian, Nina. *Tyre Through the Ages.* Beirut: Dar El-Mashreq Publishers, 1969.

75. Josephus, *Antiquities.* 15. 11. 5.

76. Josephus, Flavius. "Flavius Josephus Against Apion." *Josephus' Complete Works.* Translated by William Whiston. Grand Rapids: Kregel Publications, 1960.

77. Kenyon, Frederic G. *The Story of the Bible.* Grand Rapids: Wm. B. Eerdmans Publishing Company, 1967.

78. Kenyon, Frederic G. *Our Bible and the Ancient Manuscripts.* New York: Harper & Brothers, 1941.

79. Kenyon, Frederic G. *The Bible and Archaeology.* New York: Harper & Row Publishers, 1940.

80. Kenyon, Frederic G. *Handbook to the Textual Criticism of the New Testament.* London: Macmillan and Company, 1901.

81. Kitchen, K. A. *The Ancient Orient and the Old Testament.* Chicago: InterVarsity Press, 1966.

82. Kümmel, Werner Georg. *Introduction to the New Testament.* Rev. ed. Howard Clark Kee, translator. Nashville: Abingdon Press, 1875.

83. Lea, John W. *The Greatest Book in the World.* Philadelphia: n.pub., 1929.

84. Leach, Charles. *Our Bible: How We Got It.* Chicago: Moody Press, 1898.

85. Maier, Paul. *First Easter.* New York: Harper & Row Publishers, 1973.

86. McAfee, Cleland B. *The Greatest English Classic.* New York: n.pub., 1912.

87. McDowell, Josh. *Evidence That Demands a Verdict,* Vol. I. San Bernardino, CA: Here's Life Publishers, 1979.

88. McDowell, Josh. *Evidence That Demands a Verdict,* Vol.II. San Bernardino, CA: Here's Life Publishers, 1981.

89. McDowell, Josh and Wilson, Bill. *He Walked Among Us: Evidence for the Historical Jesus.* San Bernardino, CA: Here's Life Publishers, 1988.

90. Metzger, Bruce M. *Chapters in the History of New Testament Textual Criticism.* Grand Rapids: Wm. B. Eerdmans Publishing Co., 1963.

91. Metzger, Bruce M. *The Text of the New Testament.* New York and Oxford: Oxford University Press, 1968.

92. Meyers, Eric M., and Strange, James F. *Archaeology, the Rabbis and Early Christianity.* Nashville: Abingdon Press, 1981.

93. *Mishnah,* Aboth 3. 9.

94. Montgomery, John W. (ed.). *Christianity for the Tough Minded.* Minneapolis: Bethany Fellowship Inc., 1973.

95. Montgomery, John Warwick. *History and Christianity.* Downer's Grove, IL: InterVarsity Press, 1971.

96. Montgomery, John Warwick. *History and Christianity.* Downer's Grove, IL: InterVarsity Press, 1971 (summarizing Aristotle, *Art of Poetry,* 1460*b*-61*b).*

97. Morris, Henry M. *The Bible and Modern Science.* Rev. ed. Chicago: Moody Press, 1956.

98. Murphy, Cullen. "Who Do Men Say That I Am?" *Atlantic Monthly.* December 1986.

99. Myers, Philip Van Ness. *General History for Colleges and High Schools.* Boston: Ginn and Company, 1889.

100. Nelson, Nina. *Your Guide to Lebanon.* London: Alvin Redman, Ltd., 1965.

101. Orr, James, ed. *International Standard Bible Encyclopedia.* Grand Rapids: William B. Eerdmans Publishing Co., 1960.

102. Peters, F. E. *The Harvest of Hellenism.* New York: Simon & Schuster, 1971.

103. Pinnock, Clark. *Set Forth Your Case.* New Jersey: The Craig Press, 1968.

104. Price, I. M. *The Monuments and the Old Testament.* Philadelphia: Judson Press, 1925.

105. Rackl, Hans-Wolf. *Archaeology Underwater.* Translated by Ronald J. Floyd. New York: Charles Scribner's Sons, 1968.

106. Radmacher, Earl. Conversation with Dr. Radmacher. Dallas, Texas, June 1972.

107. Ramm, Bertrand. "Can I Trust My Old Testament?" *The King's Business.* February 1949.

108. Ramm, Bertrand. *Protestant Christian Evidences.* Chicago: Moody Press, 1957.

109. Ramsay, W. M. *St. Paul the Traveller and the Roman Citizen.* Grand Rapids: Baker Book House, 1962.

110. Ramsay, W. M. *The Bearing of Recent Discovery on the Trustworthiness of the New Testament.* Grand Rapids: Baker Book House, 1953.

111. Raven, John H. *Old Testament Introduction.* London: Fleming H. Revell Co., 1910.

112. Reicke, Bo. *The Roots of the Synoptic Gospels.* Philadelphia: Fortress Press, 1986.

113. Rhodes, A. B. "The Book of Daniel." In *Interpretation* 4. 1952.

114. Riesenfeld, Harold. *The Gospel Tradition.* Philadelphia: Fortress Press, 1970.

115. Robinson, John A. T. *Time,* March 21, 1977.

116. Robinson, George Livingston. *The Sarcophagus of an Ancient Civilization.* New York: Macmillan Company, 1930.

117. Rowley, H. H. *The Growth of the Old Testament.* London: Hutchinson's University Library, 1950.

118. Sanders, C. *Introduction to Research in English Literary History.* New York: Macmillan Publishing Company, 1952.

119. Schaff, Philip. *History of the Christian Church.* New York: Charles Scribner's Sons, 1882.

120. Sherwin-White, A. N. *Roman Society and Roman Law in the New Testament.* Grand Rapids: Baker Book House, 1963.

121. Smith, Wilbur M. *The Incomparable Book.* Minneapolis: Beacon Publications, 1961.

122. Smith, George. *The Book of Prophecy.* London: Longmain, Green, Reader and Dyer, 1865.

123. Stewart, Herbert. *The Stronghold of Prophecy.* London: Marshall, Morgan and Scott Publications, Ltd., 1941.

124. Stoner, Peter W. *Science Speaks: An Evaluation of Certain Christian Evidences.* Chicago: Moody Press, 1963.

125. Turner, E. G. *Greek Manuscripts of the Ancient World.* Princeton: Princeton University Press, 1971.

126. Unger, Merrill F. *Unger's Bible Dictionary.* Rev. ed. Chicago: Moody Press, 1971.

127. Unger, Merrill F. *Archaeology and the Old Testament.* Grand Rapids: Zondervan, 1954.

128. Urquhart, John. *The Wonders of Prophecy.* New York: Charles C. Cook, n.d.

129. Vos, Howard Frederick. *Genesis and Archaeology.* Chicago: Moody Press, 1963.

130. Vos, Howard Frederick. *Can I Trust My Bible?* Chicago: Moody Press, 1963.

131. Vos, Howard Frederick. *Fulfilled Prophecy in Israel, Jeremiah, and Ezekiel.* Unpublished doctoral dissertation, Dallas Theological Seminary, 1950.

132. Wilson, Robert Dick. Quoted in "The Incomparable Wilson: The Man Who Mastered Forty-Five Languages and Dialects" by H. W. Coray. *Which Bible?* Ed. by David Otis Fuller. Grand Rapids: Grand Rapids International Publishers, 1971.

133. Wilson, Joseph D. *Did Daniel Write Daniel?* New York: Charles C. Cook, n.d.

134. Wilson, Ian. *Jesus: The Evidence.* San Francisco: Harper & Row Publishers, 1984.

135. Wright, G. Ernest. "The Present State of Biblical Archeology," *The Study of the Bible Today and Tomorrow.* Edited by Harold R. Willoughby. Chicago: University of Chicago Press, 1947.

136. Young, Edward J. "The Authority of the Old Testament." *The Infallible Word* (a symposium). Philadelphia: Presbyterian and Reformed Publishing Co., 1946.

Part Two
ANSWERING THE BIBLE'S CRITICS

CHAPTER 10 *How Can You Believe the Miracles in the Bible?*

(RF/16-19, A/80)

One attitude surfaces repeatedly when we explore history. It is what I call the "Hume hangover." It is the argument by David Hume that belief can be justified by probability and that probability is based upon the uniformity or consistency of nature. In other words, we are right to believe an experience that conforms to normal, ordinary human experiences. Anything that is unique so far as normal human experience is concerned—such as a miracle—"should be rejected."

For example, which is more probable: The witnesses of Christ's resurrection were mistaken, or Jesus was raised from the dead?

According to Hume's "modern scientific attitude" the answer is obvious, because miracles simply can't happen.

Another way of expressing this biased view of history is that we live in a closed universe in which every event (past, present and future) must have a natural explanation. This rules out totally the intervention of the supernatural. No matter what happens or how strong the evidence, the miraculous must be rejected.

Dr. Lawrence Burkholder, chairman of the Department of the Church at the Harvard Divinity School, admits that his approach to history had been greatly influenced by Hume. However, after realizing that every historical event is to some extent or in some way unique, he confessed, "I'm beginning to feel the limitations of Hume." 19/6

Dr. Burkholder says that Hume's argument against miracles limits

> the possibility of accepting what in later times and events I find to have been a fact. He is telling me I really can't believe anything unless it corresponds to past experience. But I find myself increasingly refusing to predict the future. I find myself becoming much more modest when it comes to saying what is possible and what is not possible, what may happen in the future and what may not happen. And this same modesty is beginning to take the form of a reluctance on my part to say what could have happened in the past and what could not have happened. 19/6

Professor Clark Pinnock, speaking of a confidence in Hume's methodology and his need to naturalize all historical events, points out,

> The experience against miracles is uniform only if we know that all the reports about miracles are false, and this we do not know. No one has an infallible knowledge of "natural laws," so that he can exclude from the outset the very possibility of unique events. Science can tell us what *has* happened, but it cannot tell us what *may* or *may not* happen. It observes events; it does not create them. The historian does not dictate what history can contain; he is open to whatever the witnesses report. An appeal to Hume bespeaks ignorance of history. 63/8

Dr. Wolfhart Pannenberg of the University of Munich adds, "The question . . . whether something happened or not at a given time some thousand years ago can be settled only by historical argument." 63/10

Hume's argument:

> A miracle is a violation of the laws of nature; and as a firm and unalterable experience has established these laws, the proof against a miracle, from the very nature of the fact, is as entire as any argument from experience can possibly be imagined. . . . Nothing is esteemed a miracle if it ever happens in the common course of nature. 35/126-27

C. S. Lewis cogently answers this last assertion. He writes:

> Now of course we must agree with Hume that, if there is absolutely "uniform experience" against miracles, if, in other words, they have never happened, why then they never have. Unfortunately, we know the experience against them to be uniform only if we know that all the reports of them are false. And we can know all the reports of them to be false only if we know already that miracles have never occurred. In fact, we are arguing in a circle. 42/105

Merald Westphal, in his review of "The Historian and the Believer," writes:

> If God exists, miracles are not merely logically possible, but really and

> genuinely possible at every moment. The only condition hindering the actualization of this possibility lies in the divine will. 78/280; 49/11-12

Here is an appropriate historical example of this folly of ruling out something ahead of time because it does not fit with one's view of the world: When explorers first came to Australia, they encountered an animal that defied all known laws of taxonomy. They discovered a semiaquatic, egg-laying mammal, having a broad, flat tail, webbed feet and a snout resembling a duck's bill. They named this animal the platypus.

Upon returning to their native land, they related their finding to the world. The people regarded their report as a hoax, since no such animal with the above characteristics could possibly exist. Even though there was reputable eyewitness testimony, it was rejected because of their world view.

The explorers went back a second time to Australia, and returned with the hide of a dead platypus. The people accused them of rigging a hoax again. It seems that those people took Benjamin Disraeli's dictum seriously, "I make it a rule only to believe what I understand." 48/76

However, as Charles Caleb Colton has pointed out, "He that will believe only what he can fully comprehend must have a very long head or a very short creed." 48/76

The basis for believing in the miraculous goes back to the biblical concept of God. The very first verse of the Bible decides the issue: "In the beginning God created the heavens and the earth" (Genesis 1:1, RSV).

If this verse can be accepted at face value, that in the beginning an infinite-personal God actually did create the universe, then the rest should not be a problem. If He has the ability to do this, then a virgin birth, walking on water, feeding 5,000 people with a few loaves and fish, and other biblical miracles, become not only possible but expected.

CHAPTER 11 *What About All Those Contradictions?*

How can you believe a Bible that is full of contradictions? (A/15-17)

People ask this question so often it amazes me. The question assumes that the Bible is filled with so many obvious discrepancies it would be impossible to believe it has a divine origin. It is a popular idea to maintain that the Bible disagrees with itself, and so, unfortunately, casts considerable doubt on its own trustworthiness.

If, indeed, the Bible does contain demonstrable errors, it would show that at least those parts could not have come from a perfect, all-knowing God. We do not argue with this conclusion, but we do disagree with the initial premise that the Scriptures are full of mistakes. It is easy to accuse the Bible of inaccuracies, but it is quite another matter to prove it.

Certain passages at first glance can appear to be contradictory, but further investigation will show this is not the case.

One of the things for which we appeal with regard to possible contradictions is fairness. We should not minimize or exaggerate the problem, and we must always begin by giving the author the benefit of the doubt. This is the rule in other literature, and we ask that it also be the rule here. So often people want to employ a different set of rules in examining the Bible, and to this we immediately object.

What constitutes a contradiction? The law of non-contradiction, which is the basis of all logical thinking, states that a thing cannot be both *a* and *non-a* at the same time, in the same place, and in the same manner. It cannot be both raining and not raining at the same time in the same location.

If one can demonstrate a violation of this principle from Scripture, then and only then can he prove a contradiction. For example, if the Bible said—which it does not—that Jesus died by crucifixion both at Jerusalem and at Nazareth at the same time, this would be a provable error.

When facing possible contradictions, it is important to remember that two statements can differ from each other without being contradictory. Some people fail to make a distinction between contradiction and difference.

Take, for example, the case of the blind men at Jericho. Matthew relates how two blind men met Jesus, while both Mark and Luke mention only one. However, neither of these statements denies the other. Rather they are complementary.

Suppose you talk to the mayor of your city and the chief of police at city hall. Later, you see your friend, Jim, and tell him you talked to the mayor today. An hour after that, you see another friend, John, and tell him you talked to both the mayor and the chief of police.

Your friends compare notes, and there seems to be a contradiction—but there is not. Since you had not told Jim you talked *only* to the mayor, you did not contradict what you told John.

The statements you made to Jim and John were different, not contradictory. Many biblical statements fall into this category, and people sometimes think they find errors in passages when actually they simply do not read the passages correctly.

In the Book of Judges we have the account of the death of Sisera. Judges 5:25-27 is supposed to represent Jael as having slain him with her hammer and tent peg while he was drinking milk. Judges 4:21 says she did it while he was asleep. However, a closer reading of the Judges 5 passage reveals that it does not state he was drinking milk at the moment of impact—and the discrepancy disappears.

Sometimes two passages appear contradictory because the translation is not as accurate as it could be. A knowledge of the original languages of the Bible can immediately solve these difficulties, for both Greek and Hebrew—as all languages—have peculiarities that are difficult to render into English or any other language.

A classic example concerns the accounts of Paul's conversion recorded in the Book of Acts. Acts 9:7 (KJV) states: "The men which journeyed with him stood speechless, hearing a voice, but seeing no man." Acts 22:9 (KJV) reads: "And they that were with me saw indeed the light, and were afraid; but they heard not the voice of Him that spake to me."

These statements seem contradictory, with one saying Paul's companions heard a voice and the other saying no voice was heard. However, a knowledge of Greek solves this difficulty. As the Greek scholar, W. F. Arndt, explains:

> The construction of the verb "to hear" (*akouo*) is not the same in both accounts. In Acts 9:7 it is used with the genitive, in Acts 22:9 with the accusative. The construction with the genitive simply expresses that something is being heard or that certain sounds reach the ear; nothing is indicated as to whether a person understands what he hears or not.
>
> The construction with the accusative, however, describes a hearing which includes mental apprehension of the message spoken. From this it becomes evident that the two passages are not contradictory.
>
> Acts 22:9 does not deny that the associates of Paul heard certain sounds; it simply declares that they did not hear in such a way as to understand what was being said. Our English idiom in this case simply is not so expressive as the Greek. 15/13-14

It also must be stressed that when a possible explanation is given to a Bible difficulty, it is unreasonable to state that the passage contains a demonstrable error. Some difficulties in Scripture result from our inadequate knowledge about the circumstances, and only prove that we are ignorant of the background. As historical and archaeological studies proceed, new light is being shed on difficult portions of Scripture and many "errors" have disappeared with the new understanding. We need a wait-and-see attitude on the problems.

ADDITIONAL REFERENCE SOURCES ON THIS SUBJECT

Gleason L. Archer, *Encyclopedia of Bible Difficulties* (Grand Rapids: Zondervan Publishing House, 1982).

W. F. Arndt, *Bible Difficulties* (St. Louis: Concordia Press, 1971).

W. F. Arndt, *Does the Bible Contradict Itself?* 5th ed. revised (St. Louis: Concordia Press, 1955).

John J. Davis, *Biblical Numerology* (Grand Rapids: Baker Book House, 1968).

John W. Haley, *Alleged Discrepancies of the Bible* (Grand Rapids: Baker Book House, 1977 reprint).

Robert L. Thomas and Stanley N. Gundry, *A Harmony of the Gospels* (San Francisco: Harper & Row, 1978). See pages 313-19 for four different explanations of the alleged contradiction between the genealogies of Jesus given by Matthew and Luke.

Doesn't Matthew make a mistake by attributing a prophecy to Jeremiah when it actually was given by Zechariah? (A/86-88)

In the Gospel according to Matthew, Judas Iscariot, after betraying Jesus, feels remorse because of his evil deeds, throws the betrayal money into the sanctuary, and commits suicide. Matthew goes on to relate how this money was taken by the priests and used to buy a potter's field.

Matthew concludes:

> Then was fulfilled that which was spoken by Jeremiah, the prophet, saying, And they took the thirty pieces of silver, the price of him that was valued . . . and gave them for the potter's field, as the Lord appointed me (27:9,10, KJV).

The problem is that verse 9 attributes the prophecy to Jeremiah, when it appears that it was Zechariah who gave this prediction. When Matthew 27:9 is examined closely in light of Zechariah 11:12,13, it is clear that this prophecy is the one fulfilled. Why then does Matthew assign it to Jeremiah?

A possible solution is Jeremiah's priority in the Talmud. 43/362 Jeremiah was placed first in the ancient rabbinic order of the prophetic books. Matthew was then quoting from the collection of the books of the prophets, and cited Jeremiah since it was the first and therefore the identifier. The same thing is done in Luke 24:44, where Psalms is used when the entire third division of the Hebrew canon is in mind.

Perhaps the best solution would be to understand that Matthew is combining two prophecies, one from Jeremiah and one from Zechariah, with a mention of only one author in the composite reference, namely Jeremiah, the major prophet.

Zechariah says nothing concerning the buying of a field, but Jeremiah states that the Lord appointed him to buy a field (Jeremiah 32:6-8) as a solemn guarantee by the Lord Himself that fields and vineyards would be bought and sold in the land in a future day (Jeremiah 32:15,43*ff*).

One of the fields which God had in mind was the potter's field. Zechariah adds the details of the thirty pieces of silver and the money thrown down on the floor of the Temple. So we see that Matthew takes the details of both prophets, but stresses Jeremiah as the one who foretold these events.

Dr. J. E. Rosscup of Talbot Seminary adheres to a view consistent with the above. In classroom lectures he pointed out:

> Matthew felt that two passages were fulfilled, one typical (Jeremiah 19:1-13) and one explicit (Zechariah 11:13), and mentions only one author in the composite reference, a practice that sometimes occurred, according to Robert Gundry. 32/124-25

John N. Cool also concludes that Matthew used Zechariah chiefly, but had Jeremiah 19 prominently in mind as well, especially due to its theme of judgment on Israel. 23/56-62,66-67

Cool says,

> Both (valley, Jeremiah 19; field, Matthew 27) become burial grounds and both their names are changed to remind the people of God's judgment. [This is] confirmed by the traditional location of the potter's field . . . within the valley of Hinnom where Jeremiah pronounced his judgment by changing its name to 'valley of slaughter.'
>
> Second, Matthew's consistent use of Isaiah and Jeremiah in his formula quotations reminds his readers of God's salvation and judgment for His people. Isaiah was associated with salvation, Jeremiah . . . with judgment.
>
> The use of *tote* in Matthew 2:17 and 27:9 instead of the purposeful *Hina* or *Houtos* found in other formula introductions also underscores the judgment motif by referring to Christ's enemies as fulfilling prophecy. 23/66-67

Gundry says that Matthew's reference to Jeremiah in the introduction formula makes certain that readers will take note of the connection with Jeremiah 19, which might be overlooked. 31/125

How would you explain the inaccuracy between Judas "went away and hanged himself" in Matthew 27:5 and "falling headlong, he burst open" in Acts 1:18? (A/84-85)

This question of the manner in which Judas died is one with which we are constantly confronted in our travels. Many people point to the apparent discrepancy in the two accounts as an obvious, irreconcilable error.

Some have gone so far as to say that the idea of an inerrant Bible is destroyed by these contradictory accounts. However, this is not the case at all.

Matthew relates that Judas hanged himself, while Peter tells us he fell and was crushed by the impact. The two statements are indeed different, but do they necessarily contradict each other?

Matthew does not say that Judas did not fall; neither does Peter say that Judas did not hang himself. This is not a matter of one person calling something black and the other person calling it white. Both accounts can be true and supplementary.

A possible reconstruction would be this: Judas hanged himself on a tree on the edge of a precipice that overlooked the valley of Hinnom. After he hung there for a time, the limb of the tree snapped or the rope gave way and Judas fell down the ledge, mangling his body in the process.

The fall could have been before *or* after death as either would fit this explanation. This possibility is entirely natural when the terrain of the valley of Hinnom is examined. From the bottom of the valley, you can see rocky terraces 25 to 40 feet in height and almost perpendicular.

There are still trees that grow around the ledges and a rocky pavement at the bottom. Therefore, it is easy to conclude that Judas struck one of the jagged rocks on his way down, tearing his body open.

Three days and three nights in the tomb? (RF/121-23)

Many people have questioned the accuracy of Jesus' statement that "just as Jonah was three days and three nights in the belly of the sea monster, so shall the Son of Man be three days and three nights in the heart of the earth" (Matthew 12:40).

They ask, "How could Jesus have remained in the tomb three days and three nights if He was crucified on Friday and rose on Sunday?"

The accounts of His death and resurrection as given in the Gospels of Matthew, Mark, Luke and John indicate that Jesus was crucified and buried on Friday, before sundown, which is the beginning of the next day for the Jews, and resurrected on the first day of the week, which is our Sunday, before sunrise.

This puts Jesus in the grave for part of Friday, the entire Sabbath, and part of Sunday. In other words, He was in the tomb two full nights, one full day and part of two days. Since this is clearly not three full, 24-hour days, do we have a problem of conflict with the prophecy of Jesus in Matthew 12:40?

Jesus is recorded as saying, "The Son of man will rise again after three days" (Mark 8:31); and, "He will be raised again on the third day" (Matthew 16:21)—expressions that are used interchangeably. Also, Jesus spoke of His resurrection in John 2:19-22, stating that He would be raised up *in* three days (not the fourth day).

Matthew 27:63 gives weight to this idiomatic usage. After the Pharisees tell Pilate of the prediction of Jesus ("After three days I will rise again"), they ask for a guard to secure the tomb until the third day.

If the phrase, "after three days," had not been interchangeable with the "third day," the Pharisees certainly would have asked for a guard for the fourth day.

That the expression "one day and one night" was an idiom employed by the Jews for indicating a day, even when only a part of a day was indicated, can be seen also in the Old Testament.

For example, 1 Samuel says, "For he had not eaten bread or drunk water for three days and three nights," and in the next verse, "My master left me behind . . . three days ago" (1 Samuel 30:12,13).

Just as clearly, Genesis 42:17 shows this idiomatic usage. Joseph imprisoned his brothers for three days; in verse 18, he speaks to them and releases them, all on the third day.

The phrases, "after three days" and "on the third day," are not contradictory, either to each other or to Matthew 12:40, but simply idiomatic, interchangeable terms, a common mode of Jewish expression.

Another way to look at "three days and three nights" is to take into consideration the Jewish method of reckoning time. The Jewish writers have recorded in the commentaries on the Scriptures the principle governing the reckoning of time. Any part of a period was considered a full period. Any part of a day was reckoned as a complete day. The *Babylonian Talmud* (Jewish commentaries) relates that, "The portion of a day is as the whole of it." 54

The *Jerusalem Talmud* (so designated because it was written in Jerusalem) says, "We have a teaching, 'A day and a night are an Onah and the portion of an Onah is as the whole of it.' " 53 An *Onah* simply means, "a period of time."

Even today we often use the same principle in reference to time. For example: Many couples hope their child will be born before midnight December 31. If born at 11:59 P.M., the child will be treated by the IRS as being born 365 days and 365 nights of that year. This is true even if 99.9 percent of the year has elapsed.

Don't the resurrection accounts repeatedly contradict themselves?

(HW/285-86)

Although Pinchas Lapide argues for the actual bodily resurrection of Jesus, he nevertheless follows the lead of other critical scholars when he says of the resurrection in the Gospels:

> In no other area of the New Testament narrative are the contradictions so glaring. Nowhere else are the opposites so obvious and the contrasting descriptions so questionable as in the realm of the resurrection of Jesus. 41/34-35

Ian Wilson accuses, "The various accounts of the scene at the empty tomb on the first Easter morning are so full of inconsistencies that it is easy to deride them."

In actuality, those who see contradictions in the resurrection accounts often betray the fact that they have studied the accounts only superficially. Wilson, for example, charges, "The writer of the John gospel describes Mary Magdalene arriving at the tomb alone. . . . The Matthew author relates that Mary Magdalene was accompanied by 'Mary the mother of James and Joseph.' " 79/138

There is in fact no contradiction here. One could resolve the problem just by saying that John focused on Mary Magdalene alone, while Matthew focused on the group. In actuality, the apparent contradiction is one of a series of clues which help answer such questions as where the different women stayed on the Sabbath and what routes they took to the tomb on Sunday morning.

The whole scenario is impressively revealed by the outstanding British New Testament scholar, John Wenham, in his book, *Easter Enigma.* 77 In it he pieces together the available evidence to demonstrate that the crucifixion and resurrection reports contain, not contradictions, but clues to the many individual and group activities of the key witnesses to those events.

Any attorney who has faced the task of piecing together apparently conflicting courtroom testimony can understand how difficult it is to reconcile an apparent contradiction between two witnesses. For many years, until his retirement, Sir Norman Anderson was the Director of the Institute of Advanced Legal Studies at the University of London. As one thoroughly acquainted with apparent conflicts in the testimony of different witnesses, he states:

> I must confess that I am appalled by the way in which some people—biblical scholars among them—are prepared to make the most categorical statements that this story cannot possibly be reconciled with that, or that such and such statements are wholly irreconcilable, when a little gentle questioning of the witnesses, were this possible, might well have cleared up the whole problem. Sometimes, indeed, a tentative solution may not be very far to seek even without such questioning, although the suggested reconciliation cannot, of course, be proved; and in others there may well be a perfectly satisfactory solution which evades us. 10/139

Solutions to apparent Bible contradictions provide confidence that other alleged conflicts also have solutions. Often the solutions reveal just how precisely God has communicated to us in the Bible. Apparent contradictions become assuring confirmations of the Bible's minute accuracy and trustworthiness.

CHAPTER 12 *What Is Higher Criticism?*

(HW/126-27, ME/37)

Higher criticism is a division of biblical criticism, and *Harper's Bible Dictionary* defines biblical criticism as the "study and investigation of biblical writings that seeks to make discerning and discriminating judgments about these writings." 2 It is meant to be neither positive nor negative.

Biblical criticism may be divided into lower and higher criticism as indicated on this chart:

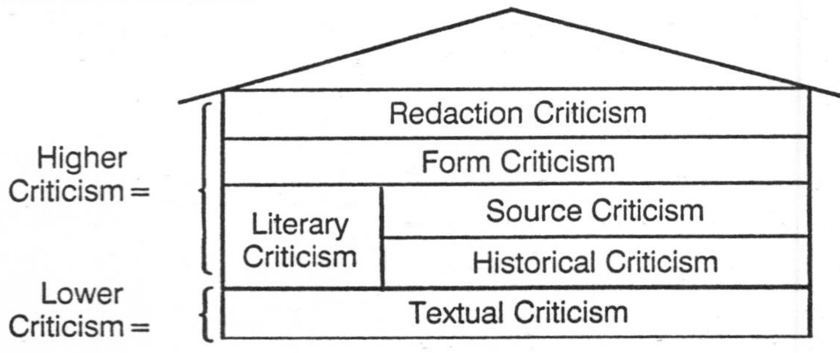

Lower criticism is identified with textual criticism since textual criticism is foundational to all other forms of biblical criticism. **Textual criticism** seeks to *determine the original wording of the biblical text,* especially since we do not have the original documents (called "autographs") themselves. Anyone who can read engages in textual criticism. If, for example, you noticed a typographical error while reading this page, you would correct the error in your mind, knowing that it was not originally intended by the authors. This process is essentially textual criticism.

Building upon lower or textual criticism, **higher criticism** uses other means to *evaluate the text* which lower criticism establishes as the most authentic version of the original. Thus, as in building a house, higher criticism builds on top of the foundation established by lower criticism.

Higher criticism can be divided into two broad disciplines, historical criticism and literary criticism. **Historical criticism** *studies the setting of the times* when the text was composed. It addresses such questions as: (1) When and where was it written? (2) Who wrote it? (3) What circumstances surrounded the author or authors? (4) To whom was it written?

Growing out of historical criticism, **source criticism** emerged to a position of prominence among higher critics in the eighteenth century as many critical scholars rallied around the "documentary hypothesis." This theory proposed that at least four *sources* (tagged *J, E, P,* and *D)* lay behind the formation of the first five books of the Old Testament. The same methodology was then applied to the gospels during the nineteenth century to suggest various sources (for example, *Q, Mark,* and *Proto-Luke)* behind the Gospel accounts.

Literary criticism seeks to *analyze the text as a finished piece of literature.* It evaluates the meanings of words, the grammar, and the style of the text. It also seeks to determine the meaning of the text, and has been used to speculate about the life setting and circumstances of the writer.

The **form critical school** likewise held that the Pentateuch was the product of a compilation process and not the work of Moses. But it differed from the Documentary Hypothesis (see next chapter) in that it *held the individual documents were themselves compilations* developing from early oral tradition and being placed in writing only during or after the exilic period (586 B.C.).

Form criticism of the New Testament originated in Germany immediately after World War I. Relying much on source criticism, form criticism combined methods from both historical and literary criticism.

Where form criticism postulated the work of the "creative community" to formulate all the various pericopes (pericope: an extract or selection from a book), **redaction criticism**, growing out of form criticism, *focused on the final redactors (or compilers)* of the Gospels as authors in their own right. Norman Perrin, a redaction critic, defines redaction criticism as "concerned with studying the theological motivation of the author as this is revealed in the collection, arrangement, editing, and modification of traditional material, and in the composition of new material or the creation of new forms within the traditions of early Christianity." 59/1

NOTE: In the next chapter, the claims and errors of the documentary hypothesis are discussed. A similar treatment of the errors of New Testament form criticism is found in *He Walked Among Us,* pages 175-97. An understanding of the material, condensed from *Evidence That Demands a Verdict,* Vol. II, pages 185-326, is vital in withstanding critics' contentions that the New Testament is unreliable.

CHAPTER 13 *The Documentary Hypothesis*

Introduction (ME/29-32)

Julius Wellhausen in 1895 added the finishing touches to a hypothesis which is prevalent in modern biblical circles. It is known as the documentary or *JEDP* hypothesis. Using literary criticism as its basis for argument, this hypothesis sets forth the idea that the Pentateuch (Genesis to Deuteronomy) was not written by Moses, as the Bible claims, but was completed years after Moses died.

Those adhering to the documentary hypothesis teach that the first five books of the Bible were written close to a thousand years after Moses' death and were the result of a process of writing, rewriting, editing and compiling by various anonymous editors or redactors.

Citing literary variations within the text (divine names, doublets, repetition of accounts), style and diction, the documentarians assert that there are four different documents, *J, E, D* and *P,* which make up the Pentateuch. The *J* stands for the divine name YHWH which is the name for God characteristically used by the anonymous *J* writer. This writer had a flowing style and a peculiar vocabulary. *E* denotes the Elohist document which is known for its use of Elohim as the name for God. *J* and *E* are often difficult to separate within the text so they are often referred to as one source, *JE*. The letter *D* describes the Deuteronomic code which was found in 621 B.C. Finally, *P* represents the Priestly writer. This writer was the last compiler to work with the Old Testament. He put the finishing touches on it. *P* is characterized by its use of the name Elohim for God and its acrid style. "Its language is that of a jurist, rather than a historian." 25/12 *P* is not to be confused with the Elohist document which has a fresh flowing style. Chronologically these came in the same order as *J, E, D,* and *P*.

Herbert Livingston gives an excellent summary of the dates of the four documents of Wellhausen's theory:

> How then did the Wellhausen theory date the four documents? Since the *D* document was declared to be written in the seventh century and made public in Josiah's reform of 621 B.C., that document became the keystone for the procedure. It was decided that *D* knew about the contents of *J* and *E,* but not of the contents of *P;* hence, *J* and *E* were written before 621 B.C., and *P* at a later date.
>
> Dialectically, the *J* document, with its naive concepts, could be dated before *E,* and the early phases of the divided kingdom seemed to provide a good historical setting. It could be argued that *J* was the kingdom of Judah's reaction against the establishment of the kingdom of north Israel. The purpose of *J*, then, was to provide Judah with an "historical" document that would justify Judah's and Jerusalem's claim to be the governmental center of all Israel. Likewise, *E* would be the antithetical production of the kingdom of north Israel, led by the tribe of Ephraim, to show that there were historical antecedents in the Patriarchs and in Joshua for the governmental center to be located in the north.
>
> The theory continued to conclude that after the destruction of the northern kingdom of Israel, in 721 B.C., broadminded men during the reign of Manasseh (first half of seventh century B.C.) felt that the *E* document was too valuable to lose, so they blended it with the *J* document. This new *JE* document became a new thesis and the *D* document its antithesis. The thinking of the *D* document is said to have triumphed, substantially, during the Exile in Babylon and colored the composition of the historical books Joshua through 2 Kings. However, the "Holiness Code," tied with Ezekiel, arose as another antithesis to *D;* and slowly, for perhaps a century, the priests in exile and then in Jerusalem put together the *P* document and made it the framework of a grand synthesis, the Pentateuch.
>
> In summary, the *J* document is dated a bit later than 900 B.C., and the *E* document somewhat later in the ninth century B.C. The two were put together about 650 B.C., and were written about that same time and made public in 621 B.C. The *P* document appeared in the fifth century and the Pentateuch composed in approximately its present form about 400 B.C. 44/228-29

As a result of the above assertions, those adhering to the documentary hypothesis reject the Mosaic authorship of the Pentateuch.

Moses, who may be dated around 1400 B.C., purports to have written the Pentateuch. The documentarians reject this date and say it was not completed until sometime between the eighth and fifth centuries B.C.

The documentary hypothesis calls into question the credibility of the entire Old Testament. One would have to conclude, if their assertions are correct, that the Old Testament is a gigantic literary fraud. Either God did speak to and through Moses or we have to acknowledge that we possess a *belles-lettres* hoax. The whole issue calls into question the trustworthiness of Jesus, the accuracy of both the Old and New Testament writers and the integrity of Moses himself.

Livingston makes an acute observation:

> Almost every book that promotes the theory has a listing of chapters and verses originally belonging to the independent documents. All isolated fragments that are left over are attributed, much too easily, to redactors or compilers. It should be understood, however, that there are no literary references, no extant manuscripts of any kind, which mention the *J, E, D,* or *P* documents, either singly or as a group. They have been created by separating them, with the aid of the above mentioned criteria, from the extant of the Pentateuch. 44/227

Livingston gives consequences of adherence to the theory of the documentary hypothesis:

> **(a)** Mosaic authorship is rejected, with only bits of the Pentateuch attributed to the Mosaic period; **(b)** for many of the scholars who accept the Wellhausen view, the men and women of the Pentateuch were not actual human beings—at best they were idealized heroes; **(c)** the Pentateuch does not give us a true history of ancient times, but it reflects instead the history of the divided kingdom through the early part of the postexilic period; **(d)** none of the people in the Pentateuch were monotheistic, and it was the postexilic priests who made them look like believers in one God; **(e)** God never spoke to any individuals in ancient times, but again, it was the work of the priests that gives that impression; **(f)** very few of the laws in the Pentateuch were prekingdom in origin; **(g)** very few of the cultic practices recorded in the Pentateuch were prekingdom, and many were postexilic; **(h)** the early Israelites never had a tabernacle such as described in Exodus; **(i)** all claims in the Pentateuch that God acted redemptively and miraculously in behalf of Israel are erroneous; **(j)** any concept that the present structural unity of the five books was original with Moses is erroneous; and finally, **(k)** the skepticism inherent in the theory creates a credibility gap with the ordinary layman to the extent that the Pentateuch becomes practically useless to him. 44/229

NOTE: For a brief history on the development of the documentary hypothesis, see *Evidence That Demands a Verdict, Vol. II,* pp. 43-46.

Ground Rules (ME/47-49)

The ancient oriental environment of the Old Testament provides many close literary parallels. Many people ignore it, but no one can well deny the truth that principles found valid in the study of ancient oriental history and literature should be applied to the Old Testament history and literature. Principles that are decidedly false when applied to ancient Near Eastern literature and history should not be applied to Old Testament literature or history. 36/28

Three elementary principles should permeate this investigation:

1. *Approach the Hebrew Scriptures as other ancient literature—harmonistically.*

Kitchen emphasizes:

> It is normal practice to assume the general reliability of statements in our sources, unless there is good, explicit evidence to the contrary. . . . The basic harmony that ultimately underlies extant records should be sought out, even despite apparent discrepancy. Throughout ancient history, our existing sources are incomplete and elliptical. 36/28-33

Allis labels this approach the "harmonistic method," and elaborates on its application to the Hebrew writings:

> It has two obvious advantages. The **one** is that it does justice to the intelligence and common sense of the writers of the Bible. To claim that the writers, compilers, editors of the biblical records would introduce or combine conflicting accounts of the same event into a narrative is to challenge their intelligence, or their honesty, or their competence to deal with the data which they record. The **second** is that it is the biblical method of interpretation. The many times and various ways in which the biblical writers quote or refer to one another implies their confidence in the sources quoted. Their method is a harmonistic method. 7/35

2. *Exercise an open mind.*

Brewer, a firm defendant of the documentary position, has provided an outstanding exposition of this principle:

> A truly scientific criticism never stops. No question is ever closed for it. When new facts appear or a new way of understanding old facts is shown, the critic is ready to reexamine, to modify or to overthrow his theory if it does not account for all the facts in the most satisfactory way. For he is interested in the truth of his theory, and indifferent to the label, old or new, orthodox or heterodox, conservative, liberal or radical, that others may place upon it. 17/305

The direction in which the facts lead may not be palatable, but it must be followed. Kitchen reasons: "While one must indeed never prefer mere orthodoxy to truth, it is also perverse to deny that orthodox views can be true." 36/173

The highly respected Jewish scholar Cyrus Gordon, formerly of Brandeis University and New York University, concludes that "a commitment to any hypothetical source structure like *JEDP* is out of keeping with what

I consider the only tenable position for a critical scholar: to go wherever the evidence leads him." 31/3

3. *Submit to external, objective controls.*

These all-important facts to which our minds must necessarily remain open are discovered by an archaeological examination of the ancient Orient. Cassuto exhorts us to

> conduct our investigation without prejudgment or anticipatory fear, but to rely on the objective examination of the texts themselves and the help afforded by our knowledge of the ancient East, in the cultural environment of which the children of Israel lived when the Torah was written. Let us not approach the Scriptural passages with the literary and aesthetic criteria of our time, but let us apply to them the standards obtaining in the ancient East generally and among the people of Israel particularly. 22/12

Kitchen establishes his axiom: "Priority must always be given to tangible, objective data, and to external evidence, over subjective theory or speculative opinions. Facts must control theory, not vice versa." 36/28-33

Faulty Methods and Assumptions (ME/51-71)

Priority of Source Analysis Over Archaeology

One of the major weaknesses of the radical higher critical school was that, in much of their analysis and isolation of alleged documents, conclusions were based almost exclusively upon their own subjective theories. These theories, regarding the history of Israel and probable development and compilation process of supposed sources, had little reference to the more objective and verifiable information being provided by archaeology.

Harrison points out:

> Whatever else may be adduced in criticism of Wellhausen and his school, it is quite evident that his theory of Pentateuchal origins would have been vastly different (if, indeed, it had been formulated at all) had Wellhausen chosen to take account of the archaeological material available for study in his day, and had he subordinated his philosophical and theoretical considerations to a sober and rational assessment of the factual evidence as a whole. While he and his followers drew to some extent upon the philological discoveries of the day and manifested a degree of interest in the origins of late Arabic culture in relation to Semitic precursors, they depended almost exclusively upon their own view of the culture and religious history of the Hebrews for purposes of biblical interpretation. 34/509

Harrison continues:

> Wellhausen took almost no note whatever of the progress in the field of Oriental scholarship, and once having arrived at his conclusions, he never troubled to revise his opinion in the light of subsequent research in the general field. 34/509

A. H. Sayce comments:

> Time after time the most positive assertions of a skeptical criticism have been disproved by archaeological discovery, events and personages that were confidently pronounced to be mythical have been shown to be historical, and the older writers have turned out to have been better acquainted with what they were describing than the modern critic who has flouted them. 68/23

Evolutionary View of Israel's Religion and History

G. E. Wright explains the view of Wellhausen and other radical critics:

> The Graf-Wellhausen reconstruction of the history of Israel's religion was, in effect, an assertion that within the pages of the Old Testament we have a perfect example of the evolution of religion from animism in patriarchal times through henotheism to monotheism. The last was first achieved in pure form during the sixth and fifth centuries. The patriarchs worshipped the spirits in trees, stones, springs, mountains, etc. The God of pre-prophetic Israel was a tribal deity, limited in his power to the land of Palestine. Under the influence of Baalism, he even became a fertility god and sufficiently tolerant to allow the early religion of Israel to be distinguished from that of Canaan. It was the prophets who were the true innovators and who produced most, if not all, of that which was truly distinctive in Israel, the grand culmination coming with the universalism of II Isaiah. 81/89-90

Here we note the critics' actual interpretation of Israel's history. Gleason Archer, a graduate of Harvard University, Suffolk Law School, Princeton Theological Seminary, and currently chairman of the Department of Old Testament at Trinity Evangelical Divinity School, provides us with an introduction to this point:

> An evolutionary understanding of history and an anthropocentric view of religion dominated the 19th century. The prevailing thinkers viewed religion as devoid of any divine intervention, explaining it as a natural development produced by man's subjective needs. Their verdict was that the Hebrew religion, as its neighbor religions, certainly must have begun with animism and then evolved through the stages of polydemonism, polytheism, menolatry, and finally monotheism. 13/132-33

W. F. Albright, W. W. Spence Professor of Semitic Languages from 1929-1958 at John Hopkins University and a sometime director of the American Schools of Oriental Research in Jerusalem, was, until his death in 1971, considered by many to be the foremost biblical archaeologist in the world. His work has forced many critics to completely reassess their conclusions regarding the history of Israel. About Wellhausen's application of Hegel's philosophical theories to the history of Israel, Albright said:

> Wellhausen's structure was so brilliant and afforded such a simple, apparently uniform interpretation that it was adopted almost universally by liberal Protestant scholars, and even largely by Catholic and Jewish

scholars. There were, of course, some exceptions, but in nearly all places where men were thoroughly schooled by learning Hebrew and Greek and absorbing the critical method, they also learned Wellhausenian principles. Unfortunately all of this was developed in the infancy of archaeology, and was of very little value in interpreting history. 5/15

Some Theoretical Assumptions

Following are a few assumptions of those who advocate an evolutionary development of Israel's religion:

- MONOTHEISM A LATE DEVELOPMENT

DOCUMENTARY ASSUMPTION: Not until the time of Amos did monotheism find a beginning in Israel's religion and definitely not during the Mosaic age (ca 1400 B.C.).

BASIC ANSWER: William F. Albright says that "it is precisely between 1500 and 1200 B.C., i.e., in the Mosaic age, that we find the closest approach to monotheism in the ancient Gentile world before the Persian period." 3/178

Joseph Free continues that an

> examination of the archeological inscriptional material shows that a monotheistic type of worship of the god Aton came into Egypt in the period between 1400 and 1350 B.C. Monotheistic tendencies in Babylonia are evidenced in the period 1500—1200 B.C. in a famous Babylonian text which identifies all important Babylonian deities with some aspect of the great god Marduk; Zababa is Marduk of battle, Sin is Marduk as illuminer of night, Adad is Marduk of rain. There is one great God, with various functions. Monotheistic tendencies also appear in Syria and Canaan in this same period of the fourteenth century B.C. Certain names were given to gods worshiped in many different places, all of whom were considered as variant forms of one great deity: there was a Teshup of Nirik, a Teshup of Khalab (Aleppo), a Teshup of Shamukha; it seems that finally Teshup was thought of as the great and sole god, who manifested himself in many places. 30/334-35

Ronald Youngblood adds:

> It cannot be shown that there is a universal tendency on the part of polytheistic religions to gradually reduce the number of deities until finally arriving at one deity. In some instances, in fact, such a religion may even add *more* deities as its adherents become aware of more and more natural phenomena to deify! 84/19

Waltke adds:

> Many scholars argue for a devolution in religion from monotheism to polytheism.
>
> The thesis of an original monotheism has been upheld more recently and with more convincing arguments by scholars of such varied outlook as

Andrew Lang, N. Soederblom, R. Pettazzoni, Father W. Schmidt and Geo Widengren, Upsala and finally, and on the particular grounds of the religion of Israel, I. Enguell believes that El, the supreme god of the Caupanites, was a "high god" who was worshiped in the whole of the west Semitic world under the names of El Shadday, El Elyon, Shaelem, and Hadad. (E. Jacobs, *Theology of the Old Testament,* 1958, pp. 44*ff.*) 6/2

- THE SECOND COMMANDMENT A LATE DEVELOPMENT

DOCUMENTARY ASSUMPTION: The second commandment, although attributed to Moses, could not have been a part of the early Israelite religions because of its prohibition of images. The radical critics reject Mosaic authorship and early dating of the decalogue because it is believed that they in fact did worship images.

BASIC ANSWER: Obviously, if the prohibition of image worship was a late addition to the Pentateuch, and the Israelites worshipped images, then one should find images of Jehovah.

However, this has not been the case. G. E. Wright records that the excavation of Megiddo by the University of Chicago failed to turn up any images of Jehovah. He says a tremendous amount of "debris was moved from the first five town levels (all Israelite), and not a single example has been found as far as this writer is aware." 82/413

Wright continues:

> There is no image of deity ever mentioned in patriarchal worship, nor in connection with the institution of the Tabernacle which served as the central shrine of the tribal amphictyony, nor in the Temple of Solomon. On the other hand, we know from archaeology that Israelites possessed small plaques or figures of the Canaanite fertility and mother goddesses in great number. This indicates the widespread syncretism which went on in early Israel, precisely as the literature frankly testifies. 80/124

- MORAL LEVEL TOO HIGH FOR MOSES' TIME

DOCUMENTARY ASSUMPTIONS: The laws, moral tone, and social level ascribed to Moses are too lofty to be found so early in Israel's development.

BASIC ANSWER: Various archaeological discoveries have discouraged the continuation of this assumption. Millar Burrows writes:

> The standards represented by the ancient law codes of the Babylonians, Assyrians, and Hittites, as well as the high ideals found in the Egyptian Book of the Dead and the early Wisdom Literature of the Egyptians, have effectively refuted this assumption. 20/46

- THE PRIESTLY CODE A LATE DEVELOPMENT

DOCUMENTARY ASSUMPTION: "The Priestly Code," writes Pfeiffer, "like all legislation, notwithstanding its deliberate timelessness and fictitious Mosaic background, bears the earmarks of its age, the first half of the Persian period (538–331 B.C.)." 60/257

BASIC ANSWER: Archer counters:

> It can hardly be objected that the Israelites were too primitive to be governed by laws such as these back in Moses' time, since according to their own explicit record they had been living in the midst of one of the most advanced civilizations of ancient times for over four hundred years, and would naturally have entertained more advanced concepts of jurisprudence than tribes indigenous to the desert. 13/162

Also it seems the other half of the skepticism comes from the belief that no primitive civilization could have written such a work as the code we have today. J. P. Free takes issue with this view:

> Archaeological discoveries, however, have shown that the advanced laws of Deuteronomy and the rest of the Pentateuch do not have to be dated late in accordance with the supposition of the critical school. The Code of Hammurabi (written within the period 2000–1700 B.C.) was found by a French archaeological expedition under the direction of M. Jacques de Morgan in 1901–1902 at the site of ancient Susa, to the east of the region of Mesopotamia. 29/121

Archer states that the

> Babylonian Code of Hammurabi . . . shows numerous similarities to the provisions in Exodus, Leviticus and Numbers relative to the punishment of crimes and the imposition of damages for torts and breaches of contract. 13/161

Joseph P. Free says:

> The fact that the Ras Shamra Tablets [Ras Shamra is a Canaanite city located on the Syro-Palestinian coast just opposite the tip of Cyprus], dating back to about 1400 B.C., record several laws similar to those of Leviticus shows that the liberal has no right to deny the possibility of such a code of sacrificial laws as early as the time of Moses. 29/112

Waltke quotes S. N. Kramer concerning the Lipit-Ishtar Law Code:

> All seven pieces date from the Early Post-Sumerian period, that is, they were actually inscribed sometime in the first half of the *second* millennium B.C. As for the first compilation of the code, it must have taken place sometime during the eleven-year reign of Lipit-Ishtar, who ruled probably during the first half of the nineteenth century B.C. It thus antedates the Hammurabi Code by more than a century and a half. 39/159

The same can be said of the Eshnunna law code of the old Babylon period (1830–1550 B.C.). Hammurabi apparently incorporated some of this code into his own system. Two tablets found in 1945 and 1947 near Baghdad contain these ancient laws.

- NO WRITING IN ISRAEL AT MOSES' TIME (ca 1500–1400 B.C.)

DOCUMENTARY ASSUMPTION: Writing was virtually unknown in

Israel during Moses' time and consequently Moses could not have written the Pentateuch.

Schultz, in 1983, states in his book *Old Testament Theology:*

> Of the legendary character of the pre-Mosaic narrators, the time of which they treat is a sufficient proof. It was a time prior to all knowledge of writing, a time separated by an interval of more than four hundred years, of which there is absolutely no history, from the nearest period of which Israel had some dim historical recollection, a time when in civilized countries writing was only beginning to be used for the most important matters of state. 69/25-26

BASIC ANSWER: The British Assyriologist A. H. Sayce evaluates this late date of writing theory. He claims that

> this supposed late use of writing for literary purposes was merely an assumption, with nothing more solid to rest upon than the critic's own theories and presuppositions. And as soon as it could be tested by solid fact it crumbled into dust. 68/28-29

Albright, speaking of the various writing systems that existed in the ancient Orient even during pre-Mosaic patriarchal times, says:

> In this connection it may be said that writing was well known in Palestine and Syria throughout the Patriarchal Age (Middle Bronze, 2100–1500 B.C.). No fewer than five scripts are known to have been in use: Egyptian hieroglyphs, used for personal and place names by the Canaanites; Accadian cuneiform; the hieroglyphiform syllabary of Phoenicia, used from the 23rd century or earlier (as known since 1935); the linear alphabet of Sinai, three inscriptions in which are now known from Palestine (this script seems to be the direct progenitor of our own); the cuneiform alphabet of Ugarit (used also a little later in Palestine), which was discovered in 1929. This means that Hebrew historical traditions need not have been handed down through oral transmission alone. 4/186

Evidence for Mosaic Authorship (ME/95-120)

1. Internal Evidence

The Pentateuch itself clearly states that these portions were written by Moses:

- BOOK OF THE COVENANT, extending from Exodus 20:22–23:33

  And Moses wrote down all the words of the LORD. Then he arose early in the morning, and built an altar at the foot of the mountain with twelve pillars for the twelve tribes of Israel. . . . Then he took the book of the covenant and read it in the hearing of the people; and they said, "All that the LORD has spoken we will do, and we will be obedient!" (Exodus 24:4,7).

- RENEWAL OF THE COVENANT, referring to Exodus 34:10-26

  Then the LORD said to Moses, "Write down these words, for in accordance with these words I have made a covenant with you and with Israel" (Exodus 34:27).

- DEUTERONOMIC CODE, which comprises the bulk of Deuteronomy 5–30

  So Moses wrote this law and gave it to the priests, the sons of Levi who carried the ark of the covenant of the LORD, and to all the elders of Israel (Deuteronomy 31:9).

  And it came about, when Moses finished writing the words of this law in a book until they were complete, that Moses commanded the Levites who carried the ark of the covenant of the LORD, saying, "Take this book of the law and place it beside the ark of the covenant of the LORD" (Deuteronomy 31:24-26).

Such a passage cannot be used to prove that Moses wrote the whole Pentateuch; but it does presuppose a considerable book which at least refers to Deuteronomy 5–26, and indicates a large amount of literary activity by Moses. 65/86

- GOD'S JUDGMENT OF AMALEK

  Then the LORD said to Moses, "Write this in a book as a memorial, and recite it to Joshua, that I will utterly blot out the memory of Amalek from under heaven" (Exodus 17:14).

- ITINERARY OF ISRAELITES FROM RAMSES TO MOAB

  And Moses recorded their starting places according to their journeys by the command of the LORD, and these are their journeys according to their starting places (Numbers 33:2).

- THE SONG OF MOSES IN DEUTERONOMY 32

  Now therefore write this song for yourselves, and teach it to the sons of Israel; put it on their lips, in order that this song may be a witness for Me against the sons of Israel (Deuteronomy 31:19).

THE LEGAL DOCUMENTS IN THESE PASSAGES ATTRIBUTE THEIR AUTHORSHIP TO MOSES

in either the superscription or subscription:

Exodus 12:1-28; 20–24; 25–31; 34

Leviticus 1–7; 8; 13; 16; 17–26; 27

Numbers 1; 2; 4; 6:1-21; 8:1-4; 8:5-22; 15; 19; 27:6-23; 28; 29; 30; 35

Deuteronomy 1–33

MOSES CERTAINLY WAS IN A POSITION TO WRITE THE PENTATEUCH

He grew up in Pharaoh's house and was, as Stephen said, "learned in all the wisdom of the Egyptians" (Acts 7:22). All now agree that this learning would have included the knowledge of writing.

That Moses was pre-eminently prepared to author a work such as the Pentateuch is witnessed by the following qualifications:

(a) *Education*—he was trained in the royal Egyptian court in their highly developed academic disciplines. This without a doubt included a knowledge of writing, for even the women's toilet articles of the time were inscribed.

(b) *Tradition*—he undoubtedly received the Hebrew traditions of their early history and encounters with God.

(c) *Geographical familiarity*—Moses possessed an intimate knowledge of the climate and geography of Egypt and Sinai as displayed in the Pentateuch.

(d) *Motivation*—as the founder of the Commonwealth of Israel, he had more than adequate incentive to provide the nation with concrete moral and religious foundations.

(e) *Time*—40 long years of wandering in the Sinai wilderness easily allowed ample opportunity to write this work.

At a time when even uneducated slaves working at the Egyptian turquoise mines were inscribing their records on the tunnel walls, it is inconceivable that a man of Moses' background would fail to record the details of one of history's most significant epochs.

WITNESS OF THE OTHER OLD TESTAMENT BOOKS

These Old Testament verses record that the Torah or "the Law," was from Moses:

Joshua 8:32 speaks of "the Law of Moses, which he had written."

(The verses marked by an asterisk refer to an actual written "Law of Moses," not simply an oral tradition):

Joshua 1:7,8*; 8:31*,34*; 23:6*

1 Kings 2:3*

2 Kings 14:6*; 23:25

1 Chronicles 22:13

2 Chronicles 5:10; 23:18*; 25:4*; 30:16; 33:8; 34:14; 35:12*

Ezra 3:2; 6:18*; 7:6

Nehemiah 1:7,8; 8:1*,14*; 9:14; 10:29; 13:1*

Daniel 9:11,13*

Malachi 4:4

WITNESS OF THE NEW TESTAMENT

The New Testament held that the Torah or "law" came from Moses·

The **apostles** believed that "Moses wrote for us a law" (Mark 12:19).

John was confident that "the Law was given through Moses" (John 1:17).

Paul, speaking of a Pentateuchal passage, asserts "Moses writes" (Romans 10:5).

Other passages which insist on this include:

Luke 2:22; 20:28

John 1:45; 8:5; 9:29

Acts 3:22; 6:14; 13:39; 15:1,21; 26:22; 28:23

1 Corinthians 9:9

2 Corinthians 3:15

Hebrews 9:19

Revelation 15:3

Jesus believed the Torah to be from Moses:

Mark 7:10; 10:3-5; 12:26

Luke 5:14; 16:29-31; 24:27,44

John 7:19,23

Notice especially John 5:45-47:

> Do not think that I will accuse you before the Father; the one who accuses you is Moses, in whom you have set your hope. For if you believed Moses, you would believe Me; for he wrote of Me. But if you do not believe his writings, how will you believe My words?

Eissfeldt states:

> The name used in the New Testament clearly with reference to the whole Pentateuch – the Book of Moses – is certainly to be understood as meaning that Moses was the compiler of the Pentateuch. 27/158

NOTE: When we speak of Moses as having "written" the Pentateuch or being its "author," it should be noted, as has previously been stated, that in accord with ancient Mesopotamian practice, this does not necessarily mean he wrote the words with his own hand, although he may have. It is quite possible that the bulk of the Pentateuch was, like Hammurabi's Law Code, dictated to scribes. This in no way undermines the essential Mosaic authorship of its contents.

2. External Evidence

See *Evidence That Demands a Verdict, Vol. II,* pages 98-99 for a list of early Jewish and early Christian testimony to Mosaic authorship of the Pentateuch. Notice especially Philo (A.D. 20): "But I will . . . tell the story of Moses as I have learned it, both from the sacred books, the wonderful monuments of his wisdom which he has left behind him, and from some of the elders of the nation." 62/279

COVENANT-FORM ANALYSIS

In 1954 George Mendenhall published an epochal article in which he described the ancient suzerainty treaties which were established between victorious Near Eastern kings and their vanquished subjects. He pointed out striking similarities between these treaties and certain treaty forms in the Hebrew Scriptures. Meredith Kline took his work further by demonstrating the correlation of these treaties to the Book of Deuteronomy as a whole.

- DEUTERONOMY AND THE SECOND MILLENNIUM B.C. TREATY/HITTITE SUZERAINTY TREATY OF THE SECOND MILLENNIUM B.C.

(1) *Preamble or title,* identifying the author of the covenant.

(2) *Historical prologue* or retrospect, mentioning previous relations between the two parties involved; past benefactions by the suzerain as a basis for the vassal's gratitude and future obedience.

(3) *Stipulations* basic and detailed; the obligations laid upon the vassal by the sovereign.

(4) (a) *Deposition* of a copy of the covenant in the vassal's sanctuary; and

(b) *periodic public reading* of the covenant terms to the people.

(5) *Witnesses,* a long list of gods invoked to witness the covenant.

(6) (a) *Curses* invoked upon the vassal if he breaks the covenant; and

(b) *blessings* invoked upon the vassal if he keeps the covenant.

Nearly all the known treaties of the fourteenth/thirteenth centuries B.C. follow this pattern closely. Sometimes some elements are omitted, but the order of them is almost invariable, whenever the original texts are sufficiently well preserved to be analyzed. This is, therefore, a stable form in the period concerned. Earlier than this, the pattern was apparently somewhat different. 36/92-93

- DEUTERONOMIC COVENANT

  Sinai Covenant in Deuteronomy

  (1) *Preamble*—1:1-5

  (2) *Historical prologue*—1:6—3:29

  (3) *Stipulations*—4—11 (basic); 12—26 (detailed)

  (4) (a) *Deposition of text*—31:9,24-26

  (b) *Public reading*—31:10-12

  (5) *Witnesses*—since pagan gods are excluded here, ancient oriental godlists are absent. Moses' song could have been the witness (31:16-30; 32:1-47), as Kitchen suggests.

  (6) *Curses and Blessings*—28:1-14 (blessings); 28:15-68 (curses); the sequence here is blessings—curses—witness, as opposed to the witness—curses—blessings sequence of ancient oriental treaties, possibly due to the different nature of the witness here in Deuteronomy. 36/96-97

- DEUTERONOMY AND THE FIRST MILLENNIUM B.C. TREATIES

If we find no appreciable differences between the treaty forms of the first and second millennia B.C., then there is no reason, on the basis of this particular investigation, to assign to Deuteronomy the traditional early date as opposed to the sixth-seventh century B.C. date given by the radical critics. But this is not the case.

As early as 1954, Mendenhall recognized that the covenant type found in the second millennium B.C. in Deuteronomy

> cannot be proven to have survived the downfall of the great empires of the late second millennium B.C. When empires again arose, notably Assyria, the structure of the covenant by which they bound their vassals was entirely different. Even in Israel, the writer submits that the older form of covenant was no longer widely known after the united monarchy. 51/30

In a recent article, Kitchen presents a forceful summary:

> The present writer cannot see any legitimate way of escape from the crystal-clear evidence of the correspondence of Deuteronomy with the remarkably stable treaty or covenant form of the fourteenth-thirteenth centuries B.C. Two points follow here. First, the basic structure of Deuteronomy and much of the content that gives specific character to that structure *must* constitute a recognizable literary entity; second, this is a literary entity *not* of the eighth or seventh century B.C. but rather from ca 1200 B.C. *at latest*. 37/4

- ANTIQUITY OF DEUTERONOMY

The crucial role Deuteronomy plays in the entire documentary scheme is recognized by all. There is also little disagreement among scholars of all positions that the book which was discovered in the Temple in 621 B.C., sparking the reforms of King Josiah (2 Kings 22 and 23), was essentially the book we now call Deuteronomy. There is much disagreement, though, over the date of its original authorship: The radical critics assign it to a time not long before the 621 discovery, while others insist that it must be dated from the time of Moses.

- GEOGRAPHICAL STATEMENTS DEMONSTRATING ANTIQUITY

Manley's words quite aptly summarize the geographical attestations for the antiquity of Deuteronomy:

> The account of the journeyings in chapters i–iii is altogether realistic and quite unlike an introduction prefixed to a collection of old laws; it bears every sign of originality. The views described and the features of the Moabite country reproduced must have been seen by human eyes. . . . The omissions also are significant: There is no hint of Jerusalem, nor of Ramah, dear to Samuel's heart, not even of Shiloh, where the Tabernacle came to rest. Everything points to its historical character and early date. 46/64

- ANSWERS TO ARGUMENTS AGAINST ANTIQUITY

(a) The phrase "beyond Jordan" to refer to the region east of the Jordan. It is contended that, since Deuteronomy claims to have been written in that region, "beyond the Jordan" could only refer to Canaan proper on the western side. However, it has been adequately demonstrated that this phrase was simply a technical term for that region, even as it was known as Paraea ("The Other-Side Land") during the New Testament times and has more recently been known as Transjordania (even to its inhabitants). 13/244; 46/49

(b) The phrase "until this day." Here it is urged that this indicates a great lapse of time since the event mentioned. Yet in each instance of its usage, it is highly appropriate that Moses use this phrase in light of only the previous forty-year period, to indicate that a situation has persisted until these final days of his life. 13/243

(c) The account of Moses' death in Deuteronomy 34. But it is quite reasonable to assume that Joshua included this account, just as often an obituary is added to the final work of a man of great letters. /244 And it is worthy of note here that the other events of the book cover all of Moses' life, and never transgress that limit. 46/172

3. Additional Evidence

There is a substantial amount of internal evidence that the Pentateuch, both in its form and content, is very much older than the ninth-fifth century B.C. dating scheme assigned to it by the critics.

Exodus, Leviticus, and Numbers are quite obviously aimed at a people wandering in the desert, not a nation of farmers settled for centuries in their promised land. Otherwise, the frequent and detailed descriptions of the portable tabernacle are absurd. The meticulous instructions for encampment (Numbers 2:1-31) and for marching (Numbers 10:14-20) would be irrelevant for a settled nation, but eminently practical for the desert experience. Desert references are abundant, including sanitary instructions for desert life (Deuteronomy 23:12,13) and the sending of the scapegoat into the desert (Leviticus 16:10). 13/106-8

Much of the material in Genesis and Exodus has an obvious Egyptian background. We would expect this if it were written by Moses (reared in an Egyptian court) shortly after the Israelites' Exodus from Egypt. It would hardly be explainable had it been written, as the documentarians claim, more than 400 years after the Hebrews left Egypt. [An ambitious work which discusses the Egyptian background of the stories of Moses and Joseph in Egypt is Abraham Yahuda's *The Language of the Pentateuch in Its Relationship to Egyptian* (1933).]

This intimacy with Egyptian geography is especially noticeable in the case of the second book. The writer of Exodus had a thorough knowledge of Egyptian territory. He knew the Egyptian papyrus (Exodus 2:3), the character of the Nile bank, and was well acquainted with the sandy desert (Exodus 2:12). He knew of such places as Ramses, Succoth (Exodus 12:37), Etham (Exodus 13:20) and Pi-Hahiroth (Exodus 14:2). The mention in Exodus 14:3 that "the wilderness had shut them in" shows an intimate knowledge of the geography of Egypt. In fact, chapter 14 cannot be understood without knowledge of Egyptian geography. 65/109

It is worthy of note here also that the antiquity of the Old Testament is supported in the mention of royalty wearing a signet ring and a chain of gold as a token of authority (Genesis 41:42; Esther 3:10,12; 8:2,8,10; Daniel 5:29). This was unknown to Israel but existed in ancient Egypt, Persia and Babylon.

This body of evidence should also include the fact that there are places in the Old Testament where trivial details are mentioned that a later author would be unlikely to include. For example, when Joseph and the Egyptians were separated from Joseph's brothers at the table, an explanatory note is included: "The Egyptians could not eat bread with the Hebrews, for that is loathsome to the Egyptians" (Genesis 43:32). Would a later author include this? 65/109

Archer discusses the antiquity of land transactions. Genesis 23 describes Abraham's reluctance in purchasing an entire tract of land from Ephron the Hittite, desiring rather only the cave of Machpelah itself and the immediate grounds. The discovery of the Hittite Legal Code (dating from 1300 B.C.) provides amazing parallels, and explains that the owner of an entire parcel must carry out the duties of feudal service, including pagan religious observances. Thus, Abraham plainly refused to purchase any more than a portion of the tract so he could avoid any involvement with gods other than Yahweh. This narrative reflects a grasp of Hittite procedure that makes it highly probable that it preceded the fall of the Hittites in the thirteenth century B.C. 13/161

CONCLUSIONS:

About the Pentateuch Albright says: "New discoveries continue to confirm the historical accuracy or the literary antiquity of detail after detail in it." 6/225

John Bright makes this statement about the patriarchal narratives: "No evidence has come to light contradicting any item in the tradition." 18/67

Albright warns: "It is . . . sheer hypercriticism to deny the substantial Mosaic character of the Pentateuchal tradition." 6/224

Meredith Kline gives an appropriate conclusion:

> The story of twentieth century biblical archaeology is the story of the silencing of the clamorous voice of the modern western Wellhausen by the voiceless witnesses emerging from ancient eastern mounds. The plot of the story would be clearer were it not for the reluctance of critical scholars to part with their traditional teachings. But all are now obliged to admit that far from the biblical narratives of patriarchal and Mosaic days being alien to the second millennium B.C. where the biblical chronology locates them, they would be completely out of place in the first millennium B.C. The biblical sequence of Law and Prophets has been vindicated. 38/139

The Phenomenon of Divine Names (ME/121-134)

Selective Usage

ELOHIM occurs 33 times in the first 34 verses of Genesis. It is followed by JEHOVAH (YHWH) ELOHIM 20 times in the next 45 verses, and finally by JEHOVAH (YHWH) 10 times in the following 25 verses. Such selective usage of divine names seems more than coincidental. 8/23

DOCUMENTARY ASSUMPTION: Critics have held that the isolated use of various divine names [i.e., Jehovah (English pronunciation) or Yahweh (Hebrew Pronunciation) and Elohim] indicated more than one author. This is what initially led Astruc to the conclusion that various sources lay intertwined and combined in the Pentateuch. Notice this statement in his *Conjectures,* cited by *The Encyclopedia of Religion and Ethics:*

> In the Hebrew text of Genesis, God is designated by two different names. The first is Elohim, for, while this name has other meanings in Hebrew, it is especially applied to the Supreme Being. The other is Jehovah *[YHWH]*, the great name of God, expressing His essence. Now one might

suppose that the two names were used indiscriminately as synonymous terms, merely to lend variety to the style. This, however, would be an error. The names are never intermixed; there are whole chapters, or large parts of chapters, in which God is always called Elohim, and others, at least as numerous, in which He is always named Jehovah. If Moses were the author of Genesis, we would have to ascribe this strange and harsh variation to himself. But can we conceive such negligence in the composition of so short a book as Genesis? Shall we impute to Moses a fault such as no other writer has committed? Is it not more natural to explain this variation by supposing that Genesis was composed of two or three memoirs, the authors of which gave different names to God, one using that of Elohim, another that of Jehovah or Jehovah Elohim? 28/315

ANSWER: SPECIFIC USES OF VARIOUS DIVINE NAMES. Umberto Cassuto, the Jewish scholar and late professor at the Hebrew University, observes,

> First consider the characters of the two Names. They are not of the same type. The designation 'Elohīm was originally a common noun, an appellative, that was applied both to the One God of Israel and to the heathen gods (so, too, was the name 'El). On the other hand the name YHWH is a proper noun, the specific name of Israel's God, the God whom the Israelites acknowledged as the Sovereign of the universe and as the Divinity who chose them as His people. 22/18

Cassuto sets forth these rules as an explanation for the use of divine names.

YHWH	ELOHIM
1. It selected the name YHWH when the text reflects the Israelite conception of God, which is embodied in the portrayal of YHWH and finds expression in the attributes traditionally ascribed to Him by Israel, particularly in His ethical character.	1. It preferred the name ELOHIM when the passage implies the abstract idea of the Deity prevalent in the international circles of "wise men"—God conceived as the Creator of the physical universe, as the Ruler of nature, as the Source of life.
2. YHWH is used, when expression is given to the direct intuitive notion of God, which characterizes the simple faith of the multitude or the ardour of the prophetic spirit.	2. The name Elohim when the concept of thinkers who meditate on the lofty problems connected with the existence of the world and humanity is to be conveyed.
3. The name YHWH occurs when the context depicts Divine attributes in relatively lucid and, as it were, palpable terms, a clear picture being conveyed.	3. Elohim, when the portrayal is more general, superficial and hazy, leaving an impression of obscurity.
4. YHWH is found when the Torah seeks to arouse in the soul of the reader or the listener the feeling of	4. Elohim, when it wishes to mention God in an ordinary manner or when the expression or thought

the sublimity of the Divine Presence in all its majesty and glory.	may not, out of reverence, be associated directly with the Holiest name.
5. The YHWH is employed when God is presented to us in His personal character and in direct relationship to people or nature.	5. Elohim, when the Deity is alluded to as a Transcendental Being who exists completely outside and above the physical universe.
6. YHWH appears when the reference is to the God of Israel relative to His people or to their ancestors.	6. Elohim, when He is spoken of in relation to one who is not a member of the Chosen people.
7. YHWH is mentioned when the theme concerns Israel's tradition.	7. Elohim, when the subject-matter appertains to the universal tradition.

> Sometimes, of course, it happens that two opposite rules apply together and come together in conflict with each other; then, as logic demands, the rule that is more material to the primary purport of the relevant passage prevails. 22/30-41

Archer states that a careful study of the use of Yahweh and Elohim in the book of Genesis will reveal the purpose that the writer had in mind. Elohim (which is perhaps derived from a root meaning "strong," "powerful" or "foremost") refers to God as the almighty Creator and Lord of the universe. Thus Elohim is appropriate for Genesis 1 because God is in the role of the almighty Creator, whereas Yahweh is the name of God when He is in the covenant engagement. Thus in Genesis 2 Yahweh is almost exclusively used because God is dealing with Adam and Eve in a covenant relationship. In Genesis 3 when Satan appears, the name for God changes back to Elohim because God has no covenant relationship with Satan. Thus, both the serpent and Eve refer to Him as Elohim. The name changes back to Jehovah as He calls out to Adam (3:9) and reproves Eve (3:13), and it is the covenant God that puts the curse on the serpent (3:14). 13/112

Archaeology provides an answer for the compound name Yahweh-Elohim.

One of the major assumptions of the *JEDP* hypothesis is that the use of Jehovah is typical of a *J* document and Elohim of an *E* document. The combination of these two documents is the ground used by the radical critics to account for the compound name Yahweh-Elohim. Cyrus Gordon cites his personal experience on the subject: "All this is admirably logical and for years I never questioned it. But my Ugaritic studies destroyed this kind of logic with relevant facts." 31/132

At Ugarit, deities were found with compound names. For example: Qadish-Amrar is the name of one and Ibb-Nikkal another. Most of the time "and" was put between the two parts, but the conjunction can be omitted. So it was common to use compound names for a god.

Amon-Re, the most famous god with a compound name, was a deity that resulted from the Egyptian conquest under the eighteenth dynasty. Amon was the god of the city of Thebes where the political power existed, while Re was the universal sun god. Because of the political leadership in Thebes and the universalism of Re, these two gods were combined. Yet Amon-Re is one god. This sheds light on the combination of Yahweh-Elohim. Yahweh refers to the specifics of the deity, while Elohim speaks more of the general or universal designation of the deity. This consolidation of Yahweh-Elohim may be demonstrating that Yahweh equals Elohim, which can be restated "Yahweh is God." Yet the documentarians tell us Yahweh-Elohim is the result of combining the two documents *J* and *E*. This is as unfounded as using an *A* document and *R* document to explain the compound deity of Amon-Re. 31/132-33

Exegesis of Exodus 6:3

DOCUMENTARY ASSUMPTION: This view is stated by the British scholar, H. H. Rowley:

> Exodus 6:2*ff.* says: "I am Jehovah, and I appeared unto Abraham, unto Isaac, and unto Jacob as El Shaddai, but by my name Jehovah I was not known to them." Yet there are several passages in the book of Genesis which declare that God *was* known to the patriarchs by the name Jehovah. The name is known to Abram (Genesis 15:2,8), to Sarai (16:2), to Laban (24:31); it is used by angelic visitors in conversations with Abraham (18:14) and with Lot (19:13); and God is represented as saying, "I am Jehovah" to Abram (14:7) and to Jacob (28:13). 67/20-21

ANSWER: "The word *to know* in the Old Testament," states Raven,

> generally includes the idea of apprehension, and the expression "to know the name of Jehovah" is used many times in this fuller sense of apprehending the divine attributes (1 Kings 8:43; Psalms 9:11; 91:14; Isaiah 52:6; 64:1; Jeremiah 16:21; Ezekiel 39:6,7). All this shows the meaning to be that Abraham, Isaac and Jacob knew God as a God of power but not as the God of the covenant. 65/121

Archer argues similarly that the radical critics reject the method of founding Christian doctrine on proof-text, yet they founded one of their primary doctrines upon this very method. This method seeks a literal interpretation of two verses without considering context or the analogy of other scriptural teaching. This is found in Exodus 6:2,3. Archer states:

> With a proper understanding both of the verb "to know" (yadra) and of the implications in Hebrew of knowing someone's name, it becomes clear that the meaning is not literal. All ten plagues were surely not for the mere purpose that the Egyptians might know that the God of the Israelites was named Yahweh (Exodus 14:4: "And the Egyptians will know that I am Yahweh"). Rather, the intent of the plagues is that the Egyptians might witness the covenant faithfulness of God to His people and thus know Him by experience as Yahweh, the covenant God. (See also Exodus 6:7: "You shall know that I am Yahweh your God, who brought you out from under the

burdens of the Egyptians.") Hebrew usage therefore indicates clearly enough that Exodus 6:3 teaches that God, who in earlier generations had revealed Himself as El Shaddai (God Almighty) by deeds of power and mercy, would now in Moses' generation reveal Himself as the covenant-keeping Jehovah by His marvelous deliverance of the whole nation of Israel. 13/113-14

Furthermore, the critics use this verse as the basis for their division of the *J* document which uses the name Jehovah, from the *E* document which uses Elohim. Yet this verse distinguishes, not Elohim from Jehovah, but El-Shaddai from Jehovah, as Merrill Unger points out:

> That this supposition regarding the meaning of Exodus 6:2,3 is totally unwarranted and has no foundation outside the exigencies of the critical hypothesis is apparent *first, because of the clear distinction indicated in the passage itself:* "God spake unto Moses, and said unto him, I am the LORD: and I appeared unto Abraham, unto Isaac, and unto Jacob, by the name of God Almighty (El Shaddai); but by my name Jehovah was I not known to them." Significantly, the reference does not distinguish Jehovah from Elohim (occurring over two hundred times in Genesis) but from El Shaddai (occurring five times in Genesis), the name denoting the particular character in which God revealed Himself to be to the patriarchs (Genesis 17:1; 28:3; 35:11; 43:14; 48:3). 73/251

Motyer adds: "The patriarchs called God Yahweh, but knew Him as El Shaddai; their descendants will both call Him and know Him by His name Yahweh." 56/14

Given the documentarians' interpretation of this passage, we are left with a most difficult question: Why did not one of the many alleged redactors involved in the compilation of the Pentateuch reconcile the obvious contradiction between the use of the name Jehovah by the patriarchs in Genesis and the statement in Exodus 6:3 that the name was first revealed to Moses at Sinai?

"The redactor of the Pentateuch, if such there were," Raven notes, "could not have considered the statement of Exodus 6:3 inconsistent with the frequent use of the name Jehovah by the patriarchs. Otherwise he would either have changed the statement in Exodus or the name Jehovah in Genesis." 65/121

Finally, it should be noted that the divine name criterion cannot be applied to any material after Exodus 6:3 since from that point on, according to the critics, *E* and *P*, like *J*, are free to use Jehovah.

Difficulties With the Documentarians' Manipulation of Divine Names

According to documentarians, the divine name Yahweh indicates *J* source, Elohim indicates *E* source, *P* source used Elohim up to Exodus 6:3 but thereafter used Jehovah also.

The following sample passages contain divine names that do not correspond with the right source from which the passage is supposed to come:

a. Elohim occurs in these *J* source passages:
   (1) Genesis 31:50
   (2) Genesis 33:5,11

b. Yahweh occurs in these *P* source passages before Exodus 6:3
   (1) Genesis 17:1
   (2) Genesis 21:1

c. Yahweh occurs in these *E* source passages:
   (1) Genesis 21:33
   (2) Genesis 22:4,11
   (3) Genesis 28:21
   (4) Exodus 18:1,8,9,10,11

The critics' answer to these obvious contradictions is that the redactors (those who compiled and edited the documents) either made a mistake by copying in the wrong name or took the liberty to arbitrarily interchange the names here and there. The second explanation is of course appealed to more than the first.

Raven points out the fallacious circular reasoning of the critics' appeal to redactors:

> Sometimes they sweep aside difficulties by asserting that *R* altered the name, at others that the text is evidently corrupt. Neither of these suppositions however has any basis outside of the exigencies of the hypothesis. The hypothesis is said to be derived from the phenomena of the text, as we have it; but if those phenomena do not suit the hypothesis, they are rejected as worthless. May we not reasonably ask: If the text is corrupt how can we trust the hypothesis which is derived from it? The very existence of *R* and several *R's* is a baseless assumption made necessary by the difficulties of the divisive hypothesis. 65/120

The implication of all this is well-stated by Allis when he concludes, "It is to be noted, therefore, that every appeal to the redactor is a tacit admission on the part of the critics that their theory breaks down at that point." 8/39

Even single verses are chopped up into "sources." Nearly a hundred verses in Genesis, Exodus, and Numbers are divided up into at least two sources by the documentarians.

Says Professor F. Dornseiff of Germany, a student of Greek philology:

> Who can picture the genesis of a first-rate literary work like the Greek

Homer or the Pentateuch by "redactors" cutting "sources" into small pieces, and compacting these separate sentences into a new unit, and that in following out such a method they met with a great literary success? 1/28

Conclusion to the Documentary Hypothesis (ME/169-175)

The renowned Jewish scholar, Cyrus Gordon, relates the almost blind adherence of many critics to the documentary theory:

> When I speak of "commitment" to *JEDP*, I mean it in the deepest sense of the word. I have heard professors of Old Testament refer to the integrity of *JEDP* as their "conviction." They are willing to countenance modifications in detail. They permit you to subdivide (D_1, D_2, D_3, and so forth) or combine *(JE)* or add a new document designated by another capital letter but they will not tolerate any questioning of the basic *JEDP* structure.
>
> I am at a loss to explain this kind of "conviction" on any grounds other than intellectual laziness or inability to reappraise. 31/131

Gordon cites a striking example of this unquestioned allegiance to the documentary hypothesis:

> A professor of Bible in a leading university once asked me to give him the facts on *JEDP*. I told him essentially what I have written above. He replied: "I am convinced by what you say but I shall go on teaching the old system."
>
> When I asked him why, he answered: "Because what you have told me means I should have to unlearn as well as study afresh and rethink. It is easier to go on with the accepted system of higher criticism for which we have standard textbooks." 31/134

Critics readily admit that any criterion by which the Pentateuch is divided into sources is not, by itself, a convincing argument. However, when taken collectively, these criteria are said to present a powerful case for composite authorship.

Yet as Kitchen points out:

> It is a waste of time to talk about the "cumulative force" of arguments that are each invalid; 0 + 0 + 0 + 0 = 0 on any reckoning. The supposed concordance of assorted criteria whose independence is more apparent than real has had to be rejected . . . on evidence far too bulky to include in this book. 36/125

The Jewish scholar, M. H. Segal, after an investigation of the Pentateuchal problem in his book, *The Pentateuch—Its Composition and Its Authorship,* concludes:

> The preceding pages have made it clear why we must reject the documentary theory as an explanation of the composition of the Pentateuch. The Theory is complicated, artificial and anomalous. It is based on un-

proved assumptions. It uses unreliable criteria for the separation of the text into component documents.

To these defects may be added other serious faults. It carries its work of analysis to absurd lengths, and neglects the synthetic study of the Pentateuch as a literary whole. By an abnormal use of the analytical method, the theory has reduced the Pentateuch to a mass of incoherent fragments, historical and legalistic, to a collection of late legends and of traditions of doubtful origin, all strung together by late compilers on an artificial chronological thread. This is a fundamentally false evaluation of the Pentateuch. Even a cursory reading of the Pentateuch is sufficient to show that the events recorded therein are set out in logical sequence, that there is some plan combining its various parts and some purpose unifying all its contents, and that this plan and purpose find their realization in the conclusion of the Pentateuch which is also the end of the Mosaic age. 71/22

Thus, Wellhausen's documentary hypothesis must, in the final analysis, be regarded as unsuccessful in attempting to substantiate its denial of Mosaic authorship in favor of the *JEDP* source theory.

CHAPTER 14 *Is The New Testament Filled With Myths?* (HW/175-97)

Did the Gospel writers give us an accurate description of the Jesus who lived in history? Can we sincerely believe the supernatural aspects of the life they attributed to Him? One major argument against the historicity of the Jesus of the New Testament has been the similarity of mythological elements found in pagan religions during the same time the early Christian church was active. One source asks:

> If you Christians believe the stories of Jesus' miracles, if you believe the story of Jesus' miraculous birth, if you believe the story that Jesus was raised from the dead and ascended into Heaven, then how can you refuse to believe precisely the same stories when they are told of the other Savior Gods: Herakles, Asklepios, the Dioscuri, Dionysos, and a dozen others I could name? 21/17

Christian college students are often devastated to hear of ancient religions which contained stories of resurrections, dying saviors, baptismal initiations, miraculous births, and the like. The inference, of course, is that the early Christian writers borrowed these stories and attributed them to Jesus as they formulated the Christian religion. Jewish scholar Pinchas

Lapide states:

> If we add to all these disturbing factors the statement that in the ancient world there were not less than a round dozen of nature deities, heroes, philosophers, and rulers who, all long before Jesus, suffered and died, and rose again on the third day, then the skepticism of most non-Christians can easily be understood . . .
>
> The imprisonment of the savior of the world, his interrogation, the condemnation, the scourging, the execution in the midst of the criminals, the descent into hell—yes, even the heart blood of the dying gushing out of a spear wound, all these details were believed by millions of believers of the Bel-Marduk mystery religion whose central deity was called the savior sent by the Father, the one who raises the dead, the Lord and the Good Shepherd. 41/40-41

Did the early Christians turn a human Jesus into a supernatural figure by borrowing supernatural elements from the mystery religions? In this section, we will attempt to answer that question by (1) examining some specific alleged mythical roots of central Christian doctrine and practice; (2) identifying some fallacies committed by those who link Christianity with mystery religions; and (3) observing the uniqueness of the gospel description of Jesus when compared to the literature of the mystery religions.

Alleged Mythical Roots of Christian Doctrine and Practice

1. The Taurobolium

The taurobolium was primarily associated with the cult of Cybele and Attis. It has been suggested as the source of inspiration for Revelation 7:14: "and they have washed their robes . . . in the blood of the lamb"; and 1 Peter 1:2: "that you may obey Jesus Christ and be sprinkled with His blood." It also has been suggested as the inspiration for Christian baptism as explained in Romans 6. The rite, as described by the ancient writer, Prudentius, called for the high priest being consecrated to be led down into a deep pit. The top of the pit is covered over by a wooden mesh grating. Then a huge bull, draped with flowers, has its breast pierced

> with a sacred spear; the gaping wound emits a wave of hot blood, and the smoking river flows into the woven structure beneath it and surges wide.
>
> . . . The falling shower rains down a foul dew, which the priest buried within catches, putting his shameful head under all the drops, defiled both in his clothing and in all his body.
>
> Yea, he throws back his face, he puts his cheeks in the way of the blood, he puts under it his ears and lips, he interposes his nostrils, he washes his very eyes with the fluid, nor does he even spare his throat but moistens his tongue, until he actually drinks the dark gore.

> . . . The pontiff, horrible in appearance, comes forth, and shows his wet head, his beard heavy with blood, his dripping fillets and sodden garments.
>
> This man, defiled with such contagions and foul with the gore of the recent sacrifice, all hail and worship at a distance, because profane blood and a dead ox have washed him while concealed in a filthy cave. 64/1011-50

There are several reasons the taurobolium cannot be the source for any Christian doctrine or practice.

First, the passage describes the consecration of a high priest, not a new convert.

Second, there is no indication that the early Christians used actual blood in their rituals. Blood was simply a symbol of Jesus pouring His life out for His own, as can be seen when we fill in the words to Revelation 7:14 which we omitted in the first paragraph under this point: "and they have washed their robes *and made them white* in the blood of the Lamb."

Third, Christians (especially Jewish Christians) would have been repulsed by the practice. Prudentius was a Christian, and his words "foul dew," "shameful head," "defiled both in his clothing and in all his body," indicate that he considered the whole rite to be crude and blasphemous.

Fourth, and most important, the taurobolium post-dates the New Testament writings by almost a hundred years. The German scholar Günter Wagner has written the definitive work on Christianity and the mystery religions. In it he explains:

> The taurobolium in the Attis cult is first attested in the time of Antoninus Pius for A.D. 160. As far as we can see at present it only became a personal consecration at the beginning of the third century A.D. The idea of a rebirth through the instrumentality of the taurobolium only emerges in isolated instances toward the end of the fourth century A.D.; it is not originally associated with this blood-bath. 75/266

Nash concludes his investigation by saying:

> It is clear, then, that the New Testament emphasis on the shedding of blood should not be traced to any pagan source. The New Testament teaching should be viewed in the context of its Old Testament background—the Passover and the Temple sacrifices. 57/156

In view of the late date of the taurobolium, if any borrowing was done, we suspect it was **from** the Christians, not **by** the Christians.

2. Baptism

Ceremonial washings have been observed as a means of purification by religions all over the world and from long before the time of Jesus. It has therefore been suggested that Christians copied their rite of baptism from pagan religions around them. But this is a gross oversimplification.

Even to draw a strict parallel with Jewish baptism would be an over-simplification. For a thorough treatment of this subject, Günter Wagner's, *Pauline Baptism and the Pagan Mysteries,* should be consulted.

Christian baptism is a demonstration of the believer's identification with Jesus in His death, burial and resurrection. For the mystery cults it was different. Herman Ridderbos, professor of New Testament at Kampen Seminary in The Netherlands, states that "nowhere in the mystery religions is such a symbolism of death present in the 'baptism' ritual." 66/24

More important, the chronology once again does not agree with a syncretistic view. Nash indicates:

> Ceremonial washings that antedate the New Testament have a different meaning from New Testament baptism, while pagan washings after A.D. 100 come too late to influence the New Testament and, indeed, might themselves have been influenced by Christianity. 57/151

The evidence points to the practice of Christian baptism originating in Jewish baptism, having its meaning rooted in the historical events of the death, burial and resurrection of Jesus.

3. Resurrection

An alleged example of resurrection in ancient myth is provided by the early Egyptian cult of Isis and Osiris. The myth has Osiris being murdered by his brother Seth who then sinks the coffin containing Osiris's body in the Nile River. Osiris's wife, Isis, the goddess of heaven, earth, sea, and the unseen world below, discovers her husband's body and returns it to Egypt. Seth, however, regains the body, cuts it into fourteen pieces, and scatters it abroad. Isis counters by recovering the pieces. Nash continues:

> It is at this point that the language used to describe what follows is crucial. Sometimes those telling the story are satisfied to say that Osiris came back to life. (As I shall point out later, even this statement claims too much.) But some writers go much too far and refer to Osiris's "resurrection." 57/137

Nash's later discussion continues:

> Which mystery gods actually experienced a resurrection from the dead? Certainly no early texts refer to any resurrection of Attis. Attempts to link the worship of Adonis to a resurrection are equally weak. Nor is the case for a resurrection of Osiris any stronger. After Isis gathered together the pieces of Osiris's dismembered body, he became "Lord of the Underworld." As Metzger comments, "Whether this can be rightly called a resurrection is questionable, especially since, according to Plutarch, it was the pious desire of devotees to be buried in the same ground where, according to local tradition, the body of Osiris was still lying." One can speak then of a "resurrection" in the stories of Osiris, Attis, and Adonis only in the most extended of senses. And of course no claim can be made that Mithras was a dying and rising god. French scholar Andre Boulanger concludes: "The conception

that the god dies and is resurrected in order to lead his faithful to eternal life is represented in no Hellenistic mystery religion." 57/172-73

If the "savior-gods" mentioned above can be spoken of as resurrected, then we need to differentiate Jesus' resurrection from theirs. Jesus was a person of history who rose from the dead never to die again. He appeared in the flesh several times before His ascension, and the story was told by eyewitnesses. James D. G. Dunn concludes:

> The parallel with visions of Isis and Asclepius . . . is hardly close. These were mythical figures from the dim past. In the sightings of Jesus we are talking about a man who had died only a few days or weeks earlier. 26/71

Another issue related to the resurrection has to do with the amount of time between the crucifixion and the resurrection. Attis is supposed to have come back to life four days after his death, one account has Osiris being reanimated two or three days after his death, and it is even suggested that Adonis may have been "resurrected" three days after his death. In the case of all three, there is no evidence earlier than the second century A.D. for the supposed "resurrection" of these mystery gods. Norman Anderson states that

> if borrowing there was by one religion from another, it seems clear which way it went. There is no evidence whatever, that I know of, that the mystery religions had any influence in Palestine in the early decades of the first century. And the difference between the mythological experiences of these nebulous figures and the crucifixion "under Pontius Pilate" of one of whom eyewitnesses bore testimony to both his death and resurrection is again obvious. 9/53-54

4. Rebirth

In 1925, Samuel Angus wrote:

> Every Mystery-Religion, being a religion of redemption, offered means of suppressing the old man and of imparting or vitalizing the spiritual principle. Every serious *mystes* (initiate) approached the solemn sacrament of Initiation believing that he thereby became "twice-born," a "new creature," and passed in a real sense from death unto life by being brought into a mysterious intimacy with the deity. 11/95-96

Others also have claimed that the concept of rebirth is central to the mystery religions and that Christianity depended on them for its doctrine of the new birth. But the evidence for such claims is slim. The ceremonial washings of the Eleusinian cult were never attached to the idea of rebirth. There is only one reference attaching "rebirth" to the cult of Cybele and Attis. The reference is a fourth-century A.D. interpretation from Sallustius, whom one would expect was influenced by Christianity, not vice-versa. Only two debatable references, both from the second century A.D. "use the imagery of rebirth." Nash continues:

> While there are several sources that suggest that Mithraism included a notion of rebirth, they are all post-Christian. The earliest . . . dates from the end of the second century A.D. . . .
>
> The most frequently discussed evidence alleged to prove the presence of rebirth in a mystery religion is an inscription on a Roman altar that appears to connect the taurobolium with a belief in rebirth. The Latin inscription *taurabolio criobiolioque in aeternum renatus* can be translated "reborn for eternity in the taurobolium and criobolium."
>
> . . . But the problems connected with this hypothesis are enormous. For one thing, the Roman altar containing the inscription dates from A.D. 376. 57/174-76

Before Nash, Machen had recounted this observation:

> It may come as a shock, therefore, to readers of recent discussions to be told that as a matter of fact the phrase does not appear until the fourth century, when Christianity was taking its place as the established religion of the Roman world. If there is any dependence, it is certainly dependence of the taurobolium upon Christianity, and not of Christianity upon the taurobolium. 45/240-41

5. Sacrificial Death of the Deity

From the earliest Greek mythologies all the way through Roman times, it was common to ascribe deity to outstanding individuals. Some of these were fictional mythological characters, others were elevated humans, usually Greek philosophers or Roman emperors. This practice was normal in polytheistic cultures.

The Jews were different. For them there was only one God. It is therefore remarkable that Palestinian Jews, and among them one of the most respected of their Pharisees, would begin proclaiming the deity of one who had walked among them. It would have been hard enough to begin proclaiming the message within the Roman world. But to start in Jerusalem, among the Jews—that was ridiculous! Still the evidence shows that the Christian gospel sprouted first among the Jews.

Is it possible that these Jews could have shaped their message from the mystery cults? Not likely. The claim to deity in the mystery religions did often spring from the stories concerning the so-called god's death and return to life again (at least spiritually). We have already seen that Jesus' resurrection is not paralleled in the mystery religions except where these religions tried to copy Christianity. Nash gives six differences between the deaths of the so-called savior-gods and that of Jesus:

(1) None of the so-called savior-gods died for someone else. The notion of the Son of God dying in place of His creatures is unique to Christianity.

(2) Only Jesus died for sin. It is never claimed that any of the pagan deities died for sin. As Wagner observes, to none of the

pagan gods, "has the intention of helping men been attributed. The sort of death that they died is quite different (hunting accident, self-emasculation, etc.)."

(3) Jesus died once and for all (Hebrews 7:27; 9:25-28; 10:10-14). In contrast, the mystery gods were vegetation deities whose repeated death and resuscitation depict the annual cycle of nature.

(4) Jesus' death was an actual event in history. The death of the god described in the pagan cults is a mythical drama with no historical ties.

(5) Unlike the mystery gods, Jesus died voluntarily. Nothing like the voluntary death of Jesus can be found in the mystery cults.

(6) And finally, Jesus' death was not a defeat but a triumph. Christianity stands entirely apart from the pagan mysteries in that its report of Jesus' death is a message of triumph. 57/171-72

Fallacies of Linking Christianity With Mystery Religions

The first to plead his case seems just, until another comes and examines him (Proverbs 18:17).

At first sight, some of the similarities between Christianity and various mystery religions are so striking that one feels compelled to believe Christianity borrowed certain phrases, stories, doctrines or practices from them. Skeptical critics, by ignoring or withholding certain facts, often give a distorted picture of Christianity's alleged relationship with the mystery religions.

The evidence shows that the early Christian spokesmen steadfastly refused to accept anything contrary to the gospel which had been revealed to them. Look at Paul and Barnabas in Lystra. No sooner had a lame man been healed at Paul's command than the whole city rushed out raising

> their voice, saying in the Lycaonian language, "The gods have become like men and have come down to us."
>
> And they began calling Barnabas, Zeus, and Paul, Hermes, because he was the chief speaker.
>
> And the priest of Zeus, whose temple was just outside the city, brought oxen and garlands to the gates, and wanted to offer sacrifice with the crowds (Acts 14:11-13).

What an opportunity! If ever the early Christians had wanted to borrow from the mystery religions (even if just to attract more people to the faith), they could have made Christianity polytheistic right then and there! But no. It took Paul, formerly Saul the Pharisee, up to three years in Arabia and Damascus to reconcile the idea of a suffering, rising, divine Messiah with his Old Testament monotheistic convictions. And so,

> when the apostles, Barnabas and Paul, heard of it, they tore their robes and rushed out into the crowd, crying out and saying, "Men, why are you doing these things? We are also men of the same nature as you, and preach the gospel to you in order that you should turn from these vain things to a living God, WHO MADE THE HEAVEN AND THE EARTH AND THE SEA, AND ALL THAT IS IN THEM." . . . And even saying these things, they with difficulty restrained the crowds from offering sacrifice to them (Acts 14:14,15,18).

The fickle multitude was so disappointed, the very next day they were persuaded to stone Paul and leave him for dead outside the gates of their city.

Having already observed some specific alleged mystery religion roots of Christianity, we want to now pull out several main fallacies of those who allege that mystery religions influenced Christianity.

Fallacy 1: Combinationalism or Universalism

This is the error of first combining all the characteristics of all mystery religions from the fifteenth century B.C. all the way up to the fifth century A.D., and then comparing this caricature to Christianity. Even Albert Schweitzer recognized this error years ago when he wrote:

> Almost all the popular writings fall into this kind of inaccuracy. They manufacture out of the various fragments of information a kind of universal mystery-religion which never actually existed, least of all in Paul's day. 70/n.p.

Obviously, something true of one mystery religion in the fifteenth century B.C. but which ceased to be a part of it or any other religion by 1000 B.C. is probably not going to strongly influence Christianity. Or something true of a religion in another culture or area of the world may be thoroughly repulsed by the Jewish culture in Palestine. Again, elements from different religions when combined may look like something in Christianity even though the combined trait never really existed as such until practiced or believed by Christians.

Fallacy 2: Coloring the Evidence

Nash attributes the cause of this error to careless language. He observes:

> One frequently encounters scholars who first use Christian terminology to describe pagan beliefs and practices and then marvel at the awesome parallels they think they have discovered. One can go a long way toward "proving" early Christian terminology. A good recent example of this can be

found in Godwin's book *Mystery Religions in the Ancient World,* which describes the *criobolium* as a "blood baptism" in which the initiate is "washed in the blood of the lamb." An uninformed reader might be stunned by this remarkable similarity to Christianity (see Revelation 7:14), whereas a more knowledgeable reader will regard Godwin's description as the reflection of a strong, negative bias against Christianity. 57/126

The criobolium was essentially the same as the taurobolium except that rams, instead of bulls, were used, probably for economic reasons. References to it likewise postdate Christian sources!

Fallacy 3: Oversimplification

Critics also tend to use exaggeration and oversimplification in order to parallel Christianity and the mystery cults. Nash cautions:

> One will encounter exaggerated claims about alleged likenesses between baptism and the Lord's Supper and similar "sacraments" in certain mystery cults. Attempts to find analogies between the resurrection of Christ and the alleged "resurrections" of the mystery deities involve massive amounts of oversimplification and inattention to detail. Furthermore, claims about the centrality of a notion of rebirth in certain mysteries are greatly overstated. 57/126-27

Fallacy 4: Who's Influencing Whom?

This error is probably the most serious methodological fallacy committed by those charging that Christianity borrowed its doctrine and practices from the mystery religions. The error here is to propose that Christianity adopted a particular feature of a mystery religion when there is no evidence that the feature existed in the particular religion until after Christianity had begun. What many fail to recognize is that the growth of the church was so explosive that other religions adopted Christian elements in order to attract Christians and to prevent the loss of their adherents to Christianity. Metzger attests:

> In what T. R. Glover aptly called the "conflict of religions in the Early Roman Empire," it was to be expected that the hierophants of cults which were beginning to lose devotees to the growing Church should take steps to stem the tide. 52/11

The key here is dating. Most of the alleged parallels between Christianity and mystery religions, upon close scrutiny will show that Christian elements predate mythological elements. In cases where they do not, it is often Jewish elements which predate both Christianity and the myth, and which lent themselves to both religions.

Nash explains,

> Of all the mystery cults, only Mithraism had anything that resembled the Lord's Supper. A piece of bread and a cup of water were placed before

initiates while the priest of Mithra spoke some ceremonial words. . . . Any quest for the historical antecedents of the Lord's Supper is more likely to succeed if it stays closer to the Jewish foundation of the Christian faith than if it wanders off into the practices of the pagan cults. As noted in the case of Christian baptism, the Lord's Supper looked back to a real, historical person and something He did in history during the Last Supper. And as every student of the New Testament knows, the occasion for Jesus' introduction of the Christian Lord's Supper was the Jewish Passover feast. 57/159

According to available evidences, Mithraism did not gain a foothold in the Roman Empire until after A.D. 100. M. J. Vermaseren, a specialist on the cult of Mithra, certifies:

No Mithraic monument can be dated earlier than the end of the first century A.D., and even the more extensive investigations at Pompeii, buried beneath the ashes of Vesuvius in A.D. 79, have not so far produced a single image of the god. 74/29

Likewise, Historian Edwin Yamauchi concluded after several investigations:

Apart from the visit of the Armenian King, who was a worshiper of Mithra, to Nero, there is no evidence of the penetration of Mithra to the west until the end of the first century A.D. 83/112

No wonder Justin Martyr, as Nash notes, "referred to the Mithraic meal as a satanic imitation of the Lord's supper." 47/n.p. In view of the late date for the cult of Mithra in the Roman Empire, we can safely dismiss it as a possible influence on Christian origins.

Uniqueness of the Gospel Portrayals of Jesus

Scholars and lay people alike have recognized for almost two millennia a clear distinction between the reports of the Gospel writers and the creators of the myths of the mystery religions. For example, Walter Künneth, professor of systematic theology at Erlangen University in Germany, states concerning the exclusiveness of the gospel:

The message of the resurrection did not appear to the contemporary world to be one of the customary cult legends, so that Jesus Christ would be a new cult hero standing harmoniously side by side with other cult heroes. But the message was in terms of strict exclusiveness: One alone is the Kyrios ("Lord"). Here every analogy fails. This witness, in contrast to the tolerance of the whole mythical world, comes with an intolerant claim to absoluteness which calls in question the validity and truth of all mythology. 40/62

Cartlidge and Dungan recognize the same:

If Christians utilized familiar concepts and terms in order to communicate their faith, they often gave them an exclusive significance. When they worshiped Jesus as their Savior, the effect was a powerful negation: "Neither Caesar, nor Asklepios, nor Herakles, nor Dionysos, nor Ptolemy, nor any other God is the Savior of the world—Jesus Christ is!" 21/21

Read through a number of the Greek myths and then read through the Gospel accounts and you will notice a marked difference in the overall flavor of the material. Concerning the Gospel of John, often the most criticized of the Gospel narratives, Blaiklock says:

> I read him often in his simple Greek without translating and always gain an overwhelming impression of his directness, his intimacy with theme and reader. Simply read the story of the wedding at Cana (but correctly rendering, "Mother, what is that to do with me?") and feel the homely atmosphere, Mary's embarrassment, the best man's feeble joke (chapter 2). Follow on to the story of the rabbi (chapter 3) who came in the night and was annoyed at first because the answer to the question he was not allowed to ask was given by allusion to the books of Ezekiel and Numbers (Ezekiel 36:25-27; Numbers 21:4-9). And then read the story of the conversation at Sychar's well, with the Samaritan fighting her losing battle of words with the strangest Jew she had ever met (chapter 4). Read on to the poignant account of the Passion Week with its climax in the vivid resurrection stories, paralleled for simple reality only by the narrative in Luke. Simply read. These men were not writing fiction. This is not what myth sounds like. This is history and only thus set down because it was reporting. 16/77-78

New Testament translator and scholar J. B. Phillips describes his experience this way:

> I have read, in Greek and Latin, scores of myths, but I did not find the slightest flavour of myth here. There is no hysteria, no careful working for effect, and no attempt at collusion. . . . One sensed again that understatement which we have been taught to think is more "British" than Oriental. There is an almost childlike candour and simplicity, and the total effect is tremendous. 61/77

Conclusions

Though statements abound in popular literature that Christianity borrowed its gospel story from the myths of the pagan world, the tide of scholarly opinion has turned against this thesis. Moreland puts it:

> It cannot be emphasized enough that such influences are seen by current New Testament scholars to have little or no role in shaping the New Testament picture of Jesus in general or the resurrection narratives in particular. Both the general milieu of the Gospels and specific features of the resurrection narratives give overwhelming evidence that the early church was rooted in Judaism. Jesus, the early church, and its writings were born in Jewish soil and Gentile influence was minimal. 55/181

Even when the hypothesis of syncretism was in its heyday, many of the top scholars were unconvinced. Probably the most influential German church historian and theologian of his day, Adolf von Harnack, shortly after the turn of the century, wrote:

> We must reject the comparative mythology which finds a causal connection between everything and everything else, which tears down solid barriers, bridges chasms as though it were child's play, and spins combinations from superficial similarities. . . . By such methods one can turn Christ into a sun god in the twinkling of an eye, or one can bring up the legends attending the birth of every conceivable god, or one can catch all sorts of mythological doves to keep company with the baptismal dove; and find any number of celebrated asses to follow the ass on which Jesus rode into Jerusalem; and thus, with the magic wand of "comparative religion," triumphantly eliminate every spontaneous trait in any religion. 57/118-19

Why did the mystery religions competing with Christianity eventually perish, leaving Christianity as the primary religion of the Roman Empire? There are a number of answers, but a primary one is that Christians preached the resurrection of an actual, recent person of history. The mythological stories of the mystery religions just couldn't compete.

CHAPTER 15 *Inspiration of the Bible*

A charge frequently leveled against the Bible is that Christians who defend it argue in circles: "Christians claim the Bible is the inspired Word of God and, as proof of this contention, they quote a passage from the Bible that says it is."

This type of argumentation is known as begging the question, or "circular reasoning." Nothing is actually proved here. It is based on assuming something to be true, using the assumption as fact to prove another assumption and then using that second "proved" assumption to "prove" your original assumption!

Are Christians Guilty of Circular Reasoning? (A/147-48)

Some Christians (and many non-Christians!) do argue in circles, but about the Bible they certainly don't need to.

Instead of assuming the Bible is the Word of God, we can begin by demonstrating that the Scriptures are basically reliable and trustworthy historical documents. This is confirmed by applying the ordinary test of historical criticism to the Scriptures.

Once it is established that the Bible is a valid historical record, the next point is realizing Jesus Christ claimed to be the unique Son of God and He based this claim on His forthcoming resurrection from the dead.

Next, we examine the evidence for the resurrection contained in this historic document and find that the arguments overwhelmingly support the contention that Christ has risen from the dead. If this is true, then He is the unique Son of God as He claimed to be. If He is indeed God, then He speaks with authority on all matters.

Since Jesus considered the Old Testament to be the Word of God (Matthew 15:1-6; 5:17,18) and promised His disciples, who either wrote or had control over the writing of the New Testament books, that the Holy Spirit would bring all things back to their remembrance (John 14:26), we can insist, with sound and accurate logic, that the Bible is God's word. This is not circular reasoning. It is establishing certain facts and basing conclusions on the sound logical outcome of these facts. The case for Christianity can be established by ordinary means of historical investigation.

What Does "The Bible Is Inspired" Mean? (R/19-20)

Some contend the Bible is inspired in the same way all great literature is. "It challenges the human heart to reach new heights," they say. However, this does not make the Bible unique. Many other books, including those of Shakespeare, Milton, Homer and Dickens, have produced similar results. In other words, they see the Bible as only a human literary masterpiece, not as being divine in origin.

Others believe the Bible is inspired because it *contains* the Word of God—along with myths, mistakes and legends. These people hold that it is wrong to identify the Bible *as* the Word of God; rather, they say, it is a witness of God speaking to mankind. Putting it another way, the Word of God can be found in the Bible but the Word of God is not synonymous with the Bible.

These two views are inadequate when the biblical evidence is considered. The Bible makes it plain that it is not merely inspiring literature or a fallible record of God speaking, but that it is the infallible Word of God.

Two important verses speak to the heart of the matter: 2 Timothy 3:16 and 2 Peter 1:21. The former reads: "All Scripture is inspired by God and profitable for teaching, for reproof, for correction, for training in righteousness" (NASB). The word *inspired* is a translation of the Greek word *theopneustos,* meaning God-breathed. Thus the origin of Scripture is God, not man; it is God-breathed.

The second verse, 2 Peter 1:21, says, "For no prophecy was ever made by an act of human will, but men moved by the Holy Spirit spoke from God" (NASB). This also confirms that the writers were moved by God to record that which God desired. Mechanical dictation was not employed, as some claim. Rather, God used each individual writer and his personality to accomplish a divinely authoritative work.

The process of inspiration extended to every word ("all Scripture"), refuting the idea of myth and error. Since God is behind the writings, and since He is perfect, the result must be infallible. If it were not infallible, we could be left with God-inspired error.

Sometimes it is easier to understand the concept of inspiration when it is compared with revelation. *Revelation* relates to the origin and actual giving of truth (1 Corinthians 2:10). *Inspiration,* on the other hand, relates to the receiving and actual recording of truth. Inspiration means that "God the Holy Spirit worked in a unique supernatural way so that the written words of the Scripture writers were also the words of God."

The human authors of Scripture wrote spontaneously using their own minds and experiences, yet their words were not merely the words of men but actually the words of God. God's control was always with them in their writings with the result being the Bible—the Word of God in the words of men.

To What Extent Is the Bible Inspired? (R/21-23)

If a person recognizes that the Bible is the inspired Word of God, he often questions the degree of inspiration. Does it include every book, every word? Does it extend to historical matters? How about scientific statements? Does it include manuscript copies and translations?

A classic statement on the extent of inspiration is given by B. B. Warfield, a reformed theologian:

> The Church has held from the beginning that the Bible is the Word of God in such a sense that its words, though written by men and bearing indelibly impressed upon them the marks of their human origin, were written, nevertheless, under such an influence of the Holy Ghost as to be also the words of God, the adequate expression of His mind and will. It has always recognized that this conception of co-authorship implies that the Spirit's superintendence extends to the choice of the words by the human authors (verbal inspiration, but not mechanical dictation!) and preserves its product from everything inconsistent with a divine authorship—thus securing, among other things, that entire truthfulness which is everywhere presupposed in and asserted for Scripture by the biblical writers (inerrancy).
>
> The doctrine of plenary inspiration holds that the original documents of the Bible were written by men, who, though permitted to exercise their own personalities and literary talents, yet wrote under the control and

> guidance of the Spirit of God, the result being in every word of the original documents a perfect and errorless recording of the exact message which God desired to give to man. 76/173

Two words describe the extent of inspiration according to the Bible: *verbal* and *plenary*.

Plenary means "full, complete extending to all parts." The apostle Paul says in 2 Timothy 3:16, "All Scripture is inspired of God." And Paul told the Thessalonians, "For this reason we also constantly thank God that when you received from us the word of God's message, you accepted it not as the word of men, but for what it really is, the Word of God" (1 Thessalonians 2:13, NASB).

The Bible ends with this warning:

> I testify to everyone who hears the words of the prophecy of this book: if anyone adds to them, God shall add to him the plagues which are written in this book; and if anyone takes away from the words of the book of this prophecy, God shall take away his part from the tree of life and from the holy city, which are written in this book (Revelation 22:18,19, NASB).

The entire Bible is inspired, not just certain parts!

Inspiration extends not only to all parts of the Bible, but it also extends to the very words,

> Which things we also speak, not in words taught by human wisdom, but in those taught by the Spirit, combining spiritual thoughts with spiritual words (1 Corinthians 2:13, NASB).

Sometimes the biblical writers base their arguments on a particular expression or a single word. For example, in Galatians 3:16 the apostle Paul cites Genesis 13:15 and 17:8 when God said to Abraham, "Unto your seed (*descendant*) will I give this land," not unto your descendants, plural. Paul's whole argument is based on the noun being singular rather than plural. Rene Pache gives a pertinent summary of this idea. We may agree with him that "very often the meaning of a whole passage rests entirely on one word, a singular or a plural number, the tense of a verb, the details of a prophecy, the precision of a promise and the silence of the text on a certain point." 58/77

It is of monumental importance to identify the extent of inspiration to include every book of Scripture, each part of every book, and every word in each book as given in the original. This does not include any manuscript copy or any translation which is a reproduction.

No one manuscript or translation is inspired, only the original. However, for all intents and purposes, they are virtually inspired since, with today's great number of manuscripts available for scrutiny, the science of textual criticism can render us an adequate representation. Therefore, we can be assured that when we read the Bible we are reading the inspired Word of God.

Charles Wesley, one of the founders of Methodism, wrote:

> The Bible must be the invention either of good men or angels, bad men or devils, or of God. Therefore:
>
> 1. It could not be the invention of good men or angels, for they neither would nor could make a book, and tell lies all the time they were writing it, saying, "Thus saith the Lord," when it was their own invention.
> 2. It could not be the invention of bad men or devils, for they would not make a book which commands all duty, forbids all sin, and condemns their souls to hell to all eternity.
> 3. Therefore, I draw this conclusion, that the Bible must be given by divine inspiration. (Robert W. Burtner and Robert E. Chiles, *A Compendium of Wesley's Theology,* p. 20.)

The evidence that the *very words* of the Bible are God-given may be briefly summarized as follows:

- This is the claim of the classical text (2 Timothy 3:16).
- It is the emphatic testimony of Paul that he spoke in "words . . . taught by the Spirit" (1 Corinthians 2:13).
- It is evident from the repeated formula, "It is written."
- Jesus said that what was written in the whole Old Testament spoke of Him (Luke 24:27,44; John 5:39; Hebrews 10:7).
- The New Testament constantly equates the Word of God with the Scripture (writings of the Old Testament; cf. Matthew 21:42; Romans 15:4; 2 Peter 3:16).
- Jesus indicated that not even the smallest part of a Hebrew word or letter could be broken (Matthew 5:18).
- The New Testament refers to the written record as the "oracles of God" (Romans 3:2; Hebrews 5:12).
- Occasionally the writers were even told to "diminish not a word" (Jeremiah 26:2, AV). In fact, John pronounced an anathema upon all who would add to or subtract from the "words of the prophecy of this book" (Revelation 22:18,19).

CHAPTER 16 *Interpreting the Bible*

There Are So Many Different Interpretations of the Bible, Why Should I Believe Yours? (A/13-14)

One of the complaints we hear often is, "Everyone has a different interpretation of the Bible." Because people arrive at varying conclusions when they read the Bible, there is supposedly no way to get a consensus. People point to the variety of denominations as an example that there can be no unanimity of agreement between Bible believers.

This idea neglects to take into account certain facts. One is that the great majority of Bible readers have no problem with agreement on the central teachings of the Bible. Even those who do not believe the Bible to be true have no difficulty whatsoever discerning the main message.

Within all branches of Christianity, we find the same basic understanding as to what the Bible teaches. They usually all accept the same creeds that assert such basic truths as that God made man in His image, with freedom of choice, and that man chose to rebel against God, thus bringing sin into the world.

God, because of His everlasting love, became a man in the person of

Jesus Christ and died a substitutionary death on our behalf, paying the penalty for sin. Any person can have his (or her) relationship with God restored through placing his faith in Jesus Christ.

The message of the Bible is clear for those who will read it and seek to find out its meaning. The problem comes when people bring their preconceived notions to the Bible and attempt to make the Word fit their ideas. This is not the fault of the Bible, but of the persons who force the Bible to say what they want it to say.

As to the various denominations, it must be stressed that they are not formed because of division over the central teachings of Christianity. The differences are a result of a variety of factors, including cultural, ethnic and social. When closely compared with one another, the doctrinal differences are not always that crucial.

Some people use this argument as an excuse for not believing in Jesus, but like all other excuses it does not prove valid. Jesus made the main issue crystal clear: "He who believes in the Son has eternal life: but he who does not obey the Son shall not see life, but the wrath of God abides on him" (John 3:36, NASB). Often the disagreement is not so much with the interpretation of the Scriptures, but with the application.

Is Everything in the Bible to Be Taken Literally? (R/36-37)

When we say we take the Bible literally, we do not mean that figurative language is absent from the Bible. However, we must find a good reason in the passage to justify interpreting figuratively.

Some types of writing by their very nature tend to exclude the possibility of figurative language. These include laws, historical writings, and philosophic writings—although these sometimes have figurative language where it is sensible. (One example would be, "Martin Luther was like a bull in a china shop.") Some literature—poetry, for example—also is figurative in nature. A good rule for interpretation is:

If the literal sense makes good sense,
seek no other sense
lest you come up with nonsense.

The words of a given text should be interpreted literally if possible. If not possible, one should move to figurative interpretation.

Usually there are clues in the context. Sometimes there will be a definition. For example, when the Book of Revelation speaks of the dragon in 12:9, the dragon is defined for the reader. Knowing the culture also helps, for the more one knows about the language and thought forms of a particular period, the better chance he has to be able to interpret a given passage appropriately.

Many a person has built a straw man out of the teaching of literal interpretation, alleging that we have to take everything in the Bible literally, even something like: "The trees of the field shall clap their hands" (Isaiah 55:12).

The Bible contains a number of definite types of figurative language including metaphor, simile, hyperbole and anthropomorphism.

A *metaphor* is a comparison by direct statement. In John 15:1 Jesus states, "I am the true vine." This does not mean He is a literal vine, but that He can be compared to one.

A *simile* is a comparison using the words *like* or *as*. Exodus 24:17 states, "The glory of the Lord was like a consuming fire on the mountain top."

An *hyperbole* is an exaggeration for emphasis. In John 21:25 we find an example of this: "And there are also many other things which Jesus did, which if they were written in detail, I suppose that even the world itself would not contain the books which were written."

Anthropomorphism, which is found particularly in the Old Testament, is attributing to God human characteristics or experiences. This can be seen in statements such as, "It repented the LORD that He had made man" (Genesis 6:6, KJV); and, "The eyes of the LORD move to and fro throughout the earth that He may strongly support those whose heart is completely His" (2 Chronicles 16:9, NASB).

Therefore, figurative language does have a place in Scripture, but only when certain factors indicate that the passage in question is not to be interpreted literally.

ADDITIONAL REFERENCE SOURCES ON THIS SUBJECT

I. Howard Marshall (ed.), *New Testament Interpretation* (Grand Rapids: Wm B. Eerdmans Publishing Co., 1977).

A. Berkeley Mickelsen, *Interpreting the Bible* (Grand Rapids: Wm. B. Eerdmans Publishing Co., 1963).

Bernard Ramm, *Protestant Biblical Interpretation* (Grand Rapids: Baker Book House, 1970.

Samuel J. Schultz and Morris A. Inch, *Interpreting the Word of God* (Chicago: Moody Press, 1976).

R. C. Sproul, *Knowing Scripture* (Downers Grove: InterVarsity Press, 1977).

Milton S. Tery, *Biblical Hermeneutics* (Grand Rapids: Zondervan Publishing House, 1974).

NOTE: See *Josh McDowell's Know Your Bible* (Scripture Press, 1990) for a step-by-step method of effectively interpreting and applying Scripture to your life.

1 THE BIBLE

Part Two: Bibliography

1. Aalders, G. A. *A Short Introduction to the Pentateuch.* Chicago: InterVarsity Christian Fellowship, n.d. (originally published in 1949).

2. Achtemeier, Paul (ed.). "Biblical Criticism." *Harper's Bible Dictionary.* San Francisco: Harper & Row Publishers, 1985.

3. Albright, William F. *Archaeology and the Religion of Israel.* Baltimore: Johns Hopkins Press, 1942.

4. Albright, William F. "Archaeology Confronts Biblical Criticism." *The American Scholar* 7 (April 1988).

5. Albright, William F. *Archaeology, Historical Analogy, and Early Biblical Tradition.* Baton Rouge: Louisiana State University Press, 1966.

6. Albright, William F. *The Archaeology of Palestine.* Baltimore: Penguin Books, revised 1960.

7. Allis, Oswald T. *The Old Testament, Its Claims and Its Critics.* Nutley, NJ: The Presbyterian and Reformed Publishing Company, 1972.

8. Allis, Oswald T. *The Five Books of Moses.* Philadelphia: The Presbyterian and Reformed Publishing Co., revised 1969.

9. Anderson, Norman. *Christianity and World Religions.* Downers Grove, IL: InterVarsity Press, 1984.

10. Anderson, Norman. *Jesus Christ: The Witness of History.* Downers Grove, IL: InterVarsity Press, 1985.

11. Angus, Samuel. *Mystery-Religions and Christianity.* London: J. Murray, 1925. Reprint, New Hyde Park, NY: University Books, 1967.

12. Archer, Gleason L. *Encyclopedia of Bible Difficulties.* Grand Rapids, MI: Zondervan Publishing House, 1982.

13. Archer, Gleason, Jr. *A Survey of Old Testament Introduction,* Chicago: Moody Press, 1964, 1974.

14. Arndt, W. F. *Bible Difficulties.* St. Louis: Concordia Press, 1971.

15. Arndt, W. F. *Does the Bible Contradict Itself?* 5th ed., revised. St. Louis: Concordia Press, 1955.

16. Blaiklock, E. M. *Jesus Christ: Man or Myth?* Nashville: Thomas Nelson Publishers, 1984.

17. Brewer, Julius; Paton, Lewis Bayles; and Dahl, George. "The Problem of Deuteronomy: A Symposium." *Journal of Biblical Literature* 47 (1929-30).

18. Bright, John. *A History of Israel.* Philadelphia: The Westminster Press, 1959.

19. Burkholder, Lawrence. "A Dialogue on Christ's Resurrection." *Christianity Today* 12 (April 12, 1968).

20. Burrows, Millar. *What Mean These Stones?* New York: Meridian Books, 1957.

21. Cartlidge, David R., and Dungan, David L. *Documents for the Study of the Gospels.* Philadelphia: Fortress Press, 1980.

22. Cassuto, V. *The Documentary Hypothesis.* Jerusalem: Magnes Press, 1941. First English edition, 1961.

23. Cool, John N. "A Study of Matthew 27:9,10. " M.A. thesis, Talbot Theological Seminary, 1975.

24. Davis, John J. *Biblical Numerology.* Grand Rapids: Baker Book House, 1968.

25. Driver, S. R. *Introduction to the Literature of the Old Testament.* New York: Charles Scribner's Sons, 1913.

26. Dunn, James D. G. *The Evidence for Jesus.* Philadelphia: The Westminster Press, 1985.

27. Eissfeldt, Otto. *The Old Testament—An Introduction.* New York: Harper & Row Publishers, Inc., 1965.

28. *Encyclopedia of Religion and Ethics.* Edited by James Hastings. Edinburgh: T. & T. Clark, 1935.

29. Free, Joseph P. *Archaeology and Bible History.* Wheaton, IL: Scripture Press, 1969.

30. Free, Joseph P. "Archaeology and Liberalism." *Bibliotheca Sacra* 113 (July 1956).

31. Gordon, Cyrus H. "Higher Critics and Forbidden Fruit." *Christianity Today* 4 (November 23, 1959).

32. Gundry, Robert. *The Use of the Old Testament in St. Matthew's Gospel.*

33. Haley, John W. *Alleged Discrepancies of the Bible,* reprint. Grand Rapids, MI: Baker Book House, 1977.

34. Harrison, R. K. *Introduction to the Old Testament.* Grand Rapids, MI: Wm. B. Eerdman's Publishing Company, 1970.

35. Hume, David. *An Enquiry Concerning Human Understanding.* Chicago: Open Court, 1958.

36. Kitchen, K. A. *Ancient Orient and the Old Testament.* Chicago: InterVarsity Press, 1966.

37. Kitchen, K. A. "Ancient Orient, 'Deuteronism' and the Old Testament." *New Perspectives on the Old Testament.* Ed. by J. Barton Payne. Waco, TX: Word Books, 1970.

38. Kline, Meredith. "Is the History of the Old Testament Accurate?" *Can I Trust My Bible?* Edited by Howard Vos. Chicago: Moody Press, 1963.

39. Kramer, S. N. *ANET.* 1953.

40. Künneth, Walter. *The Theology of the Resurrection.* London: SCM Press Ltd., 1965.

41. Lapide, Pinchas. *The Resurrection of Jesus: A Jewish Perspective.* Minneapolis: Augsburg Publishing House, 1983.

42. Lewis, C. S. *Miracles.* New York: Macmillan, 1947.

43. Lightfoot, J. B. *Horae Hebraicae et Talmudicae* II (citing Baba Bathra 14*b).*

44. Livingston, G. Herbert. *The Pentateuch in Its Cultural Environment.* Grand Rapids, MI: Baker Book House, 1974.

45. Machen, J. Gresham. *The Origin of Paul's Religion.* New York: Macmillan Publishing Co., 1925.

46. Manley, G. T. *The Book of the Law.* London: The Tyndale Press, 1957.

47. Martyr, Justin. *First Apology* 66.

48. McDowell, Josh, and Stewart, Don. *Answers to Tough Questions Skeptics Ask About the Christian Faith.* Wheaton, IL: Tyndale House Publishers, Inc., 1986.

49. McDowell, Josh. *Evidence That Demands a Verdict* 2. San Bernardino, CA: Here's Life Publishers, Inc., 1986.

50. McDowell, Josh, and Wilson, Bill. *He Walked Among UsD: Evidence for the Historical Jesus.* San Bernardino, CA: Here's Life Publishers, Inc., 1988.

51. Mendenhall, George E. *Law and Covenant in Israel and the Ancient Near East.* Pittsburgh: Biblical Colloquium, 1955.

52. Metzger, Bruce M. "Mystery Religions and Early Christianity." In *Historical and Literary Studies.* Leiden, Netherlands: E. J. Brill, 1968.

53. *Mishnah,* Tractate "J. Shabbath," chapter IX, par. J.

54. *Mishnah,* Third Tractate, "B. Pesachim," *4a.*

55. Moreland, J. P. *Scaling the Secular City.* Grand Rapids, MI: Baker Book House, 1987.

56. Motyer, J. A. *The Revelation of the Divine Name.* London: The Tyndale Press, 1959.

57. Nash, Ronald. *Christianity and the Hellenistic World.* Grand Rapids: Zondervan Publ. House, 1984.

58. Pache, Rene. *The Inspiration and Authority of Scripture.* Chiocago: Moody Press, 1970.

59. Perrin, Norman. *What Is Redaction Criticism?* Philadelphia: Fortress Press, 1969.

60. Pfeiffer, R. H. *Introduction to the Old Testament.* New York: Harper and Brothers Publishers, 1948.

61. Phillips, J. B. *The Ring of Truth.* New York: Macmillan Publishing Co., 1967.

62. Philo, Judaeus. *The Works of Philo.* vol. 4. Translated by F. H. Colson. Cambridge: Harvard University Press, 1935.

63. Pinnock, Clark. "The Tombstone That Trembled." *Christianity Today* 12 (April 12, 1968).

64. Prudentius, *Peristephanon* 10. 1011-50.

65. Raven, John Howard. *Old Testament Introduction.* New York: Fleming H. Revell Company, 1906, revised 1910.

66. Ridderbos, Herman N. *Paul: An Outline of His Theology.* Grand Rapids: Wm. B. Eerdmans Publishing Co., 1975.

67. Rowley, H. H. *The Growth of the Old Testament.* London: Hutchinson's University Library, Hutchinson House, 1950.

68. Sayce, A. H. *Monument Facts and Higher Critical Fancies.* London: Religious Tract Society, 1904.

69. Schultz, Hermann. *Old Testament Theology.* Translated from the fourth edition by H. A. Patterson. Edinburgh: T. & T. Clark, 1898.

70. Schweitzer, Albert. *Paul and His Interprter.* London: 1912.

71. Segal, M. H. *The Pentateuch—Its Composition and Its Authorship.* Jerusalem: Magnes Press, Hebrew University, 1967.

72. Thomas, Robert L., and Gundry, Stanley N. *A Harmony of the Gospels.* San Francisco: Harper & Row, 1978. (See pp. 313-19 for four different explanations of the alleged contradiction between the genealogies of Jesus given by Matthew and Luke.)

73. Unger, Merrill F. *Introductory Guide to the Old Testament.* Grand Rapids: Zondervan Publishing House, 1956.

74. Vermaseren, M. J. *Mithras: The Secret God.* London: Chatto and Windus, 1963.

75. Wagner, Günter. *Pauline Baptism and the Pagan Mysteries.* Edinburgh: Oliver and Boyd, 1967.

76. Warfield, B. B. *The Inspiration and Authority of the Bible.* Grand Rapids: Baker Book House, n. d.

77. Wenham, John W. *Easter Enigma.* Grand Rapids, MI: Zondervan Publishing House, 1984.

78. Westphal, Merold. "The Historian and the Believer." *Religious Studies* 2, no. 2 (1967).

79. Wilson, Ian. *Jesus: The Evidence.* San Francisco: Harper & Row Publishers, Inc., 1984.

80. Wright, G. Ernest. *The Old Testament Against Its Environment.* Chicago: Henry Regnery Co., 1950.

81. Wright, G. Ernest. "The Present State of Biblical Archaeology." *The Study of the Bible Today and Tomorrow.* Edited by Harold R. Willoughby. Chicago: University of Chicago Press, 1947.

82. Wright, G. Ernest. "The Terminology of Old Testament Religion and Its Significance." *Journal of Near Eastern Studies* 1, no. 4 (October 1942).

83. Yamauchi, Edwin M. *Pre-Christian Gnosticism.* 2nd ed. Grand Rapids: Baker Book House, 1983.

84. Youngblood, Ronald. *The Heart of the Old Testament.* Grand Rapids: Baker Book House, 1971.

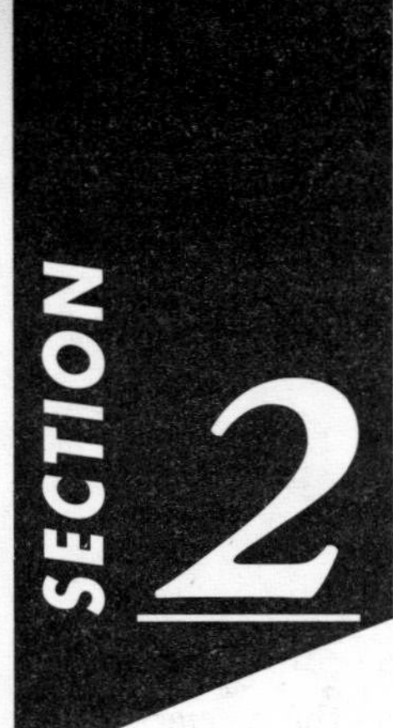

JESUS

His Humanity and his Deity

Introduction (C/1, E/24)

Why is it that you can talk about God and nobody gets upset, but as soon as you mention Jesus, people often want to stop the conversation? Why have men and women down through the ages been divided over the question, "Who is Jesus?"

> This Jesus of Nazareth, without money and arms, conquered more millions than Alexander, Caesar, Mohammed, and Napoleon; without science and learning, He shed more light on things human and divine than all philosophers and scholars combined; without the eloquence of schools, He spoke such words of life as were never spoken before or since, and produced effects which lie beyond the reach of orator or poet; without writing a single line, He set more pens in motion, and furnished themes for more sermons, orations, discussions, learned volumes, works of art, and songs of praise than the whole army of great men of ancient and modern times. 70

Yale Historian, Kenneth Scott Latourette, says:

> It is evidence of His importance, of the effect that He has had upon history and presumably, of the baffling mystery of His being, that no other life ever lived on this planet has evoked so huge a volume of literature among so many peoples and languages, and that, far from ebbing, the flood continues to mount. 47/44

CHAPTER 17 *Was Jesus Born of a Virgin?*

(A/55-59)

A Fact of History

The miracle of the virgin birth of Jesus Christ has perplexed many people, and actually has kept them from accepting the truth of Christianity. However, the Bible declares that God decided His Son would have a miraculous entrance into humanity.

Seven hundred years before the birth of Christ, the prophet Isaiah said, "Therefore the Lord Himself will give you a sign: Behold, the virgin will be with child and bear a son, and she will call His name Immanuel" (Isaiah 7:14, NASB).

The New Testament records the fulfillment of Isaiah's prophecy:

> Now in the sixth month the angel Gabriel was sent from God to a city of Galilee called Nazareth, to a virgin engaged to a man whose name was Joseph, of the descendants of David; and the virgin's name was Mary . . . And the angel said to her, "Do not be afraid, Mary: for you have found favor with God. And behold, you will conceive in your womb, and bear a son, and you shall name Him Jesus . . . "

> And Mary said to the angel, "How can this be, since I am a virgin?"
>
> And the angel answered and said to her, "The Holy Spirit, will come upon you, and the power of the Most High will overshadow you; and for that reason the holy offspring shall be called the Son of God . . . For nothing will be impossible with God" (Luke 1:27-37, NASB).

The virgin birth is set down in the Bible as an historical fact. The writers who recorded the story were Matthew—an eyewitness to the events in the life of Jesus—and Luke, the doctor, who presents many things in the life of Christ from Mary's viewpoint. The passages in both Matthew and Luke are authentic, with no evidence at all that they were later additions to the text.

The doctrine of the virgin birth has been believed by the church from its inception. Ignatius, who lived at the start of the second century, wrote to the Ephesians: "For our God, Jesus the Christ, was conceived in the womb by Mary, according to a dispensation, of the seed of David but also of the Holy Ghost."

A Necessary Fact of History

There are several reasons the virgin birth was a necessity. The Bible teaches that the Word who became flesh was with God from the very beginning (John 1:1). The fact of the pre-existence of Christ is confirmed many times in the New Testament (John 8:58; Philippians 2:5-11; Colossians 1:15,16).

When Jesus came into the world, He was not a newly created individual such as we are, but was rather the eternal Son of God. To be born into this world, of the virgin Mary, required divine intervention, and this is exactly what the Gospels record.

Another reason Jesus needed to be virgin-born was His sinless nature. A basic New Testament teaching is that from the day He was born until the day He died, Jesus was without sin. To be a perfect sacrifice, He must Himself be perfect—without sin. Since our race is contaminated with sin, a miraculous entrance into the world would be required, hence the virgin birth.

Moreover, if Jesus had been sired by Joseph, He would not have been able to claim the legal rights to the throne of David. According to the prophecy of Jeremiah 22:28-30, there could be no king in Israel who was a descendant of King Jeconiah, and Matthew 1:12 relates that Joseph was from the line of Jeconiah. Jesus would have been of the cursed lineage.

The virgin birth of Christ is not only an historical fact, but it was also a *necessary* historical fact when one considers all the data.

Objections to the Virgin Birth

The main problem people have with the virgin birth is its miraculous nature. Scripture does not treat this event as an ordinary occurrence but rather as a supernatural act of God. The miracle of the virgin birth should not pose any special problem if one grants the possibility of miracles.

Why, we may ask, is the virgin birth any greater miracle than, say, the feeding of the five thousand or Jesus walking on water? If an all-powerful God who spoke all creation into existence does exist, a virgin birth would not be beyond His capability.

A common objection to the virgin birth is that it is a biological impossibility, acceptable only because of people's ignorance of these things. C. S. Lewis made some pertinent observations on this view:

> Thus you will hear people say, "The early Christians believed that Christ was the son of a virgin, but we know that this is a scientific impossibility." Such people seem to have an idea that belief in miracles arose at a period when men were so ignorant of the course of nature that they did not perceive a miracle to be contrary to it.
>
> A moment's thought shows this to be foolish, with the story of the virgin birth as a particularly striking example. When Joseph discovered that his fiancée was going to have a baby, he naturally decided to repudiate her. Why? Because he knew just as well as any modern gynecologist that in the ordinary course of nature women do not have babies unless they have lain with men.
>
> No doubt the modern gynecologist knows several things about birth and begetting that Joseph did not know. But those things do not concern the main point—that a virgin birth is contrary to the course of nature. And Joseph obviously knew that. 50/48

Some have attempted to account for the virgin birth by tracing it to Greek or Babylonian mythology. They argue that the Gospel writers borrowed this story from the mythology of their day. This view does not fit the facts, for there is not any hero in pagan mythology for which a virgin birth is claimed, and moreover it would be unthinkable to the Jewish mind to construct such a story from mythology.

Many deities among Greeks, Babylonians and Egyptians were reported born in an unusual manner, but for the most part these beings never actually existed. The accounts are filled with obvious mythological elements which are totally absent from the Gospel narratives. They are reports of a god or goddess being born into the world by sexual relations between some heavenly being and an earthly woman, or by some adulterous affair among the gods and goddesses.

Dr. Thomas Thorburn comments appropriately:

> All these various stories of supernatural conceptions and births, which we meet with in folklore and the history of mythology, have this one point in common—they serve to point not so much to the similarity as to the complete contrast and dissimilarity which exists between the Christian birth-story and the tales which are current in various pagan circles. 78/158

Thus when we closely consider the objections to the virgin birth, we become more convinced that it did indeed occur just as the historical record in the Gospels states.

ADDITIONAL REFERENCE SOURCES ON THIS SUBJECT

Arthur Custance, *The Virgin Birth and the Incarnation* (Grand Rapids: Zondervan, 1976).

Robert Gromacki, *The Virgin Birth* (New York: Thomas Nelson, Inc., 1974).

J. Gresham Machen, *The Virgin Birth of Christ* (New York: Harper and Brothers, 1930).

Wilbur Smith, *The Supernaturalness of Christ* (Boston: W. A. Wilde Co., 1943).

CHAPTER 18 *The Historicity of Jesus*

Journalist Louis Cassels wrote in 1973:

> You can count on it. Every few years, some "scholar" will stir up a short-lived sensation by publishing a book that says something outlandish about Jesus . . .
>
> The amazing thing about all these debunk-Jesus books is that they accept as much of the recorded Gospels as they find convenient, then ignore or repudiate other parts of the same document which contradict their notions. 13/7A

Why Not More First Century Non-Christian References to Christ?

(HW/23-24)

Recently we received a letter from an individual who wrote, "I'm an almost believer, but I do not wish to believe on blind faith. . . . Can you document for me nonbiblical historical accounts of the resurrection of Christ?"

One correspondent with Professor F. F. Bruce, former Rylands Professor of Biblical Criticism and Exegesis at the University of Manchester, posed the question a little more broadly:

> What collateral proof is there in existence of the historical fact of the life of Jesus Christ? 11/17

Should we in fact expect the secular history records of Jesus' day to have preserved any mention of the life of Jesus, and if so, what kind of references should we expect?

What About Reports from Pilate?

If the Bible accurately portrays the life, death and resurrection of Jesus, wouldn't Pontius Pilate, of all people, have made some reports about it? Bruce answers:

> People frequently ask if any record has been preserved of the report which, it is presumed, Pontius Pilate, prefect of Judea, sent to Rome concerning the trial and execution of Jesus of Nazareth. The answer is none. But let it be added at once that no official record has been preserved of **any** report which Pontius Pilate, **or any other Roman governor of Judea,** sent to Rome about **anything**. And only rarely has an official report from any governor of any Roman province survived. They may have sent in their reports regularly, but for the most part these reports were ephemeral documents, and in due course they disappeared. 11/17

It is interesting that even though today we have no reports about anything from Pilate or any other Roman governor of Judea, the early Christians apparently knew about Pilate's records concerning Jesus. Justin Martyr, writing in approximately A.D. 150, informs emperor Antoninus Pius of the fulfillment of Psalm 22:16:

> But the words, "They pierced my hands and feet," refer to the nails which were fixed in Jesus' hands and feet on the cross; and after He was crucified, His executioners cast lots for His garments, and divided them among themselves. That these things happened you may learn from the "Acts" which were recorded under Pontius Pilate. 57/7-9

Justin also says:

> That He performed these miracles you may easily satisfy yourself from the "Acts" of Pontius Pilate. 58/3

Bruce continues:

> Similarly both Justin and Tertullian, another Christian apologist of a generation or two later, were sure that the census which was held about the time of our Lord's birth was recorded in the official archives of the reign of Augustus, and that anyone who took the trouble to look these archives up would find the registration of Joseph and Mary there. 11/20

Justin's statement is a bold one if in fact no record existed. Can you imagine a respected scholar writing the President of the United States a letter, which he knows will be carefully scrutinized, and building his case on official federal documents which do not exist? It did, however, apparently bother fourth century Christians that this record was not available in their day. An obviously forged "Acts of Pilate" was manufactured at that time. One indication of its falsity: It was addressed to Claudius even though

Tiberias was emperor when Pilate governed Judea.

But why would someone in the fourth century want to forge a document from the first century? Aside from a warped view of what the Scriptures taught about honesty, part of the reason lies in the fact that first century documents were quite rare.

Just how much survived?

How much nonbiblical material on any subject actually survived from the first century? And of that material, in what parts would we expect to find references to Jesus? Again, Bruce relates:

> When we are asked what "collateral proof" exists of the life of Jesus Christ, would it be unfair to begin by asking another question? In which contemporary writers—in which writers who flourished, say, during the first fifty years after the death of Christ—would you expect to find the collateral evidence you are looking for? Well, perhaps it would be rather unfair, as the man in the street can hardly be expected to know who was writing in the Graeco-Roman world during those fifty years; the classical student himself has to scratch his head in an attempt to remember who they were. It is surprising how few writings, comparatively speaking, have survived from those years of a kind which might be even remotely expected to mention Christ. (I except, for the present, the letters of Paul and several other New Testament writings.) 11/17

One prolific writer and contemporary of Jesus was Philo. He was born circa 15 B.C. and lived in Alexandria, Egypt, until his death sometime after A.D. 40 His works consist primarily of philosophy and commentary on Jewish Scripture and religion as they relate to Greek culture and philosophy. His family was one of the wealthiest in Alexandria. A reading of the fifteenth edition of the Encyclopedia Britannica article on Philo will readily confirm Daniel-Rop's conclusion: "It is not unduly surprising that such a person should not pay much attention to an agitator sprung from the humblest of the people, whose doctrine, if he had one, had no connection with philosophy." 1/17-18

E. M. Blaiklock has catalogued the non-Christian writings of the Roman Empire (other than those of Philo) which have survived the first century and which do not mention Jesus. As you will see from our summary of Blaiklock in the following paragraphs, there is very little.

From the decade of the thirties practically nothing has survived. Velleius Paterculus, a retired army officer of Tiberias, published what was considered an amateurish history of Rome in A.D. 30. Only part of it has survived. Jesus was just beginning His ministry. 38/n.p. Considering the time of the writing, and especially the segregation between Jewish and Roman towns in Galilee, it is unlikely that Paterculus ever even heard of Jesus. The Gospel writers give no evidence that Jesus ever set foot in Tiberias or any other Roman town in Galilee. Also surviving from the thirties is an inscription of Caesarea bearing two-thirds of Pilate's name.

All that is left from the forties are the fables written by Phaedrus, a Macedonian freedman.

Of the fifties and sixties, Blaiklock says:

> Bookends set a foot apart on this desk where I write would enclose the works from those significant years. Curiously, much of it comes from Spanish emigrants in Rome, a foretaste of what the Iberian peninsula was to give to her conqueror—senators, writers, and two important emperors, Trajan and Hadrian. Paul had foresight when he set a visit to Spain in his program. 9/13

The works of this period include the philosophical treatises and letters of Roman statesman, writer and tutor of Nero, Seneca; the long poem of his nephew Lucan on the civil war between Julius Caesar and Pompey; a book on agriculture by the retired soldier, Columella; and large fragments of the novel *Satyricon* by the voluptuary, Gaius Petronius. Also surviving from this period are a few hundred lines of Roman satirist, Persius; the Elder Pliny's *Historia Naturalis* ("a collection of odd facts about the world of nature"); some fragments of Asconius Pedianus' commentary on Cicero; and the history of Alexander the Great by the little known Quintus Curtius. Blaiklock asks:

> Of this handful of writers, would any have been likely to mention Christ? Perhaps Seneca, if in fact he met and talked with Paul. But there is small likelihood that this pleasant medieval legend is true. Besides, in A.D. 64, in the summer of which year Nero took hostile note of Rome's Christians, Seneca was a distracted and tormented man. A year later he was dead, driven to suicide by the mad young tyrant whom he had sought in vain to tame. 9/16

Check the works of the seventies and eighties to see if they might be candidates for mentioning a Jewish religious rabble rouser now dead for forty years: Tacitus, who would become a great historian, published a minor work on oratory in A.D. 81. Several hundred witty poems or epigrams written by Martial in Rome survive but do not clearly mention the Christians. After Nero's mass killing of Christians in A.D. 64, it is no wonder that few Christians wanted to remain in Rome.

Josephus wrote during this period, and we will look at his comments about Jesus shortly. Two of his works, for good reasons, do not mention Jesus: *Against Apion,* an apologetic work contrasting the Jewish faith with Greek thought, and *Wars of the Jews,* a general history of the Jewish Wars from the time of the Maccabees to A.D. 70. A reading of both works is enough to show that any reference to Jesus in either one would have been out of place.

In the nineties, the poet Statius published *Silvae*, Quintilian published twelve books on oratory and Tacitus published two small books, one a monograph of his father-in-law, Agricola, and the other a monograph about what is now Germany. The subject matter of none of these would be expected to include anything about Jesus. Juvenal began his writings of satire just prior to the turn of the century. He does not mention the Christians. This again is not surprising. They were outlawed in Rome and therefore had to keep out of sight. A writer always increases his popularity by poking fun at those in the limelight rather than at those whom nobody knows.

There were, in addition, some writings from Qumran in the first century. Again, it is no big surprise—but expected—that they fail to mention Jesus. F. F. Bruce observes:

> The Qumran community withdrew as far as possible from public life and lived in its wilderness retreat; Jesus carried on His ministry in places where people lived and worked, mixing with all sorts and conditions, and by preference (it appears) with men and women whose society pious men like those of Qumran would rather avoid. And, more important still, practically all the Qumran texts dealing with religious topics (so far as they have been published to date) are assigned on paleographical grounds to the pre-Christian decades. 11/66-67

When you consider the quantity and content of first-century writings which have survived, you can understand why we do not possess more non-Christian references to Jesus. R. T. France puts it this way:

> From the point of view of Roman history of the first century, Jesus was a nobody. A man of no social standing, who achieved brief local notice in a remote and little-loved province as a preacher and miracle-worker, and who was duly executed by order of a minor provincial governor, could hardly be expected to achieve mention in the Roman headlines. 30/82 (See vol. 1, pp. 81-87.)

Some first-century works which did not survive almost certainly did not contain any references to Jesus. The one work with the best opportunity of mentioning Jesus but which apparently did not was the *Chronicle* by Justus of Tiberias. He was born at about the time Jesus died. Photius, in the ninth century, comments that his silence was due to his non-Christian bias as a Jew. 1/18 When a writer of antiquity sought to discredit someone, he often used the common device of not mentioning him. As a result, his memory would not be preserved. In some areas of the Middle East, especially in Egypt, new rulers commonly attempted to erase all evidence of a previous ruler's existence by destroying all inscriptions and writings about him. Whether Justus consciously chose to ignore Jesus of Nazareth is impossible to tell since his work can't be analyzed. Living in Tiberias may have colored what he viewed as important. He may also have ignored Jesus along with a host of other messianic pretenders common in that day.

So one reason it is surprising that we have any non-Christian references to Jesus in the first century at all is that not much about anything of that day has survived to the present time. What did survive indicates the writers would not have known about or been interested in the person of Jesus.

What News Was Hot?

If the biblical description of Jesus' activities is accurate, wouldn't Jesus have attracted sufficient attention to be mentioned in first century writings? Aside from what was said above, we can also agree with G. A. Wells when he says, "Today Christianity has been so important for so long that one is apt to assume that it must have appeared important to educated pagans who lived A.D. 50-150." 81/15

The journalists of the first century, at least those whose works have been preserved to the present day, indicated they were concerned about such things as the major political events of the day. Read through portions of the works of Tacitus, Suetonius, even Josephus and others of that time period, and you will notice very quickly that they concerned themselves almost completely with the major political and international events of the day. When it came to religious events, only those which had bearing on the "more important" national and international affairs were mentioned.

A perfect example is Acts 25:19 where Festus, one of the closest political figures to the events of first-century Christianity, says, in speaking of the Jews and Paul, "They simply had some points of disagreement with him about their own religion and about a certain dead man, Jesus, whom Paul asserted to be alive." What Luke preserves here is the relatively small degree of importance which ruling officials attached to the religious events in first-century Palestine, at least those which seemed to have no political consequences. As a result, we ought to expect that the secular press of the day in Rome concerned itself more with the Roman attempts to protect its borders than with what was considered to be minor disagreements about religion. As France puts it:

> Galilee and Judaea were at the time two minor administrative areas under the large Roman province of Syria, itself on the far eastern frontier of the empire. The Jews, among whom Jesus lived and died, were a strange, remote people, little understood and little liked by most Europeans of the time, more often the butt of Roman humor than of serious interest. Major events of Jewish history find their echo in the histories of the period, but was the life of Jesus, from the Roman point of view, a major event? The death of a failed Jewish insurrectionary leader was a common enough occurrence, and religious preachers were two a penny in that part of the empire, a matter of curiosity, but hardly of real interest, to civilized Romans. 29/20

There is another factor which pushes Christianity even further down the list of priorities in terms of hot news items. More conflicts are recorded in the Gospels between Jesus and the Pharisees than between Jesus and any other group of people, yet increasing discoveries reveal that Jesus' teaching was closer in content to at least one of the schools of the Pharisees than to any other group in Israel at that time. We may therefore reasonably conclude that even a major confrontation between Jesus and the Pharisees probably was only a meaningless religious squabble to any first-century historian—including Josephus.

Was Christianity a hot news item in the first century? For Christians it was—but for those in government and for the press, not really.

Is Absence of Evidence Evidence of Absence?

No one denies that the Christian church existed in the first century. Scholars recognize that even though Christianity did not attract much attention from first-century writers, it still would be impossible to deny its existence. Some scholars, therefore, are inconsistent when they argue for the lack of historicity of Jesus. As France brings out:

> Those who suspect the historicity of the Jesus of the Gospels on the grounds that there are so few early non-Christian references to Him, must surely, by the same argument, be even more skeptical as to whether the Christian church existed in the first century. But not even George Wells wishes to deny this! As has so often been noted, absence of evidence is not evidence of absence. 29/44

In view of what has been discussed in this chapter, consider two questions: (1) What kind of reference to Jesus by a non-Christian would need to exist to incontrovertibly prove His existence? (2) Is it likely that any such reference survives today?

An incontrovertible reference to Jesus would first of all have to be from an eyewitness. But outside of Christian testimony, no surviving historical literature could even be expected to contain eyewitness references to Him. So the modern historian must seek non-Christian evidence for Jesus the same way he does for every other person of antiquity who was considered insignificant by the authorities of his day. He must analyze the credibility of secondhand reports.

Combine secondhand reports of Jesus (both non-Christian and Christian) with the eyewitness accounts recorded in the Gospels, and you will find that Jesus compares extremely favorably with other people in history whose historicity is **not** doubted. Professor of Philosophy and Religion at Liberty University, Gary Habermas, states concerning Jesus:

> We can perceive all the more how groundless the speculations are which deny His existence or which postulate only a minimal amount of facts concerning Him. Much of ancient history is based on many fewer sources which are much later than the events which they record. . . . While some believe that we know almost nothing about Jesus from ancient, non-New Testament sources, this plainly is not the case. Not only are there many such sources, but Jesus is one of the persons of ancient history concerning whom we have a significant amount of quality data. His is one of the most-mentioned and most-substantiated lives in ancient times. 35/169

Blaiklock adds:

> Historians would be glad to have authentic, multiple, congruent evidence on more personalities and events of ancient history. 9/12

Early Non-Christian References to Jesus (E/81-87)

> **NOTE:** The material below is considerably expanded in *He Walked Among Us,* pages 35-70. In addition, one should not overlook the fact that our most reliable historical sources on the life of Jesus are the four Gospel narratives of the New Testament. This fact is also thoroughly documented in *He Walked Among Us.*

Ancient Secular Writers

CORNELIUS TACITUS (born A.D. 52-54)

A Roman historian, in A.D. 112, Governor of Asia, son-in-law of Julius Agricola, who was Governor of Britain A.D. 80-84. Writing of the reign of Nero, Tacitus alludes to the death of Christ and to the existence of Christians at Rome:

> But not all the relief that could come from man, not all the bounties that the prince could bestow, nor all the atonements which could be presented to the gods, availed to relieve Nero from the infamy of being believed to have ordered the conflagration, the fire of Rome. Hence to suppress the rumor, he falsely charged with the guilt, and punished with the most exquisite tortures, the persons commonly called Christians, who were hated for their enormities. Christus, the founder of the name, was put to death by Pontius Pilate, procurator of Judea in the reign of Tiberius: but the pernicious superstition, repressed for a time broke out again, not only through Judea, where the mischief originated, but through the city of Rome also (*Annals,* XV. 44).

Tacitus has a further reference to Christianity in a fragment of his *Histories,* dealing with the burning of the Jerusalem Temple in A.D. 70, preserved by Sulpicius Severus (*Chron.* ii. 30. 6).

LUCIAN OF SAMOSATA

A satirist of the second century, who spoke scornfully of Christ and the Christians. He connected them with the synagogues of Palestine and alluded to Christ as

> the man who was crucified in Palestine because He introduced this new cult into the world. . . . Furthermore, their first lawgiver persuaded them that they were all brothers one of another after they have transgressed once for all by denying the Greek gods and by worshipping that crucified sophist Himself and living under His laws (*The Passing Peregrinus).*

Lucian also mentions the Christians several times in his *Alexander the False Prophet,* sections 25 and 29.

FLAVIUS JOSEPHUS (born A.D. 37)

A Jewish historian, became a Pharisee at age 19; in A.D. 66 he was the commander of the Jewish forces in Galilee. After being captured, he was attached to the Roman headquarters. He says in a hotly contested quotation:

> Now there was about this time Jesus, a wise man, if it be lawful to call Him a man, for He was a doer of wonderful works, a teacher of such men as receive the truth with pleasure. He drew over to Him both many of the Jews, and many of the Gentiles. He was the Christ, and when Pilate, at the suggestion of the principal men among us, had condemned Him to the cross, those that loved Him at the first did not forsake Him; for He appeared to them alive again in the third day; as the divine prophets had foretold these and ten thousand other wonderful things concerning Him. And the tribe of Christians so named from Him are not extinct at this day (*Antiquities,* xviii. 33. [early second century]).

The Arabic text of this passage is as follows:

> At this time there was a wise man who was called Jesus. And His conduct was good, and [He] was known to be virtuous. And many people from among the Jews and the other nations became His disciples. Pilate condemned Him to be crucified and to die. And those who had become His disciples did not abandon His discipleship. They reported that He had appeared to them three days after His crucifixion and that He was alive; accordingly, He was perhaps the Messiah concerning whom the prophets have recounted wonders.

The above passage is found in the Arabic manuscript entitled: "Kitab Al-Unwan Al-Mukallal Bi-Fadail Al-Hikma Al-Mutawwaj Bi-Anwa Al-Falsafa Al-Manduh Bi-Haqaq Al-Marifa." The approximate translation would be: "Book of History Guided by All the Virtues of Wisdom. Crowned with Various Philosophies and Blessed by the Truth of Knowledge."

The above manuscript composed by Bishop Agapius in the tenth century has a section commencing with: "We have found in many books of the philosophers that they refer to the day of the crucifixion of Christ." Then he gives a list and quotes portions of the ancient works. Some of the works are familiar to modern scholars and others are not. 64/n.p.

We also find from Josephus a reference to James the brother of Jesus. In *Antiquities* XX 9:1 he describes the actions of the high priest Ananus:

> But the younger Ananus who, as we said, received the high priesthood, was of a bold disposition and exceptionally daring; he followed the party of the Sadducees, who are severe in judgment above all the Jews, as we have already shown. As therefore Ananus was of such a disposition, he thought he had now a good opportunity, as Festus was now dead, and Albinus was still on the road; so he assembled a council of judges, and brought before it the brother of Jesus the so-called Christ, whose name was James, together

> with some others, and having accused them as law-breakers, he delivered them over to be stoned. 10/107

SUETONIUS (A.D.120)

Another Roman historian, a court official under Hadrian, annalist of the Imperial House, Suetonius says: "As the Jews were making constant disturbances at the instigation of Chrestus [another spelling of Christus], he expelled them from Rome" (*Life of Claudius*, 25. 4).

He also writes: "Punishment by Nero was inflicted on the Christians, a class of men given to a new and mischievous superstition" (*Lives of the Caesars*, 26. 2)

PLINIUS SECUNDUS, PLINY THE YOUNGER

Governor of Bithynia in Asia Minor (A.D. 112), Pliny was writing the emperor Trajan seeking counsel as to how to treat the Christians.

He explained that he had been killing both men and women, boys and girls. There were so many being put to death that he wondered if he should continue killing anyone who was discovered to be a Christian, or if he should kill only certain ones. He explained that he had made the Christians bow down to the statues of Trajan. He goes on to say that he also "made them curse Christ, which a genuine Christian cannot be induced to do." In the same letter he says of the people who were being tried:

> They affirmed, however, that the whole of their guilt, or their error, was that they were in the habit of meeting on a certain fixed day before it was light, when they sang in alternate verse a hymn to Christ as to a god, and bound themselves to a solemn oath, not to any wicked deeds, but never to commit any fraud, theft, adultery, never to falsify their word, not to deny a trust when they should be called upon to deliver it up (*Epistles*, X. 96).

TERTULLIAN (Regarding Pilate and Tiberius)

Jurist-theologian of Carthage, in a defense of Christianity (A.D. 197) before the Roman authorities in Africa, mentions the exchange between Tiberius and Pontius Pilate:

> Tiberius accordingly, in whose days the Christian name made its entry into the world, having himself received intelligence from the truth of Christ's divinity, brought the matter before the senate, with his own decision in favor of Christ. The senate, because it had not given the approval itself, rejected his proposal. Caesar held to his opinion, threatening wrath against all the accusers of the Christians (*Apology*, V. 2).

Some historians doubt the historicity of this passage. Also, cf. Justin Martyr (*Apology*, 1. 35).

THALLUS, the Samaritan-born historian

One of the first Gentile writers who mentions Christ is Thallus, who wrote in A.D. 52. However, his writings have disappeared and we only know of them from fragments cited by other writers. One such writer is Julius Africanus, a Christian writer about A.D. 221. One very interesting passage relates to a comment from Thallus. Julius Africanus writes:

> "Thallus, in the third book of his histories, explains away this darkness as an eclipse of the sun—unreasonably, as it seems to me" (unreasonably, of course, because a solar eclipse could not take place at the time of the full moon, and it was the season of the Paschal full moon that Christ died).

Thus, from this reference we see that the Gospel account of the darkness which fell upon the land during Christ's crucifixion was well known and required a naturalistic explanation from those non-believers who witnessed it. 10/113

PHLEGON, a first-century historian

His *Chronicles* have been lost, but a small fragment of that work, which confirms the darkness upon the earth at the crucifixion, is also mentioned by Julius Africanus. After his (Africanus') remarks about Thallus' unreasonable opinion of the darkness, he quotes Phlegon that "during the time of Tiberius Caesar an eclipse of the sun occurred during the full moon." 60/n.p.

Phlegon is also mentioned by Origen in *Contra Celsum,* Book 2, sections 14, 33, 59.

Philopon [De. opif. mund. II 21] says: "And about this darkness... Phlegon recalls it in the *Olympiads* [the title of his history]." He says that "Phlegon mentioned the eclipse which took place during the crucifixion of the Lord Jesus Christ, and no other [eclipse], it is clear that he did not know from his sources about any [similar] eclipse in previous times . . . and this is shown by the historical account itself of Tiberius Caesar." 41/1165

LETTER OF MARA BAR-SERAPION

F. F. Bruce records that there is

> in the British Museum an interesting manuscript preserving the text of a letter written some time later than A.D. 73, but how much later we cannot be sure. This letter was sent by a Syrian named Mara Bar-Serapion to his son Serapion. Mara Bar-Serapion was in prison at the time, but he wrote to encourage his son in the pursuit of wisdom, and pointed out that those who persecuted wise men were overtaken by misfortune. He instances the deaths of Socrates, Pythagoras and Christ.
>
> What advantage did the Athenians gain from putting Socrates to death? Famine and plague came upon them as a judgment for their crime. What advantage did the men of Samos gain from burning Pythagoras? In a moment their land was covered with sand. What advantage did the Jews gain from executing their wise King? It was just after that that their kingdom was abolished. God justly avenged these three wise men: the Athenians died of hunger; the Samians were overwhelmed by the sea; the Jews, ruined and driven from their land, live in complete dispersion. But

Socrates did not die for good; he lived on in the teaching of Plato. Pythagoras did not die for good; he lived on in the statue of Hera. Nor did the wise King die for good; He lived on in the teaching which He had given. 10/114

References From the Rabbis

> **NOTE:** See *He Walked Among Us,* pp. 55*ff.,* for an explanation of the various kinds of rabbinic literature.

Comments in the *Baraia* are of great historical value:

> On the eve of Passover they hanged Yeshu (of Nazareth) and the herald went before him for forty days saying (Yeshu of Nazareth) is going forth to be stoned in that he hath practiced sorcery and beguiled and led astray Israel. Let everyone knowing aught in His defence come and plead for Him. But they found in Him naught in His defence and hanged Him on the eve of Passover (Babylonia *Sanhedrin* 43a).—"Eve of Passover."

The Amoa "Ulla" ("Ulla" was a disciple of R. Youchanan and lived in Palestine at the end of the third century) adds:

> And do you suppose that for (Yeshu of Nazareth) there was any right of appeal? He was a beguiler, and the Merciful One hath said: "Thou shalt not spare neither shalt thou conceal him." It is otherwise with Yeshu, for He was near to the civil authority.

The Jewish authorities did not deny that Jesus performed signs and miracles (Matthew 9:34; 12:24; Mark 3:22) but they attributed them to acts of sorcery. 46/23

"The *Talmud,*" writes the Jewish scholar Joseph Klausner, "speaks of hanging in place of crucifixion, since this horrible Roman form of death was only known to Jewish scholars from Roman trials, and not from the Jewish legal system. Even Paul the apostle (Galatians 3:13) expounds the passage 'for a curse of God is that which is hanged' (Deuteronomy 22:23) as applicable to Jesus." 46/28

Sanhedrin 43*a* also makes references to the disciples of Jesus *(Yeb.* IV 3. 49*a):*

> R. Shimeon ben Azzai said [concerning Jesus]: "I found a genealogical roll in Jerusalem wherein was recorded, Such-an-one is a bastard of an adulteress."

Klausner adds to the above:

> Current editions of the *Mishnah* add: "To support the words of R. Yehoshua" (who, in the same *Mishnah,* says: What is a bastard? Everyone whose parents are liable to death by the Beth Din). That Jesus is here referred to seems to be beyond doubt. 46/35

An early *Baraita,* in which R. Eliezer is the central figure, speaks of

Jesus by name. The brackets are within the quote. Eliezer speaking:

> He answered, Akiba, you have reminded me! Once I was walking along the upper market (*Tosefta* reads "street") of Sepphoris and found one [of the disciples of Jesus of Nazareth] and Jacob of Kefar Sekanya (*Tosefta* reads "Sakkanin") was his name. He said to me, It is written in your Law, "Thou shalt not bring the hire of a harlot, etc." What was to be done with it—a latrine for the High Priest? But I answered nothing. He said to me, so [Jesus of Nazareth] taught me (*Tosefta* reads, "Yeshu ben Pantere"): "For of the hire of a harlot hath she gathered them, and unto the hire of a harlot shall they return"; from the place of filth they come, and unto the place of filth they shall go. And the saying pleased me, and because of this I was arrested for *Minuth*. And I transgressed against what is written in the Law; "Keep thy way far from her"—that is *Minuth;* "and come not nigh the door of her house"—that is the civil government. 46/38

The above brackets are found in *Dikduke Sof'rim* to *Aboda Zara* (Munich Manuscript, ed. Rabinovitz).

Klausner, commenting on the above passage, says:

> There can be no doubt that the words, "one of the disciples of Jesus of Nazareth," and, "thus Jesus of Nazareth taught me," are, in the present passage both early in date and fundamental in their bearing on the grounds of the slight variations in the parallel passages; their variants ("Yeshu ben Pantere" or "Yeshu ben Pandera," instead of "Yeshu of Nazareth") are merely due to the fact that, from an early date, the name "Pantere," or "Pandera," became current among the Jews as the name of the reputed father of Jesus. 46/38

Encyclopedia Britannica

The fifteenth edition of the *Encyclopedia Britannica* uses 20,000 words in describing this person, Jesus. His description took more space than was given to Aristotle, Cicero, Alexander, Julius Caesar, Buddha, Confucious, Mohammed or Napoleon Bonaparte.

Concerning the testimony of the many independent secular accounts of Jesus of Nazareth, it records:

> These independent accounts prove that in ancient times even the opponents of Christianity never doubted the historicity of Jesus, which was disputed for the first time and on inadequate grounds by several authors at the end of the 18th, during the 19th, and at the beginning of the 20th centuries. 22/145

The Jewishness of Jesus (HW/233-242)

Just after World War II, a Scottish minister, R. A. Stewart, wrote: "A proper historical understanding of the New Testament is impossible without a detailed knowledge of Jewish literature and thought." 73/5

His words proved almost prophetic—many Jewish scholars today are in the forefront of affirming the historicity of Jesus. Geza Vermes, David Flusser, S. Safrai and Pinchas Lapide lead the way in reclaiming Jesus as a striking Jewish person of the first century. Vermes even asserts that "no objective and enlightened student of the Gospels can help but be struck by the incomparable superiority of Jesus." 80/224

Professor Donald A. Hagner, Associate Professor of New Testament at Fuller Theological Seminary, has written a detailed analysis of the current reclamation of Jesus in Jewish scholarship. Concerning the contributions provided from the Hebrew perspective, he states:

> It will be obvious that Jewish scholars are in a particularly advantageous position to understand the teaching of Jesus. Familiar with the Bible (Old Testament), the development of early Judaism, the Jewish background of the Gospels, and often learned in the difficult world of rabbinic literature, they are often able not only to place Jesus in historical context but also to enter the mental world of Jesus and to capture every Jewish nuance in His words. 36/27

The Jewishness of Jesus and the pervasive Hebraic quality of His surroundings repeatedly surface in the Gospel accounts. Yet much of past New Testament scholarship has failed to deal with this critical aspect of the life of the historical Jesus. If one is to see Jesus of Nazareth as He actually was when He traversed the land of Palestine, then one cannot ignore the evidence of His Jewishness.

Jewish scholarship has helped most to identify Jesus' Jewishness by showing the parallels between His teaching and rabbinic teaching. When you compare these teachings, you can begin to see how far-fetched the idea is that the life of Jesus was made up by zealous churchmen of the second and third centuries. As the leadership of the church shifted from Jerusalem to Antioch to Rome between the first and fourth centuries, there also was a predominant shift from a Jewish Christianity to a Gentile Christianity. In fact, the history of the first two centuries of the church confirms that it was primarily Gentile in character by the beginning of the second century A.D. It would therefore be highly unlikely for a Gentile of the second century or later to mold an account of the life of Jesus which so thoroughly reflected the first-century Hebrew culture.

The Jews of Jesus' day were meticulous educators, as they have been throughout most of their history. A passage from the *Mishnah* (Aboth 5. 15) demonstrates their active concern about what their students absorbed:

> There are four types of people who sit in front of the sages: The sponge, the funnel, the strainer and the sifter. The sponge—it soaks up everything; the funnel—it takes in at one end and lets out at the other; the strainer—it lets out the wine and retains the dregs; and the sifter—it lets out the bran dust and retains the fine flour.

In order to stimulate the student not to just "memorize the right answers," the teacher, or rabbi, would ask questions of his students. Not only were the students expected to be able to answer the questions, but they also were expected to answer them by phrasing equally good questions, showing that they had thought through the original questions thoroughly. Perhaps this is why Rabbi Hillel said, "A timid student does not learn." (Aboth 2.6) David Bivin, the director of the Jerusalem School of Synoptic Studies, writes:

> This pattern of answering questions with questions was so common that in the Hebrew of Jesus' day the word for "question" came to be a synonym for "answer." 8/5

Biven gives several examples which illustrate the deep Jewish roots of Jesus' learning and teaching styles:

> Twelve-year-old Jesus was lost and finally discovered by His parents, "sitting in the Temple among the rabbis, listening to them and asking them questions" (Luke 2:46). The Gospel writer comments in the following verse, "And all those listening to Him were amazed at His wise answers." If Jesus was only asking questions, how is it that the listeners were impressed by His answers? This would seem very strange indeed if one did not know that in the rabbinic world in which Jesus lived, a student's answers were given in the form of questions. . . .
>
> Jesus answered a question with a question on other occasions as well. When He was asked by the Temple authorities what right He had to do "these things" (cleansing the Temple), He answered by saying, "I will also ask you something. Now tell me, was John's baptism of God or of men?" (Luke 20:3-4) . . .
>
> The best example in the teaching of Jesus of the kind of question a rabbi commonly would ask his students is found in Luke 20:41-44, in which he asked:
>
> > How can one say that the Messiah is the descendant (literally "son") of David? David himself says in the book of Psalms, "the LORD said to my lord, "Sit here at my right hand until I make your enemies your footstool." David calls Him Lord, so how can He be His descendant?
>
> This is a typical rabbinic riddle based on a seeming contradiction in a passage of Scripture. 8/5

The first of Hillel's rules of interpretation was called *kal vachomer* (simple and complex). 7/1 This principle has to do with deducing something that is not very apparent from something that is apparent or already known. It often uses the words *how much more* as in "Silence becomes a scholar; *how much more* a fool" (Tosefta: Pesachim 9:2).

Mishnah: Sanhedrin 6.5 is another example:

> Rabbi Meir said, "While the man is in agony, what does the Tongue say? 'My head is hurting! My arm is hurting!' If the Scripture has thus spoken: 'I agonize over the blood of the wicked,' *how much more* over the blood of the righteous that is shed?"

Jesus used this same rabbinic device in His teaching. One example is found in Matthew 7:9-11 where He says:

> Or what man is there among you, when his son shall ask him for a loaf, will give him a stone? Or if he shall ask for a fish, he will not give him a snake, will he? If you then, being evil, know how to give gifts to your children, *how much more* shall your Father who is in heaven give what is good to those who ask Him!

In Matthew 6:28-30, Jesus says:

> But if God so arrays the grass of the field, which is alive today and tomorrow is thrown into the furnace, will He not *much more* do so for you, O men of little faith?

Jesus, being Jewish and thoroughly acquainted with the teachings of the rabbis, makes a number of statements which have close parallels in the rabbinic literature. Professor Gustaf Dalman, founder of the Institute for the Study of Antiquity in the Holy Land, gives the following among many others: 17/225-29

> And by your standard of measure, it shall be measured to you (Matthew 7:2, Mark 4:24, Luke 6:38).

vs.

> With the measure with which one measures, it will be measured unto him (Sot. 1. 7; Tos. Sot. 3.1,2; Siphre, 28*b*).

> Therefore whatever you want others to do for you, do so for them; for this is the Law and the Prophets (Matthew 7:12, Luke 6:31).

vs.

> What is hateful to thee, do it not unto thy neighbor. This is the whole Law and the rest is the interpretation thereof (Hillel. b. Sab. 31a). [The "Golden Rule" has been taught in many different forms. Jesus' version is unique in that it is a positive rather than negative approach. He does not say "Don't do what you don't want others to do to you," like Hillel. This approach only keeps one from doing harmful actions. Rather, Jesus says, "Do what you would like others to do for you." This approach, while eliminating harmful actions, also adds the responsibility to do acts of kindness, benevolence, etc. to others.]

> Blessed are the merciful, for they shall receive mercy (Matthew 5:7).

vs.

> Whenever thou art merciful, God is merciful to thee (p. Bab. k. 6*c*).

While the similarities of Jesus' teaching to that of the rabbis provides substantial evidence for the historicity of Jesus as a first-century teacher, some may wonder if there was anything at all unique about Jesus. Rabbi H. G. Enelow has observed the following tension between Jewish and Christian writers:

> Jewish writers have tried to prove that anything taught by Jesus may be found in Jewish literature, and that therefore He could not be called original; while Christians have deemed it necessary to defend Jesus against the charge of borrowing or reproducing from Jewish sources, lest His originality be impugned. 23/14

Traditionally Jewish people have been taught that anything good in the Gospels is nothing new; anything new is nothing good. The truth is that there is much that flows out of the teaching of the rabbis, and there is much that is unique to Jesus. A good example is in Jesus' use of parables as a teaching device.

The two standard authoritative reference works on the parables of Jesus are C. H. Dodd's *The Parables of the Kingdom* and Göttingen professor of New Testament and late Jewish religion, Joachim Jeremias's *The Parables of Jesus*. Both affirm that readers must interpret Jesus' parables within their original life setting. They defend the parables as being authentically from Jesus, for the content of the parables emerges from the historical Jewish situation of Jesus as opposed to the situation of the early church.

Christians and non-Christians alike have almost universally appreciated the parables of Jesus as a supreme teaching device. But it is important to realize that this mode of instruction was not unique to Jesus. Jewish literature preserves more than four thousand rabbinic parables. Here is an example of one such parable:

> A person in whom there are good deeds and who has studied the Torah extensively, what is he like? A man who builds first [of] stones and then afterwards [of] mud bricks. Even if a large quantity of water were to collect beside the stones, it would not destroy them. But a person in whom there are not good deeds, though he has studied Torah, what is he like? A man who builds first [of] mud and then afterwards [of] stones. Even if only a little water collects, it immediately undermines them. 6/5

Now, compare the above parable with the parable which Jesus gives in Matthew 7:24-27:

> Therefore everyone who hears these words of Mine, and acts upon them, may be compared to a wise man, who built his house upon the rock. And the rain descended, and the floods came, and the winds blew, and burst against that house; and yet it did not fall, for it had been founded upon the rock. And everyone who hears these words of Mine, and does not act upon them, will be like a foolish man, who built his house upon the sand. And the rain descended, and the floods came, and the winds blew, and burst against that house; and it fell, and great was its fall.

So what makes Jesus so different? What was it that Jesus said that seems to have caught the attention of the world for nearly two thousand years? How was He different from the rabbis who preceded Him? David Bivin answers that question here:

> It was not the way He taught or even the general content of His teaching that made Jesus unique among the rabbis. What *was* unique about Jesus was who He claimed to be, and He rarely ever taught without claiming to be not only God's Messiah, but more startlingly, *Immanuel,* "God with us."
>
> It is just this claim that marks a difference between Jesus' parable of the house built on bedrock and all other rabbinic parables which deal with the same theme. All the other rabbis spoke of knowing and doing the words of Torah, but Jesus introduced His parable with the words, "A person who hears *these words of mine* and does them . . . " No other rabbi is recorded as ever having spoken like that or having made the claims inherent in Jesus' words. He was clearly speaking as only God would speak, and none of His contemporaries could have missed or ignored that fact. 6/5

The rabbinic parallels to sayings of Jesus confirm again that the Gospel accounts give us a reliable picture of the historical Jesus. The Jesus of the Gospels was not a Jesus made up by the early church, but a thoroughly Jewish teacher from within the Jewish culture, yet one who spoke out in a uniquely prophetic fashion.

CHAPTER 19 Messianic Prophecies Fulfilled in Jesus

(C/101-10)

NOTE: For a much more detailed treatment of this subject, see *Evidence That Demands a Verdict, Vol I,* pp. 141-76. Additional information also can be found in *He Walked Among Us,* pp. 305-8, particularly an answer to those who claim that the servant of Isaiah 53 refers to the nation of Israel and not to the Messiah.

Will the Real Messiah Please Stand Up?

Jesus had various credentials to support His claims to being Messiah, God's son. One credential often overlooked, one of the most profound, is the fulfillment of prophecy in His life.

Over and over again Jesus appealed to the prophecies of the Old Testament to substantiate His claims as the Messiah. Galatians 4:4 says, "But when the fullness of the time came, God sent forth His Son, born of a woman, born under the Law." Here we have reference to the prophecies being fulfilled in Jesus Christ.

> And beginning with Moses and with all the prophets He explained to them the things concerning Himself in all the Scriptures (Luke 24:27).

Jesus said to them, "These are My words which I spoke to you while I was still with you, that all things which are written about Me in the Law of Moses and the Prophets and the Psalms must be fulfilled" (Luke 24:44). He said, "For if you believed Moses, you would believe Me; for he wrote of Me" (John 5:46). He also said, "Abraham rejoiced to see My day" (John 8:56).

The apostles, the New Testament writers, etc., constantly appealed to fulfilled prophecy to substantiate the claims of Jesus as the Son of God, the Savior, the Messiah.

> But the things which God announced beforehand by the mouth of all the prophets, that His Christ should suffer, He has thus fulfilled (Acts 3:18).

> And according to Paul's custom, he went to them, and for three Sabbaths reasoned with them from the Scriptures [meaning the Old Testament], explaining and giving evidence that the Christ had to suffer and rise again from the dead, and saying, "This Jesus whom I am proclaiming to you is the Christ" (Acts 17:2,3).

> For I delivered to you as of first importance what I also received, that Christ died for our sins according to the Scriptures [in other words, Christ's death was prophesied in the Old Testament], and that He was buried, and that He was raised on the third day according to the Scriptures (1 Corinthians 15:3,4).

In the Old Testament there are sixty major messianic prophecies and approximately 270 ramifications that were fulfilled in one person, Jesus Christ. It is helpful to look at all these predictions fulfilled in Christ as His "address." You've probably never realized how important the details of *your* name and address are—and yet these details set you apart from the five billion other people who also inhabit this planet.

An Address in History

With even greater detail, God wrote an address in history to single out His Son, the Messiah, the Savior of mankind, from anyone who has ever lived in history—past, present, or future. The specifics of this address can be found in the Old Testament, a document written over a period of a thousand years, which contains more than three hundred references to His coming. Using the science of probability, we find the chances of just forty-eight of these prophecies being fulfilled in one person to be right at one in 10^{157} (a one followed by 157 zeros!).

The task of matching up God's address with one man is further complicated by the fact that all the prophecies of the Messiah were made at least 400 years before He was to appear. Some might disagree and say that these prophecies were written down after the time of Christ and fabricated to coincide with His life. This might sound feasible until you realize that the Septuagint, the Greek translation of the Hebrew Old Testament, was translated around 150–200 B.C. This Greek translation shows that there was at least a two-hundred-year gap between the prophecies being recorded and their fulfillment in Christ.

Certainly God was writing an address in history that only the Messiah could fulfill. Approximately forty major claims to be the Jewish Messiah have been made by men. Only one—Jesus Christ—appealed to fulfilled prophecy to substantiate His claims, and only His credentials back up those claims.

What were some of those details? And what events had to precede and coincide with the appearance of God's Son?

To begin, we need to go way back to Genesis 3:15. Here we have the first messianic prophecy. In all of Scripture, only one man was "born of the seed of a woman"—all others are born of the seed of a man. Here is the one who will come into the world and undo the works of Satan ("bruise His head").

In Genesis 9 and 10 God narrowed the address down further. Noah had three sons, Shem, Japheth, and Ham. Today all of the nations of the world can be traced back to these three men. But in this passage, God effectively eliminated two-thirds of them from the line of Messiahship. The Messiah will come through the lineage of Shem.

Continuing on to the year 2000 B.C., we find God calling a man named Abraham out of Ur of the Chaldees. With Abraham, God became still more specific, stating that the Messiah will be one of his descendants (Genesis 12; 17; 22). All the families of the earth will be blessed through Abraham. Abraham had two sons, Isaac and Ishmael, but many of his descendants were eliminated when God selected his second son, Isaac (Genesis 17;21).

Isaac had two sons, Jacob and Esau, and God chose the line of Jacob (Genesis 28; 35:10-12; Numbers 24:17). Jacob had twelve sons, out of whom developed the twelve tribes of Israel. God singled out the tribe of Judah for Messiahship and eliminated 11/12ths of the Israelite tribes. And of all the family lines within Judah's tribe, the line of Jesse was the divine choice (Isaiah 11:1-5). One can see the probability of Jesus being the Messiah building.

Jesse had eight children and in 2 Samuel 7:12-16 and Jeremiah 23:5 God eliminated 7/8ths of Jesse's family line: We read that God's man will not only be of the seed of a woman, the lineage of Shem, the race of the Jews, the line of Isaac, the line of Jacob, the tribe of Judah, but that He will also be of the house of David.

A prophecy dating 1012 B.C. (Psalm 22:6-18; cf. Zechariah 12:10 and

Galatians 3:13) also predicts that this man's hands and feet will be pierced (i.e., He will be crucified). This description was written eight hundred years before crucifixion began to be practiced by the Romans.

Isaiah 7:14 adds that this man will be born of a virgin—a natural birth of unnatural conception, a criterion beyond human planning and control. Several prophecies recorded in Isaiah and the psalms describe the social climate and response that God's man will encounter: His own people, the Jews, will reject Him and the Gentiles will believe in Him (Isaiah 8:14; 28:16; 49:6; 50:6; 52:53; 60:3; Psalms 22:7,8; 118:22). There will be a forerunner for Him (Isaiah 40:3; Malachi 3:1), a voice in the wilderness, one preparing the way before the Lord, a John the Baptist.

Thirty Pieces of Silver

Notice, too, the seven ramifications of a prophecy (Zechariah 11:11-13; cf. Psalm 41, Jeremiah 32:6-15, and Matthew 27:3-10) that narrows the drama down even further. Here God indicates the Messiah will be (1) betrayed, (2) by a friend, (3) for thirty pieces, (4) of silver, that will be (5) cast onto the floor, (6) of the Temple, and (7) used to buy a potter's field.

In Micah 5:2 God eliminated all the cities of the world and selected Bethlehem, with a population of less than a thousand, as the Messiah's birthplace.

Then through a series of prophecies He even defined the time sequence that would set His man apart. For example, Malachi 3:1 and four other Old Testament verses (Psalm 118:26; Daniel 9:26; Zechariah 11:13; Haggai 2:7-9) require the Messiah to come while the Temple of Jerusalem is still standing. This is of great significance when we realize that the Temple was destroyed in A.D. 70 and has not since been rebuilt.

The precise lineage; the place, time, and manner of birth; people's reactions; the betrayal; the manner of death. These are just a fraction of the hundreds of details that made up the address to identify God's Son, the Messiah, the Savior of the world.

Objection: Such Fulfilled Prophecy Was Coincidental

"Why, you could find some of these prophecies fulfilled in Kennedy, King, Nassar, etc." replies a critic. Yes, one could possibly find one or two prophecies fulfilled in other men, but not all 60 major prophecies and 270 ramifications. H. Harold Artzler, of the American Scientific Affiliation, in the foreword of a book by Peter W. Stoner writes:

> The manuscript for *Science Speaks* has been carefully reviewed by a committee of the American Scientific Affiliation members and by the Executive Council of the same group and has been found, in general, to be dependable and accurate in regard to the scientific material presented. The

mathematical analysis included is based upon principles of probability which are thoroughly sound, and Professor Stoner has applied these principles in a proper and convincing way. 74

The following probabilities are taken from that book to show that coincidence is ruled out by the science of probability. Stoner says that by using the modern science of probability in reference to just eight prophecies, "we find that the chance that any man might have lived down to the present time and fulfilled all eight prophecies is 1 in 10^{17}." That would be 1 in 100,000,000,000,000,000. In order to help us comprehend this staggering probability, Stoner illustrates it by supposing that

> we take 10^{17} silver dollars and lay them on the face of Texas. They will cover all of the state two feet deep. Now mark one of these silver dollars and stir the whole mass thoroughly, all over the state. Blindfold a man and tell him that he can travel as far as he wishes, but he must pick up one silver dollar and say that this is the right one. What chance would he have of getting the right one? Just the same chance that the prophets would have had of writing these eight prophecies and having them all come true in any one man, from their day to the present time, providing they wrote them in their own wisdom.
>
> Now these prophecies were either given by inspiration of God or the prophets just wrote them as they thought they should be. In such a case the prophets had just one chance in 10^{17} of having them come true in any man, but they all came true in Christ.
>
> This means that the fulfillment of these eight prophecies alone proves that God inspired the writing of those prophecies to a definiteness which lacks only one chance in 10^{17} of being absolute.74/106-112

Objection: Jesus Tried to Fulfill Prophecies

Another objection is that Jesus deliberately attempted to fulfill the Jewish prophecies. This objection seems plausible until we realize that many of the details of the Messiah's coming were totally beyond human control.

For example, the place of birth. I can just hear Jesus in Mary's womb as she rode on the donkey: "Mom, we won't make it!"

When Herod asked the chief priests and scribes, "Where is the Christ to be born?" they said, "In Bethlehem of Judea, for so it has been written by the prophet" (Matthew 2:5). The time of His coming. The manner of His birth. Betrayal by Judas and the betrayal price. The manner of His death. The people's reaction. The mocking and spitting, the staring. The casting of dice for His clothes. The non-tearing of His garment, etc. Half the prophecies are beyond His fulfillment. He couldn't work it out to be born of the seed of the woman, the lineage of Shem, the descendants of Abraham, etc. No wonder Jesus and the apostles appealed to fulfilled prophecy to substantiate His claim.

Why did God go to all this trouble? I believe He wanted Jesus Christ to have all the credentials He needed when He came into the world. Yet the most exciting thing about Jesus Christ is that He came to change lives. He alone proved the hundreds of Old Testament prophecies that described His coming to be correct. He alone can fulfill the greatest prophecy of all for those who will accept it—the promise of new life: "I will give you a new heart and put a new spirit within you" (Ezekiel 36:25-27). "Therefore if any man is in Christ, he is a new creature; the old things passed away; behold, new things have come" (2 Corinthians 5:17).

CHAPTER 20 *The Resurrection of Jesus*

You Can't Keep a "Good Man" Down (C/89-90)

And Jesus said to him, "Why do you call me good? No one is good except God alone" (Luke 18:19).

A student at the University of Uruguay said to me, "Professor McDowell, why can't you refute Christianity?"

I answered, "For a very simple reason—the resurrection of Jesus Christ."

After more than 700 hours of studying this subject and thoroughly investigating its foundation, I came to the conclusion that the resurrection of Jesus Christ is either one of the most wicked, vicious, heartless hoaxes ever foisted upon people, or it is the most important fact of history.

The resurrection issue takes the question, "Is Christianity valid?" out of the realm of philosophy and makes it a question of history. Does Christianity have an historically acceptable basis? Is sufficient evidence available to warrant belief in the resurrection?

Obvious Observations (RF/10-31)

In my attempt to refute Christianity, I made five acute observations of the resurrection that I previously had been totally unaware of.

OBSERVATION 1–Testimony of History

Before my research, I had never realized there was so much positive historical, literary and legal testimony supporting its validity.

ROMAN HISTORY SCHOLAR

Professor Thomas Arnold, for fourteen years the headmaster of Rugby, author of the three-volume *History of Rome,* and holder of the chair of modern history at Oxford, was well acquainted with the value of evidence in determining historical facts.

This great scholar said,

> I have been used for many years to study the histories of other times, and to examine and weigh the evidence of those who have written about them, and I know of no one fact in the history of mankind which is proved by better and fuller evidence of every sort, to the understanding of a fair inquirer, than the great sign which God hath given us that Christ died and rose again from the dead. 3/324

TEXTUAL CRITIC

Brooke Foss Wescott, English scholar, said, "Taking all the evidence together, it is not too much to say that there is no historic incident better or more variously supported than the resurrection of Christ." 82/4-6

PROFESSOR OF ANCIENT HISTORY

Dr. Paul L. Maier, professor of ancient history at Western Michigan University, concluded that, "If all the evidence is weighed carefully and fairly, it is indeed justifiable, according to the canons of historical research, to conclude that the tomb in which Jesus was buried was actually empty on the morning of the first Easter. And no shred of evidence has yet been discovered in literary sources, epigraphy or archaeology that would disprove this statement." 56/A-10

CHIEF JUSTICE

Lord Caldecote, Lord Chief Justice of England, has written:

> My faith began with and was grounded on what I thought was revealed in the Bible. When, particularly, I came to the New Testament, the Gospels and other writings of the men who had been friends of Jesus Christ seemed to me to make an overwhelming case, merely as a matter of strict evidence, for the fact therein stated . . . The same approach to the cardinal test of the claims of Jesus Christ, namely, His resurrection, has led me, as often as I have tried to examine the evidence, to believe it as fact beyond dispute. 40/14

LEGAL AUTHORITY

One man who was highly skilled at dealing with evidence was Dr. Simon Greenleaf. He was the famous Royall Professor of Law at Harvard University and succeeded Justice Joseph Story as the Dane Professor of Law in the same university. The rise of Harvard Law School to its eminent position among the legal schools of the United States is to be ascribed to the efforts of these two men. Greenleaf produced his famous three-volume work, *A Treatise on the Law of Evidence,* which still is considered one of the greatest single authorities on this subject in the entire literature of legal procedure.

Greenleaf examined the value of the historical evidence for the resurrection of Jesus Christ to ascertain the truth. He applied the principles contained in his three-volume treatise on evidence. His findings were recorded in his book, *An Examination of the Testimony of the Four Evangelists by the Rules of Evidence Administered in the Courts of Justice.*

Greenleaf came to the conclusion that, according to the laws of legal evidence used in courts of law, there is more evidence for the historical fact of the resurrection of Jesus Christ than for just about any other event in history.

RATIONALISTIC LAWYER

Dr. Frank Morrison, a lawyer who had been brought up in a rationalistic environment, had come to the opinion that the resurrection was nothing but a fairy-tale happy ending which spoiled the matchless story of Jesus. He felt that he owed it to himself, and to others, to write a book that would present the truth about Jesus and dispel the myth of the resurrection.

Upon studying the facts, however, he, too, came to a different conclusion. The sheer weight of the evidence compelled him to conclude that Jesus actually did rise from the dead. Morrison wrote his book—but not the one he had planned. It is titled, *Who Moved the Stone?* The first chapter, very significantly, is called, "The Book That Refused to Be Written."

LITERARY GENIUS

The literary scholar, C. S. Lewis, former professor of Medieval and Renaissance literature at Cambridge University, when writing about his conversion to Christianity, indicated that he had believed Christians "to be wrong."

The last thing Lewis wanted was to embrace Christianity. However, "Early in 1926 the hardest boiled of all atheists I ever knew sat in my room on the other side of the fire and remarked that the evidence for the historicity of the Gospels was really surprisingly good. 'Rum thing,' he went on. 'All that stuff of Frazer's about the Dying God. Rum thing. It almost looks as if it had really happened once.'

"To understand the shattering impact of it, you would need to know the man (who has certainly never since shown any interest in Christianity). If he, the cynic of cynics, the toughest of the toughs, were not—as I would still have put it—'safe,' where could I turn? Was there then no escape?"

After evaluating the basis and evidence for Christianity, Lewis concluded that in other religions there was "no such historical claim as in Christianity." His knowledge of literature forced him to treat the Gospel record as a trustworthy account. "I was by now too experienced in literary criticism to regard the Gospels as myth."

Finally, contrary to his strong stand against Christianity, Professor Lewis had to make an intelligent decision:

"You must picture me alone in that room in Magdelen, night after night, feeling, whenever my mind lifted even for a second from my work, the steady, unrelenting approach of Him whom I so earnestly desired not to meet. That which I greatly feared had at last come upon me. In the Trinity Term of 1929 I gave in, and admitted that God was God, and knelt and prayed: perhaps, that night, the most dejected and reluctant convert in all England." 52/211, 215, 223

OBSERVATION 2—Resurrection Foretold

Christ actually predicted He would rise on the third day. His claims are substantiated throughout the four Gospels. When Jesus was going up to Jerusalem, He took the twelve disciples aside and said to them, "We are going up to Jerusalem. And the Son of Man will be delivered to death. They will deliver Him to the Gentiles to mock, and to scourge, and to crucify Him. And on the third day He will be raised up" (Matthew 16:21; Mark 8:31; Luke 9:22).

Mark points out in his Gospel that "He began to teach them that the Son of Man must suffer many things, and be rejected by the elders, and the chief priests, and the scribes, and be killed, and after three days rise again" (Mark 8:31).

John confirms this when he writes: "Jesus answered and said to them, 'Destroy this temple, and in three days I will raise it up.' The Jews therefore said, 'It took forty-six years to build this Temple, and will You raise it up in three days?' But He was speaking of the temple of His body" (John 2:19-21).

OBSERVATION 3—Basis of Christianity

The historical fact of the resurrection is the very basis for the truth of Christianity. To put it simply, the resurrection of Jesus Christ and Christianity stand or fall together. One cannot be true without the other.

The apostle Paul emphasized this point when he wrote:

> But if there is no resurrection of the dead, not even Christ has been raised;

> and if Christ has not been raised, then our preaching is in vain; your faith also is in vain. Moreover we are even found to be false witnesses of God, because we witnessed against God that He raised Christ, whom He did not raise, if in fact the dead are not raised. For if the dead are not raised, not even Christ has been raised; and if Christ has not been raised, your faith is worthless (1 Corinthians 15:13-17).

OBSERVATION 4–Intelligent Faith

My fourth observation on Christianity was quite an eye-opener. The more I studied the historical/biblical Christian faith the more I realized it was an "intelligent faith." When an individual in the Scriptures was called upon to exercise faith, it was to be that intelligent faith. Jesus said, "You shall know the truth [not ignore it] and the truth shall make you free" (John 8:32).

A lawyer asked Jesus, "Which is the greatest commandment?"

Jesus replied, "[To] love the Lord your God with all your heart . . . and with all your mind" (Matthew 22:37).

Never is an individual called upon to commit intellectual suicide in trusting Christ as Savior and Lord. Instead, a believer is instructed to be ready always to give an answer (an intelligent one) as to why he believes (1 Peter 3:15).

In his work, *I Believe in the Resurrection,* Dr. George Eldon Ladd observes that faith does not mean a leap in the dark, an irrational credulity, a believing against evidences and against reason. It means believing in the light of historical facts, consistent with evidences, on the basis of witnesses.

OBSERVATION 5–Historical Criteria

The resurrection of Christ must be examined by the same criteria as is any other past event in history. The faith of the early church was founded on experiences in the factual realm. For example, the followers of Christ said He showed Himself alive to them by "many convincing proofs" (Acts 1:3). Luke used the word *tekmerion.* That connotes a "demonstrable proof."

It became apparent to me that my research would have to include the historical criteria for truth if I were to discover what really happened that first Easter.

Sufficient Evidence Needed

Wolfhart Pannenberg is a professor of systematic theology at the University of Munich, Germany. He has been concerned primarily with questions of the relationship between faith and history. This brilliant scholar says, "Whether the resurrection of Jesus took place or not is an historical question, and . . . at this point is inescapable. And so the question has to be decided on the level of historical argument." 62/10

The evidence must be approached with an honest, fair view of history and the investigation must not be prejudiced by preconceived notions or conclusions. There is a compelling need to let the evidence speak for itself. Historian Ronald Sider writes about the need for objectivity in historical research:

> What does the critical historian do when his evidence points very strongly to the reality of an event which contradicts his expectations and goes against the naturalistic view of reality? I submit that he must follow his critically analyzed sources. It is unscientific to begin with the philosophical presupposition that miracles cannot occur. Unless we avoid such one-sided presuppositions, historical interpretation becomes mere propaganda.
>
> We have a right to demand good evidence for an alleged event which we have not experienced, but we dare not judge reality by our limited experience. And I would suggest that we have good evidence for the resurrection of Jesus of Nazareth. 71/27-31

Proper Approach

The Erlangen historian Ethelbert Stauffer gives further suggestions on how to approach history:

> What do we (as historians) do when we experience surprises which run counter to all our expectations, perhaps all our convictions and even our period's whole understanding of truth? We say as one great historian used to say in such instances: "It is surely possible." And why not? For the critical historian nothing is impossible. 72/17

Historian Philip Schaff adds to the above: "The purpose of the historian is not to construct a history from preconceived notions and to adjust it to his own liking, but to reproduce it from the best evidences and to let it speak for itself." 69/175

The ultimate test historically concerning the resurrection is whether the purported facts are supported by the evidence.

NOTE: Much of what follows is based on the eye-witness reports recorded in the Gospel narratives of Matthew, Mark, Luke and John. For evidence concerning the reliability of this material, see "Section I: The Bible and Its Reliability" of this book. For further evidence of the reliability of the resurrection reports in the New Testament, see *He Walked Among Us*, pp. 278-90. The points covered there are: (1)the early origination of the reports, including evidence that 1 Corinthians 15:3-8 originated within three years of the death and resurrection of Jesus; (2) the historical nature of the reports; and (3) the fact that the actual resurrection of Jesus is the only way to explain the early Christian belief in the resurrection of Jesus.

Security Precautions (RF/37-60)

SECURITY PRECAUTION 1—The Trial

Jesus was brought for trial before the Roman governor, Pontius Pilate. All available evidence shows Pilate to have been an extremely cruel and merciless despot. Philo records that he was responsible "for countless atrocities and numerous executions without any previous trial." **63/38**

Six Trials

One needs to realize that Jesus Christ went through six distinct trials. One was before Annas, the high priest (John 18:13), another was before Caiaphas (Matthew 26:57), the third before the Sanhedrin (Matthew 26:59), the fourth before Pilate (Matthew 27:2), the fifth before Herod (Luke 23:7), and the sixth was back before Pilate (Luke 23:11-25). There were three Jewish trials and three Roman trials.

The Jewish legal system was made up of two different Sanhedrins. One Sanhedrin was composed of 23 members who tried cases involving capital punishment. **86/335** The other Sanhedrin of 71 could serve as a trial court for cases involving the head of state, the high priest, or for offenses against the state or the Temple. The Sanhedrin of 71 could not try a case involving capital punishment. It was probably the Sanhedrin of 23 that tried Jesus. One was located in every major city in Judea. **86/n.p.**

Finally after three Jewish trials and three Roman trials, the Jewish authorities, in conjunction with the Roman authorities, delivered Jesus to be crucified (Matthew 27:26).

Various "security precautions" were taken to make sure that when Jesus was dead He would remain dead and buried.

SECURITY PRECAUTION 2—Death by Crucifixion

Alexander the Great introduced crucifixion into the Mediterranean world—mainly Egypt and Carthage. From all indications, the Romans learned the practice from the Carthaginians.

A Cruel Death

Death by crucifixion developed into one of the world's most disgraceful and cruel methods of torture. Cicero called it "the most cruel and hideous of tortures." **15/64** Will Durant wrote that "even the Romans . . . pitied the victims." **21/572**

Flavius Josephus, the Jewish historian, who was an advisor to Titus during the siege of Jerusalem, had observed many crucifixions and called them "the most wretched deaths." **44**

The Custom of Whipping

After the verdict of crucifixion was pronounced by the court, it was customary to tie the accused to a post at the tribunal. The criminal was stripped of his clothes, then severely whipped by the lictors or scourgers.

The whip, known as a flagrum, had a sturdy handle to which were attached long leather thongs of varying lengths. Sharp, jagged pieces of bone and lead were woven into them. The Jews were limited by their law to 40 lashes. The Pharisees, with their emphasis on strict adherence to the law, would limit their lashes to 39, so that if they miscounted they would not break their law. The Romans had no such limitations. Out of disgust or anger, the Romans could totally ignore the Jewish limitation, and probably did so in the case of Jesus.

A Medical Perspective

Dr. C. Truman Davis, a medical doctor who has meticulously studied crucifixion from a medical perspective, describes the effects of the Roman flagrum used in whipping:

> The heavy whip is brought down with full force again and again across [a person's] shoulders, back and legs. At first the heavy thongs cut through the skin only. Then, as the blows continue, they cut deeper into the sub-cutaneous tissues, producing first an oozing of blood from the capillaries and veins of the skin, and finally spurting arterial bleeding from vessels in the underlying muscles. The small balls of lead first produce large, deep bruises which are broken open by subsequent blows. Finally the skin of the back is hanging in long ribbons and the entire area is an unrecognizable mass of torn, bleeding tissue. When it is determined by the centurion in charge that the prisoner is near death, the beating is finally stopped. 18/185

Eusebius, a third-century historian, confirms Dr. Davis's description when he writes: "The sufferer's veins were laid bare, and the very muscles, sinews, and bowels of the victim were open to exposure." 24/n.p.

A Crown of Thorns

After placing the crown of thorns on Christ's head, they began to mock Him saying, "Hail, the King of the Jews." They also spit on Him and beat Him with a rod. Then they led Him away to be crucified.

The Crossbar Burden

A man condemned to be crucified had to carry his own crossbar from prison to the place of his execution.

Dr. Pierre Barbet points out that "they began to use a long piece of wood, which was used for barring doors and was called the *patibulum* (from *patere,* to be open)." 4/44 The patibulum weighed approximately 110 pounds and was strapped to the victim's shoulders.

Crucifixion With Nails

Upon reaching the execution site, the condemned person was nailed or bound by ropes to the cross. Many have questioned the historical accuracy of the nailing of the hands and feet. The reason for this skepticism is that there has been almost zero evidence of it in history.

Dr. J. W. Hewitt, in his *Harvard Theological Review* article entitled, "The Use of Nails in the Crucifixion," said, "To sum up, there is astonishingly little evidence that the feet of a crucified person were ever pierced by nails." 39/29-45 He went on to say that the victim's hands and feet were bound by ropes to the cross.

For years Dr. Hewitt's statement was quoted as the final word. The conclusion, therefore, was that the New Testament account of Christ being nailed to the cross was false and misleading. Crucifixion by use of nails was considered legendary. It was believed that nails would have ripped the flesh and could not have supported a body on the cross.

A Dead Man Speaks

Then, a revolutionary archaeological discovery was made in June 1968. Archeologist V. Tzaferis, under the direction of the Israeli Department of Antiquities and Museums, discovered four cave-tombs at the site of Giv'at ha-mivtar (Ras el-Masaref) just north of Jerusalem near Mt. Scopus.

In Ossuary 4 of Tomb I, inscribed with the name Yohanan Ben Ha'galgal, were found the bones of an adult male and of a child. A large 7-inch spike had been driven through the heel bone, and both legs had been fractured. Haas reported: "Both the heel bones were found transfixed by a large iron nail. The shins were found intentionally broken. Death caused by crucifixion." 34/39

The bones in Ossuary 4 confirm another passage in the New Testament:

> The soldiers therefore came, and broke the legs of the first man, and of the man who was crucified with Him; but coming to Jesus, when they saw that He was already dead, they did not break His legs (John 19:32,33).

Purpose for Breaking the Legs

To understand why the legs were broken, one must study the means of execution. The soldiers would feel for the depression at the front of the wrist, then drive the heavy wrought-iron spike through at that point. Next, the legs were placed together and a large nail was driven through them. The knees were left moderately flexed, and a seat (known as a *sedecula*) was attached to the cross for the buttocks of the victim.

Dr. Truman Davis, the M.D. whom I quoted before, describes what happens to the human body after a short time of exposure on the cross:

> As the arms fatigue, great waves of cramps sweep over the muscles, knotting them in deep, relentless, throbbing pain. With these cramps comes the inability to push Himself upward. Hanging by His arms, the pectoral muscles are paralyzed and the intercostal muscles are unable to act. Air can be drawn into the lungs, but cannot be exhaled. Jesus fights to raise Himself in order to get even one short breath. Finally, carbon dioxide builds up in the lungs and in the bloodstream and the cramps partially subside. Spasmodically, He is able to push Himself upward to exhale and bring in the life-giving oxygen. 18/186

After a while, orthostatic collapse through insufficient blood circulating to the brain and heart would follow. The only way the victim could avoid this was to push up by his feet so the blood could be returned to some degree of circulation in the upper part of his body.

When the authorities wanted to hasten death or terminate the torture, the victim's legs were broken below the knees with a club. This prevented him from pushing himself upward to relieve the tension on the pectoral or chest muscles. Either rapid suffocation or coronary insufficiency followed. In the case of Christ, the legs of the two thieves crucified with Him were broken, but Christ's were not because the executioners observed He already was dead.

Spilling of Blood and Water

One of the executioners thrust a spear into Christ's side, and, as recorded in John 19:34, "Immediately there came out blood and water."

Davis relates that there was "an escape of watery fluid from the sac surrounding the heart. We, therefore, have rather conclusive post-mortem evidence that [Christ] died, not the usual crucifixion death by suffocation, but of heart failure due to shock and constriction of the heart by fluid in the pericardium." 18/186

A Job Well Done

Pilate required certification of Christ's death before the body could be turned over to Joseph of Arimathea. 21/573 He consented to Christ's being removed from the cross only after four executioners had certified His death.

The efficiency of execution by crucifixion was quite well-known in the time of Christ. Dr. Paul L. Maier, professor of ancient history at Western Michigan University, writes,

> True, there is a recorded instance of a victim being taken down from a cross and surviving. The Jewish historian Josephus, who had gone over to the Roman side in the rebellion of A.D. 66, discovered three of his friends

being crucified. He asked the Roman general Titus to reprieve them, and they were immediately removed from their crosses.

Still, two of the three died anyway, even though they apparently had been crucified only a short time. In Jesus' case, however, there were the additional complications of scourging and exhaustion, to say nothing of the great spear thrust that pierced His rib cage and probably ruptured His pericardium. Romans were grimly efficient about crucifixions: Victims did *not* escape with their lives. 54/122

SECURITY PRECAUTION 3–Solid Rock Tomb

The body of Christ was placed in a new tomb, hewn out of a solid rock, in a private burial area. Jewish tombs usually had an entrance 4-1/2 to 5 feet high.

SECURITY PRECAUTION 4–Jewish Burial

The New Testament is very clear that the burial of Christ followed the customs of the Jews.

In preparing a body for burial, the Jews would place it on a stone table in the burial chamber. The body first would be washed with warm water.

It was the custom, as verified in the New Testament, to prepare the corpse (after cleansing) with various types of aromatic spices.

In the case of Christ's burial, 75 pounds of spices were used. One might regard this as substantial, but it was no great amount for a leader. For example, Gamaliel, grandson of the distinguished Jewish scholar Hillel, also was a contemporary of Jesus. Saul of Tarsus studied under him. When Gameliel died, 86 pounds of spices were used in his burial. Josephus, the Jewish historian, records that when Herod died, it required 500 servants to carry the spices for his body. 43 So the 75 pounds for Jesus was not at all unusual.

After all the members of the body were straightened, the corpse was clothed in grave vestments made out of white linen. There could not be the slightest ornamentation or stain on the cloth. 5/261 The grave linens were sewn together by women. No knots were permitted. For some this was to indicate that the mind of the dead was "disentangled of the cares of this life" 5/261–to others, it indicated the continuity of the soul through eternity. No individual could be buried in fewer than three separate garments.

At this point, the aromatic spices, composed of a fragrant wood pounded into a dust known as aloes, were mixed with a gummy substance known as myrrh. Starting at the feet, they would wrap to the armpits, put the arms down, then wrap to the neck. A separate piece was wrapped around the head. I would estimate an encasement weighing a total of between 92 and 95 pounds.

John Chrysostom, in the fourth century A.D., commented that "the myrrh used was a drug which adheres so closely to the body that the graveclothes could not easily be removed." 14/321

SECURITY PRECAUTION 5–Very Large Stone

Matthew records in his writings that a large stone was rolled against the front of the tomb (Matthew 27:60). Mark said the stone was extremely large (Mark 16:1-4). In today's language, he would have said, "Wow! Get a loada' that rock!"

Just how large was that "Wow, get a loada' that rock" stone?

In the Mark 16:4 portion of the Bezae manuscripts in the Cambridge Library in England, a parenthetical statement was found that adds, "And when He was laid there, he (Joseph) put against the tomb a stone which *20 men could not roll away.*"

The significance of this statement is realized when one considers the rules for transcribing manuscripts. It was the custom that if a copier was emphasizing his own interpretation, he would write his thought in the margin and not include it within the text. One might conclude, therefore, that the insert in the text was copied from a text even closer to the time of Christ, perhaps, a first-century manuscript. The phrase, then, could have been recorded by an eyewitness who was impressed with the enormity of the stone which was rolled against Jesus' sepulcher.

One and a Half to Two Tons

After my lecture at Georgia Tech, two engineering professors went on a tour of Israel with other Georgia Tech faculty members. They remembered the comments I had made about the large size of the stone. So, being engineers, they considered the type of stone used in the time of Christ and calculated the size needed to roll against a 4-1/2 to 5-foot doorway.

Later, they wrote me a letter containing all the technical terms, but they put their conclusions in simple language on the back of it.

They said a stone of that size would have to have had a minimum weight of 1-1/2 to 2 tons. No wonder Matthew and Mark said the stone was extremely large.

One might ask, "If the stone were that big, how did Joseph move it into position in the first place?" He simply gave it a push and let gravity do the rest. It had been held in place with a wedge as it sat in a groove or trench that sloped down to the front of the tomb. When the wedge was removed, the heavy circular rock just rolled into position.

SECURITY PRECAUTION 6–Roman Security

Jewish officials panicked, because thousands were turning to Christ. To avoid a political problem, it was to the advantage of both the Romans and the Jews to make sure Jesus was put away for good.

So the chief priests and Pharisees gathered together and said to Pilate, "Sir, we remember that when He was still alive that deceiver said, 'After three days I am to rise again.' Therefore, give orders for the grave to be made secure until the third day, lest the disciples come and steal Him away and say to the people, 'He has risen from the dead,' and the last deception will be worse than the first" (Matthew 27:63).

Pilate said to them, "You have a guard; go, make it as secure as you know how." And so "they went and made the grave secure, and along with the guard they set a seal on the stone" (verse 65).

Some people would argue that Pilate said, "Look, you have your Temple police. You take your Temple police, and go make it secure."

The Temple Police

Now, if you want to say it's a Temple guard, you need to realize who made up that guard. It consisted of a group of 10 Levites who were placed on duty at different places at the Temple. The total number of men on duty was 270. This represented 27 units of 10 each. The military discipline of the Temple guard was quite good. In fact, at night, if the captain approached a guard member who was asleep, he was beaten and burned with his own clothes. A member of the guard also was forbidden to sit down or lean against something when he was on duty.

A Roman Guard

However, I am convinced it was the Roman guard that was placed at the grave of Christ to secure it.

A. T. Robertson, noted Greek scholar, says this phrase is in the present imperative and can refer only to a Roman guard, and not the Temple police. According to him, Pilate literally said, "Have a guard."

Robertson adds that the Latin form *koustodia* occurs as far back as the Oxyrhynchus papyrus in reference to the Roman guard. The Jews knew Pilate wanted to keep the peace, so they were sure he'd give them what they wanted.

What was the Roman guard?

A Roman "custodian" did a lot more than care for a building. The word "custodian" represented the guard unit of the Roman Legion. This unit was probably one of the greatest offensive and defensive fighting machines ever conceived.

One helpful source for understanding the importance of the Roman guard is Flavius Vegitius Renatus. His friends called him Vegitius. A military historian, he lived several hundred years after the time of Christ when the Roman army started to deteriorate in its discipline. He wrote a manual to the Roman Emperor Valentinian to encourage him to instill the methods of offensive and defensive warfare used by the Romans during the time of Christ. Called *The Military Institutes of the Romans,* it is a classic today.

Vegitius wanted to see the Roman armies restored to the efficiency and might which characterized them at the time of Christ. These armies were great because they were highly disciplined. He wrote, "Victory in war does not depend entirely upon numbers or mere courage; only skill and discipline will insure it. We find that the Romans owed . . . the conquest of the world to no other cause than continual military training, exact observation of discipline in their camps and unwearied cultivation of the other arts of war."

There are two other excellent sources. At Indiana University, Dr. George Currie did his doctoral dissertation on the Roman custodian, and Dr. Smith edited a dictionary entitled, *Dictionary of Greek and Roman Antiquities.*

The Force of the Roman Guard

These and other sources point out that the Roman guard was not a one-, two-, or three-man force. Supercilious pictures of the tomb of Jesus Christ show one or two men standing around with wooden spears and mini-skirts. That's really laughable.

A Roman guard unit was a 4- to 16-man security force. Each man was trained to protect six feet of ground. The 16 men in a square of 4 on each side were supposed to be able to protect 36 yards against an entire battalion and hold it.

Normally what they did was this: 4 men were placed immediately in front of what they were to protect. The other 12 were asleep in a semi-circle in front of them with their heads pointing in. To steal what these guards were protecting, thieves would first have to walk over those who were asleep. Every four hours, another unit of 4 was awakened, and those who had been awake went to sleep.

They would rotate this way around the clock.

Historian Dr. Paul Maier writes, "Peter would be guarded by four squads of four men each when imprisoned by Herod Agrippa (Acts 12), so sixteen would be a minimum number expected *outside* a prison. Guards in ancient times always slept in shifts, so it would have been virtually impossible for a raiding party to have stepped over all their sleeping faces" without waking them. 54/111

High Priest Offers Bribe

Even Matthew records that it was a multi-man force when he wrote that *"some* of the guard came into the city and reported to the chief priests all that had happened" (Matthew 28:11).

A critic at this point might say, "See, they came to the high priest. It shows that they were the Temple guard." The context is clear, however, that they came to the high priest because he had influence with the Roman authority and because it was the only possible way to save their necks. The high priest tried to bribe them (which would have been a mockery if they had been Temple police). He gave them money and told them what to tell the people. When the news reached Pilate, the high priest said he would keep them from being killed. Normally, they would receive the death penalty, because the story was to be that they had fallen asleep while guarding the tomb.

It is significant that the governor had to be satisfied, because I have not been able to find any account in history—secular, Jewish or Christian—indicating that the Roman governor had anything at all to do with the Temple police.

Even if the guard at the tomb had been made up of Temple police, the security would have been no less thorough.

A Fighting Machine

T. G. Tucker, in his book, *Life in the Roman World of Nero and St. Paul,* describes one of these Roman guards:

> Over his breast, and with flaps over the shoulders, he will wear a corset of leather covered with hoop-like layers, or maybe scales, of iron or bronze. On his head will be a plain pot-like helmet, or skull-cap, of iron.
>
> In his right hand he will carry the famous Roman pike. This is a stout weapon, over 6 feet in length, consisting of a sharp iron head fixed in a wooden shaft, and the soldier may either charge with it as a bayonet, or he may hurl it like a javelin and then fight at close quarters with his sword.
>
> On the left arm is a shield, which may be of various shapes. The shield is not only carried by means of a handle, but may be supported by a belt over the right shoulder. In order to be out of the way of the shield, the sword—a thrusting rather than a slashing weapon, approaching 3 feet in length—is hung at the right side by a belt passing over the left shoulder .... On the left side, the soldier wears a dagger at his girdle. 79/340-42

Polybius, the Greek historian of the second century B.C., records that, in addition to all this,

> the men are adorned with a crown made of feathers and with three upright feathers, either purple or black, about a foot and a half high; when they add these on the head along with the other arms, the man appears twice as big as he really is, and his appearance is striking and terrifying to the enemy.

> The men of the lowest property classes also wear a bronze plate, 8 inches square, which they place in front of their chests and call the heart guard; this completes their armament. But those worth more than 10,000 drachmae, instead of wearing the heart guard, along with the rest of their equipment, wear a coat of mail. 66/37-38

SECURITY PRECAUTION 7–Roman Seal

Matthew records that along with the guard they set a "seal on the stone" (Matthew 27:66). A. T. Robertson says this could be placed on the stone only in the presence of the Roman guards who were left in charge. Vegitius indicates the same thing. The purpose of this procedure was to prevent anyone from tampering with the grave's contents.

After the guard inspected the tomb and rolled the stone in place, a cord was stretched across the rock. This was fastened at either end with sealing clay. Finally, the clay packs were stamped with the official signet of the Roman governor.

A parallel to this is seen in Daniel: "And a stone was brought and laid over the mouth of the den; and the king sealed it with his own signet ring and with the signet rings of his nobles, so that nothing might be changed in regard to Daniel" (Daniel 6:17).

Purpose of the Seal

Henry Sumner Maine, member of the Supreme Council of India, formerly regius professor of the civil law at the University of Cambridge, speaking on the legal authority attached to a Roman seal, said, "Seals in antiquity were actually considered as a mode of authentication."

To authenticate something simply means to prove that it is real or genuine. So this seal on Jesus' tomb was a public testimony that Jesus' body was actually there. In addition, because the seal was Roman, it verified the fact that His body was protected from vandals by nothing less than the power and authority of the Roman Empire.

Anyone trying to move the stone from the tomb's entrance would have broken the seal and thus incurred the wrath of Roman law and power.

Grave Robbers Warned

In Nazareth, a marble slab was discovered with a very interesting inscription—a warning to grave robbers. It was written in Greek and says, "Ordinance of Caesar. It is my pleasure that graves and tombs remain perpetually undisturbed for those who have made them for the cult of their ancestors or children or members of their house. If, however, anyone charges that another has either demolished them, or has in any other way extracted the buried, or has maliciously transferred them to other places in order to wrong them, or has displaced the sealing or other stones, against such a one I order that a trial be instituted, as in respect of the gods, so in regard to the cult of mortals. For it shall be much more obligatory to honor the buried. Let it be absolutely forbidden for anyone to disturb them. In case of violation I desire that the offender be sentenced to capital punishment on charge of violation of sepulcher." 54/119

Maier observes, "All previous Roman edicts concerning grave violation set only a large fine, and one wonders what presumed serious infraction could have led the Roman government to stiffen the penalty precisely in Palestine and to erect a notice regarding it specifically in Nazareth or the vicinity." 54/118-19 It well could be a response to the commotion caused by Christ's resurrection.

Facts to Be Reckoned With (RF/64-74)

Now, something happened. Something happened almost two thousand years ago that changed the course of history from B.C. (Before Christ) to A.D. (the Latin *Anno Domini*—the year of our Lord).

That "something" was so dramatic it completely changed eleven men's lives, so that all but one died a martyr's death.

That something was an empty tomb! An empty tomb that a 15-minute walk from the center of Jerusalem would have confirmed or disproved.

Even after the two thousand years since that time, mankind hasn't forgotten the empty tomb nor the resurrection appearances of Jesus Christ.

If you wish to rationalize away the events surrounding Christ and His resurrection, you must deal with certain imponderables. In fact, you might say that both the Jews and the Romans outwitted themselves when they took so many precautions to make sure Jesus was dead and remained in the grave. These "security precautions"—taken with the trial, crucifixion, burial, entombment, sealing and the guarding of Christ's tomb—make it very difficult for critics to defend their position that Christ did not rise from the dead!

Consider these seven facts:

FACT 1–Broken Roman Seal

The first obvious fact was the breaking of the seal that stood for the power and authority of the Roman Empire. The consequences of breaking the seal were severe. The FBI and CIA of the Roman Empire were called into action to find the man or men responsible. When they were apprehended, it meant automatic execution by crucifixion upside down. Your guts ran into your throat. So people feared the breaking of the seal. Even the disciples displayed signs of cowardice, and hid themselves.

FACT 2–The Empty Tomb

Another obvious fact after the resurrection was the empty tomb. The disciples of Christ did not go off to Athens or Rome to preach Christ raised from the dead; they went right back to the city of Jerusalem where, if what they were teaching were false, their message would have been disproved. The resurrection could not have been maintained for a moment in Jerusalem if the tomb had not been empty.

Dr. Paul Maier says,

> Where did Christianity first begin? To this the answer must be: "Only one spot on earth–the city of Jerusalem." But this is the very *last* place it could have started if Jesus' tomb remained occupied, since anyone producing a dead Jesus would have driven a wooden stake through the heart of an incipient Christianity inflamed by His supposed resurrection.
>
> What happened in Jerusalem seven weeks after the first Easter could have taken place only if Jesus' body were somehow missing from Joseph's tomb, for otherwise the Temple establishment, in its embroglio with the Apostles, would simply have aborted the movement by making a brief trip over to the sepulcher of Joseph of Arimathea and unveiling exhibit A. They did not do this, because they knew the tomb was empty. Their official explanation for it–that the disciples had stolen the body–was an admission that the sepulcher was indeed vacant. 55/5

There are both Jewish and Roman sources and traditions that acknowledge an empty tomb. These sources range from the Jewish historian Josephus to a compilation of fifth-century Jewish writings called the *Toledoth Jeshu.* Maier calls this "positive evidence from a hostile source, which is the strongest kind of historical evidence. In essence, this means that if a source admits a fact decidedly *not* in its favor, then that fact is genuine." 55/5

Gamaliel, who was a member of the Sanhedrin, put forth the suggestion that the Christian movement was of God (Acts 5:34-42); he could not have done this if the tomb had been occupied, or if the Sanhedrin had known the whereabouts of Christ's body.

Even Justin Martyr in his *Dialogue With Trypho* relates that the Jerusalem authorities sent special representatives throughout the Mediterranean world to counteract the story of the empty tomb with the explanation that His followers stole the body. Why would the Jewish authorities bribe the Roman guard and propagate the "stolen body" explanation if the tomb was occupied? Historian Ron Sider concluded that: "If the Christians and their Jewish opponents both agreed that the tomb was empty, we have little choice but to accept the empty tomb as an historical fact." 71/29

FACT 3—Large Stone Moved

On that Sunday morning, the first thing that impressed the people who approached the tomb was the unusual position of that 1-1/2- to 2-ton stone that had been lodged in front of the doorway. All the Gospel writers mentioned the removal of the large stone.

Up an Incline

For example, in Matthew 27, it is said that a "large stone was *rolled* against the entrance of the tomb." Here the Greek word used for roll is *kulio,* meaning "to roll." Mark used the same root word *kulio.* However, in Mark 16, he added a preposition to explain the position of the stone after the resurrection.

In Greek, as in English, to change the direction of a verb or to intensify it, you add a preposition. He added the preposition *ana,* which means "up or upward." So, *anakulio* can mean "to roll something up a slope or an incline." For Mark, then, to have used that verb, there would have had to be a slope or an incline coming down to the front of that tomb.

Away From

In fact, that stone was so far "up a slope" that Luke used the same root word *kulio,* but added a different preposition, *apo. Apo* can mean, according to the Greek lexicons, "a separation from," in the sense of "a distance from." *Apokulio,* then, means to roll one object away from another object in a sense of "separation" or "distance from it." Now, they saw the stone moved away in a sense of distance *from* "what"?

Let's go back to Mark 16. On Sunday morning, the women were coming to the tomb.

You might say, "Wait a minute! Why were those women coming to the tomb Sunday morning?" One reason was to anoint the body over the graveclothes with a mixture of spices and perfume. Another might ask, "Why would they come since the Roman security unit was there guarding the grave?"

That's quite simple. The guard did not examine the body and secure the sepulcher until Saturday afternoon. On Friday afternoon the women had watched as the body was prepared in a private burial area. They lived in the suburb of Bethany and therefore were not aware of the Roman and Jewish actions about putting extra security at the place of Christ's burial.

Let's go back to Mark 16 again.

The women are saying, "Who will roll away the stone for us from the entrance of the tomb?" Here, they used the Greek word for entrance That's logical, isn't it? *But,* when they got there they said, "Who rolled the stone away from . . . ?" and here they changed the Greek word for "the entrance" to the word used for the entire massive sepulcher. *Apokulio,* then, means "away from" in the sense of at a "distance from the entire massive sepulcher."

Picked Up and Carried

In fact, the stone was in such a position up a slope away from the entire massive sepulcher that John (chapter 20) used a different Greek verb, *airo,* which (according to the Arndt and Gingrish Lexicon) means "to pick something up and carry it away."

Now, I ask you, if the disciples had wanted to come in, tiptoe around the sleeping guards, then roll the stone over and steal the body, why would they have moved a 1-1/2- to 2-ton stone up a slope away from the entire massive sepulcher to such a position that it looked like someone had picked it up and carried it away? Those soldiers would have had to be deaf not to have heard that stone being moved.

FACT 4–Roman Guard Goes AWOL

The Roman guard fled. They left their place of responsibility. This has to be explained away because the military discipline of the Romans was exceptionally good. Justin, in his *Digest #49,* mentions all offenses which required the penalty of death: a scout remaining with the enemy (-3.4), desertion (-3.11; -5.1-3), losing or disposing of one's arms (-3.130), disobedience in war time (-3.15), going over the wall or rampart (-3.17), starting a mutiny (-3.19), refusing to protect an officer or deserting one's post (-3.22), a drafted man hiding from service (-4.2), murder (-4.5), laying hands on a superior or insult to a general (-6.1), leading flight when the example would influence others (-6.3), betraying plans to the enemy (-6.4; -7), wounding a fellow soldier with a sword (-6.6), disabling self or attempting suicide without reasonable excuse (-6.7), leaving the night watch (-10.1), breaking the centurion's staff or striking him when being punished (-13.4), escaping guard house (-13.5), and disturbing the peace (-16.1). To the above, one can add "falling asleep." If it was not apparent which soldier had failed in duty, then lots were drawn to see who would be punished with death for the guard unit's failure.

Fear of Punishment

One way a guard was put to death was by being stripped of his clothes, then burned alive in a fire started with the garments. The entire unit certainly would not have fallen asleep with that threat hanging over their heads. The history of Roman discipline and security testifies to the fact that if the tomb had not been empty the soldiers never would have left their position, nor would they have gone to the high priest. The fear of the wrath of their superiors and the possibility of the death penalty meant they paid close attention to the most minute details of their job. Dr. George Curie, who studied carefully the military discipline of the Romans, wrote that fear of punishment "produced flawless attention to duty, especially in the night watches." 16/41-43

Dr. Bill White is in charge of the Garden Tomb in Jerusalem. His responsibilities have caused him to study quite extensively the resurrection and the events following the first Easter. White makes several critical observations about the Jewish authorities bribing the Roman guard.

> If the stone were simply rolled to one side of the tomb, as would be necessary to enter it, then they might be justified in accusing the men of sleeping at their posts, and in punishing them severely. If the men protested that the earthquake broke the seal and that the stone rolled back under the vibration, they would still be liable to punishment for behavior which might be labeled cowardice.
>
> But these responsibilities do not meet the case. There was some undeniable evidence which made it impossible for the chief priests to bring any charge against the guard. The Jewish authorities must have visited the scene, examined the stone, and recognized its position as making it humanly impossible for their men to have permitted its removal. No twist of human ingenuity could provide an adequate answer or scapegoat and so they were forced to bribe the guard and seek to hush things up. 83/n.p.

FACT 5–Graveclothes Tell a Tale

In a literal sense, the tomb was not actually empty. Instead, an amazing phenomenon occurred. After visiting the grave and seeing the stone rolled away, the women ran back and told the disciples. Then Peter and John took off running. John outran Peter, and upon arriving at the tomb he did not enter. Instead, he leaned over and looked in and saw something so startling that he immediately believed.

He looked over to the place where the body of Jesus had lain. There were graveclothes, in the form of a body, slightly caved in and empty–like the empty chrysalis of a caterpillar's cocoon. That was enough to make a believer out of anybody! He never did get over it!

The first thing that stuck in the minds of the disciples was not the empty tomb–but the empty graveclothes, undisturbed in their form and position.

FACT 6–Appearances of Christ Confirmed

On several occasions, Christ appeared alive after the cataclysmic events of that first Easter.

A Principle to Remember

When studying an event in history, it is important to investigate whether enough people who were participants or eyewitnesses to the event were alive when the facts about the event were published. This is helpful to validate the accuracy of the published report. If the number is substantial, the event can be fairly well established. For instance, if we all witness a murder, and in a week the police report turns out to be composed of fabricated lies, we as eyewitnesses can refute it.

In other words, when a book is written about an event, the accuracy of its contents can be validated if enough people are alive at the time it is published who have been either eyewitnesses of, or participants in, the events recorded.

Several very important factors often are overlooked when investigating Christ's post-resurrection appearances to individuals. The first is the large number of witnesses of Christ after that first Sunday morning.

Fifty Hours of Eyewitnesses

One of the earliest records of Christ's appearing after the resurrection is by Paul (1 Corinthians 15). The apostle appeals to his audience's knowledge of the fact that Christ had been seen by more than five hundred people at one time. Paul reminds them that the majority of these people were still alive and could be questioned.

Dr. Ewin M. Yamauchi, associate professor of history at Miami University in Oxford, Ohio, emphasizes:

> What gives a special authority to the list [of witnesses] as historical evidence is the reference to most of the five hundred brethren being still alive. St. Paul says in effect, "If you do not believe me, you can ask them." 85/13

Let's take the more than five hundred witnesses who saw Jesus alive after His death and burial and place them in a courtroom. Do you realize that if each of these five hundred people were to testify only six minutes each, including cross-examination, you would have an amazing fifty hours of firsthand eyewitness testimony? Add to this the testimony of many other eyewitnesses and you could well have the largest and most lopsided trial in history.

Variety of People

The second factor often overlooked is the variety of locations and people involved in Jesus' appearances.

Professor Merrill C. Tenney of Wheaton College writes:

> It is noteworthy that these appearances are not stereotyped. No two of

> them are exactly alike. The appearance to Mary Magdalene occurred in early morning; that to the travelers to Emmaus in the afternoon; and to the apostles in the evening, probably after dark. He appeared to Mary in the open air. Mary was alone when she saw Him; the disciples were together in a group; and Paul records that on one occasion He appeared to more than five hundred at one time (1 Corinthians 15:6).
>
> The reactions also were varied. Mary was overwhelmed with emotion; the disciples were frightened; Thomas was obstinately incredulous when told of the Lord's resurrection, but worshiped Him when He manifested Himself. Each occasion had its own peculiar atmosphere and characteristics, and revealed some different quality of the risen Lord. 77/59

In no way can anyone say His appearances were stereotyped.

Hostile Viewers

A third factor very crucial to interpreting Christ's appearance is that He also appeared to those who were hostile or unconvinced. Over and over again I have read or heard people comment that Jesus was seen alive after His death and burial only by His friends and followers. Using this argument, they attempt to water down the overwhelming impact of the eyewitness accounts—but this line of reasoning is so pathetic it hardly deserves comment.

No author or informed individual would regard Saul of Tarsus to have been a follower of Christ. The facts show the exact opposite. He despised Christ and persecuted Christ's followers (Acts 8:1; 9:1,2; Philippians 3:5,6). For Paul it was a life-shattering experience when Christ appeared to him (Acts 9:3-6). Although Paul was not at the time a disciple, he later became one of the greatest witnesses for the truth of the resurrection.

No one acquainted with the facts can accurately say that Jesus appeared to just "an insignificant few."

FACT 7—Women Saw Him First

Another authenticating feature of the resurrection narrative is that the first appearances of the risen Christ were not to His disciples, but rather to women—to Mary Magdalene and the other women. This must have been an embarrassment to the apostles, Christ's inner circle. They were likely quite jealous.

According to Jewish principles of legal evidence women were invalid witnesses. They did not have a right to give testimony in a court of law.

Unreliable Testimony

Dr. Maier accurately observes that since the testimony of a woman was deemed unreliable, the "initial reaction of the Eleven was understandably one of suspicion and disbelief. Again, if the resurrection accounts had been manufactured . . . women would *never* have been included in the story, at least, not as first witnesses." 54/98

> **NOTE:** For answers to several attempted explanations of the resurrection of Jesus, see *The Resurrection,* pages 75-103.

It Changed Their Lives (RF/109-11)

The changed lives of those early Christian believers is one of the most telling testimonies to the fact of the resurrection. We must ask ourselves: What motivated them to go everywhere proclaiming the message of the risen Christ?

Had there been visible benefits accruing to them from their efforts—such as prestige, wealth or increased social status—we might logically account for their actions. As a reward, however, for their wholehearted and total allegiance to this "risen Christ," these early Christians were beaten, stoned to death, thrown to the lions, tortured, crucified and subjected to every conceivable method of stopping them from talking. Yet they were the most peaceful of men, who physically forced their beliefs on no one. Rather they laid down their very lives as the ultimate proof of their complete confidence in the truth of their message.

Those Hardest to Convince

There was the skeptical family of Jesus (John 7:1-5). His brothers did not believe in Him. They were embarrassed to hear their brother say to the people, "I am the way, the truth and the life, no man cometh unto the Father but by Me," and "I am the vine, you are the branches," and "I'm the shepherd, you are the sheep" (John 14:6; 15:5; 10:11). What would you do if your brother did that?

There was James, His brother. He was found in the company of the Pharisees. James and his brothers mocked Jesus.

However, after Jesus went to that degrading death on the cross, disgracing the family, and was buried, where do we find those hardest to convince—His own family?

We find them in the upper room with the disciples waiting for the Holy Spirit to be sent (Acts 1:13,14). Now, since they mocked Him while He was alive, what happened in a matter of a few days to turn their lives upside down?

James became a leader in the early church and wrote an epistle stating, "I James, a bond-servant of God and of the Lord Jesus Christ [his brother] . . . " (James 1). Eventually, for the cause of Christ, James died a martyr's death—he was stoned. 42/n.p.

What happened?

The best explanation I know is recorded by Paul: "Then He appeared to James" (1 Corinthians 15:7).

His Cowardly Followers

What about the fearful disciples of Jesus? When the authorities captured Jesus in the Garden of Gethsemane, "all the disciples left Him and fled" (Matthew 26:56; Mark 14:50). During Christ's trial, Peter went out and denied Him three times (John 18:15-27; Mark 14:66-72). After Christ was crucified, the fearful disciples hid themselves in an upper room and locked the doors (John 20:19). But something happened within days to totally change this group of cowardly followers into a bold band of enthusiasts who faced martyrdom without fear or hesitation. Peter, who had denied Jesus, was imprisoned for his persistency in preaching a "risen Christ" and later was himself crucified upside down.

What happened? The most logical explanation is that the resurrected Jesus "appeared to Cephas [Peter] . . . then to all the Apostles" (1 Corinthians 15:5-7).

A Jewish Fanatic Converted

And how about Paul, the religious persecutor of the Christians? This Jewish fanatic so hated the followers of Christ that he obtained special permission to go to other cities and incarcerate Christ's disciples. He ravaged the church (Acts 8:1-3; 9:1,2; 22:3-5).

But something happened to this persecutor. He turned from an antagonist to a protagonist of Jesus. He was transformed from a murderer to a Christian missionary. He changed from a bitter interrogator of Christians to one of the greatest propagators of the Christian faith.

The irony is that Paul began to confound the Jewish authorities "by proving Jesus is the Christ," the Son of God (Acts 9:22). He was eventually killed for his devotion to Christ.

What happened? This historical explanation is Paul's statement that Jesus "appeared to me also" (1 Corinthians 15:8; Acts 9:3-22).

It would be very difficult to explain the transformation of these men if the resurrection were not true. Professor Robert Grant says: "The origin of Christianity is almost incomprehensible unless such an event took place." 32/302

A Resurrection Explains All the Facts

Harvard law professor Simon Greenleaf, a man who lectured for years on how to break down testimony and determine whether or not a witness is lying, concludes:

> It was therefore impossible that they could have persisted in affirming the truths they have narrated, had not Jesus actually risen from the dead, and had they not known this fact as certainly as they knew any other fact.
>
> The annals of military warfare afford scarcely an example of the like heroic constancy, patience, and unflinching courage. They had every possible motive to review carefully the grounds of their faith, and the evidences of the great facts and truths they asserted. 33/29

A believer in Jesus Christ today can have the complete confidence, as did those first Christians, that his faith is based not on myth or legend but on the solid historical fact of the empty tomb and the risen Christ.

CHAPTER 21 *The Trilemma–Lord, Liar or Lunatic?*

(C/25-34)

Jesus' distinct claims of being God eliminate the popular ploy of skeptics who regard Him as just a good moral man or a prophet who said a lot of profound things. So often that conclusion is passed off as the only one acceptable to scholars or as the obvious result of the intellectual process. The trouble is, many people nod their heads in agreement and never see the fallacy of such reasoning.

C. S. Lewis, who was a professor at Cambridge University and once an agnostic, understood this issue clearly. He writes:

> I am trying here to prevent anyone saying the really foolish thing that people often say about Him: "I'm ready to accept Jesus as a great moral teacher, but I don't accept His claim to be God." That is the one thing we must not say. A man who was merely a man and said the sort of things Jesus said would not be a great moral teacher. He would either be a lunatic—on a level with the man who says he is a poached egg—or else he would be the Devil of Hell. You must make your choice. Either this man was, and is, the son of God: or else a madman or something worse.

Then Lewis adds:

> You can shut Him up for a fool, you can spit at Him and kill Him as a demon; or you can fall at His feet and call Him Lord and God. But let us not come up with any patronizing nonsense about His being a great human teacher. He has not left that open to us. He did not intend to. 49/40-41

In the words of Kenneth Scott Latourette, historian of Christianity at Yale University: "It is not His teachings which make Jesus so remarkable, although these would be enough to give Him distinction. It is a combination of the teachings with the man Himself. The two cannot be separated." 47/44,48

Jesus claimed to be God. He didn't leave any other option open. His claim must be either true or false, so it is something that should be given serious consideration. Jesus' question to His disciples, "But who do you say that I am?" (Matthew 16:15) has several alternatives.

First, suppose that His claim to be God was false. If it was false, then we have only two alternatives. He either knew it was false or He didn't know it was false. We will consider each one separately and examine the evidence.

Was He a Liar?

If, when Jesus made His claims, He knew that He was not God, then He was lying and deliberately deceiving His followers. But if He was a liar, then He was also a hypocrite because He told others to be honest, whatever the cost, while He himself taught and lived a colossal lie. More than that, He was a demon, because He told others to trust Him for their eternal destiny. If He couldn't back up His claims and knew it, then He was unspeakably evil. Last, He would also be a fool because it was His claims to being God that led to His crucifixion.

Many will say that Jesus was a good moral teacher. Let's be realistic. How could He be a great moral teacher and knowingly mislead people at the most important point of His teaching—His own identity?

You would have to conclude logically that He was a deliberate liar. This view of Jesus, however doesn't coincide with what we know either of Him or the results of His life and teachings. Wherever Jesus has been proclaimed, lives have been changed for the good, nations have changed for the better, thieves are made honest, alcoholics are cured, hateful individuals become channels of love, unjust persons become just.

William Lecky, one of Great Britain's most noted historians and a dedicated opponent of organized Christianity, writes:

> It was reserved for Christianity to present to the world an ideal character which through all the changes of eighteen centuries has inspired the hearts of men with an impassioned love; has shown itself capable of acting on all ages, nations, temperaments and conditions; has been not only the highest pattern of virtue, but the strongest incentive to its practice. . . . The

> simple record of these three short years of active life has done more to regenerate and soften mankind than all the disquisitions of philosophers and all the exhortations of moralists. 48/8-9

Historian Philip Schaff says:

> How, in the name of logic, common sense, and experience, could an imposter—that is a deceitful, selfish, depraved man—have invented, and consistently maintained from the beginning to end, the purest and noblest character known in history with the most perfect air of truth and reality? How could He have conceived and successfully carried out a plan of unparalleled beneficence, moral magnitude, and sublimity, and sacrificed His own life for it, in the face of the strongest prejudices of His people and age? 70/94-95

If Jesus wanted to get people to follow Him and believe in Him as God, why did He go to the Jewish nation? Why go as a Nazarene carpenter to a country so small in size and population and so thoroughly adhering the undivided unity of God? Why didn't He go to Egypt or, even more, to Greece, where they believed in various gods and various manifestations of them?

Someone who lived as Jesus lived, taught as Jesus taught, and died as Jesus died could not have been a liar. What other alternatives are there?

Was He a Lunatic?

If it is inconceivable for Jesus to be a liar, then couldn't He actually have thought Himself to be God, but been mistaken? After all, it's possible to be both sincere and wrong. But we must remember that for someone to think himself God, especially in a fiercely monotheistic culture, and then to tell others that their eternal destiny depended on believing in him, is no light flight of fantasy but the thoughts of a lunatic in the fullest sense. Was Jesus Christ such a person?

Someone who believes he is God sounds like someone today believing himself Napoleon. He would be deluded and self-deceived, and probably he would be locked up so he wouldn't hurt himself or anyone else. Yet in Jesus we don't observe the abnormalities and imbalance that usually go along with being deranged. His poise and composure would certainly be amazing if He were insane.

Noyes and Kolb, in a medical text, describe the schizophrenic as a person who is more autistic than realistic. 61/62 The schizophrenic desires to escape from the world of reality. Let's face it; claiming to be God would certainly be a retreat from reality.

In light of the other things we know about Jesus, it's hard to imagine that He was mentally disturbed. Here is a man who spoke some of the most profound sayings ever recorded. His instructions have liberated many individuals from mental bondage.

Clark H. Pinnock asks:

> Was He deluded about His greatness, a paranoid, an unintentional deceiver, a schizophrenic? Again, the skill and depth of His teachings support the case only for His total mental soundness. If only we were as sane as He! 65/62

A student at a California university told me that his psychology professor had said in class that "all he has to do is pick up the Bible and read portions of Christ's teaching to many of his patients. That's all the counseling they need."

Psychiatrist J. T. Fisher states:

> If you were to take the sum total of all authoritative articles ever written by the most qualified of psychologists and psychiatrists on the subject of mental hygiene—if you were to combine them and refine them and cleave out the excess verbiage—if you were to take the whole of the meat and none of the parsley, and if you were to have these unadulterated bits of pure scientific knowledge concisely expressed by the most capable of living poets, you would have an awkward and incomplete summation of the Sermon on the Mount. And it would suffer immeasurably through comparison. For nearly two thousand years the Christian world has been holding in its hands the complete answer to its restless and fruitless yearnings. Here . . . rests the blueprint for successful human life with optimism, mental health, and contentment. 25/273

C. S. Lewis writes:

> The historical difficulty of giving for the life, sayings and influence of Jesus any explanation that is not harder than the Christian explanation is very great. The discrepancy between the depth and sanity . . . of His moral teaching and the rampant megalomania which must lie behind His theological teaching unless He is indeed God has never been satisfactorily explained. Hence the non-Christian hypotheses succeed one another with the restless fertility of bewilderment. 51/113

Philip Schaff reasons:

> Is such an intellect—clear as the sky, bracing as the mountain air, sharp and penetrating as a sword, thoroughly healthy and vigorous, always ready and always self-possessed—liable to a radical and most serious delusion concerning His own character and mission? Preposterous imagination! 70/97

Was He Lord?

I cannot personally conclude that Jesus was a liar or a lunatic. The only other alternative is that He was the Christ, the Son of God, as He claimed.

When I discuss this with most Jewish people, it's interesting how they respond. They usually tell me that Jesus was a moral, upright, religious leader, a good man, or some kind of prophet. I then share with them the claims Jesus made about Himself and then the material in this chapter on the trilemma (liar, lunatic, or Lord). When I ask if they believe Jesus was a liar, there is a sharp "No!"

Then I ask, "Do you believe He was a lunatic?"

The reply is, "Of course not."

"Do you believe He is God?"

Before I can get a breath in edgewise, there is a resounding, "Absolutely not."

Yet one has only so many choices.

The issue with these three alternatives is not which is possible, for it is obvious that all three are possible. Rather, the question is, "Which is more probable?" Who you decide Jesus Christ is must not be an idle intellectual exercise. You cannot put Him on the shelf as a great moral teacher. That is not a valid option. He is either a liar, a lunatic, or Lord and God. You must make a choice. "But," as the apostle John wrote, "these have been written that you may believe that Jesus is the Christ, the Son of God; and"—more important—"that believing you might have life in His name" (John 20:31).

The evidence is clearly in favor of Jesus as Lord. Some people, however, reject this clear evidence because of moral implications involved. They don't want to face up to the responsibility or implications of calling Him Lord.

CHAPTER 22 *Is Jesus Both Messiah and God?*

(HW/291-318)

The thought that Jewish writers might ascribe deity to another human being has brought much criticism to the Gospel accounts. Ian Wilson, in his book *Jesus: The Evidence,* has one chapter called, "How He Became God." In it he claims that "no Gospel regarded Jesus as God, and not even Paul had done so." 84/168 According to Wilson, the deifying of Jesus was primarily a product of the fourth-century Council of Nicea, not the belief of early Christians.

It is therefore necessary to sort out the historical details related to Jesus' alleged messiahship and deity. Did He think of Himself as Messiah and Son of God? What did He mean by the term "Son of God"? What did the people understand Him to mean? In order to answer these questions, we first must understand what the people expected the coming Messiah to be like.

Messianic Expectations

For about a hundred years, beginning in 164 B.C., the Jewish people tasted independence. Professor Jim Fleming, reflecting on the final loss of Jewish national sovereignty, states:

> Although this period had found its abrupt termination with the campaign of the Romans and General Pompey (63 B.C.), hope for its restoration had never been given up completely. Jesus was born into a time when the people anticipated the coming of the Messiah (cf. Song of Songs 17) and freedom from the Roman yoke. 27/5

One of the best analyses of first-century messianic expectations has been done by Geza Vermes. He observes that at this time there was both a widespread popular belief about what Messiah would be like and a number of minority splinter opinions: "It would seem more appropriate to bear in mind the difference between general messianic expectations of Palestinian Jewry, and peculiar messianic speculations characteristic of certain learned and/or esoterical minorities." 80/130

In order to determine what kind of Messiah the Jewish masses generally expected, Vermes advises, "A reliable answer is to be found in the least academic, and at the same time most normative, literary form: prayer."

Therefore, one of the best surviving sources regarding messianic expectation during this time is the *Psalms of Solomon* (a book of Jewish prayers), probably written just after the Roman conquest of Judaea in 63 B.C. These psalms (obviously not written by Solomon) reflect the common view of a righteous, reigning Messiah who would militarily reestablish Israel's sovereignty and restore a just government over the nation:

> Behold, O Lord, and raise up unto them their king, the son of David . . . And gird him with strength, that he may shatter unrighteous rulers . . . With a rod of iron he shall break in pieces all their substance, He shall destroy the godless nations with the word of his mouth . . . And he shall gather together a holy people . . . He shall have the heathen nations to serve him under his yoke . . . And he shall be a righteous king, taught by God . . . And there shall be no unrighteousness in his days in their midst. For all shall be holy and their king the Anointed (of) the Lord. 80/251

Psalm of Solomon 18 speaks of God's Anointed who will "use His 'rod' to instill the 'fear of the Lord' into every man and direct them to 'the works of righteousness.' " 80/131

Vermes concludes:

> Ancient Jewish prayer and Bible interpretation demonstrate unequivocally that if in the intertestamental era a man claims, or was proclaimed, to be "the Messiah," his listeners would as a matter of course have assumed that he was referring to the Davidic Redeemer and should have expected to find before them a person endowed with the combined talents of soldierly prowess, righteousness and holiness. 80/134

It is therefore understandable why, especially in view of the Roman occupation of Israel's land, most Jewish people would not see in Jesus what they expected of the Messiah.

Millar Burrows of Yale wrote, "Jesus was so unlike what all Jews expected the son of David to be that His own disciples found it almost impossible to connect the idea of Messiah with Him." 12/68

And finally, as the Jewish scholar Samuel Sandmel puts it,

> Any claims made, during the lifetime of Jesus, that He was the Messiah whom the Jews had awaited, were rendered poorly defensible by His crucifixion and by the collapse of any political aspect of His movement, and by the sad actuality that Palestine was still not liberated from Roman dominion. 67/33

The popular concept of Messiah as a reigning military deliverer, then, was a natural deterrent for most Jewish people to consider Jesus as Messiah. The question is: Was the popular concept the correct concept?

It is clear that not all Jewish people of Jesus' day held the majority opinion. Vermes observes,

> In addition to the royal concept, messianic speculation in ancient Judaism included notions of a priestly and prophetic Messiah, and in some cases, of a messianic figure who would perform all these functions in one. 80/135

The important point is that not everyone held to the popular concept of the awaited Messiah. There was enough obscurity in what Messiah was to be that a number of the especially religious Jews found the charisma of Jesus to fit with their picture of the Messiah. The fact that they also expected Him to deliver Israel from Roman oppression made Jesus' primary mission more complicated.

The big problem was the Romans. They were completely aware of the popular messianic expectations of the Jewish people. Tacitus (writing at the beginning of the second century A.D.) reports: "There was a firm persuasion . . . that at this very time the East was to grow powerful, and rulers coming from Judea were to acquire a universal empire." 76

At about the same time, writing about the decade following the destruction of the Temple in A.D. 70, Suetonius wrote, "There had spread over all the Orient an old established belief, that it was fated at that time for men coming from Judea to rule the world." 75

It is obvious that the Romans were ready at a minute's notice to squash any messianic uprising. No wonder Jesus did not go around blurting out, "I am the Messiah." As we will see, He had much more effective ways of making that announcement.

The Gospels often reveal the messianic expectations of the people. From the beginning of Jesus' earthly life, when Simeon in the Temple identifies Jesus as the long-awaited Messiah, to the end, when many honor Him as Messiah at the triumphal entry into Jerusalem, the Gospel accounts accurately reflect these expectations.

The messianic expectations of the Jewish people provide one of the strongest reasons for trusting the accuracy of the Gospel accounts as they describe Jesus' activities. Skeptics often claim that the life of Jesus described in the Gospels is too supernatural to be believed. What is often forgotten is that the great cause of the disciples died on the cross. Jesus certainly did not fulfill the messianic expectations of His disciples. Something had to happen, something no less powerful than what the Gospel accounts record, in order to motivate Jewish men and women to risk their lives to propagate this message which was so diametrically opposed to the prevailing messianic opinion of the day.

Did Jesus Think He Was Messiah?

Even as early as age twelve, Jesus refers to God as "My Father" (Luke 2:49). He continues to use the term throughout the Gospel accounts—a total of forty times! Jerusalem scholar, Dr. Robert Lindsey, explains the significance of this expression:

> Synagogue prayers contain the expression, "Our Father [*Avinu*] who is in heaven," many times, and Jesus taught His disciples to pray a prayer which also begins, "Our Father who is in heaven." The expression, "My Father [*avi*]," however, almost certainly must have seemed improper to the Jews of that period. Only once in the Hebrew Scripture is God referred to as "my Father," and that is in Psalm 89, which speaks of the coming Messiah. Verse 26 reads, "He will call to me, *'Avi ata'*—'You *are* my Father.' " The Messiah has the right to call God "my Father." I am quite sure that the rabbis of Jesus' day taught the people to say "*Our* Father who is in heaven," because they say "my Father" was reserved for the Messiah alone.
>
> Second Samuel 7:14 also contains a prophecy about the Messiah: "I will be to him a father, and he will be to me a son." This verse marks the beginning of a coming Messiah who is the son of God.
>
> It was known from Psalm 89:26, 2 Samuel 7:14 and Psalm 2:7 that the Messiah would be the son of God, but these verses do not contain the expression "son of God." What is used is, "He will call to me, 'You are my Father' "; "I will be a father to him, he will be a son to me"; and, "You are my son, this day I have brought you forth." This is the Hebraic way of expressing messiahship—it is the way the Holy Spirit spoke and the way Jesus spoke. 53/11

Jesus also declared Himself Messiah by the things He did. Look at John the Baptist in John 11. He sits in Herod's prison, and with free time on his hands he begins to review the events of his life. He especially reflects on whether or not he should have been referring his disciples to Jesus several months back (John 1:35-37). Having some doubts, he sends a question to Jesus by way of his disciples: "Are you the coming one, or shall we look for someone else?" (Matthew 11:3). Jesus tells John's disciples:

> Go and report to John the things which you hear and see: the blind receive sight and the lame walk, the lepers are cleansed and the deaf hear, and the dead are raised up, and the poor have the gospel preached to them (Matthew 11:5).

Jesus drew these words from two verses found in Isaiah. The first, 35:5, occurs in the midst of a passage speaking of the arrival of the kingdom of God in Zion. The second, 61:1, is found in a context announcing the favorable year of the Lord. John, therefore, would have understood Jesus as saying not only "Yes, I am the Messiah," but also, "Here, I'm willing to give you proof no one else can bring that my claims are true." In this sense, every time Jesus healed someone or performed some attesting sign, He was declaring Himself to be Messiah.

Jesus declared Himself to be Messiah by His triumphal entry into Jerusalem. A verse in the *Babylonian Talmud,* Menahoth 78*b*, has Rabbi Yohanan explaining that "outside the wall" of Jerusalem means not further than the wall of Bethphage. When Jesus mounts the donkey foal in Bethphage and rides into Jerusalem, He is making a very definite statement that He understands Himself to be the Messiah. He clearly intends to fulfill Zechariah 9:9:

> Rejoice greatly, O daughter of Zion!
> Shout in triumph, O daughter of Jerusalem!
> Behold your King is coming to you;
> He is just and endowed with salvation,
> Humble, mounted on a donkey,
> Even on a colt, the foal of a donkey.

The people clearly understood Jesus' intentions. Fleming states:

> The palm became a symbol of Jewish nationalism. But on Palm Sunday the poor population of Jerusalem was feeling the heavy arm of Rome over them. There was a popular understanding by Jews of Jesus' day that Messiah would come during the passover season. (Do you remember in John's Gospel that, after Jesus fed the 5,000, the people "wanted to make Him king because it was Passover"?) The role Messiah would play in the hopes of the populace was that He would deliver the people from oppression . . . as in the days of the exodus from Egypt. By bringing the palm branches the people were in a way saying, "Jesus, we are all with you . . . you see you have enough of a following to do something about the Roman garrison in Jerusalem." 26/7

In John 4, Jesus spoke with a Samaritan woman outside the city of Sychar. In the course of their conversation,

> the woman said to Him, "I know that Messiah is coming (He who is called Christ); when that one comes, He will declare all things to us" (John 4:25).

Jesus probably felt more freedom in Samaria about disclosing His identity. Messianic expectations were quite subdued since the Samaritans believed only in the Pentateuch. Jesus therefore revealed to the woman, "I who speak to you am He" (John 4:26).

There was no question about it. Jesus clearly declared Himself to be the Messiah.

Another declaration of Jesus that He was the Messiah occurred at His trial before the high priest Caiaphas, the chief priests, and the elders and scribes (Matthew 26:57-68; Mark 14:53-65). In Mark's account, the high priest finally asked Jesus directly, "Are you the Christ, the Son of the Blessed One?" and Jesus responded, "I am; and you shall see the Son of Man sitting at the right hand of power, and coming with the clouds of heaven." Notice that Jesus clearly spoke of Himself.

The term "Son of Man" was the way He usually referred to Himself. Son of Man occurs 81 times in the Gospel accounts. Notice also that Jesus clearly identified Himself as the one about whom Daniel prophesied when He revealed,

> I kept looking in the night visions,
> And behold, with the clouds of heaven
> One like a Son of Man was coming,
> And he came up to the Ancient of Days
> And was presented before Him. And to Him was given dominion,
> Glory and a kingdom,
> That all the peoples, nations, and men of every language
> Might serve Him.
> His dominion is an everlasting dominion
> Which will not pass away;
> And His kingdom is one
> Which will not be destroyed (Daniel 7:13,14).

In this passage Daniel reveals this coming one, and Jesus claims for Himself: (1) that He will come with or on the clouds of heaven; and (2) He will be given supreme authority over all mankind for all eternity. For the Sadducees, who controlled the Sanhedrin at this time and for whom "the Messianic hope played no role," 37/n.p. this claim was tantamount to blasphemy. (Blasphemy meant not just a claim to be God, but also slander against God or even against other persons.) Though the concept of Messiah would have been interpreted differently by Jesus, the scribes, Pharisees and Sadducees, there can be no doubt that Jesus clearly claimed He was that Son of Man to come, the Messiah.

That Jesus claimed to be Messiah is confirmed by the report which the Sanhedrin must have delivered to Pilate in view of that claim. Norman Anderson explains:

> The crucifixion, however, does seem to provide convincing proof of one point about which New Testament scholars have been much divided—and to which passing reference has already been made: namely, that Jesus Himself did believe that He was the Messiah. It is true that He did not make any such claim explicitly in His public preaching—partly, no doubt, for political reasons, but largely because of the mistaken expectations this would have aroused among His hearers. But it was clearly as a potential threat to Rome that Pilate and his minions delivered Him to a death largely reserved for the armed robber and the political insurgent. This is explicit in the inscription on the cross: "JESUS OF NAZARETH, THE KING OF THE JEWS" (John 19:19), which would seem to echo the Evangelists'

report that part of the conversation between Pilate and Jesus had been about this very point (Matthew 27:11; Mark 15:2; Luke 23:3; John 18:33-37). And this, in its turn, must have been prompted by the fact that the "blasphemy" for which the Sanhedrin had condemned Him was His reply to the question (put to Him on oath by the high priest), "Are you the Christ, the Son of the Blessed One?" with the words: "I am . . . And you will see the Son of Man sitting at the right hand of the mighty one and coming on the clouds of heaven" (Mark 14:61-64)—an affirmation that had naturally been reported by the chief priests to Pilate in explicitly political terms. 2/82-83

Though a number of Jewish scholars in the past have attempted to deny that Jesus thought of Himself as the Messiah, others now support His messianic consciousness. One is Samuel Sandmel, recognized as the leading U. S. Jewish authority in the New Testament and early Christianity. He was a professor at Yale, then at Hebrew Union College in Cincinnati up to his death in 1979. Sandmel concluded, "I believe that He believed Himself to be the Messiah, and that those scholars who deny this are incorrect." 68/109

David Flusser, professor of comparative religion at Hebrew University in Jerusalem, like other Jewish scholars, sees "inauthentic" passages in the Gospel texts. Still he maintains that "other apparently authentic sayings of Jesus can be understood only if it is assumed that Jesus thought Himself to be the Son of Man." 28/254 For Flusser, Jesus' concept of "Son of Man" was both messianic and divine.

Was Jesus the Messiah?

In the Old Testament, there are hundreds of prophesies alluding to the coming Messiah. The brilliant nineteenth-century Oxford professor, Canon Henry Liddon, found 332 "distinct predictions which were literally fulfilled in Christ." [See *Evidence That Demands a Verdict,* pp. 145-175, for specific prophecies.]

For example, Daniel 9:25,26 indicates that the Messiah had to come before the second Temple was destroyed (A.D. 70). Micah 5:2 speaks of the Messiah's birthplace as Bethlehem Ephrathah, the town where Jesus was born. Isaiah 35:5,6 speaks of the blind, deaf, lame and dumb being healed. Isaiah 42:6 and 49:6 speak of the Messiah as a light to the Gentiles. Zechariah 9:9 predicts that the Messiah would come humbly, "mounted on a donkey, even on a colt, the foal of a donkey." Psalm 22 provides a graphic description of one undergoing crucifixion (even though crucifixion was unknown to the psalmist), and Jesus quoted its opening verse as He hung on the cross. Zechariah 12:9,10 even mentions in one passage the two separate comings of the Messiah:

> And it will come about in that day that I will be about to destroy all the nations that come against Jerusalem [second coming]. And I will pour out

> on the house of David and on the inhabitants of Jerusalem, the Spirit of grace and of supplication, so that they will look on Me whom they have pierced [occurred at the first coming]; and they will mourn for Him, like the bitter weeping over a first-born.

But the Christian must be careful not to overstate the case. There are hundreds of additional messianic prophecies in the Old Testament which have not yet found their fulfillment in Jesus. This is by necessity, for if it is prophesied that the Messiah had to suffer and die and yet is also to subsequently reign over an eternal kingdom (at least part of which is established on earth) then it follows that Messiah must somehow rise from the dead and come again. The most important and overlooked question is: Does the Old Testament predict that the Messiah must first suffer and die?

Christians and critics alike today are often so focused on the issue of Jesus' resurrection that they forget the other half of the apostles' preaching. Peter preached in the Temple, "But the things which God announced beforehand by the mouth of all the prophets, that His Christ **should suffer**, He has thus fulfilled" (Acts 3:18).

Paul reasoned with the Thessalonians in their synagogue. He was "explaining and giving evidence that the Christ *had to suffer* and rise again from the dead, and saying, 'This Jesus whom I am proclaiming to you is the Christ' " (Acts 17:3). Before King Agrippa Paul reported:

> And so, having obtained help from God, I stand to this day testifying both to small and great, stating nothing but what the Prophets and Moses said was going to take place; that the Christ *was to suffer,* and that by reason of His resurrection from the dead He should be the first to proclaim light both to the Jewish people and to the Gentiles (Acts 26:22,23).

The apostles were saying nothing new. Jesus Himself repeatedly stated that He had to go to Jerusalem to suffer, die and be raised from the dead (Matthew 16:21; 17:12; Mark 8:31; 9:12; Luke 9:22; 17:25; 22:15; 24:26,46). But where in the Old Testament was this prophesied?

Many Jewish people today are surprised to find the following passage in the Jewish Bible, what Christians call the Old Testament:

> See, my servant will act wisely; he will be raised and lifted up and highly exalted. Just as there were many who were appalled at him—his appearance was so disfigured beyond that of any man and his form marred beyond human likeness—so will he sprinkle many nations, and kings will shut their mouths because of him. For what they were not told, they will see, and what they have not heard, they will understand.
>
> Who has believed our message and to whom has the arm of the LORD been revealed? He grew up before him like a tender shoot, and like a root out of dry ground. He had no beauty or majesty to attract us to him, nothing in his appearance that we should desire him. He was despised and rejected by men, a man of sorrows, and familiar with suffering. Like one from whom men hide their faces he was despised, and we esteemed him not.

> Surely he took up our infirmities and carried our sorrows, yet we considered him stricken by God, smitten by him, and afflicted. But he was pierced for our transgressions, he was crushed for our iniquities; the punishment that brought us peace was upon him, and by his wounds we are healed. We all, like sheep, have gone astray, each of us has turned to his own way; and the LORD has laid on him the iniquity of us all.
>
> He was oppressed and afflicted, yet he did not open his mouth; he was led like a lamb to the slaughter, and as a sheep before her shearers is silent, so he did not open his mouth. By oppression and judgment he was taken away. And who can speak of his descendants? For he was cut off from the land of the living; for the transgression of my people he was stricken. He was assigned a grave with the wicked, and with the rich in his death, though he had done no violence, nor was any deceit in his mouth.
>
> Yet it was the LORD's will to crush him and cause him to suffer, and though the LORD makes his life a guilt offering, he will see his offspring and prolong his days, and the will of the LORD will prosper in his hand. After the suffering of his soul, he will see the light of life and be satisfied; by his knowledge my righteous servant will justify many, and he will bear their iniquities. Therefore I will give him a portion among the great, and he will divide the spoils with the strong, because he poured out his life unto death, and was numbered with the transgressors. For he bore the sin of many, and made intercession for the transgressors (Isaiah 52:13–53:12, NIV, written ca 700 B.C.).

For more than 1700 years, the Jewish rabbis interpreted this passage almost unanimously as referring to the Messiah. This fact is thoroughly documented in S. R. Driver and Adolf Neubauer's *The Fifty-Third Chapter of Isaiah According to the Jewish Interpreters.* 19/37-39 They quote numerous rabbis during this period who equated the servant of Isaiah 53 with the Messiah.

Not until the twelfth century A.D., no doubt under the suffering of the Jews at the hand of the Crusaders, did any Jewish interpreter say that Isaiah 52:13–53:12 refers to the whole nation of Israel, the most common interpretation today among Jewish scholars. Even after Rashi (Rabbi Solomon Yazchaki) first proposed this interpretation, however, many other Jewish interpreters have held, even to the present, the traditional Talmudic view that Isaiah 53 speaks of the Messiah. One of the most respected Jewish intellectuals of all history, Moses Maimonides (A.D. 1135–1204) rejected Rashi's interpretation, and he taught that the passage was messianic. 59/364-65

Rashi and other Jewish interpreters are not necessarily grasping at straws to suggest that the servant is the nation of Israel. Isaiah 43:10 (NIV) says to the people of Israel: " 'You are My witnesses,' declares the LORD, 'and My servant whom I have chosen.' " Surely, then, the servant must be Israel.

That this interpretation is in error can first be seen in Isaiah 52:14

where the nation of Israel is compared to the servant: "Just as many were astonished at you, My people, so his appearance was marred more than any man." In 53:8, the servant bears punishment that should have been born by "my people" (obviously Israel). It makes no sense for the nation of Israel to bear substitutionary punishment for the nation of Israel. Therefore Israel cannot be the servant of Isaiah 52:13–53:12.

But what about Isaiah 49:3: "And He said to Me, 'You are My Servant, Israel, in Whom I will show My glory' "? Good point! We're glad you brought it up. The key to identifying the servant in Isaiah 52:13–53:12 is to see who he is in the three previous "servant songs" of Isaiah: 42:1-9; 49:1-12; and 50:4-9. Since these passages spoke of the servant, for example, establishing justice in the earth (Isaiah 42:4) and regathering the Jewish people from worldwide exile (Isaiah 49:8-13), Jewish interpreters have traditionally held the servant songs to be speaking of the Messiah, not the nation of Israel. Even Isaiah 49:3 does not say that Israel is the servant; rather it says that the servant (Messiah) is the true Israel! In verse 5 and 6 we see: "Now says the LORD, who formed Me from the womb to be His servant . . . 'to raise up the tribes of Jacob, and to restore the preserved ones of Israel.' " The point is that Jacob (Israel) had gone astray, especially from the commission God gave to him: "In you and in your descendants shall all the families of the earth be blessed" (Genesis 28:14). The Servant (Messiah) was now to stand in Israel's place to do two things: (1) to bring the nation of Israel back to God (Isaiah 49:5); and (2) to be a light to the nations, as seen in verse 6:

> It is too small a thing that You should be My Servant. . . . I will also make You a light of the nations so that My salvation may reach to the end of the earth.

If you caught what is going on here in Isaiah, you probably realize why Jesus so often appealed or alluded to this prophet. The Servant is the Messiah. The Messiah had to suffer and die for many. He also had to be raised from the dead (Psalm 16:10). When the monumental event of the resurrection did occur and the disciples were filled at Pentecost with the Spirit of God, they preached everywhere the message "that Messiah died for our sins according to the Scriptures, and that He was buried, and that He was raised on the third day according to the Scriptures" (1 Corinthians 15:3,4). To judge from the earliest surviving Christian literature, 1 Thessalonians, they also preached that the Messiah would come again.

Was Jesus the Messiah? If not, then there is to be no Messiah. No one prior to A.D. 70 had His credentials. All the prophecies which could be fulfilled in His first coming were fulfilled in Jesus. And He sealed it all with His own resurrection from the dead. It is therefore fitting to refer to Jesus as the Christ if one uses Greek terminology, or as the Messiah if one uses Hebrew terminology.

Did Jesus Really Believe He Was God?

Those who wrote the historical accounts of Jesus' life were thoroughly Jewish. The accounts themselves clearly certify that the witnesses' natural tendency was to see Jesus in a conquering messianic, not a divine messianic, posture. Even on the night of Jesus' arrest, the disciples brought swords to Jesus (Luke 22:38). As devoted worshippers of Yahweh, it must have been quite difficult for them to report some of the things Jesus said and did which attributed deity to Himself. Vermes states concerning the alleged deity of Jesus, "The identification of a contemporary historical figure with God would have been inconceivable to a first-century A.D. Palestinian Jew." 80/212 The thrust of Vermes' conclusions is that Jesus Himself never would have imagined that He was God. Let's look at the evidence.

In Matthew 12:6, Jesus says to the Pharisees, "I say to you, that something greater than the Temple is here." How much greater? Look at verse 8. Referring to Himself, Jesus asserts, "The Son of Man is Lord of the Sabbath." How can anyone be Lord of the Sabbath except God who instituted it? This is a direct claim to deity.

In Matthew 23:37, Jesus speaks as though He has personally observed the whole history of Jerusalem:

> O Jerusalem, Jerusalem, who kills the prophets and stones those who are sent to her! How often I wanted to gather your children together, the way a hen gathers her chicks under her wings, and you were unwilling.

In Mark 2:1,2, Jesus tells a paralyzed man, "My son, your sins are forgiven." Some scribes sitting there caught the obvious intent of Jesus' words and reasoned:

> Why does this man speak in this way? He is blaspheming; who can forgive sins but God alone?

Jesus challenged them:

> Which is easier, to say to the paralytic, "Your sins are forgiven"; or to say, "Arise, and take up your pallet and walk"? But in order that you may know that the Son of Man has authority on earth to forgive sins . . .

And then Jesus healed the paralytic. The implication was obvious. No one forgives sin but God. Anyone could say he is able to forgive sin; but Jesus proved He had the authority to forgive sin when He healed the paralytic. Jesus was clearly claiming deity for Himself.

Back again in Matthew, at the end of the Sermon on the Mount (7:21-23), Jesus speaks of Himself as the ultimate judge who will have authority to deny entrance into the kingdom of heaven.

In the next paragraph, rather than say, "Everyone who hears the words of God or Torah will lay a strong foundation for their lives," Jesus states, "Everyone who hears these words of Mine . . . "

David Biven, a researcher of the Hebraic background of the Gospel accounts, concludes:

> It was not the way He taught or even the general content of His teaching that made Jesus unique among the rabbis. What *was* unique about Jesus was who He claimed to be, and He rarely ever taught without claiming to be not only God's Messiah, but more startlingly, *Immanuel*, "God with us." 6/5

It is surprising how critics try to reject Jesus' constant references to Himself as deity. Ian Wilson, for example, writes:

> In the Mark Gospel, the most consistent in conveying Jesus' humanity, a man is represented as running up to Jesus and addressing Him with the words "Good Master." Jesus' response is a firm rebuke: "Why do you call me good? No one is good but God alone" (Mark 10:18). 84/176

Wilson's interpretation is 180 degrees in the wrong direction. Seen within the context of the situation, Jesus is using obvious irony. In essence, He is arguing: (1) If no one is good but God alone, and (2) if I am good, then (3) I must be God. Often Jesus receives worship and does nothing to discourage it (see Matthew 14:33, John 9:38). You would think one who severely rebukes Peter for trying to keep Him from God's will of being crucified would also severely rebuke someone offering worship to Him which rightly ought to be given only to the one true living God. Paul severely reacted against being deified at Lystra (Acts 14:8-18). How much more should Jesus have reacted if He were only a mere man? Did He not quote Deuteronomy 6:13 to Satan during His temptation, "You shall worship the Lord your God, and serve Him only"?

One notable occurrence of Jesus accepting worship is in Matthew 21:15,16. Children cried out, "Hosanna to the Son of David," in praise to Jesus. "Hosanna" is used here as a cry of adoration, but some critics insist on interpreting "Hosanna" in a stiffly literal sense, rendering the statement "Save us Son of David." This interpretation cannot be accurate, though, because (1) it would actually read: "Save us *to* the Son of David," which makes little or no sense; (2) the chief priests and scribes who saw Jesus receiving the praise "became indignant and said to Him, 'Do you hear what these are saying?' " as though Jesus should have silenced the crowd (something He would be expected to do only if the crowd were worshipping Him); and most important, (3) Jesus replied by attributing to Himself something which was meant for God alone. He asked the chief priests and scribes, "Have you never read, 'Out of the mouth of infants and nursing babes Thou [God] hast prepared praise for Thyself [God]'?"

Did you catch what Jesus said? Basically it was, "When those children praise me, they are praising God."

Of all the Gospel writers, John most clearly perceived the cues Jesus gave about His identity. For his effort to report those cues, he has been the most criticized Gospel writer of all, allegedly falling under Hellenistic influence. Scholars today, however, have begun to realize the inaccuracy of this charge. In John 8:58, when Jesus proclaimed to a Jewish crowd, "Truly, truly I say to you, before Abraham was born, I Am," He was claiming two aspects of deity for Himself:

- the eternal existence of God; and
- the name of God.

Jesus was referring His listeners back to Exodus 3:13,14 where Moses tells God:

> Behold, I am going to the sons of Israel, and I shall say to them, "The God of your fathers has sent me to you." Now they may say to me, "What is His name?" What shall I say to them?

God answered Moses,

> I AM WHO I AM . . . Thus you shall say to the sons of Israel, "I AM has sent me to you."

Any Jewish person would have heard Jesus' claim to deity loud and clear. That is why the very next verse in John's account says: "Therefore they picked up stones to throw at Him" (John 8:59). In all, Jesus uses the term *I am* (Gr. *Ego eimi)* more than nineteen times in reference to Himself in the Gospel according to John. Often it is used to make claims about Himself that normally would be thought appropriate only for God. For example,

> I am the bread of life, he who comes to Me shall not hunger, and he who believes in Me shall never thirst (6:35);

> I am the light of the world; he who follows Me shall not walk in the darkness, but shall have the light of life (8:12);

> Unless you believe that I am He, you shall die in your sins (8:24);

> I am the good shepherd (10:11-14) [cf. Psalm 23:1: "The LORD is my shepherd"];

> I am the resurrection, and the life; He who believes in Me shall live even if he dies (11:25).

Other Scriptures on this subject include John 4:26; 6:41,48,51; 8:18, 28,58; 10:7,9; 13:19; 14:6; and 15:1.)

Earlier, in John 5:17, Jesus claimed to be continuing the work of the Father. He also called God "My Father." In John 10:28-30 Jesus again called God "My Father." He also claimed at one time to be the giver of eternal life and at another time to be one with the Father. On both those occasions, the Jewish crowds picked up stones to stone Him because, as they put it, "You, being a man, make Yourself out to be God" (John 10:33;

cf. 5:18).

In John 14:6, Jesus did not just claim to be teaching mankind the truth; He claimed that He **was** the truth. In John 14:9, Jesus admonished Philip, "He who has seen Me has seen the Father." In Isaiah 42:8, God said, "I am the LORD, that is My name; I will not give My glory to another." But in John 17:5, Jesus prayed, "And now, glorify Thou Me together with Thyself, Father, with the glory which I ever had with Thee before the world was."

In John 5:19*ff.*, Jesus delivers a long monologue in which He makes repeated claims to be on the same level of authority as God the Father.

"Even in His parables," says Norman Geisler, "Jesus claimed functions reserved only for *Yahweh* in the Old Testament, such as being Shepherd (Luke 15), Rock (Matthew 7:24-27), and Sower (Matthew 13:24-30)." 31/14

C. S. Lewis puts all these claims in the right perspective when he reminds his readers that Jesus was a Jew among Jews:

> Among these Jews there suddenly turns up a man who goes about talking as if He was God. He claims to forgive sins. He says He has always existed. He says He is coming to judge the world at the end of time. Now let us get this clear. Among pantheists, like the Indians, anyone might say that he was a part of God, or one with God: there would be nothing very odd about it. But this man, since He was a Jew, could not mean that kind of God. God, in their language, meant the Being outside the world who had made it and was infinitely different from anything else. And when you have grasped that, you will see that what this man said was, quite simply, the most shocking thing that has ever been uttered by human lips. 50/54-55

Was Jesus the God He Thought He Was?

The question, Is Jesus God? is fundamentally different from the question, Is God Jesus? In the latter, God is limited to earth during the earthly life of Jesus. In the former, God simply manifests Himself in human flesh. Of course this means that a trinitarian theology (or at least a dual-personality theology) must be adopted in order to keep God from vacating His sovereign rule over the universe during the life of Jesus. Many Jewish scholars today no longer criticize Christians for being tritheists. Though these scholars almost universally reject the doctrine of the trinity, they do not generally deny the logical possibility of a single God manifesting Himself in more than one personality.

This is not the place to demonstrate the doctrine of the trinity, but it is necessary to see that such a concept is **not** ruled out by the Old Testament Scriptures. If the Old Testament did rule out such a doctrine, it would be ridiculous to think of Jesus possibly being God.

The fact is, the Old Testament suggests a plurality of personalities in one God from the very beginning. Genesis 1:26 states: "Then God said, 'Let Us make man in Our image, according to Our likeness.' "

Old Testament scholars Keil and Delitzsch have reviewed the arguments proposed against this verse and found them wanting. 45/1:61-62 It is enough to say that if the passage doesn't demand the multiple person view, it certainly allows for it, and the most natural reading of the passage supports it.

One of the greatest objections to the trinity usually comes from the most often recited verse among the Jewish people, Deuteronomy 6:4: "Hear, O Israel! The LORD is our God, the LORD is one!" The Hebrew word used here for "one" is *echod,* meaning a "composite unity." It is the same word used in Genesis 2:24 where the husband and wife are commanded to become *one* flesh. Had the writer of Deuteronomy 6:4 wished to express an absolute unity, he could have used the Hebrew word, *yachid.*

A number of other passages also either suggest or require that the Messiah be seen as deity. Psalm 45, for example, begins as a song celebrating "the King's marriage." In verse 3 it moves to a Messiah-type figure and in verses 6 and 7 it reads:

> Thy throne, O God, is forever and ever;
> A scepter of uprightness is the scepter of Thy kingdom.
> Thou hast loved righteousness, and hated wickedness;
> Therefore God, Thy God, has anointed Thee
> with the oil of joy above Thy fellows.

Sir Norman Anderson reviews a number of other passages concerning the Messiah:

> His sway was to be not only universal (Psalm 2:8) but [also] eternal (Isaiah 9:7), and even divine (Psalm 45:6,7). The prophet Micah speaks of His pre-existence (Micah 5:2); Jeremiah describes Him as "The LORD our Righteousness" (Jeremiah 23:6); and Isaiah speaks of Him as "Wonderful, Counselor, Mighty God, Eternal Father, Prince of Peace" (Isaiah 9:6) . . . And it is interesting in this context to note that the statement in Hebrews 1:6 ("And when He again brings the first-born into the world, He says, 'And let all the angels of God worship him' ") almost certainly represents a quotation taken from the "Septuagint" Greek version of the Old Testament of words omitted from the end of Deuteronomy 32:43 in the now official Hebrew or "Massoretic" text, but present in that of the Dead Sea Scrolls. 2/73-74

Psalm 2:12 commands that the Messiah should be worshipped:

> Do homage to the Son, lest He become angry, and you perish in the way,
> For His wrath may soon be kindled. How blessed are all who take refuge in Him!

In Zechariah 12:10, God says, "They will look on Me whom they have pierced." How can one pierce God unless He manifests Himself in the flesh? Of the ten other places where "pierce" is used, at least nine times a person is either thrust through or pierced to death; the remaining occurrence refers to wounded soldiers.

In Daniel 7:14, the Messiah is given an everlasting kingdom, "that all the peoples, nations, and men of every language might serve Him." But if everyone is serving the Messiah, then no one would be left to serve the Lord unless the Lord and the Messiah are somehow united.

We can say then that the Old Testament in some places at least allowed for and in other places required that the Messiah to come should be identified as God eternal. Thus, if Jesus was Messiah, and if Messiah was God, then Jesus had to be God.

Returning to the first disciples, E. M. Blaiklock observes:

> One of the sources of youth's disillusionment is the fading halo around the head of some human hero it has hastily sought to worship. Not so with Christ and His disciples. For three years they trod together the lanes and byways of Galilee and Judea. They climbed together the rough roads up to Jerusalem, sat together in the lush grass above Tabgha. Together they bore the heat of Jericho and the cold winds of the Galilean lake. They shared His chill rest beneath the stars, His breakfast on the beach. Together they bore storms and tensions in the holy city, together they enjoyed Bethany's hospitable home. Surely, this was test enough if shrewd men were to know Him. What happened? Far from detecting the hidden flaw, the human burst of annoyance at the end of a weary day, personal ambition betrayed by a chance word or unwise confidence, far from finding in Him disappointing blemishes, they found that their sense of wonder and reverence grew. 9/85

It is an amazing fact that the message of Jesus, including His deity, was spread abroad by these Jewish men and women. As James D. G. Dunn, Professor of Divinity at the University of Durham in England, states:

> The testimony comes not from Gentiles to whom the deification of an emperor was more like a promotion to "the upper chamber." It comes from Jews. And Jews were the most fiercely monotheistic race of that age. For a Jew to speak of a man, Jesus, in terms which showed Him as sharing in the deity of God, was a quite astonishing feature of earliest Christianity. 20/61-62

It is remarkable enough that a Jew like Thomas would come to the point of calling Jesus "My Lord and my God!" (John 20:28). But then there is Paul. It is unbelievable how critics tend to forget he was a Jew *par excellence.* He was trained in Judaism by none other than Rabbi Gamaliel. He was so zealous for his monotheistic faith that he began persecuting the Christians. His goal in life was to help bring to pass Isaiah 45:22,23 where God says through the prophet, "I am God, and there is no other . . . *to me every knee will bow,* every tongue will swear allegiance" [emphasis ours]. And then Paul discovered that this One had stepped out of eternity and into time. Now Paul writes of Him:

> He existed in the form of God . . . but emptied Himself . . . being made in

> the likeness of men . . . He humbled Himself by becoming obedient to the point of death, even death on a cross . . . that at the name of Jesus *every knee should bow* . . . and that every tongue should confess that Jesus Christ is Lord (Philippians 2:6-11, emphasis ours).

That Paul meant "God" by the term *Lord* is clear from Romans 10:13 where he quotes Joel 2:32: "Whoever calls on the name of the LORD will be delivered." In Joel 2:32, the LORD is clearly God.

These first-century Jewish men and women came to accept Jesus as the God of their monotheistic faith. Why? Certainly they had been attracted to Him by His teaching and attesting miracles. At some point they obviously put two and two together to see that Jesus, the Son of Man, was also the Messiah, that Messiah was God and therefore that He must also be God. But it was the resurrection that solidified their conviction. Norman Anderson summarizes:

> He frequently made claims which would have sounded outrageous and blasphemous to Jewish ears, even from the lips of the greatest of prophets. He said that He was in existence before Abraham and that He was "lord" of the sabbath; He claimed to forgive sins; He frequently identified Himself (in His work, His person and His glory) with the one He termed His heavenly Father; He accepted men's worship; and He said that He was to be the judge of men at the last day, when their eternal destiny would depend on their attitude to Him. Then He died. It seems inescapable, therefore, that His resurrection must be interpreted as God's decisive vindication of these claims, while the alternative—the finality of the cross—would necessarily have implied the repudiation of His presumptuous and even blasphemous assertions. 2/113-14

CHAPTER 23 *Conclusion–A New Beginning*

(HW/335-36)

To know Jesus from history is to know Him from afar. It is only to know **about** Him rather than to actually **know** Him. Yet the historical record of His life reveals that He intensely desired that "all mankind" might know Him personally. On the eve of His crucifixion, when He knew death was imminent and the most important thoughts filled His mind, we find Him praying before His disciples:

> Father, the hour has come; glorify Your Son, that the Son may glorify You, even as You gave Him authority over all mankind, that to all whom You have given Him, He may give eternal life. And this is eternal life, that they may know You, the only true God, and Jesus Christ whom You have sent (John 17:1-3).

Either Jesus was supremely egotistical or He was revealing the whole purpose of His life within human history: that anyone from all mankind might come to know Him. Not just know about Him, but actually know Him in a personal way.

One of the most powerful evidences that Jesus lived, died, and rose from the dead is the changed lives of His disciples, from those of the first century down to those in the present time. Hundreds of millions of people throughout history have been able to say that they have come to know Him and that He has changed their lives.

During the nineteenth century, critical scholars put a dividing line between the Jesus of history and the Christ of faith. Our experience, along with that of Christians throughout history, is that no such barrier exists. Because of the resurrection, the historical Jesus continues to live in history. As the apostle Paul wrote, "Jesus Christ is the same yesterday and today, yes and forever" (Hebrews 13:8).

We can understand why Paul did not devote much space in his writings to the earthly life of Jesus. Knowing Jesus in the present is too exciting! If you have not made the wonderful discovery of knowing Christ personally, we invite you to read "Would You Like to Know God Personally?" beginning on page 469, to find out how. Discovering the historical Jesus in one's everyday experience is without a doubt the greatest discovery one can make!

Bibliography

1. Amiot, Francois; Brunot, Amedee; Danielou, Jean; and Daniel-Rops, Henri. *The Sources for the Life of Christ.* Translated by P. J. Hepburne-Scott. New York: Hawthorn Books, 1962.
2. Anderson, Norman. *Jesus Christ: The Witness of History.* Downers Grove, IL: InterVarsity Press, 1984.
3. Arnold, Thomas. *Sermons on the Christian Life—Its Hopes, Its Fears, and Its Close.*
4. Barbet, Pierre. *A Doctor at Calvary.* New York: P. S. Kennedy & Sons, 1953.
5. Bender, A. P. "Beliefs, Rites, and Customs of the Jews, Connected With Death, Burial, and Mourning." *The Jewish Quarterly Review* 7 (1895).
6. Biven, David. "Looking Behind Rabbinic Parables." *Through Their Eyes* 1 (November 1986).
7. Biven, David. "Principles of Rabbinic Interpretations." *Through Their Eyes* 2 (1987).
8. Biven, David. "Question for Question." *Through Their Eyes* 2 (January 1987).
9. Blaiklock, E. M. *Jesus Christ: Man or Myth?* Nashville: Thomas Nelson Publishers, 1984.
10. Bruce, F. F. *The New Testament Documents: Are They Reliable?* 5th revised edition. Downers Grove, IL: InterVarsity Press, 1972.
11. Bruce, F. F. *Jesus and Christian Origins Outside the New Testament.* Grand Rapids: Wm. B. Eerdmans Publishing Co., 1985.
12. Burrows, Millar. *More Light on the Dead Sea Scrolls.* New York: Viking, 1958.
13. Cassels, Louis. "Debunkers of Jesus Still Trying." *Detroit News.* June 23, 1973.
14. Chrysostom, John. *Homilies of St. John.* Grand Rapids: Wm. B. Eerdmans Publishing Co., reprint 1969.
15. Cicero. *Vin Verrem,* 64.
16. Currie, George. *The Military Discipline of the Romans From the Founding of the City to the Close of the Republic.* Abstract of thesis published under auspices of Graduate Council of Indiana University, 1928.
17. Dalman, Gustaf. *Jesus—Jeshua.* Translated by Paul P. Levertoff (first published in 1929). New York: Ktav Publishing House, 1971.
18. Davis, C. Truman. "The Crucifixion of Jesus." *Arizona Medicine.* March 1965.
19. Driver, S. R., and Neubauer, Adolf. *The Fifty-Third Chapter of Isaiah According to the Jewish Interpreters.* New York: Ktav Publishing House, 1969. Reprint of Oxford, 1876-77 edition.
20. Dunn, James D. G. *The Evidence for Jesus.* Philadelphia: The Westminster Press, 1985.
21. Durant, Will. *Caesar and Christ.* New York: Simon & Schuster, 1944.
22. Encyclopedia Britannica. 15th edition. 1974.
23. Enelow, H. G. *A Jewish View of Jesus.* New York: Macmillan Publishing Co., 1920.
24. Eusebius. "The Epistle of the Church in Smyrna." *Trials and Crucifixion of Christ.* A. P. Stout, ed. Cincinnati: Standard Publishing, 1886.
25. Fisher, J. T., and Hawley, L. S. *A Few Buttons Missing.* Philadelphia: Lippincott, 1951.

26. Fleming, Jim. Lecture at the Jerusalem Center for Biblical Studies, Jerusalem, Israel, January 1987.

27. Fleming, Jim. Lecture on cassette tape and booklet entitled "Survey of the Life of Jesus." P.O. Box 71055, Jerusalem, Israel.

28. Flusser, David. "Jesus," *Encyclopedia Judaica.* 10:14. Edited by C. Roth. 1971.

29. France, R. T. *The Evidence for Jesus.* Downers Grove, IL: InterVarsity Press, 1986.

30. France, R. T. "The Gospels as Historical Sources of Jesus, the Founder of Christianity." *Truth* 1.

31. Geisler, Norman L. "The Importance of the Christological Issues." A paper read at the "Jesus Christ: God and Man" conference, an international colloquium of Christian scholars held in Dallas, November 13-16, 1986.

32. Grant, Robert. *Historical Introduction to the New Testament.* New York: Harper & Row, 1963.

33. Greenleaf, Simon. *An Examination of the Testimony of the Four Evangelists by the Rules of Evidence Administered in the Courts of Justice.* Grand Rapids: Baker Book House, 1965. Reprint of 1874 ed., New York: J. Cockroft & Co.

34. Haas, N. "Anthropological Observations on the Skeletal Remains From Giv' at ha-Mivtar." *Israel Exploration Journal* 20 (1970).

35. Habermas, Gary R. *Ancient Evidence for the Life of Jesus.* Nashville: Thomas Nelson Publishers, 1984.

36. Hagner, Donald A. *The Jewish Reclamation of Jesus.* Grand Rapids: Zondervan Publishing House, 1984.

37. Hagner, Donald A. "Sadducees." *Zondervan Pictorial Encyclopedia.*

38. Heohner, Harold W. *Chronological Aspects of the Life of Christ.* Grand Rapids: Zondervan Publishing House, 1977.

39. Hewitt, J. W. "The Use of Nails in the Crucifixion." *Harvard Theological Review* 25 (1932).

40. Irwin, Linton H. *A Lawyer Examines the Bible.* Grand Rapids: Baker Book House, 1943.

41. Jacoby, Felix. *Die Fragmente der Griechischen Historiker.* Berlin: Wiedmann, 1923.

42. Josephus, Flavius. *Antiquities of the Jews,* 3, book 20, chap. 9, sec. 1.

43. Josephus, Flavius. *Antiquities of the Jews,* 3. 8. 3.

44. Josephus, Flavius. *De Bello Judaico,* 7. 202-3.

45. Keil, C. F., and Delitzsch, F. *Commentary on the Old Testament.* 10 volumes. Edinburgh: T. & T. Clark, 1866. Reprint ed. Grand Rapids: William B. Eerdmans Publishing Co., 1980.

46. Klausner, Joseph. *Jesus of Nazareth.* New York: Menorah Publishing Co., 1925.

47. Latourette, Kenneth Scott. *A History of Christianity.* New York: Harper & Row, 1953.

48. Lecky, William E. *History of European Morals From Augustus to Charlemagne* 2. New York: D. Appleton and Co., 1903.

49. Lewis, C. S. *Mere Christianity.* New York: Macmillan Publishing Co., Inc., 1960.

50. Lewis, C. S. *Miracles.* New York: Macmillan Publishing Co., 1960. Macmillan paperback edition, 1978.

51. Lewis, C. S. *Miracles, a Preliminary Study.* New York: Macmillan, 1947.

52. Lewis, C. S. *Surprised by Joy.* London: Geoffrey Bles, 1955.

53. Lindsey, Robert. "On Jesus' Messianic Claims." *Through Their Eyes* 1 (November 1986).

54.Maier, Paul L. *First Easter.* New York: Harper & Row, 1973.

55. Maier, Paul L. "The Empty Tomb as History." *Christianity Today* 19 (March 28, 1975).

56. Maier, Paul L. *Independent Press Telegram.* Long Beach, CA: April 21, 1973.

57. Martyr, Justin. *First Apology,* 35. 7-9.

58. Martyr, Justin. *First Apology,* 48. 3.

59. Morais, Sabato. "A Letter by Maimonides to the Jews of South Arabia Entitled 'The Inspired Hope.' " *Jewish Quarterly Review* 25 (July 1934-April 1935).

60. Moyer, Elgin. *Who Was Who in Church History.* Chicago: Moody Press, 1968.

61. Noyes, Arthur P., and Kolb, Lawrence C. *Modern Clinical Psychiatry.* 5th ed. Philadelphia: Saunders, 1958.

62. Pannenberg, Wolfhart. "A Dialogue on Christ's Resurrection." *Christianity Today* 12 (April 12, 1968).

63. Philo. *Logatio and Gaium* 38.

64. Pines, Shlomo. *An Arabic Version of the Testimonium Flavianum and Its Implications.* Jerusalem: Jerusalem Academic Press, 1971.

65. Pinnock, Clark H. *Set Forth Your Case.* New Jersey: The Craig Press, 1967.

66. Polybius VI. 37-38.

67. Sandmel, Samuel. *A Jewish Understanding of the New Testament.* Cincinnati: Hebrew Union College Press, 1956.

68. Sandmel, Samuel. *Jews and Jesus.* New York: Oxford University Press, 1965.

69. Schaff, Philip. *History of the Christian Church.* Grand Rapids: Wm. B. Eerdmans Publishing Co., 1962.

70. Schaff, Philip. *The Person of Christ.* New York: American Tract Society, 1913.

71. Sider, Ronald. "A Case for Easter." *His,* April 1972.

72. Stauffer, Ethelbert. *Jesus and His Story.* Translated by Dorthea M. Barton. New York: Knopf, 1960.

73. Stewart, R. A. *The Earlier Rabbinic Tradition: And Its Importance for New Testament Background.* London: InterVarsity Fellowship, 1949.

74. Stoner, Peter W., and Newman, Robert C. *Science Speaks.* Chicago: Moody Press, 1976.

75. Suetonius. *Life of Vespasian,* 4. 5.

76. Tacitus. *Histories,* 5. 13.

77. Tenney, Merrill C. "The Resurrection of Jesus Christ." *Prophecy in the Making.* Carl Henry, editor. Carol Stream, IL: Creation House, 1971.

78. Thorburn, Thomas James. *A Critical Examination of the Evidences for the Doctrine of the Virgin Birth.* London: 1908.

79. Tucker, T. G. *Life in the Roman World of Nero and St. Paul.* London: Macmillan & Co., Ltd., 1910.

80. Vermes, Geza. *Jesus the Jew: A Historian's Reading of the Gospels.* New York: Macmillan Publishing Co., 1973.

81. Wells, G. A. *Did Jesus Exist?* London: Elek/Pemberton, 1975.

82. Westcott, Brooke F. *The Gospel of the Resurrection.* 4th ed. London: n.pub., 1879.

83. White, Bill. *A Thing Incredible.* 1944, Israel: Yanetz Ltd., 1976.

84. Wilson, Ian. *Jesus: The Evidence.* San Francisco: Harper & Row Publishers, Inc., 1984.

85. Yamauchi, Edwin. "Easter—Myth, Hallucination, or History?" *Christianity Today,* March 29, 1974.

86. Zeitlin, Solomon. "The Crucifixion of Jesus Re-examined." *Jewish Quarterly Review* 31 (1940-41).

OTHER RELIGIONS

Compared with Christianity

What Is Religion? (UNR/9-10)

The term religion has many definitions. None is agreed upon by everyone, but certain common aspects and implications of religion can be observed. We define religion as that aspect of one's experience in which he attempts to live harmoniously with the power or powers he believes are controlling the world.

> **NOTE:** More details on the main distinctions between other religions and Christianity may be found in the four original books by Josh McDowell and Don Stewart (now conveniently compiled into one volume, *Concise Guide To Today's Religions*), which cover the parts of this section: (1) Non-Christian Religions; (2) Secular Religions; (3) Cults; and (4) The Occult.

Part One
NON-CHRISTIAN RELIGIONS

CHAPTER 24 *Hinduism*

(UNR/17-32)

Hinduism is not only one of the oldest of all religious systems, it is also one of the most complex. During its history Hinduism has spawned a variety of sects holding diverse beliefs; therefore, it is difficult to get an accurate picture of Hinduism without considering a vast array of history and commentary.

Gaer notes,

> But all the various sects believe in:
>
> *Brahman,* the eternal Trimutri, or Three-in-One God: *Brahma,* the Creator; *Vishnu,* the Preserver; and *Shiva,* the Destroyer;
>
> *Submission to Fate,* since man is not outside, but part of Brahman;
>
> *The Caste System,* determined by the laws of Manu;
>
> *The Law of Karma,* that from good must come good, and from evil must come evil;
>
> *Reincarnation,* as a chain of rebirths in which each soul, through virtuous living, can rise to a higher state;
>
> *Nirvana,* the final stage reached upon the emancipation of the soul from the chain of rebirths;

Yogas, the disciplines which enable the individual to control the body and the emotions; and

Dharma, the Law of Moral Order, which each individual must find and follow to reach nirvana. 10/35

John Baker observes:

> It is the essence of Hinduism that there are many different ways of looking at a single object, none of which will give the view of the whole, but each of which is entirely valid in its own right. 5/193

Hinduism is tolerant of other religions because Hindus see a sameness in all of them.

Hindu Scriptures

The Hindu scriptures, written through a period of 2,000 years (1400 B.C.—A.D. 500) are voluminous. They reflect the practices and beliefs which arose during the different long periods of Hindu history.

The word *veda* literally means wisdom or knowledge. It is the term applied to the oldest of the Hindu scriptures, originally transmitted orally and then subsequently preserved in written form. The vedas contain hymns, prayers and ritual texts composed during a period of a thousand years, beginning about 1400 B.C.

The upanishads are a collection of speculative treatises. They were composed during the period 800—600 B.C., and 108 of them are still in existence. The word *upanishad* conveys the idea of secret teaching. Its treatises mark a definite change in emphasis from the sacrificial hymns and magic formulas in the vedas to the mystical ideas about man and the universe, specifically the eternal Brahman, which is the basis of all reality, and the *atman,* which is the self or the soul. The upanishads reportedly had an influence upon Gautama Buddha, the founder of Buddhism, as can be observed in some basic similarities between the upanishads and the teachings of Mahayana Buddhism.

The *Ramayana* is one of the two major epic tales of India, the other being the *Mahabharata.* Authorship is ascribed to the sage-poet Valmiki. The work consists of 24,000 couplets based upon the life of Rama, a righteous king who was supposedly an incarnation of the God Vishnu.

The *Mahabharata* is the second epic; an immense story of the deeds of Aryan clans. It consists of some 100,000 verses and was composed over an 800-year period beginning about 400 B.C. Contained within this work is a great classic, the *Bhagavad Gita,* or the "Song of the Blessed Lord."

The Bhagavad Gita is not only the most sacred book of the Hindus, but it is also the best known and the most read of all Indian works in the entire world, despite the fact it was added late to the *Mahabharata,* sometime in the first century A.D.

The story revolves around man's duty, which, if carried out, will bring nothing but sorrow. The significance this story has on Hindu belief is its endorsement of bhakti, or devotion to a particular god, as a means of salvation, since Arjuna, the story's main character, decides to put his devotion to Vishnu above his own personal desires. The Gita ends with Arjuna devoted to Vishnu and ready to kill his relatives in battle.

This poem has inspired millions of Hindus who, because of their own situation, have identified with Arjuna and his dilemma. The poem offers hope, through the way of devotion, to all people no matter what their caste or sex. The poor and downtrodden who could not achieve salvation through the way of works or the way of knowledge can now achieve it through the way of devotion.

These two epic stories, the *Ramayana* and the *Mahabharata,* depict characters who have become ideals for the people of India in terms of moral and social behavior.

The *Puranas* are an important source for the understanding of Hinduism. They include legends of gods, goddesses, demons and ancestors, and they describe pilgrimages and rituals to demonstrate the importance of bhakti, caste and dharma.

Hindu Teachings

Moksha, also known as *mukti,* is the Hindu term used for the liberation of the soul from the wheel of karma. For the Hindu, the chief aim of the existence is to be freed from *samsara* (the binding life-cycle) and the wheel of karma with its endless cycle of births, deaths and rebirths. When one achieves this liberation, he enters into a state of fullness or completion.

The word *karma* literally means action and refers to a person's actions and the consequences thereof. In Hinduism, one's present state of existence is determined by his performance in previous lifetimes. The law of karma is the law of moral consequence, or the effect of any action upon the performer in a past, present or even future existence. As one performs righteous acts, he moves toward liberation from the cycle of successive births and deaths.

Contrariwise, if one's deeds are evil, he will move further from liberation. The determining factor is one's karma. The cycle of births, deaths and rebirths could be endless.

Samsara refers to transmigration or rebirth. It is the passing through a succession of lives based upon the direct reward or penalty of one's karma. This continuous chain consists of suffering from the results of acts of ignorance or sin in past lives. At each successive rebirth, the soul, which the Hindus consider to be eternal, moves from one body to another and carries with it the karma from its previous existence.

The rebirth may be to a higher form, i.e., a member of a higher caste or god, or down the social ladder to a lower caste or animal, since the wheel of karma applies to both man and animals.

The *caste system* is a unique feature of the Hindu religion. The account of its origin is an interesting story. Brahma created Manu, the first man. From Manu came the four different types of people, as the creator Brahma determined. From Manu's head came the Brahmins, the best and most holy people. Out of Manu's hands came the Kshatriyas, the rulers and warriors. The craftsmen came from his thighs and are called Vaisyas. The remainder of the people came from Manu's feet and are known as Sudras.

The caste system became more complicated as time went on, with literally thousands of subcastes coming into existence. Today the caste system is still an integral part of the social order of India, even though it has been outlawed by the Indian government.

From early times the Hindus *revered the cow* and considered it a possessor of great power. The following verses from the *Atharva Veda* praise the cow, identifying it with the entire visible universe:

> Worship to thee, springing to life, and worship to thee when born!
> Worship, O Cow, to thy tail-hair, and to thy hooves, and to thy form! . . .
> The Cow is Heaven, the Cow is Earth, the Cow is Vishnu, Lord of Life. . .
> He who hath given a Cow unto the Brahmans winneth all the worlds. . .
> Both Gods and mortal men depend for life and being on the Cow.
> She hath become this universe; all that the sun surveys is she (*Atharva Veda* X:10).

Hinduism and Christianity

On the subject of God, Hinduism's supreme being is the undefinable, impersonal Brahman, a philosophical absolute. Christianity, on the other hand, teaches that there is a supreme being who is the infinite, personal Creator. The God of Christianity, moreover, is loving and He is keenly interested in the affairs of mankind, quite in contrast to the aloof deity of Hinduism.

The Bible makes it clear that God cares about what happens to each one of us:

> And call upon Me in the day of trouble; I shall rescue you and you will honor Me (Psalm 50:15, NASB).

> Come to Me, all who are weary and heavy laden, and I will give you rest (Matthew 11:28, NASB).

The Hindu views man as a manifestation of the impersonal Brahman, without individual self or self-worth. Christianity teaches that man was made in the image of God with a personality and the ability to receive and give love. Although the image of God in man has been tarnished by the fall, man is still of infinite value to God. This was demonstrated by the fact that God sent His only begotten Son, Jesus Christ, to die to redeem sinful man, even while man was still in rebellion against God.

The Bible says,

> For while we were still helpless, at the right time Christ died for the ungodly. For one will hardly die for a righteous man, though perhaps for a good man someone would dare even to die. But God demonstrates His own loved toward us, in that while we were yet sinners, Christ died for us (Romans 5:6-8, NASB).

> Namely, that God was in Christ reconciling the world to Himself, not counting their trespasses against them, and He has committed to us the word of reconciliation. Therefore, we are ambassadors for Christ, as though God were entreating through us; we beg you on behalf of Christ, be reconciled to God. He made Him who knew no sin to be sin on our behalf, that we might become the righteousness of God in Him (2 Corinthians 5:19-21, NASB).

In Hinduism there is no sin against a Holy God. Acts of wrongdoing are not done against any God but are mainly a result of ignorance. These evils can be overcome by following the guidelines of one's caste and way of salvation. To the contrary, Christianity sees sin as a real act of rebellion against a perfect and Holy God. All acts of transgression are ultimately acts of rebellion against the laws of God.

The Scripture states:

> Against Thee, Thee only, I have sinned, and done what is evil in Thy sight, so that Thou art justified when Thou dost speak, and blameless when Thou dost judge (Psalm 51:4, NASB).

> For all have sinned and fall short of the glory of God (Romans 3:23, NASB).

Salvation in Hinduism can be attained in one of three general ways: the way of knowledge, knowing one is actually a part of the ultimate Brahman and not a separate entity; the way of devotion, which is love and obedience to a particular deity; or the way of works, or following ceremonial ritual. This salvation is from the seemingly endless cycle of birth, death and rebirth. By contrast, in Christianity salvation is from a potentially eternal separation from God and cannot be obtained by any number of good deeds, but rather is given freely by God to all who will receive it.

The Bible says:

> For by grace have you been saved through faith; and that not of yourselves, it is the gift of God; not as a result of works, that no one should boast (Ephesians 2:8,9, NASB).

> He saved us, not on the basis of deeds which we have done in righteousness, but according to His mercy, by the washing of regeneration and renewing by the Holy Spirit (Titus 3:5, NASB).

> He who believes in the Son has eternal life; but he who does not obey the

Son shall not see life, but the wrath of God abides on him (John 3:36, NASB).

Hinduism views the material world as transitory and of secondary importance to the realization of Brahman, while Christianity sees the world as having objective reality and its source in the creative will of God. Hindus see the world as an extension of Brahman, part of the absolute, while Christianity views the world as an entity eternally different in nature from God, not part of some universal or monistic one.

The Bible says that in the beginning God created the heavens and the earth (Genesis 1:1). Since the earth, therefore, was created by God, it is not to be identified with Him or His eternal nature.

These contradictions represent major diversities between the two religions. Many other differences remain which we cannot discuss in this small space. However, even with this limited spectrum of differences, one readily can see that the two faiths of Hinduism and Christianity never can be reconciled. The basic foundations on which each is built are mutually exclusive.

CHAPTER 25 *Buddhism*

(UNR/47-72)

Buddhism began in India about five hundred years before the birth of Christ. The people living at that time had become disillusioned with certain beliefs of Hinduism including the caste system, which had grown extremely complex. The number of outcasts (those who did not belong to any particular caste) was continuing to grow.

Moreover, the Hindu belief of an endless cycle of births, deaths and rebirths was viewed with dread. Consequently, the people turned to a variety of beliefs, including the worship of animals, to satisfy this spiritual vacuum. Many different sects of Hinduism arose, the most successful being that of Buddhism, which denies the authority of the vedas.

The Buddha

Buddhism, unlike Hinduism, can point to a specific founder. However, in Buddhism, like so many other religions, fanciful stories arose concerning events in the life of the founder, Siddhartha Gautama (fifth century B.C.).

The Buddha, or "enlightened one," was born about 560 B.C. in northeastern India. His family name was Gautama, his given name was Siddhartha. Siddhartha was the son of a rajah, or ruler. His mother died when he was just a week old and Siddhartha was cared for by his mother's sister, who was also the rajah's second wife. There was supposedly a prophecy given at the time of his birth by a sage at his father's court.

The prophecy said that the child would be a great king if he stayed at home, but if he decided to leave home, he would become a savior for mankind. This bothered his father, for he wanted his son to succeed him as king. Therefore, to keep him at home, his father surrounded him with wealth and pleasures and kept all painful and ugly things out of his sight.

Siddhartha eventually married and had a son but was still confined to the palace and its pleasures. One day he informed his father that he wished to see the world. This excursion would forever change his life, for it was during this journey that he saw "the four passing sights."

Although his father ordered the streets to be cleansed and decorated and all elderly or infirmed people to stay inside, there were those who did not get the message. The first troubling sight Siddhartha saw was that of a decrepit old man. When Siddhartha asked what happened to this man, he was told that the man was old, as everyone someday would become.

Later, he met a sick man and was told that all people were liable to be sick and suffer pain like that individual.

He then saw a funeral procession with a corpse on its way to cremation, the followers weeping bitterly. When he asked what that meant, the prince was informed that it was the way of life, for sooner or later both prince and pauper would have to die.

The last sight was that of a monk begging for his food. The tranquil look on the beggar's face convinced Siddhartha that this type of life was for him. Immediately he left his family and the palace in search of enlightenment. The night he left his home to seek enlightenment became known as the Great Renunciation.

The former prince, now a beggar, spent his time wandering from place to place seeking wisdom. Unsatisfied by the truths taught in the Hindu scriptures, he became discouraged but continued on his quest. He tried asceticism but this gave him no peace. The fateful day in his life came while he was meditating beneath a fig tree.

Deep in meditation, he reached the highest degree of God-consciousness, known as nirvana. He supposedly stayed under the fig tree for seven days. After that, the fig tree was called the bodhi, or the bo tree, the tree of wisdom. The truths he learned he would now impart to the world, no longer as Siddhartha Gautama, but as the Buddha, the enlightened one.

When the Buddha emerged from his experience under the bo tree, he met with five monks who had been his companions. It was to these monks that the Buddha began his teaching ministry with the sermon at Benares. The sermon contained the following:

> These two extremes, monks, are not to be practiced by one who has gone forth from the world. What are the two? That conjoined with the passions and luxury, which is low, vulgar, common, ignoble, and useless; and

> that conjoined with self-torture, which is painful, ignoble, and useless. Avoiding these two extremes the Blessed One has gained the enlightenment of the Middle Path, which produces insight and knowledge, and leads to calm, to higher knowledge, enlightenment, nirvana.
>
> And what, monks, is the Middle Path . . . ? It is the noble Eightfold Path: namely, right view, right intention, right speech, right action, right livelihood, right effort, right mindfulness, right concentration. 6/29-30

After the sermon at Benares, the Buddha started to spread his teachings to the people of India. The Indian people, disillusioned with Hinduism, listened intently to this new doctrine. By the time of Buddha's death, at age 80, his teachings had become a strong force in India.

Some time after his death, the Buddha was deified by some of his followers, even though veneration of the Buddha is against the basic teachings of Buddha himself.

Theravada and Mahayana Buddhism

Early Buddhism was confined largely to India and is usually referred to as Theravada Buddhism. Later Buddhism, which became very popular outside India (notably in China and Japan), became known as Mahayana Buddhism:

Buddhist Teachings

A key concept in Buddhism is nirvana, the final goal for the Buddhists. Donald K. Swearer gives insight into this important concept.

> Nirvana has been a troublesome idea for the students of Buddhism. Just what is it? The term itself does not offer much help. Like not-self (*anatta*), nirvana is a negative term. Literally, it means the "blowing out" of the flame of desire, the negation of suffering (*dukkha*). This implies that nirvana is not to be thought of as a place but as a total reorientation or state of being realized as a consequence of the extinction of blinding and binding attachment. 23/44

There are five precepts taught by Buddhism that all Buddhists should follow:

1. Kill no living thing (including insects).
2. Do not steal.
3. Do not commit adultery.
4. Tell no lies.
5. Do not drink intoxicants or take drugs.

There are other precepts that apply only to monks and nuns. These include:

6. Eat moderately and only at the appointed time.

7. Avoid that which excites the senses.
8. Do not wear adornments (including perfume).
9. Do not sleep in luxurious beds.
10. Accept no silver or gold.

Sacred Scriptures

In Theravada Buddhism there are three groups of writings considered to be holy scriptures, known as "The Three Baskets" (Tripitaka). The Vinaya Pitaka (discipline basket) contains rules for the higher class of Buddhists; the Sutta Pitaka (teaching basket) contains the discourses of the Buddha; and the Abidhamma Pitaka (metaphysical basket) contains Buddhist theology. The total volume of these three groups of writings is about 11 times larger than the Bible.

In Mahayana Buddhism the scriptures are much more voluminous, as Clark B. Offner reveals:

> "A Mahayanist is one who reads Mahayana scriptures" is the definition given by one ancient Buddhist scholar. In contrast to the comparatively limited scope of the Pali canon used by Theravada Buddhists, Mahayana scriptures have multiplied to the point where standard editions of the Chinese canon encompass over 5,000 volumes. While the oldest scriptures are based on Sanskrit and contain much that is parallel to the Pali canon, other scriptures which have no Sanskrit prototypes have been written in Nepalese, Tibetan and Chinese.
>
> Since there are no clear limits to the Mahayana "canon," comparatively recent works by later innovators are often given *de facto* canonical status in the sects which adhere to their teachings. As there are such a number and such a variety of scriptures, most Mahayana sects have chosen certain favorite ones to which they refer exclusively. The fact is that some such selection is necessary, for this extreme bulk and breadth of the scriptures makes it impossible for believers to be acquainted with, let alone understand and practice, the often contradictory teachings found in them. 18/181

Nichiren Shoshu Buddhism

One form of Buddhism that has seen a revival of sorts in the past fifty years is a Japanese mystical sect known as Nichiren Shoshu. Its recent growth has been astounding, as chronicled by Walter Martin:

> In 1960 Daisaku Ikeda was inaugurated president over 1.3 million members. Ikeda expanded NSB's evangelism in foreign countries, opening a branch in the United States in 1960. The quickly growing branch of the sect held its first convention in 1963 in Chicago, with representatives from ten chapters. By 1973, membership was more than 250,000. From 1960 to 1973, NSB in the United States increased three-hundredfold! Japanese growth was even faster. The number of practicing Japanese families grew from three thousand in 1951 to more than seven million in 1971. 16/323

The origins of Nichiren Shoshu go back to a Japanese reformer named Nichiren Daishonon, who lived in the 13th century A.D. He was convinced that the true faith was taught by Dengyo Daishi (named Saicho before his death) who had introduced Tendai Buddhism to Japan in the eighth century.

Nichiren went about preaching his newly discovered truth, condemning all others as false religions. This did not go over well with the authorities, making Nichiren the object of persecution. Nichiren was both arrested and exiled for his preaching, many times narrowly escaping with his life. At the time of his death in 1282 he had attracted many followers.

Central to Nichiren Shoshu belief is the "gohonzon." The gohonzon is a black wooden box containing the names of important people in the Lotus Sutra and is used as a private altar. The gohonzon supposedly contains universal forces that control the devotee's life. There is, they believe, a direct connection between events in a person's life and the treatment of the gohonzon.

The worship ritual practiced by Nichiren Shoshu members is called "gongyo." The practice consists of kneeling before the gohonzon, the recitation of passages from the Lotus Sutra, then the rubbing of rosary-type beads while chanting the daimoku—"nam-myoho-rengekyo."

The chief object of worship in Nichiren Shoshu Buddhism is a shrine known as the Dai-gohonzon located at the base of Mount Fuji in Japan. Individual gohonzons are mystical representations of the Dai-gohonzon.

Nichiren Shoshu's recent accelerated growth (1970 figures by the Japanese Office of Cultural Affairs put membership at over 16 million 1/208) can be attributed directly to its missionary emphasis.

Zen Buddhism

Zen is a branch of Mahayana Buddhism that has become widely known in the West.

> The Chinese added to the many schools of Buddhism a new school, whose name reveals its history. Dhyana is the Indian word for meditation; it was changed in China to Chan and in Japan to Zen, which is now the best-known title of this sect. 20/145

Zen actually developed about a thousand years after the death of the Buddha. However, it contains Buddha's emphasis on meditation which led to his enlightenment. One statement attributed to the Buddha has become a frequent reference by Zen teachers: "Look within, you are the Buddha."

One famous story tells about a man who desired to be a Zen master. He asked to be taught Zen. The Zen master did not speak but began to pour a cup of tea for his visitor, using a cup that was already filled. The extra tea overflowed and ran across the table to drip to the rice-mat-covered floor. Still the Zen master kept pouring until the pot was empty. He finally spoke: "You are like this cup," he said. "You are full. How can I pour Zen into you? Empty yourself and come back."

Central to Zen practice is *zazen*. Zazen is the method of sitting in Zen meditation, which is done daily at specific times with occasional periods of intense meditation lasting one week. The goal is final enlightenment.

In Zen the sudden illumination or enlightenment is known as *satori*. Satori is an experience beyond analyzation and communication, bringing the practitioner into a state of maturity. The experience of satori comes abruptly and momentarily, but it can be repeated. It cannot be willed into existence.

Part of Zen's attraction is that one is not required to be responsible in evaluating anything in the world or even in his own thoughts. One loses his capacity to think logically and critically. While the Bible commands Christians to test *all* things (1 Thessalonians 5:21,22), Zen mocks critical analysis.

Buddhism and Christianity

There are radical differences between Buddhism and Christianity that make any attempt of reconciliation between these two faiths impossible. The Buddhistic world view is basically monistic. That is, the existence of a personal creator and Lord is denied. The world operates by natural power and law, not divine command.

Buddhism denies the existence of a personal God.

> Any concept of God was beyond man's grasp and since Buddhism was a practical approach to life, why not deal with practical things? India, where Buddhism was born, had so many Hindu gods that no one could number them. They were often made in the image of men, but Buddhism was made in the image of concepts about life and how life should be lived. If the truth were known, you often tell yourself, Buddhism has no God in the Hindu or Christian sense, nor does it have a savior or messiah. It has the Buddha. And he was the Enlightened One, the Shower-of-the-Way. 3/47

There are those who deify the Buddha but along with him they worship other gods. The Scriptures make it clear that not only does a personal God exist, but He is to be the only object of worship.

> "You are My witness," declares the Lord, "And My servant whom I have chosen, in order that you may know and believe Me, and understand that I am He. Before Me there was no God formed, and there will be none after Me" (Isaiah 43:10, NASB).

> Thus says the Lord, the King of Israel and His Redeemer, the Lord of hosts: "I am the first and I am the last, and there is no God besides Me" (Isaiah 44:6, NASB).

> I am the Lord your God, who brought you out of the land of Egypt, out of

> the house of slavery. You shall have no other gods before Me (Exodus 20:2,3, NASB).

> Then Jesus said to him, "Begone, Satan! For it is written 'You shall worship the Lord your God, and serve him only' " (Matthew 4:10, NASB).

> Jesus therefore said to them again, "Truly, truly, I say to you, I am the door of the sheep. All who came before Me are thieves and robbers; but the sheep did not hear them. I am the door; if anyone enters through Me, he shall be saved and shall go in and out, and find pasture" (John 10:7-9, NASB).

There is no such thing in Buddhism as sin against a supreme being. In Christianity sin is ultimately against God although sinful actions also affect man and his world. The Bible makes it clear:

> Against thee, thee only, I have sinned, and done what is evil in thy sight (Psalm 51:4, NASB).

Therefore, man needs a savior to deliver him from his sins.

According to Buddhist belief, man is worthless, having only temporary existence. In Christianity man is of infinite worth, made in the image of God, and will exist eternally. Man's body is a hindrance to the Buddhist while to the Christian it is an instrument for glorifying God.

> Then God said, "Let us make man in our image, according to our likeness; and let them rule over the fish of the sea and over the birds of the sky and over the cattle and over all the earth, and over every creeping thing that creeps on the earth" (Genesis 1:26, NASB).

> Or do you not know that your body is a temple of the Holy Spirit who is in you, whom you have from God, and that you are not your own? (1 Corinthians 6:19, NASB).

Another problem with Buddhism is the many forms it takes. Consequently, there is a wide variety of belief in the different sects with much that is contradictory. John B. Noss makes an appropriate comment:

> The rather odd fact is that there ultimately developed within Buddhism so many forms of religious organization, cultus and belief, such great changes even in the fundamentals of the faith, that one must say Buddhism as a whole is really like Hinduism, a family of religions rather than a single religion. 17/146

With these and other differences, it can be seen readily that any harmonization of Christianity and Buddhism simply is not possible.

CHAPTER 26 *Confucianism* (UNR/77-93)

Confucianism, a religion of optimistic humanism, has had a monumental impact on the life, social structure and political structure of China. The founding of the religion goes back to one man, known as Confucius, born a half-millennium before Christ.

The Life of Confucius

Although Confucius occupies a hallowed place in Chinese tradition, little is verifiable about his life. The best source available is *The Analects,* the collection of his sayings made by his followers. Long after his death much biographical detail on his life surfaced, but most of this material is of questionable historical value. However, there are some basic facts that can be accepted reasonably to give an outline of his life.

Confucius was born Chiu King, the youngest of eleven children, about 550 B.C., in the principality of Lu, which is located in present-day Shantung. He was a contemporary of the Buddha (although they probably never met) and lived immediately before Socrates and Plato. Nothing is known for certain concerning his ancestors except the fact that his surroundings were humble. As he himself revealed: "When I was young I was without rank and in humble circumstances."

His father died soon after his birth, leaving his upbringing to his mother. During his youth, Confucius participated in a variety of activities, including hunting and fishing; but, "On reaching the age of 15, I bent my mind to learning."

He held a minor government post as a collector of taxes before he reached the age of 20. It was at this time that Confucius married. However, this marriage was short-lived, ending in divorce after producing a son and a daughter. He became a teacher in his early twenties, and that proved to be his calling in life.

His ability as a teacher became apparent and his fame spread rapidly, attracting a strong core of disciples. Many were attracted by his wisdom. He believed that society would not be changed unless he occupied a public office where he could put his theories into practice.

Confucius held minor posts until age 50, when he became a high official in Lu. His moral reforms achieved an immediate success, but he soon had a falling out with his superiors and subsequently resigned his post. Confucius spent the next thirteen years wandering from state to state, attempting to implement his political and social reforms. He devoted the last five years of his life to writing and editing what have become Confucian classics.

He died in Chüfou, Shantung, in 479 B.C., having established himself as the most important teacher in Chinese culture. His disciples referred to him as King Fu-tzu or Kung the Master, which has been latinized into Confucius.

China Before Confucius

It is important to understand life in China at the time of Confucius in order to develop a better appreciation of the reforms he was attempting to institute. The age in which Confucius lived was characterized by social anarchy. Huston Smith gives insight into the condition of China during this difficult period:

> Instead of nobly holding their prisoners for ransom, conquerors put them to death in mass executions. Soldiers were paid upon presenting the severed heads of their enemies. Whole populations unlucky enough to be captured were beheaded, including women, children, and the aged. We read of mass slaughters of 60,000, 80,000, 82,000, and even 400,000. There are accounts of the conquered being thrown into boiling caldrons and their relatives forced to drink the human soup. 22/166

It is easy to see how the need arose for someone like Confucius to provide answers as to how the people could live together harmoniously.

Confucius believed China could be saved if the people would seek for the good of others, a practice of their ancestors. The role Confucius would play was not as a savior or messiah but as one who would put the people back in touch with the ancients: "I transmit but do not create. I believe in and love the ancients."

The Veneration of Confucius

Like many great religious leaders, Confucius was eventually deified by his followers. The following chart traces the progress which led to his ultimate deification:

B.C.	
195	The Emperor of China offered animal sacrifices at the tomb of Confucius.
A.D.	
1	He was given the imperial title "Duke Ni, All-complete and Illustrious."
57	Regular sacrifice to Confucius was ordered at the imperial and provincial colleges.
89	He was raised to the higher imperial rank of "Earl."
267	More elaborate animal sacrifices to Confucius were decreed four times yearly.
492	He was canonized as "The Venerable, the Accomplished Sage."
555	Separate temples for the worship of Confucius were ordered at the capital of every prefecture in China.
740	The statue of Confucius was moved from the side to the center of the Imperial College, to stand with the historic kings of China.
1068–1086	Confucius was raised to the full rank of Emperor.
1906	December 31. An Imperial Rescript raised him to the rank of Co-Assessor with the deities Heaven and Earth.
1914	The worship of Confucius was continued by the first President of the Republic of China, Yuan Shi Kai. 14/117-18

The Life of Mencius

One of the central figures in Confucianism is Meng-tzu (Latinized into Mencius) who became second only to Confucius in the history of Confucian thought. Mencius, born in the state of Ch'i in 371 B.C., studied with a disciple of Confucius's grandson, Tzu-ssu.

Like his master, Mencius spent most of his lifetime traveling from state to state, seeking those in leadership who would adopt the teachings of Confucius. The feudal order in China had become worse than in the days of Confucius, and the attempts of Mencius to reverse this trend were to no avail.

Mencius, rejected by the politicians of his day, turned to teaching and developing Confucian thought. Among his accomplishments was the clarification of a question that Confucius left ambiguous: the basic nature of man. Mencius taught that man is basically good. This is still a basic presupposition of Confucian thought.

This teaching, which is dramatically opposed to the biblical doctrine of original and universal sin, has made the proclamation of the gospel that much more difficult among the people in China who accept the ideas of Mencius concerning the nature of man.

The Sources of Confucianism

The Five Classics as we have them today have gone through much editing and alteration by Confucius's disciples, yet there is much in them that can be considered the work of Confucius. *The Five Classics* are:

1. *The Book of Changes (I Ching)* The I Ching is a collection of eight triagrams and 64 hexagrams which consist solely of broken and unbroken lines. These lines were supposed to have great meaning if the key were discovered.
2. *The Book of Annals (Shu K'ing)* The history of the five preceding dynasties. The example of the ancients was crucial to Confucius's understanding of how the superior man should behave.
3. *The Book of Poetry (Shih Ching)* The book of ancient poetry was assembled by Confucius because he believed the reading of poetry would aid in making a man virtuous.
4. *The Book of Ceremonies (Li Chi)* This work taught the superior man to act in the right or traditional way. Again Confucius stressed doing things in the same way as the ancients.
5. *The Annals of Spring and Autumn (Ch'un Ch'iu)* This book, supposedly written by Confucius, gave a commentary on the events of the state of Lu at Confucius's time.

None of these works contain the unique teachings of Confucius but they are rather an anthology of works he collected and from which he taught. Confucius's own teachings have come down to us from four books written by his disciples. They include:

1. *The Analects.* This is the most important source we have on Confucius. *The Analects* are sayings of both Confucius and his disciples.
2. *The Great Learning.* This work, which deals with the education and training of a gentleman, comes not from the hand of Confucius but rather from a later period (about 250 B.C.).
3. *The Doctrine of the Mean.* This work deals with the relationship of human nature to the order of the universe. Authorship

is uncertain (part of it may be attributed to Confucius's grandson Tzu-Ssu), but it does not come from Confucius.

4. *The Book of Mencius*. Mencius wrote the first exposition of Confucian thought about 300 B.C. by collecting earlier teachings and attempting to put them down systematically. This work, which has had great influence and gives an idealistic view of life, stresses the goodness of human nature.

The Doctrines of Confucianism

A concept that was entrenched in China long before the time of Confucius is that of filial piety (*Hsaio*) which can be described as devotion and obedience by the younger members of the family toward the elders, particularly in the case of son to father. This loyalty and devotion to the family was the top priority in Chinese life. Such duty to the family, especially devotion to the elders, was continued throughout one's life.

Confucius stressed this concept in his teachings, and it was well received by the Chinese people, both then and now.

Confucianism's doctrines can be summarized by six key terms or ways. *Jen* is the golden rule; *Chun-tzu* the gentleman; *Cheng-ming* is the role-player; *Te* is virtuous power; *Li* is the standard of conduct; and *Wen* encompasses the arts of peace. A brief discussion of the six principles reveals the basic doctrinal structure of Confucianism.

1. *Jen*. *Jen* has the idea of humaneness, goodness, benevolence or man-to-manness. *Jen* is the golden rule, the rule of reciprocity; that is to say, do not do anything to others that you would not have them do to you.

   "Tzu-Kung asked, 'Is there a single word which can be a guide to conduct throughout one's life?' The master said, 'It is perhaps the word "Shu." Do not impose on others what you yourself do not desire' " 9

> **NOTE**: This negative stating of the golden rule compares with the negative way many other religions also state it. On the other hand, Jesus' positive statement of the golden rule, "Do unto others as you would have them do unto you," commands a higher degree of service to others by His followers. They were not just to avoid doing bad things to others but rather to actively seek opportunities to do good to others.

2. *Chun-tzu*. *Chun-tzu* can be translated variously as the gentleman, true manhood, the superior man, or man-at-his-best. The teachings of Confucius were aimed toward the gentleman, the man of virtue.

   Huston Smith observes, "If *Jen* is the ideal relationship

between human beings, *Chun-tzu* refers to the ideal term of such relationships." 22/180 Confucius had this to say about the gentleman:

> (Confucius:) He who in this world can practice five things may indeed be considered man-at-his-best.
>
> What are they?
>
> Humility, magnanimity, sincerity, diligence, and graciousness. If you are humble, you will not be laughed at. If you are magnanimous, you will attract many to your side. If you are sincere, people will trust you. If you are gracious, you will get along well with your subordinates. 24/110

It is this type of man who can transform society into the peaceful state it was meant to be.

3. *Cheng-ming.* Another important concept according to Confucius was *Cheng-ming,* or the rectification of names. For a society to be properly ordered, Confucious believed everyone must act his proper part. Consequently, a king should act like a king, a gentleman like a gentleman, etc.

> Confucius said, "Duke Ching of Ch'i asked Confucius about government. Confucius answered, 'Let the ruler be a ruler, the subject a subject, the father a father, the son a son.' " 8

4. *Te.* The word *te* literally means "power," but the concept has a far wider meaning. The power needed to rule, according to Confucius, consists of more than mere physical might. It is necessary that the leaders be men of virtue who can inspire their subjects to obedience through example. This concept had been lost during Confucius's time with the prevailing attitude being that physical might was the only proper way to order a society.

   Confucius looked back at history to the sages of the past, Yao and Shun, along with the founders of the Chou dynasty, as examples of such virtuous rule. If the rulers would follow the example of the past, the people would rally around the virtuous example.

5. *Li.* One of the key words used by Confucius is *li.* The term has a variety of meanings, depending upon the context. It can mean propriety, reverence, courtesy, ritual or the ideal standard of conduct.

6. *Wen.* The concept of *wen* refers to the arts of peace, which Confucius held in high esteem. These include music, poetry and art. Confucius felt that these arts of peace, which came from the earlier Chou period, were symbols of virtue that should be manifest throughout society.

Is Confucianism a Religion?

Confucianism is not a religion in the sense of man relating to the Almighty but is rather an ethical system teaching man how to get along with his fellow man. However, Confucius did make some comments on the supernatural which give insight into how he viewed life, death, heaven, etc. He once said, "Absorption in the study of the supernatural is most harmful." 11/16,94

When asked about the subject of death, he had this to say: "Chi-lu asked how the spirits of the dead and the gods should be served. The master said, 'You are not able to serve man. How can you serve the spirits?'

" 'May I ask you about death?'

" 'You do not understand even life. How can you understand death?' " 7/12

John B. Noss comments, "His position in matters of faith is this: Whatever seemed contrary to common sense in popular tradition, and whatever did not serve any discoverable social purpose, he regarded coldly." 17/291

Since Confucianism deals primarily with moral conduct and the ordering of society, it is often categorized as an ethical system rather than a religion. Although Confucianism deals solely with life here on earth rather than the afterlife, it does take into consideration mankind's ultimate concerns.

The emphasis in Confucianism was on the earthly, not the heavenly; but the heavens and their doings were assumed to be real rather than imaginary. Since Confucianism gradually assumed control over all of one's life, and it was the presupposition from which all action was decided, it necessarily permeated Chinese religious thought, belief and practice as well.

The Impact of Confucianism

The impact Confucianism has had on China can hardly be over-estimated. Huston Smith observes:

> History to date affords no clearer support for this thesis than the work of Confucius. For over two thousand years his teachings have profoundly affected a quarter of the population of this globe. 22/192

Confucianism and Christianity

The ethical system taught by Confucius has much to commend it, for virtue is something to desire highly. However, the ethical philosophy Confucius espoused was one of self-effort, leaving no room or need for God.

Confucius taught that man can do it all by himself if he only follows the way of the ancients, while Christianity teaches that man does not have the capacity to save himself but is in desperate need of a savior. Confucius also hinted that human nature is basically good. This thought was developed by later Confucian teachers and became a cardinal belief of Confucianism.

The Bible, on the other hand, teaches that man in basically sinful and, when left to himself, is completely incapable of performing ultimate good. Contrast what the Bible says about human nature and the need of a savior against Confucianism.

> The heart is more deceitful than all else and is desperately sick; Who can understand it? (Jeremiah 17:9, NASB).

> For all have sinned and fall short of the glory of God (Romans 3:23, NASB).

> For by grace you have been saved through faith; and that not of yourselves, it is the gift of God; not as a result of works, that no one should boast (Ephesians 2:8,9, NASB).

> He saved us, not on the basis of deeds which we have done in righteousness, but according to His mercy, by the washing of regeneration and renewing by the Holy Spirit (Titus 3:5, NASB).

Since Confucianism lacks any emphasis upon the supernatural, this religious system must be rejected. It must be remembered that Confucius taught an ethical philosophy that later germinated into a popular religion, though Confucius had no idea that his teachings would become the state religion in China. Nevertheless, Confucianism as a religious system is opposed to the teachings of Christianity and must be rejected summarily by Christians.

CHAPTER 27 *Shintoism*

(UNR/111-118)

Shinto, the national religion of Japan, is one of the oldest of all the world's religions. It is unlike other religions inasmuch as it is basically not a system of beliefs. It has been variously defined.

Shinto is purely a Japanese religion, the origins of which are buried in antiquity. The Japanese name for their country is *Nippon,* which means "sun origin." Until the end of World War II, Japanese children were taught at school that the emperors were descendants of the sun-goddess, *Amaterasu.* Amaterasu had allegedly given the imperial house the divine right to rule. In 1946, in a radio broadcast to the Japanese people, Emperor Hirohito repudiated his divine right to rule.

Shinto's history can be divided into a number of stages. The first period was from prehistoric times to A.D. 522 when Shinto reigned supreme among the people of Japan without any serious competition.

In A.D. 522 Buddhism started gaining in popularity among the Japanese people. In the year 645, the Emperor Kotoku embraced Buddhism and rejected Shinto.

From 800 to 1700, Shinto combined with other religions, mixing with both Buddhism and Confucianism and forming what is called *Ryobu Shinto,* or dual-aspect Shinto. Shinto, by itself, experienced a considerable decline during this period.

Around 1700 Shinto experienced a revival when the study of archaic

Japanese texts was reinstituted. One of the most learned Shinto scholars of the period was Hirata, who wrote:

> The two fundamental doctrines are: Japan is the country of the Gods, and her inhabitants are the descendants of the Gods. Between the Japanese people and the Chinese, Hindus, Russians, Dutch, Siamese, Cambodians and other nations of the world there is a difference of kind, rather than of degree.
>
> The Mikado is the true Son of Heaven, who is entitled to reign over the four seas and the ten-thousand countries.
>
> From the fact of the divine descent of the Japanese people proceeds their immeasurable superiority to the natives of other countries in courage and intelligence. They "are honest and upright of heart, and are not given to useless theorizing and falsehoods like other nations." 14/172

Japanese Emperor Meiji established Shinto as the official religion of Japan in place of Buddhism. However, since the people continued to embrace both religions, in 1877 Buddhism was allowed to be practiced by the people, with total religious liberty granted two years afterward.

Meaning of Shinto

The word Shinto comes from the Chinese word *Shen-tao,* which means "the way of the gods." This term was not applied to the religion until the sixth century A.D., when it became necessary in order to distinguish it from Buddhism. A major feature of Shinto is the notion of *kami. Kami* is a difficult term to define precisely but it refers basically to the concept of sacred power in both animate and inanimate objects. Ninian Smart elaborates upon the idea of *kami* in the following manner:

> Shintoism displayed, and still displays, a powerful sense of the presence of gods and spirits in nature. These spirits are called *kami,* literally, "superior beings," and it is appropriate to venerate them. The kami are too numerous to lend themselves to a systematic ordering or stable hierarchy, but among them the sun goddess Amaterasu has long held a central place in Shinto belief. 21/192-93

Sacred Books

Although Shinto does not consider any one volume as the wholly inspired revelation on which its religion is based, two books are considered sacred and have done much to influence the beliefs of the Japanese people. The works are *Ko-ji-ki,* the "records of ancient matters," and *Nihon-gi,* the "chronicles of Japan." They were both composed around A.D. 720 and because they report events occurring some 1300 years earlier in the history of Japan, they are considered late works.

Worship

The basic place for worship in Shinto is at one of the numerous shrines covering the country of Japan. Although many Shintoists have built altars in their homes, the center of worship is the local shrine. Since Shinto has a large number of deities, a systematic worship of all such deities is impossible. The Shinto religious books acknowledge that only a few deities are consistently worshipped, the chief being the sun-goddess, Amaterasu.

The fact that the highest object of worship from whom the divine ancestors arose is a female rather than a male deity makes Shinto unique among the larger world religions.

Shinto and Christianity

The religion of Shinto is in opposition to Christianity. In its purest form it teaches the superiority of the Japanese people and their land above all others on earth and that is diametrically opposed to the teaching of the Bible. According to the Bible, the Jews are God's chosen people through whom He entrusted His words.

> Then what advantage has the Jew? or what is the benefit of circumcision? Great in every respect. First of all, that they were entrusted with the oracles of God (Romans 3:1,2, NASB).

However, though the Jews are God's chosen people, they have never been designated better than any other people (Galatians 3:27) and they have never been taught that they were direct descendants of the gods, as Shinto teaches its people.

Shinto fosters a pride and a feeling of superiority in the Japanese people. This type of pride is condemned by God, who says, "There is none righteous, not even one" (Romans 3:10, NASB). The same lesson was learned by the apostle Peter who concluded: "I most certainly understand now that God is not one to show partiality, but in every nation the man who fears Him and does what is right, is welcome to Him" (Acts 10:34, NASB).

Since Shinto teaches the basic goodness and divine origin of its people, there is no need for a Savior. This is the natural consequence of assuming one's race is of celestial origin.

Christianity teaches that all of us need a savior because our sins need to be punished. God, through Jesus Christ, took that punishment on Himself so that all mankind could be brought back into a proper relationship with Him.

Furthermore, the *Ko-ji-ki* and *Nihon-gi,* as the basis of the Shinto myth, are found to be hopelessly unhistorical and totally unverifiable. The stories and legends contained in these works are a far cry from the historically verifiable documents of both the Old and New Testaments.

The concept of *kami* is both polytheistic and crude, surrounded by much superstition. This is in contrast to the God of the Bible whose ways are righteous and beyond reproach. Immorality abounds in the stories of Shinto while the Bible is quick to condemn acts of immorality.

Shinto finds little acceptance apart from Japan since everything of Japanese origin is exalted and that which is non-Japanese is abased. Shinto is a textbook example of a religion invented by man to explain his ancestry and environment while taking no consideration of anyone but himself.

CHAPTER 28 *Judaism*

(UNR/131-47)

To Christians, Judaism is unique among world religions. It is to historic Judaism, the Judaism of the Old Testament, that Christianity traces its roots. Christianity does not supplant Old Testament Judaism; it is the fruition of it.

One cannot hold to the Bible, Old and New Testaments, as God's divine revelation without also recognizing and honoring the place God has given historic Judaism. As the apostle Paul recited, these are some of the blessings God has given to the Jewish people:

> To whom belongs the adoption as sons and the glory and the covenants and the giving of the Law and the temple service and the promises, whose are the fathers, and from whom is Christ according to the flesh, who is over all, God blessed forever. Amen (Romans 9:4,5, NASB).

Judaism has undergone many changes throughout its long history. At times it has been very close to the true God, serving Him in spirit and in deed. At other times it has ranged far from the will of God, forsaking its promises to Him, while He has remained faithful to Israel.

Statement of Faith

One of the great figures in Jewish history was Moses Maimonides, a Spanish Jew who lived in the 12th century A.D. Maimonides, a systematic thinker, tried to condense basic Jewish beliefs into the form of a creed.

Although criticized afterward by some, his creed is still followed by the traditional forms of Judaism. The creed is expressed in these thirteen basic beliefs:

1. I believe with perfect faith that the Creator, blessed be His Name, is the Creator and Guide of everything that has been created; and He alone has made, does make, and will make all things.
2. I believe with perfect faith that the Creator, blessed be His Name, is One, and that there is no unity in any manner like unto His, and that He alone is our God, who was, and is, and will be.
3. I believe with perfect faith that the Creator, blessed be His Name, is not a body, and that He is free from all the properties of matter, and that He has not any form whatever.
4. I believe with perfect faith that the Creator, blessed be His Name, is the first and the last.
5. I believe with perfect faith that to the Creator, blessed be His Name, and to Him alone, it is right to pray, and that it is not right to pray to any being besides Him.
6. I believe with perfect faith that all the words of the prophets are true.
7. I believe with perfect faith that the prophecy of Moses, our teacher, peace be unto him, was true, and that he was the chief of the prophets, both of those who preceded and of those who followed him.
8. I believe with perfect faith that the whole *Torah,* now in our possession, is the same that was given to Moses, our teacher, peace be unto him.
9. I believe with perfect faith that this *Torah* will not be changed, and that there will never be any other Law from the Creator, blessed be His Name.
10. I believe with perfect faith that the Creator, blessed be His Name, knows every deed of children and men, and all their thoughts, as it is said. It is He that fashioned the hearts of them all, that gives heed to all their works.
11. I believe with perfect faith that the Creator, blessed be His Name, rewards those that keep His commandments and punishes those that transgress them.
12. I believe with perfect faith in the coming of the Messiah; and, though he tarry, I will wait daily for his coming.
13. I believe with perfect faith that there will be a revival of the dead at the time when it shall please the Creator, blessed be His Name,

and exalted be His Fame for ever and ever. For Thy salvation I hope, O Lord.

Jewish Holy Days

The cycle of Jewish holy days is called the sacred round. Based on the ancient Jewish calendar, these holy days serve to remind Jews regularly of significant historical events in which God displayed His covenant with them and to give them regular opportunity to display their commitment to God.

THE SABBATH

This is a holy day of rest, in commemoration of God's completed work of creation and in His later liberation of the Israelites from the bondage of Egypt. It is a day of joy and thanksgiving to God for His many blessings.

PASSOVER

Passover (*Pessah*), the festival of spring, is celebrated one month after Purim [the celebration of deliverance of the Jews from Haman's plotted massacre in the time of Esther]. It constitutes the beginning of harvest; therefore, it is a time of celebration. However, there is a deeper reason for the people to observe this holy day, as the Scriptures plainly reveal. This feast celebrates the deliverance of the children of Israel from the bondage of Egypt.

SHABUOT

Shabuot, the feast of weeks, comes seven weeks after the Passover. Shabuot commemorates the giving of the Ten Commandments. During ancient times the farmer would bring his firstfruits to the Temple on Shabuot and offer them to God. The day is also celebrated by the reading of the Ten Commandments and the recitation of the book of Ruth.

ROSH HASHANAH

Rosh Hashanah literally means "head of the year." It is the Jewish New Year, celebrated on the first two days of the month of Tishri (September-October). It is a solemn day of reflection on both the deeds of the past year and the hopes of the upcoming one.

YOM KIPPUR

Yom Kippur is the holiest day of the year, the day of atonement. It is celebrated ten days after Rosh Hashanah and is devoted to confession of sins and reconciliation with God. Problems with enemies must be reconciled before one can be right with God, and forgiving and forgetting is the order of the day. The day is spent without touching food or drink, the mind being devoted to God on the holiest of days.

SUKKOTH

Sukkoth is the feast of tabernacles, or booths. This festival, which commemorates the ingathering of the harvest, is one of three pilgrim feasts established in ancient times where yearly trips were made to the Temple of Jerusalem. It is known as the feast of the booths because the people lived in tabernacles, or temporary shelters, throughout its duration (Exodus 34:18-26). In modern times the people, for the most part, only take their meals in these tabernacles rather than living in them for the duration of the feast.

HANUKKAH

Hanukkah, observed for eight days in midwinter, is the only major feast that does not have its source in the Bible. This feast is based upon the story of the Maccabees, recorded in the Apocrypha. When Antiochus IV Epiphanes in 167 B.C. introduced the worship of the Greek gods as the state religion, a small group of Jews led by Judas Maccabee staged a revolt.

Antiochus, who, among other things desecrated the Temple by slaughtering a pig in the Holy of Holies, was finally overthrown and freedom of religion returned to the land. Hanukkah is celebrated in observance of the heroic acts of the Maccabees.

The eight-branched candlestick, the Menorah, is integral to Hanukkah worship and commemorates a miracle that took place when the Temple was cleansed from the idolatrous acts of Antiochus IV Epiphanes. The tradition states that only enough holy oil was found in the Temple to light the lamp for one night. However, because of the providence of God and as a sign that He blessed the Jewish cleansing and rededication of the Temple, God miraculously kept the lamp burning for eight days and nights.

Since Hanukkah is celebrated near the Christian Christmas holiday, it has borrowed some ideas from Christmas, including the giving of gifts (traditionally one to each child on each of the eight nights), and family gatherings. Especially among non-practicing and reform (liberal) Jews, Hanukkah is a very important holiday.

The Three Branches of Judaism

Very simply stated, modern-day Judaism can be divided into three groups: Orthodox, Conservative and Reform.

ORTHODOX

Orthodox Judaism designates the traditionalists who are united in their upholding of the Law.

Orthodox Judaism observes most of the traditional dietary and ceremonial laws of Judaism. It adheres to the inspiration of the Old Testament, although greater authority is given to the *Torah* (Law), the first five books, than to the rest.

CONSERVATIVE

Conservative Judaism is sort of a happy medium between Orthodox and Reform Judaism. Founded in the nineteenth century, the Conservative movement quickly gained strength in both Germany and the United States.

In 1918, six months after the Balfour Declaration, the Conservative movement announced:

> We hold that the Jewish people are and of right ought to be at home in all lands. Israel, like every other religious communion, has the right to live and assert its message in any part of the world. We are opposed to the idea that Palestine should be considered *the home-land* of the Jews. Jews in America are part of the American nation.
>
> The ideal of the Jew is not the establishment of a Jewish state—not the reassertion of the Jewish nationality which has been long outgrown. We believe that our survival as a people is dependent on the assertion and the maintenance of our historic religious role and not upon the acceptance of Palestine as a home-land of the Jewish people. The mission of the Jew is to witness to God all over the world.

REFORM

Reform Judaism is the liberal wing of Judaism. It is so culture- and race-oriented that it easily can neglect the spiritual and religious side of Jewish life. Rather than assuming that the religious life produces and molds the culture, Reform Judaism assumes that the culture and racial heritage of the Jews produced and molded the religious life. While belief and doctrine may be changeable or even dispensable, the cultural history of the race is vital to any continuation of Jewishness. There is little consensus on doctrinal or religious belief in Reform Judaism.

Doctrine

JUDAISM AND THE MESSIAH

While Christianity recognizes that the promise of a personal, spiritual savior is the core of biblical revelation, Judaism has long vacillated in its concept of messiahship.

In the course of Jewish history the meaning of the Messiah has undergone changes. Originally it was believed that God would send His special messenger, delivering Israel from her oppressors and instituting peace and freedom. However, today, any idea of a personal messiah has been all but abandoned by the majority of Jews. It has been substituted with the hope of a messianic age characterized by truth and justice.

GOD

The Orthodox Jewish concept of God is based upon the Old Testament. The Hebrew scholar Samuel Sandmel summarizes the biblical teaching:

> The heritage from the Bible included a number of significant components about the Deity. God was not a physical being: He was intangible and invisible. He was the Creator and Ruler, indeed, the Judge of the World. He and He alone was truly God; the deities worshipped by peoples other than Israel were not God. Idols were powerless and futile; they were unworthy of worship; and indeed, to worship what was not God was a gross and sinful disrespect of Him. 19/168-69

THE SCRIPTURES

The sacred Scriptures of Judaism consists of documents arranged in three groups known as the Law, the Prophets, and the Writings. These books were originally written in Hebrew, except for parts of Daniel and Ezra and a verse in Jeremiah which were composed in Aramaic. These books are synonymous with the 39 books of Christianity's Old Testament. Their composition was over a period of some one thousand years, from 1400–400 B.C.

The Jews do not hold each part of their writings in equal importance. *The Law,* the Torah, is the most authoritative, followed by *the Prophets,* which have lesser authority, and lastly *the Writings.*

SALVATION IN JUDAISM

Judaism, while admitting the existence of sin, its abhorrence by God, and the necessity for atonement, has not developed a system of salvation teaching as found in Christianity. Atonement is accomplished by sacrifices, penitence, good deeds and a little of God's grace. No concept of substitutionary atonement (as in Christianity in the person of Jesus Christ) exists.

ORIGINAL SIN

Judaism holds no concept of original sin. According to Christian belief, all human beings are born into the world with a sinful nature because of the transgression of Adam (Romans 5:12-21). Judaism's emphasis is not on original sin but original virtue and righteousness. Although Judaism acknowledges that man does commit acts of sin, there is not a sense of man being totally depraved or unworthy as is found in Christian theology.

Judaism and Christianity

Although there are marked differences in many areas of belief and practice between Judaism and Christianity, there is a common heritage that both religions share. The Jewish writer, Pinchas Lapide, comments:

> We Jews and Christians are joined in brotherhood at the deepest level, so deep in fact that we have overlooked it and missed the forest of brotherhood for the trees of theology. We have an intellectual and spiritual kinship which goes deeper than dogmatics, hermeneutics, and exegesis. We are brothers in a manifold "elective affinity"
>
> -in the belief in one God our Father,
> -in the hope of His salvation,
> -in ignorance of His ways,
> -in humility before His omnipotence,
> -in the knowledge that we belong to Him, and He to us,
> -in love and reverence for God,
> -in doubt about our wavering fidelity,
> -in the paradox that we are dust and yet the image of God,
> -in the consciousness that God wants us as partners in the sanctification of the world,
> -in the condemnation of arrogant religious chauvinism,
> -in the conviction that love of God is crippled without love of neighbor,
> -in the knowledge that all speech about God must remain in a stammering on our way to Him. 15/2

The book of Galatians gives us God's view of Jews and Gentiles today. Chapter 3 shows forcefully that God's blessings on the Jews were a means of showing His grace, which was fully expressed in the sacrifice of His son, Jesus Christ, on the cross for the sins of all, Jewish and Gentile. The gospel was preached beforehand to Abraham, the father of the Jews (5:8) and was given to the Gentiles in Jesus Christ (5:14).

The heritage of the Old Testament, preserved for all mankind by the Jews, points all of us, Jewish or Gentile, to Jesus Christ (5:22-24). Each man, whether of Jewish or Gentile heritage, must come to God through Jesus Christ. There is no other way to true peace with God. As Galatians 3:26-29 concludes,

> For you are all sons of God through faith in Christ Jesus. For all of you who were baptized into Christ have clothed yourselves with Christ. There is neither Jew nor Greek, there is neither slave nor free man, there is neither male nor female; for you are all one in Jesus Christ. And if you belong to Christ, then you are Abraham's offspring, heirs according to promise.

CHAPTER 29 *Islam*

(UNR/149-78)

There are an estimated 450 million members of Islam which dominate more than three dozen countries on three continents. The word *Islam* is a noun which is formed from the Arabic verb meaning "to submit, surrender or commit oneself." *Islam* means submission or surrender, and with the translation comes the idea of action, not simple stagnation. The very act of submissive commitment is at the heart of Islam, not simply a passive acceptance and surrender to doctrine. *Muslim*, another noun form of the same verb, means "the one who submits."

History of Islam

The Muslim (var. sp.: Moslem) faith is a major driving force in the lives of many of the nations in the Middle East, West Asia and North Africa. The impact of this faith on the world has been increasing steadily. Today, Islam is the fastest-growing religion in the world.

The early history of Islam revolved around one central figure, Muhammad (var. sp.: Muhammed, Mohammed).

Muhammad

Muhammad was born around A.D. 570 in the city of Mecca in Arabia. His father died before his birth. His mother died when he was six. He was raised first by his grandfather and later by his uncle. Muhammad's early background is not well known. Some scholars believe he came from a well-respected family, but this is not certain.

At the age of 25, he married a wealthy 40-year-old widow named Khadijah. Of his life Anderson related:

> There is evidence in a tradition which can scarcely have been fabricated that Muhammad suffered in early life from fits. Be that as it may, the adult Muhammad soon showed signs of a markedly religious disposition. He would retire to caves for seclusion and meditation; he frequently practiced fasting; and he was prone to dreams. Profoundly dissatisfied with the polytheism and crude superstitions of his native Mecca, he appears to have become passionately convinced of the existence and transcendence of one true God. How much of this conviction he owed to Christianity or Judaism it seems impossible to determine. Monophysite Christianity was at that time widely spread in the Arab Kingdom of Ghassan; the Byzantine Church was represented by hermits dotted about the Hijaz with whom Muhammad may well have come into contact; the Nestorians were established at al Hira and in Persia; and the Jews were strongly represented in al Madina, the Yemen and elsewhere. There can be no manner of doubt, moreover, that at some period of his life he absorbed much teaching from Talmudic sources and had contact with some form of Christianity; and it seems overwhelmingly probable that his early adoption of monotheism can be traced to one or both of these influences. 2/54

The Call

As Muhammad grew, his views changed. He came to believe in only one God, Allah, a monotheistic faith. He rejected the idolatrous polytheism of those around him. By the age of 40, the now religious Muhammad had his first vision. These revelations are what are recorded in the *Qur'an (Koran).*

Muhammad was at first unsure of the source of these visions, whether divine or demonic. His wife, Khadijah, encouraged him to believe that they had come from God. Later she became his first convert. However, his most important early convert was a wealthy merchant named Abu Bakr, who eventually became one of his successors.

The Cambridge History of Islam comments on Muhammad's revelations:

> Either in the course of the visions or shortly afterwards, Muhammad began to receive "messages" or "revelations" from God. Sometimes he may have heard the words being spoken to him, but for the most part he seems simply to have "found them in his heart." Whatever the precise "manner of revelation"—and several different "manners" were listed by Muslim scholars—the important point is that the message was not the product of Muhammad's conscious mind. He believed that he could easily distinguish between his own thinking and these revelations.
>
> The messages which thus came to Muhammad from beyond his con-

> scious mind were at first fairly short, and consisted of short verses ending in a common rhyme or assonance. They were committed to memory by Muhammad and his followers, and recited as part of their common worship. Muhammad continued to receive the messages at intervals until his death. In his closing years the revelations tended to be longer, to have much longer verses and to deal with the affairs of the community of Muslims at Medina. All, or at least many, of the revelations were probably written down during Muhammad's lifetime by his secretaries. 13/31-32

These visions mark the start of Muhammad's prophetic call by Allah. Muhammad received these visions during the following 22 years, until his death in A.D. 632.

The Hijira

The new faith encountered opposition in Muhammad's home town of Mecca. Because of his rejection in Mecca and the ostracism of his views, Muhammad and his followers withdrew to the city known as Medina, which means in full, "City of the Prophet," renamed from its original Yathrib.

The Hijira, which means "flight," marks the turning point in Islam. All Islamic calendars mark this date, July 16, 622, as their beginning. Thus, A.D. 630 would be 8 A.H. (in the year of the Hijira).

In his early years in Medina, Muhammad was sympathetic to both Jews and Christians, but they rejected him and his teaching. Upon that rejection, Muhammad turned from Jerusalem as the center of worship of Islam, to Mecca, where the famous black stone Ka'aba was enshrined. Muhammad denounced all the idols which surrounded the Ka'aba and declared it was a shrine for the one true God, Allah.

With this new emphasis on Mecca, Muhammad realized he must soon return to his home. The rejected prophet did return, in triumph, conquering the city.

Muhammad now made sure of his political and prophetic ascendancy in Arabia. Active opponents near at hand were conquered by the sword, and tribes far away were invited sternly to send delegations offering their allegiance. Before his sudden death in 632 he knew he was well on the way to unifying the Arab tribes under a theocracy governed by the will of God. 17/517

Between the return to Mecca and Muhammad's death, the prophet zealously and militantly propagated Islam, and the new faith quickly spread throughout the area.

After Muhammad's Death

When Muhammad died he had not written a will instructing the leadership in Islam about determining his successor.

Eventually a power struggle developed as different factions believed their own methods of establishing a successor were better than their rivals. The major eruption came between those who believed the Caliph should be elected by the Islamic leadership and those who believed the successor should be hereditary, through 'Alī, Muhammad's son-in-law, married to his only daughter, Fatima. This struggle, along with others, produced the main body of Islam known as the Sunnis (followers of the prophet's way) as well as numerous sects.

Sunnis

Along with the Caliphate controversy, conflict raged on another front, that of law and theology. Through this conflict eventually four recognized, orthodox schools of Islamic thought emerged. All four schools accepted the *Qur'an* (Koran), the *Sunna,* or the practice of the Prophet as expressed in the *Hadith* (traditions) and the four bases of Islamic Law *(Shari'a)*: the *Qur'an,* the *Hadith,* the *Ij'ma'* (consensus of the Muslim community) and the *Q'yas* (use of analogical reason). These four groups came to be called the Sunnis.

The Shi'a

The fourth Caliph to follow Muhammad was an early convert, along with his son-in-law, 'Alī. He was eventually murdered by Mu'awiya, who claimed the Caliphate for himself.

> The tragedy that befell the House of 'Alī, beginning with the murder of 'Alī himself and including the deaths of his two sons, grandsons of Muhammad, has haunted the lives of "the party *(Shi'a)* of 'Alī." They have brooded upon these dark happenings down the years as Christians do upon the death of Jesus. A major heretical group, they have drawn the censure and yet have also had the sympathy of Sunnis and Sufis. They are among the sects whose radical elements al-Ghazali attacked as guilty of resting their claims on false grounds and sinfully dividing Islam. And yet, although agreeing with this indictment, the Muslim world at large has suppressed its annoyance at them, because their movement goes back to the very beginnings of Islam and has a kind of perverse justification, even in orthodox eyes. 17/540

The Sufis

In any strong, legalistic, religious system, worship can become mechanical and be exercised by rote, and God can become transcendent. Such an impersonal religion often motivates people to react. Such is the case with Islam, as the Sufis, the most well-known Islamic mystics, have arisen in response to orthodox Islam and to the often loose and secularist view of Islamic leadership during some of its early days under the *Ummayad* and *Abbasid* dynasties.

The Sufis exist today and probably are best known through their Dervish Orders (e.g., "the whirling Dervish").

There are many other sects and divergent groups among Islam, too numerous to detail here. One might mention that the Baha'i Faith, although significantly different from Islam today, had its roots in Islam.

Teachings of Islam

NOTE: For a more detailed treatment of this subject, see page 110 of *The Islam Debate* by Josh McDowell and John Gilchrist.

Faith and Duty

The teachings of Islam are comprised of faith *(imam)* and practice or duty *(din)*. Sir Norman Anderson explains:

> The faith and practice of Islam are governed by the two great branches of Muslim learning, theology, and jurisprudence. . . . Muslim theology (usually called "Tawhid" from its central doctrine of the Unity of the Godhead) defines all that man should believe, while the law (Shari'a) prescribes everything that he should do. There is no priesthood and no sacraments. Except among the Sufis, Islam knows only exhortation and instruction from those who consider themselves, or are considered by others, adequately learned in theology or law. 2/78

Qur'an

The basis for Islamic doctrine is found in the Qur'an (Koran). Boa describes the central place of the Qur'an in the Islamic faith as well as the supplementary works:

> The Koran is the authoritative scripture of Islam. About four-fifths the length of the New Testament, it is divided into 114 surahs (chapters). Parts were written by Mohammed, and the rest, based on his oral teaching, was written from memory by his disciples after Mohammed's death.
>
> Over the years a number of additional sayings of Mohammed and his early disciples were compiled. These comprise the *hadith* ("tradition"), the sayings of which are called *sunna* ("custom"). The Hadith supplements the Koran much as the Talmud supplements the Law in Judaism. 4/52

The Qur'an is the Word of God in Islam, the holy scriptures. As the authoritative scripture, it is the main guide for all matters of faith and practice. The Qur'an was revealed to Muhammad as the Word of God for mankind.

As noted above, the Qur'an is comprised of 114 *surahs,* or chapters, all attributed to Muhammad. The surahs are arranged in the Qur'an by length—the longer in front, the shorter in back.

In modern times, the Qur'an has faced many of the same dilemmas as the Bible. A major issue is the inspiration of the Qur'an. Islamic scholars do not agree as a whole on how the Qur'an came to be true or how much is true, although conservative Islamic scholars accept it *all* as literally true.

Five Articles of Faith

The five articles of faith are the main doctrines of Islam. All Muslims are expected to believe these tenets.

1. *God.* There is only one true God and his name is Allah. Allah is all-knowing, all-powerful and the sovereign judge. Yet Allah is not a personal God, for he is so far above man in every way that he is not personally knowable.

   > Although Allah is said to be loving, this aspect of his nature is almost ignored, and his supreme attribute of justice is thought to overrule love. 2/79

   The emphasis of the God of Islam is on judgment, not grace; on power, not mercy. He is the source of both good and evil and his will is supreme.
2. *Angels.* The existence of angels is fundamental to Islamic teaching. Gabriel, the leading angel, appeared to Muhammad and was instrumental in delivering the revelations in the Qur'an to Muhammad. Al Shaytan is the devil and most likely a fallen angel or jinn. Jinn are those creatures between angels and men which can be either good or evil. Each man and woman has two recording angels—one which records his good deeds, the other, his bad deeds.
3. *Scripture.* There are four inspired books in the Islamic faith. They are the *Torah* of Moses, the Psalms *(Zabin)* of David, the Gospel of Jesus Christ *(Injil)* and the *Qur'an.* Muslims believe the former three books have been corrupted by Jews and Christians. Also, since the Qur'an is God's most recent and final word to man, it supercedes all the other works.
4. *Prophets.* In Islam God has spoken through numerous prophets down through the centuries. The six greatest are: Adam, Noah, Abraham, Moses, Jesus and Muhammad. Muhammad is the last and greatest of all Allah's messengers.
5. *Last Days.* The last day will be a time of resurrection and judgment. Those who follow and obey Allah and Muhammad will go to Islamic heaven, called Paradise, a place of pleasure. Those who oppose them will be tormented in hell.

   > The last day (the resurrection and the judgment) figures prominently in Muslim thought. The day and the hour is a secret to all, but

> there are to be twenty-five signs of its approach. All men will be raised; the books kept by the recording angels will be opened; and God as judge will weigh each man's deeds in the balances. Some will be admitted to Paradise, where they will recline on soft couches quaffing cups of wine handed them by the Huris, or maidens of Paradise, of whom each man may marry as many as he pleases; others will be consigned to the torments of Hell. Almost all, it would seem, will have to enter the fire temporarily, but no true Muslim will remain there forever. 2/81

Finally there is a sixth article of faith which is considered by many to belong to the five doctrines. Whether this is one of the articles or not, it is a central teaching of Islam—*the belief in God's decrees or Kismet, the doctrine of fate.* This is a very rigid view of predestination that states all good or evil proceeds from divine will.

This strong fatalism has played a central role in Muslim culture. "To this the lethargy and lack of progress which, until recently at least, has for centuries characterized Muslim countries, can be partially attributed." 2/82

Five Pillars of Faith

Besides the five major beliefs or doctrines in Islam, there are also "five pillars of faith," foundational practices or duties which every Muslim must observe. They are:

1. *The Creed (Kalima).* "There is no God but Allah, and Muhammad is the Prophet of Allah," is the bedrock of Muslim belief. One must state this aloud publicly in order to become a Muslim. It is repeated constantly by the faithful.
2. *Prayer (Salat).* Prayer as ritual is central to a devout Muslim. Boa comments:

   > . . . the practice of prayer *(salat)* five times a day (upon rising, at noon, at midafternoon, after sunset, and before retiring). The worshipper must recite the prescribed prayers (the first surah and other selections from the Koran) in Arabic while facing the Ka'aba in Mecca. The Hadith (book of traditions) has turned these prayers into a mechanical procedure of standing, kneeling, hands and face on the ground, and so forth. The call to prayer is sounded by the *muezzin* (a Muslim crier) from a tower called a *minaret* which is a part of the *mosque* (the place of public worship). 4/53

3. *Almsgiving (Zakat).* Muhammad, himself an orphan, had a strong desire to help the needy. The alms originally were voluntary, but all Muslims are legally required to give one-fortieth of their income for the destitute. There are other rules and regulations for produce, cattle, etc. Freewill offerings also can be exercised.

4. *Fasting (Ramadan).* Faithful Muslims fast from sunup to sundown each day during this holy month. The fast develops self-control, devotion to God and identity with the destitute. No food or drink may be consumed during the daylight hours; no smoking or sexual pleasures may be enjoyed, either. Many Muslims eat two meals a day during Ramadan, one before sunrise and one shortly after sunset.
5. *The Pilgrimage (Hajj).* The pilgrimage is expected of all Muslims at least once in their lifetimes. It can be extremely arduous on the old or infirm, so in their cases, they may send someone in their places. The trip is an essential part in Muslims' gaining salvation. It involves a set of ceremonies and rituals, many of which center around the Ka'aba shrine, to which the pilgrimage is directed.

There is a sixth religious duty associated with the five pillars. This is *Jihad,* the Holy War. This duty requires that when the situation warrants, men are required to go to war to spread Islam or defend it against infidels. One who dies in a *Jihad* is guaranteed eternal life in Paradise (heaven).

Cultural Expression

Islam, like Judaism, is both a religion and a cultural identity which cannot be separated from the people. In many countries the Islamic faith, though not strictly practiced, is woven into the web of society at every facet.

To their doctrine, which serves as both a religious and social foundation, can be added another unifying factor, the Arabic language. It helps weld Islamic peoples, living in different countries, together.

The family also is important in the social economy of Islam. Marriage is required for every Muslim, even the ascetics. Muhammad commanded men to marry and propagate the race, and though they may not have more than four wives, large numbers of the men cohabit with as many concubines as they choose.

Although the act of marriage is important, the sanctity of the union is not as highly regarded. A Muslim may divorce his wife at any time and for any reason. On the whole, women in Islamic culture do not enjoy the status or the privileges of the men and are very dependent on their husbands:

> Since Muslim propagandists in this country persistently deny that women are inferior to men in Islam, it is worthwhile to set out the facts. Sura 4:31 says: "Men have the authority over women because God has made the one superior to the other and because they spend their wealth [to maintain them]. So good women are obedient, guarding the unseen [parts] because God has guarded [them]. As for those from whom you fear disobedience, admonish them and banish them to beds apart and beat them; then if they obey you, seek not occasion against them." 12/71-72

Islam and Christianity

Many of the Muslim beliefs come from the Bible. Yet in spite of the influence and similarities, the differences in the beliefs of the two faiths are striking.

GOD

Islam teaches the unity of God's essence and personality, explicitly excluding the Trinity as taught in the Bible.

The emphasis on the unity of God comes across in other ways. Islam has God divorced from His creation, so unified to Himself that He cannot be associated with creation. His transcendence is so great that He acts impersonally.

Their doctrine of predestination and the fact that both evil and good came from Allah make their God very capricious. Whatever Allah chooses becomes right; this makes any true standard of righteousness or ethics hard to discern and practically impossible to establish.

This is unlike the righteous God of the Bible. The very word *righteous* means, "a standard."

The Muslim finds it difficult to divorce the concept of father from the physical realm. To them it is blasphemous to call Allah or God your father. To do so is the same as saying that your mother and Allah had sexual intercourse to produce you!

In addition, while calling God "Father" is to evoke thoughts of love, compassion, tenderness and protectiveness to Christians, it is not so to the Muslim mind. To him, a father is strict, shows no emotion, never expresses love, and is bound to his family by duty and for what his family can provide for him, not by devotion.

CHRIST

In Islam the person and work of Jesus Christ are not seen in the same way as in Christianity. For the Christian the resurrection of Jesus Christ as the incarnate Son of God is the vital cornerstone of faith, yet the Muslim does not hold either of these truths—that Christ is the Son of God or that He rose from the dead.

Islam does believe Jesus was a sinless prophet although not as great as Muhammad. While Surah 3:45-47 in the Qur'an speaks of the virgin birth of Christ, it is not the same biblical virgin birth. Jesus is certainly *not* the only begotten Son of God, and an angel—rather than the Holy Spirit—was the agency of God's power in the conception. However, the idea that Allah had a son is repugnant to them. Surah 4:171 states, "Jesus . . . was only a messenger of Allah . . . Far is it removed from His transcendent majesty that He should have a son."

John states concerning Christ,

> And the Word became flesh, and dwelt among us, and we beheld His glory, glory as of the only begotten from the Father, full of grace and truth . . . And I have seen, and have borne witness that this is the Son of God (John 1:14,34, NASB).

Christ's claim for His own deity and sonship are unequivocal. In John 10:30 He claims equality with the Father when He states, "I and the Father are one." Not only is the sonship of Christ important per se, but the deity of Christ is also an important point of difference between Christianity and Islam since Islam denies the doctrine of the Trinity.

Of the crucifixion, the Qur'an states in Surah 4:157, "They slew him not nor crucified, but it appeared so unto them . . . " Most Muslims believe Judas was put in the place of Christ, and Christ went to heaven. The Bible teaches that Christ went to the cross to pay the penalty for man's sins, that He died and was raised from the dead, and that He appeared to the disciples and *then* ascended to heaven.

Paul recounts the events this way:

> For I delivered to you as of first importance what I also received, that Christ died for our sins according to the Scriptures, and that He was buried, and that He was raised on the third day according to the Scriptures, and that He appeared to Cephas and then to the twelve. After that He appeared to more than five hundred (1 Corinthians 15:3-6, NASB).

Of the importance of the resurrection, Paul states, "And if Christ has not been raised, your faith is worthless; you are still in your sins" (2 Corinthians 15:17, NASB).

SIN AND SALVATION

The Muslim operates under a legalistic system and must earn his salvation. He holds to the *Articles of Faith* and follows the *Pillars of Faith.* For the Muslim, sin is lack of obedience to Allah. Thus man is sinful by act only, not by nature.

The Bible teaches that man is sinful by nature. Paul writes to the Romans, "For all have sinned and fall short of the glory of God" (Romans 3:23, NASB).

Summary

Historical roots tie Islam to Christianity, yet this is where the similarity ends. Islam rejects the key doctrines of the Christian faith—the Trinity, the deity of Christ, Christ's crucifixion and resurrection, and the sin nature of man and his salvation by grace alone through faith in Christ.

They also reject the Bible as the only authoritative book on which to base all matters of doctrine, faith and practice. When Islam rejects the truth of the written Word of God, they are left not only different from Christianity, but opposite from Christianity on all counts. Islam was founded by a dead prophet; Christianity was founded by a risen Savior.

Conclusion

Muhammad has based his teaching on inaccurate and untrue interpretations of the Bible. There is no historical evidence to support Muhammad's contentions that either the Jewish or Christian Scriptures have been corrupted. In addition, his teaching in the Qur'an is based on revelations which he initially believed were demonic in origin.

Islam is an aggressive and impressive world religion. It appeals to those who welcome a religious world view which permeates every facet of life. However, it is ultimately unfulfilling. The Islamic God of strict judgment, Allah, cannot offer the mercy, love, or ultimate sacrifice on mankind's behalf that the Christian God, incarnate in Jesus Christ, offers to each individual even today.

Part One: Bibliography

1. Agency for Cultural Affairs. *Japanese Religion: A Survey*. Tokyo, New York, and San Francisco: Kodansha International Ltd., 1972, 1981.

2. Anderson, Sir Norman, Ed. *The World's Religions*. Grand Rapids, MI: Wm. B. Eerdmans Publishing Co., 1975.

3. Bach, Marcus. *Had You Been Born in Another Faith*. Englewood Cliffs, NJ: Prentice-Hall, 1961.

4. Boa, Kenneth. *Cults, World Religions, and You*. Wheaton, IL: Victor Books, 1977.

5. Bowker, John. *Problems of Suffering in Religions of the World*. London: Cambridge University Press, 1970.

6. Burtt, E. A., ed. *The Teachings of the Compassionate Buddha*. New York: New American Library, 1955.

7. Confucius. D. C. Lau, trans. *The Analects* Book XI:12. London: Penguin Books, 1979.

8. Confucius. *The Analects*, XII:11.

9. Confucius. *The Analects*, XV:24.

10. Gaer, Joseph. *What the Great Religions Believe*. New York: Dodd, Mead, and Company, 1963.

11. Giles, Lionel. *Sayings of Confucius, Wisdom of the East Series* 2. London: John Murray Publ., 1917.

12. Guillaume, Alfred. *Islam*. London: Penguin Books, 1954.

13. Holt, P. M., ed. *The Cambridge History of Islam* 2. London: Cambridge University Press, 1970.

14. Hume, Robert E. *The World's Living Religions*. New York: Charles Scribner's Sons, rev. ed., 1959.

15. Lapide, Pinchas. *Israelis, Jews and Jesus*. Garden City, NJ: Doubleday & Co., Inc., 1979.

16. Martin, Walter, ed. *The New Cults*. Santa Ana, CA: Vision House Publishers Inc., 1980.

17. Noss, John B. *Man's Religions*. New York: Macmillan Company, 1969.

18. Offner, Clark B. Sir Norman Anderson, ed. *The World's Religions*. Grand Rapids: Wm. B. Eerdmans Publishing Co., 1976.

19. Sandmel, Samuel. *Judaism and Christian Beginnings*. London: Oxford University Press, 1978.

20. Seeger, Elizabeth. *Eastern Religions*. New York: Crowell, 1973.

21. Smart, Ninian. *The Religious Experience of Mankind*. New York: Charles Scribner's Sons, 1969.

22. Smith, Huston. *The Religions of Man*. New York: Harper & Row, 1965.

23. Swearer, Donald K. *Buddhism*. Niles, IL: Argus Communications, 1977.

24. Ware, James R., trans. *The Sayings of Confucius*. New York: New American Library, 1955.

Part Two
SECULAR RELIGIONS

CHAPTER 30 *Agnosticism, Atheism and Secular Humanism*

Agnosticism and Atheism (A/106-7)

Many individuals who have rejected the Christian claim have embraced other views of life. Most of these people state that there is no God as the Bible teaches, and if there is, He is unknowable. The claims of these alternatives, however, will not hold up under investigation.

An *agnostic* usually is someone who does not know whether God exists. The agnostic has not made up his mind about God. He is a doubter. Some agnostics are more aggressive than others in searching for God, and this we applaud.

The Bible promises, if anyone desires to know the truth about God, they shall. "If any man is willing to do His will, he shall know of the teaching, whether it is of God, or whether I speak from Myself" (John 7:17, NASB).

Unfortunately, most agnostics do not make a real effort to know if there is a God. They do not consider the question all that crucial. Yet it is. The very fact that an agnostic cannot be sure makes it logical that he should consider the claims of Christianity. Therefore, agnosticism is not grounds for rejecting Christianity; rather, it is grounds for examining Christianity.

Atheists affirm there is no God. Yet they cannot hold this position dogmatically. For a person to be able to make this type of statement with authority, he would have to know the universe in its entirety and to possess all knowledge. If anyone had these credentials, then by definition he would be God.

Since the atheist is not all-knowing, he cannot make a dogmatic statement on God's existence. He can state only that he is uncertain whether or not there is a God, and this view is agnosticism. We already have investigated this view and found it wanting. The atheist's claim that God does not exist crumbles under examination.

The alternative views, when soundly probed, are found not to undermine Christianity but rather to reinforce it. This is because philosophical systems and other religions, in their search for truth and meaning to life, fall short in their quest. Without God's revelation of Himself as recorded in the Bible, there is no way to determine whether or not we have the truth. It alone offers man truth and hope.

NOTE: A more detailed treatment of this subject is given in *Understanding Secular Religions,* pages 13-38.

Secular Humanism (USR/75-100)

One of the most organized, most challenging and most clearly non-Christian philosophies of today is *secular humanism*. It is ably represented and defended by a core of prominent scientists and philosophers at the forefront of new scientific and philosophical thought. Secular humanism has its own meetings, its own "clergy" of spokesmen, its own "creed" called *The Humanist Manifesto*, and its own goals toward which it desires all of humanity to work.

The term *humanism* by itself is not automatically anti-God or pro-God, as many have tried so often to maintain. Historically, during Renaissance times, the word emphasized the importance of man, not to the exclusion of God, but simply with little emphasis on God.

Sometimes humanism is defined as the study of the worth and dignity of man as such worth is given to him by God. As Christians, we must be careful not to build a false case about all uses of the word humanism and then attempt to refute that false case. In fact, this is what some secular humanist writers do when they unfairly paint a caricature of Christianity and then attempt to tear that down.

We will make a working definition of secular humanism, adapting it from the ancient Greek philosopher Protagoras, who said, "Man is the measure of all things." Today this view holds that man is the ultimate standard by which all life is measured and judged. Thus values, law, justice, good, beauty, and right and wrong all are to be judged by man-made rules with no credence to either God or the Bible. We identify this position as secular (non-theistic) humanism (in distinction to the ambiguous and broad term humanism). The humanist believes that man will be able to solve all his own problems. This creed that "man is the measure of all things" offers no concrete solution to those looking for a way out, yet today in our world, humanism is quite popular.

Humanism fails on two counts, though. **First**, man operating by himself cannot set up true standards of justice or values in the world without God. If one man decides his human view of values is correct and another man decides his view, which is different, is correct, who will decide between them?

Who would decide between the Nazis and the Jewish race in World War II? Each had a set of values, but who was right? The majority? The nicest? The meanest?

Without a higher standard of authority to go to, which is God, all of life is based on the values of the majority or of a dictator in power. They have no sure truth to turn to; it is all a matter of opinion.

Second, humanism believes man is "getting better and better every day in every way." However, with two world wars in this century and the world on the brink of nuclear holocaust, the demise of optimistic humanism is a foregone conclusion.

Thus humanism offers not hope but despair. Humanism does not solve problems; it creates them. If humanism is honestly examined, it leads man not to look to man, but beyond himself, for the answers.

Historical Perspective

One can trace the roots of modern secular humanism back to the renewed emphasis on man during the Renaissance. This revival of classical learning and emphasis on man did not exclude God as man's Maker, but it focused attention away from Him, as man made great strides on his own.

Later God was de-emphasized to the point where He was no longer seen as an intimate worker in creation and Father to mankind, and before long, deism became a prominent view. Deism affirmed belief in God, but a God who was not involved in the affairs of men. Deism soon gave way to naturalism, a world view which dismissed God completely from the scene.

Humanism entered the nineteenth century through the French philosopher, Comte, who was committed to the secularization of science, and through British utilitarianism via English deism. These serve as a backdrop for twentieth century naturalism and pragmatism. Through such men as Schiller and especially Dewey, the modern tenets of secular humanism began to take their expressed form.

Today this self-centered system of ideas exerts influence in all of our lives. Its assumptions and dogmas continue to be adopted by more and more people, and as a result, many secular humanist organizations are in existence both in Europe and in America, some of which have been around for a long time. Two prominent organizations, *The American Humanist Association* and *The British Humanist Association*, are both front-runners in the secular humanist cause. Another secular humanist-oriented organization is *The Aspen Institute for Humanistic Studies.* 4 *The Aspen Institute* is a motivator for thought and action on cultural issues affecting man and society. Committed to and rooted in a secular humanistic approach, it seeks solutions to local, national, and international problems.

Still another organization, *The Sex Information and Education Council,* is humanistic in its outlook and policy. The periodical *The Humanist*, a bi-monthly publication, is a leading outlet in America for secular humanist doctrine.

The Humanist Manifesto I

In 1933 secular humanists, drawn together by like beliefs, ideas and dreams, drafted a manifesto which became the creed of secular humanism. Drafter and philosopher Paul Kurtz explains the background of the *Humanist Manifesto I.*

> In the twentieth century, humanist awareness has developed at a rapid pace; yet it has to overcome powerful anti-humanist forces that seek to destroy it.
>
> In 1933 a group of thirty-four liberal humanists in the United States defined and enunciated the philosophical and religious principles that seemed to them fundamental. They drafted *Humanist Manifesto I,* which for its time was a radical document. It was concerned with expressing a general religious and philosophical outlook that rejected orthodox and dogmatic positions and provided meaning and direction, unity and purpose to human life. It was committed to reason, science, and democracy. 5/3

The Humanist Manifesto I reflected the general optimism of the time immediately after World War I. Mankind was convinced that it had ably weathered, in the war, the greatest evil imaginable, and that the future perfecting of humanity was now possible. Mankind had proved that it could triumph over evil.

To summarize, the *Humanist Manifesto I* dealt with fifteen major themes, or convictions, of secular humanism. Its chief assertions were that the universe was self-existing and not created; that man is a result of a continuous natural process; that mind is a projection of body and nothing more; that man is molded mostly by his culture; that there is no supernatural; that man has outgrown religion and any idea of God; that man's goal is the development of his own personality, which ceases to exist at death; that man will continue to develop to the point where he will look within himself and to the natural world for the solution to all of his problems; that all institutions and/or religions that some way impede this "human development" must be changed; that socialism is the ideal form of economics; and that all of mankind deserves to share in the fruits from following the above tenets.

The Humanist Manifesto II

World War II and Adolph Hitler rudely contradicted the unmitigated optimism of the secular humanists who signed the 1933 *Manifesto*. Not only had World War I failed to rout evil, but evil had reared its ugly head much more powerfully through the Nazi atrocities of World War II. Having rejected the supernatural and a higher Judge in favor of the basic goodness and perfectibility of man, the secular humanists turned toward modifying their previous statements. Drafters Paul Kurtz and Edwin H. Wilson explained the need for a new *Manifesto*:

> It is forty years since *Humanist Manifesto I* (1933) appeared. Events since then make that earlier statement seem far too optimistic. Nazism has shown the depths of brutality of which humanity is capable. Other totalitarian regimes have suppressed human rights without ending poverty. Science has sometimes brought evil as well as good. Recent decades have shown that inhuman wars can be made in the name of peace. The beginnings of police states, even in democratic societies, widespread government espionage, and other abuses of power by military, political, and industrial elites, and the continuance of unyielding racism, all present a different and difficult social outlook. In various societies, the demands of women and minority groups for equal rights effectively challenge our generation.
>
> As we approach the twenty-first century, however, an affirmative and hopeful vision is needed. Faith, commensurate with advancing knowledge, is also necessary. In the choice between despair and hope, humanists respond in the *Humanist Manifesto II* with a positive declaration for times of uncertainty. 5/13

The Secular Humanist Creed

A study of *Manifesto II* reveals that its 17 propositions can be categorized into six groups: Religion, Philosophy, Mankind, Society, One-World Government, and Science. (The resolutions may be found on pages 13-24 of *Human Manifesto I and II* by Kurtz.)

NOTE: *Understanding Secular Religions* deals with all six groups. We reproduce here excerpts from the first of those groups, Religion.

Religion

Religion is the topic of the first two resolutions. We quote portions of both resolutions:

> **First**: We believe . . . that traditional dogmatic or authoritarian religions that place revelation, God, ritual, or creed above human needs and experience do a disservice to the human species. Any account of nature should pass the tests of scientific evidence; in our judgment, the dogmas and myths of traditional religions do not do so. Even at this late date in human history, certain elementary facts based upon the critical use of scientific reason have to be restated. We find insufficient evidence for belief in the existence of a supernatural; it is either meaningless or irrelevant to the question of survival and fulfillment of the human race. As non-theists, we begin with humans not God, nature not deity. Nature may indeed be broader and deeper than we now know; any new discoveries, however, will but enlarge our knowledge of the natural. . . .
>
> But we can discover no divine purpose or providence for the human species. While there is much that we do not know, humans are responsible for what we are or will become. No deity will save us; we must save ourselves.
>
> **Second**: Promises of immortal salvation or fear of eternal damnation are both illusory and harmful. They distract humans from present concerns, from self-actualization, and from rectifying social injustices. Modern science discredits such historic concepts as the "ghost in the machine" and the "separable soul." Rather, science affirms that the human species is an emergence from natural evolutionary forces. As far as we know, the total personality is a function of the biological organism transacting in a social and cultural context. There is no credible evidence that life survives the death of the body. We continue to exist in our progeny and in the way that our lives have influenced others in our culture.

The world view of humanism, as expressed by these first two tenets, is diametrically opposed to Christianity. While the humanists start and end with man, the Bible starts and ends with God. It was God who was in the beginning (Genesis 1:1, John 1:1-3), not impersonal, self-creating nature from which man gradually evolved. The Bible consistently teaches that it is upon the infinite God that this finite world depends for its existence. For primordial, nonintelligent mass to produce human intelligence assumes, contrary to reason, that an effect is greater than its cause. To account for that human intelligence by a higher intelligence in whose image the human was made, and who sustains the very life of the human and his world, is reasonable—and biblical. When the apostle Paul argued with the Greek philosophers of his day he testified about this sustaining God:

> The God who made the world and all things in it, since He is both Lord of heaven and earth, does not dwell in temples made with hands; neither is He served by human hands, as though He needed anything, since He Himself gives to all life and breath and all things; . . . for in Him we live and move and exist, as even some of your own poets have said, "For we also are His offspring" (Acts 17:24-28, NASB).

For the humanists to blithely dismiss all religious philosophy and all evidence in support of the existence of God in two simple propositions does not settle the matter of God's existence. As evangelical Christians we believe that our reasoning ability was given to us by God, in whose image we were created, and that responsible use of our reasoning ability to understand the world around us can lead us to sound evidence for the existence of God.

The French philosopher Pascal stated the matter plainly:

> The evidence of God's existence and His gift is more than compelling, but those who insist that they have no need of Him, or it, will always find ways to discount the offer. 7

When *Manifesto II* says that it can find no design or purpose or providence for the human species, it devaluates man to a level below that on which God places him as His highest creation. The humanists pretend to esteem the human being above all else. In reality, as *Manifesto II* shows, the humanist takes away all worth from mankind. Unless our worth is rooted and grounded in something objective and outside ourselves, we are of value only to ourselves, and can never rise above the impermanence of our own short lives. The God of Christianity is outside our finite and transitory universe and His love for us gives us a value which transcends not only ourselves but our finite universe as well.

Humanist Manifesto II states that we must save ourselves. We believe it is not possible for an individual to save himself in all circumstances. In fact, according to the biblical definition of salvation, it is an operation undertaken because the individual *cannot* help himself. While we would grant that a man could "save himself" from falling after a slip by grabbing a rail, for example, we also recognize it is not always possible. Picture a man in the middle of a large lake. He has fallen from his boat, which is now hopelessly out of reach. He has been in the frigid water for two hours. He can no longer keep himself afloat. His body temperature is falling rapidly. He is becoming delirious. Would he find solace and genuine help in a bystander's admonition to "save himself"? Of course not. Without *outside* intervention, he will die. The spiritual (moral) condition of man is such that he is past the point of "saving himself." He needs *outside* intervention. Christians believe that intervention is from God. He alone is able to save man. Ephesians 2:8-10 reminds us:

> For by grace you have been saved through faith; and that not of yourselves, it is the gift of God; not as a result of works, that no one should boast. For

> we are His workmanship, created in Christ Jesus for good works, which God prepared beforehand, that we should walk in them (NASB).

Contrary to humanist declarations, Christianity gives true worth and dignity to man and secular humanism makes all human dignity subjective and self-centered. Francis Schaeffer comments:

> I am convinced that one of the great weaknesses in evangelical preaching in the last few years is that we have lost sight of the biblical fact that man is wonderful. We have seen the unbiblical humanism which surrounds us, and, to resist this in our emphasis on man's lostness, we have tended to reduce man to a zero. Man is indeed lost, but that does not mean he is nothing. We *must* resist humanism, but to make man a zero is neither the right way nor the best way to resist it. . . .
>
> In short, therefore, man is not a cog in a machine; he is not a piece of theater; he really can influence history. From the biblical viewpoint, *man is lost, but great.* 8/80-81

Secular humanism rejects the idea of life after death, dogmatically asserting that it is impossible to prove. On the contrary, the resurrection of Jesus Christ from the dead is a fact of history, verifiable by standard historical tests. His resurrection becomes the seal and hope of every Christian.

CHAPTER 31 *Marxism*

(USR/43-64)

Marxism is not just politics and economics. Marxism is also a world view, a way of looking at and *explaining* the world. As such, it encompasses philosophy and religion, while paradoxically and vigorously asserting its atheism and contempt for philosophy.

While Marx often strongly stressed that his system was *scientific*, and not *philosophical*, he could not escape the realm of philosophy. Because the world view of Marxism attacks the world view of Christianity, we are here addressing that challenge.

Karl Marx

The name of Karl Marx is probably the best known name of any founder of a political or economic system. While he made little difference in the societies in which he lived, his system of thought has, in the last hundred years, exerted tremendous influence on the governments and economies of hundreds of countries. The two largest nations in the world, Russia and China, claim him as their ideological father. His ideas have flourished for years, showing a greater strength and stability than the man himself, who spent most of his life in poor health, precarious psychological balance and financial insecurity.

Karl Marx was born in Trier, an ancient German city in Rhineland (sometimes claimed by France, and known as Treveri). His ancestors, Jewish on both his mother's and father's sides, were rabbis. His father, Heinrich, had converted to Protestantism in 1816 or 1817 in order to continue practicing law after the Prussian edict denying Jews to the bar. Karl was born in 1818 and baptized in 1824, but his mother, Henriette, did not convert until 1825, when Karl was 7.

While the family did not appear religious at all—it was said that not a single volume on religion or theology was in Heinrich's modest library—Karl was raised in an atmosphere of religious toleration. There was some discrimination against Jews in the area, but general religious tolerance was the standard. Karl was sent to religious school primarily for academic rather than religious training. On the whole, the family was not committed to either evangelical Protestantism or evangelical Judaism.

Marx attended the gymnasium (high school) from 1830 to 1835 and then attended Bonn University (1835-1836). He worked on his doctorate at Berlin University (1836-1841). During this time he met and associated with the Young Hegelians and suffered a nervous breakdown (1837). His doctoral dissertation was in philosophy and was titled *The Difference Between Democritean and Epicurean Philosophy of Nature*. It was accepted by Jena University. His father died in 1838.

Marx's professed atheism and his radical views may have made it difficult for him to be hired as a professor at Prussian-dominated schools, and his attention turned to political involvement. His life pattern of revolutionary involvement and intense political activism began to emerge. In 1842 he became the editor of the *Reinische Zeitung*, which was said to be a business periodical. However, this publication had strong radical political views. Marx's philosophy of dialectical materialism and class struggle was already being developed, and often appeared in the pages of the *Reinische Zeitung*.

The year 1843 was an important one for young Marx (25 years old). He met for the first time with Frederich Engles, who was to become his closest friend, benefactor, collaborator, and philosophical and political "soul-mate." He also married Jenny von Westphalen, a baroness to whom he was devoted (in spirit if not always in deed) for the rest of his life. During the same year he wrote two of his early works and they typify his thinking at the time: the "Critique of Hegel's Philosophy of Law," and "On the Jewish Question."

(It is debated whether Marx was specifically anti-Semitic or only anti-Semitic in the sense that his economic theories had no room for Jewish free enterprise and his presupposed atheism had no room for Jewish religion.)

That same year also saw the demise of the *Reinische Zeitung*—it became a victim of Prussian censorship—and the expulsion of Marx and his bride from Germany. They moved to Paris in October of 1843.

Carrying his political zeal with him, Marx published the *Deutsche Französische Jahrbücher* in Paris in 1844. This fiery publication earned him expulsion from France, and he moved to Brussels in January-February of 1845.

Marx jumped enthusiastically into the communist activity of Brussels. In 1847 he wrote for the *Deutche-Brüssler-Zeitung* and organized the *German Communist League* and *German Worker's Association*. At the request of the Brussels communists, Marx and Engles wrote their famous *Communist Manifesto* in 1848. It has become the creed and catechism of Marxist Communism. Early in 1848 Marx and Jenny were expelled from Brussels, spent a short time in Paris, and returned to Germany as revolutionaries in April. Throwing his entire energies into the workers' fight against the repressive Prussian government, Marx began to publish the *Neue Reinische Zeitung*. Less than a year later he was again expelled from Prussia, spent a month in Paris, was expelled from there and moved himself and his family to London (August 24, 1849). For nearly 30 years Marx called London his home. It was there, where he had much more literary freedom than in any country before, that he wrote his monumental work *Das Kapital* which criticized, among other things, British capitalism.

Most of the time they were in London, his family was wretchedly poor. Three of his children died, their illnesses complicated by inadequate shelter, food, and medicine. Although he loved his wife and children devotedly, it was unequal to the passion he felt for his political writing and involvement. Stumpf records:

> While his poverty was deeply humiliating, he was driven with such single-mindedness to produce his massive books that he could not deviate from this objective to provide his family with more adequate facilities. In addition to his poverty, he was afflicted with a liver ailment and, as Job, was plagued with boils. In this environment his six-year-old son died and his beautiful wife's health failed. 9/425

Marx and his wife made many trips to friends and relatives to beg and borrow enough money to pay their debts, feed their children, and finance Marx's political activities. He recognized the sad position in which he put his family, but seemed unable to turn from his profitless writing and organizing to work at any physical labor or occupation that could have provided better for them. In later years he looked back with regret on the hardships he had made his family endure, commenting:

> You know that I have sacrificed my whole fortune to the revolutionary struggle. I do not regret it. Quite the contrary. If I had to start my life over again, I would do the same. But I would not marry. 6/280

In 1851 his illegitimate son, Frederick Demuth, was born to his wife's maid. His wife and children were not told that Fredrick was Karl's son. Instead, benefactor, confidant and collaborator Engels was appointed the boy's "father." Not until after her parents' death did Karl's daughter,

Eleanor ("Tussy"), learn the truth from Engels.

The years 1849-1853 were times of desperate financial straits for the family but a time when Marx rose to the top of the exiled German Communist movement. A personal description of him by a Prussian spy recorded in 1853 reveals the two tensions, poverty and politics, in the Marx household:

> In private life he is a highly disorderly, cynical person, a poor host; he leads a gypsy existence. Washing, grooming, and changing underwear are rarities with him; he gets drunk readily. Often he loafs all day long, but if he has work to do, he works day and night tirelessly. He does not have a fixed time for sleeping and staying up; very often he stays up all night, and at noon he lies down on the sofa fully dressed and sleeps until evening, unconcerned about the comings and goings around him. . . .
>
> Marx lives in one of the worst, and thus cheapest, quarters in London. He lives in two rooms, the one with a view on the street is the living room, the one in the back is the bedroom. In the whole lodging not a single piece of good furniture is to be found; everything is broken, ragged, and tattered; everything is covered with fingerthick dust; everywhere the greatest disorder. In the middle of the living room there is a big old table covered with oilcloth. On it lie manuscripts, books, newspapers, the children's toys, the scraps of his wife's sewing, tea cups with broken rims, dirty spoons, knives, forks, candlesticks, inkwell, drinking glasses, Dutch clay pipes, tobacco ashes—in a word, everything piled up helter-skelter on the same table. **6/155-57**

As destitute as the family was, Karl and Jenny did not neglect the education of their daughters (no legitimate son lived to adulthood), paying for their education in the classics, language, music, art, business, and social graces. While they lived like Marx's beloved proletariat, their daughters were groomed to join the hated bourgeois.

While exiled from Germany, Marx resumed publication of the *Neue Reinische Zeitung*. He wrote it in London and it was printed and distributed in Germany.

From 1852 to 1862 Marx was also foreign correspondent for the New York *Daily Tribune*. He wrote his "Critique of Political Economy" in 1859. This work served as the prologue to his later *Das Kapital*. In 1860 he studied the writings of Charles Darwin and wrote of *Natural Selection*, "It is the book that contains the natural-history basis of our philosophy." **6/366** He sent a copy of the first volume of *Das Kapital* to Darwin and later requested Darwin's permission to dedicate volume two to him. (Darwin turned him down.)

Work on *Das Kapital* began in earnest in 1861. In 1864, in very poor health, Marx temporarily suspended work on it and devoted his failing energy to the founding of the communist *International Working Men's Association*. The first draft of *Das Kapital* was finished in 1865 and the book was finally published in Germany on September 14, 1867. His finances became somewhat stabilized and he began to join the ranks of the very class his new book condemned. During his stay in Germany for the release of *Das Kapital*, his hostess remarked to him, "I cannot think of you in a leveling society, as you have altogether aristocratic tastes and habits."

Marx replied, "I cannot either. That time will come, but we will be gone by then." 6/201-2

On December 2, 1881, his beloved wife Jenny died, probably from stomach cancer, and the already-ill Marx never fully recovered from losing her. In declining health, he received the news of the death of his daughter, also named Jenny, in 1883. He went into a deep depression; his health finally failed him, and he died of an abscessed lung on March 14, 1883.

Georg Wilhelm Hegel

Hegel (d. 1831) developed a system to explain change which is called "dialectics." Change and progression are accomplished through a process of thesis, antithesis, and synthesis.

Hegel himself rarely used the terms thesis, antithesis and synthesis. 2/215 However, traditional interpretations of Hegel recognize this preoccupation with triads in his philosophy and note his debt to his predecessor, Fichte, with whom the three terms were commonplace.

Marx accepted Hegel's process of dialectics, seeing reality as a process that can be understood by the mind and that proceeds by the dialectic of thesis, antithesis, and synthesis.

However, Marx flatly rejected Hegel's Spirit-goal, adopting instead a thorough-going materialism. . . . Because only the material is fundamental, and everything (even mind) proceeds from the material, and progress can only occur through dialectic change, Marx easily concluded that class reform (dealing with the material) is man's basic priority and that such reform can occur only through revolution (dialectics). How sharply this differs from Christian teaching, where the intangible is most important, where God can and does intervene for our good, and where social reform is accomplished through the transformation of individual souls from darkness into light!

Ludwig Feuerbach

Feuerbach (d. 1872) was one of the shapers of Marx's ideas about religion. His *Essence of Christianity* (1841) reduced Christianity to man's fulfillment of his desires. There is no objective religion, no objective God, no objective Jesus Christ. All religious belief is subjective, projected from man's inner needs and desires. It is because of man's miserable existence that he feels the need to invent God.

Marx went further than Feuerbach. In his typical demarcation between "philosophers" who merely observed and "revolutionaries" who acted, Marx called for revolution to bring man to the place where he no longer needed religion. He was not content to wait for man to grow out of a need for God. He was ready to join the fight himself. Marx, then, was not passive when it came to religion. The active destruction of religion and promotion of atheism was part of his plan to fulfill man through his dialectical materialism.

Against Religion

Marx saw two compelling reasons to abolish religion and promote atheism: **First**, his materialism denied the existence of the supernatural; and **second**, the very structure of organized religion had, through the ages, condoned and supported the bourgeois suppression of the proletariat.

There are some who try to synthesize Marxism and Christianity. "Liberation Theology" proponents in various areas of South America are examples. Usually such quasi-Marxists are motivated by strong social concerns. They see inequity and suffering in the world and they want to do something about it. Too often, the Marxists are the only ones who appear to be working to relieve such suffering.

Douglas Hyde

Former British communist Douglas Hyde was studying to become a missionary when he was drawn to Communism in just such a way after World War I in England. He joined his first Communist sponsored Party after reading a book by a Quaker who embraced Communism and extolled its virtues in *The Challenge of Bolshevism*. Young Hyde recounted his reaction to the book:

> It provided a bridge by means of which the man with some religious belief could cross with a clear conscience into the camp of unbelief.
>
> The author's case was that the Communists had found the Christian answer to an utterly un-Christian, bourgeois system of society. . . . In Communism the sincere Quaker found honesty of purpose, intellectual integrity, a higher morality and a system which would prepare the way for a Christianity purified and reborn. . . . It was exactly what I needed at the time. It resolved a crisis for me, clarified my position and accelerated my progress toward Communism. It was the link between my Christian past and my atheist future. I was able now to read with an "open mind" Engel's *Anti-Duhring*, *A.B.C. of Communism*, the works of Lenin and others which formerly I would have rejected because of their atheism. 3/22-23

However, as Hyde discovered, one cannot remain true to orthodox Marxism and orthodox Christianity at the same time. Hyde quickly abandoned all faith in God and was as militantly atheistic as any other Communist for more than two decades, until his disillusionment with Communism drove him to Christ.

One of the turning points came when he realized:

> It was not sufficient now to tell myself that the end justified the means. Once a Marxist begins to differentiate between right and wrong, just and unjust, good and bad, to think in terms of spiritual values, the worst has happened so far as his Marxism is concerned. 3/243

He chronicles how he and his wife searched and how they accepted Christianity intellectually before they were reborn spiritually.

> We had come to accept the intellectual case for God, to see that without it not only Catholicism but the universe itself made nonsense. We had discovered with some surprise that the great thinkers and philosophers of the church had made out a better case for God's existence than Marx and Engels had done for His non-existence.
>
> Yet we realized that that was not enough. Belief meant being able to *feel* the existence of the spiritual, to *know* God and not just to know *about* Him. Christians even said they loved Him, they talked to Him and listened to Him. That was still outside our experience and, in moments of depression, we feared that it would remain so. 3/248

Hyde and his wife made personal commitments to Jesus Christ and found the faith they had yearned for. His story ends:

> I lost my Communism because I had been shown something better. I did not find it easy to get to know my new God. And the love of God did not even then come automatically. Just as one has first to get to know a man or woman, and love comes later on a basis of common interest shared and intimacies exchanged, so, slowly, I came to know that love. But one thing is certain: My God has not failed. 3/303

Changing the Individual

A complete acceptance of Marx's dialectical materialism and theories of class struggle leads one inexorably to the denial of individual human worth. History and its march toward perfection is the Marxist god. In the struggle for the classless society, those who stand in the way must be eliminated. Absolute materialism leads, inevitably, to a form of practical totalitarianism.

Such a totalitarianism denies the worth and freedom of the individual and cuts at the heart of the gospel message. Yet the individual is so important to God that He sent His only begotten Son to die for our sins, that we may be reconciled to fellowship with God on an individual basis. Marx sought to elevate man. His system only served to degrade the individual. By attacking the evil he saw in society with class struggle, he hoped to eradicate evil from mankind. He and his philosophical descendants did not succeed. Sin is not man divorced from his social potential; it is man in willful alienation from himself and God.

As the reader can see, there is a sharp distinction between the goal and plan of Marxism and the goal and plan of Christianity. Christianity also works toward a transformed society. This working is in two major areas. Christianity recognizes that sin, within man, is action perpetrated by personal agents. It is not some nasty by-product of social birth pangs. Christianity seeks to change those personal agents through the life-transforming power of the Lord Jesus Christ. Once that personal and individual transformation has taken place, the redeemed person shows his faith through his actions by working toward social, economic, political and religious parity among his fellow men.

True freedom for mankind is possible only when the individual is considered valuable and when the root causes of injustice are removed. Such change is not brought about by violent revolution at the expense of others nor is it based on philosophy which sees man valuable only as a member of a classless society.

> It was for freedom that Christ set us free, therefore keep standing firm and do not be subject again to a yoke of slavery (Galatians 5:1, NASB).

NOTE: A more comprehensive critique of Marxism may be found in Thomas O. Kay's *The Christian Answer to Communism* (Grand Rapids, MI: Zondervan Publishing House, 1961), and Lester Dekoster's *Communism and Christian Faith* (Grand Rapids, MI: Wm. B. Eerdmans Publishing Co., 1956).

Part Two: Bibliography

1. Chambers, Claire. *The Siecus Circle: A Humanist Revolution.* Belmont, MA: Western Islands Publishing Company, 1977.

2. Copleston, Frederick. *A History of Philosophy* 7: part 1. Garden City, NY: Doubleday and Company, Inc., 1963.

3. Hyde, Douglas. *I Believed.* London: William Heinemann, Ltd., 1951.

4. Hyman, Sidney. *The Aspen Idea.* Norman, OK: University of Oklahoma Press, 1975.

5. Kurtz, Paul, ed. *Humanist Manifesto I and II.* Buffalo, NY: Prometheus Books, 1973.

6. Padover, Saul K. *Karl Marx: An Intimate Biography.* Abridged ed. New York: New American Library, 1978, 1980.

7. Pascal, Blaise. *Pense's No. 430.* H. F. Stewart, trans. NY: Random House, n.d.

8. Schaeffer, Francis. *Death in the City.* Downers Grove, IL: InterVarsity Press, 1969.

9. Stumpf, Samuel Enoch. *Socrates to Sartre: A History of Philosophy.* New York: McGraw-Hill Book Company, 1966.

Part Three CULTS

What Is a Cult? (UC/17)

A cult is a perversion, a distortion of biblical Christianity, and as such, rejects the historic teachings of the Christian Church. The apostle Paul warned there would be false Christs and a false gospel that would attempt to deceive the true church and the world:

> For if one comes and preaches another Jesus whom we have not preached, or you receive a different spirit which you have not received, or a different gospel which you have not accepted, you bear this beautifully . . . for such men are false apostles, deceitful workers, disguising themselves as apostles of Christ and no wonder for even Satan disguises himself as an angel of light. Therefore it is not surprising if his servants also disguise themselves as servants of righteousness; whose end shall be according to their deeds (2 Corinthians 11:13-15, NASB).

Walter Martin gives us a good definition of a cult when he says:

> A cult, then, is a group of people polarized around someone's interpretation of the Bible and is characterized by major deviations from orthodox Christianity relative to the cardinal doctrines of the Christian faith, particularly the fact that God became man in Jesus Christ. 27/12

CHAPTER 32 *Jehovah's Witnesses*

(UC/55-81)

History

Officially known as the Watchtower Bible and Tract Society, the Jehovah's Witnesses are a product of the life work of Charles Taze Russell, born February 16, 1852, near Pittsburgh, Pennsylvania. In 1870, while still in his teens and without formal theological education, Russell organized a Bible class whose members eventually made him "pastor."

In 1879 he founded the magazine Zion's *Watchtower* in which he published his own unique interpretation of the Bible, and in 1886, the first volume of seven books (six written by Russell) entitled *The Millennial Dawn* was published. (These later were retitled *Studies in the Scriptures.)*

By the time of his death in 1916, "Pastor" Russell, according to the Watchtower, traveled more than a million miles, gave more than thirty thousand sermons, and wrote books totalling over fifty thousand pages. 1/310

A few months after the death of Charles Taze Russell, the society's legal counselor, Joseph Franklin Rutherford, became the second President of the Watchtower Society. It was under his leadership that the name "Jehovah's Witnesses" was adopted.

Rutherford died in 1942 and was succeeded by Nathan H. Knorr. It was during Knorr's presidency that the society increased from 115,000 to more than two million members. In 1961, under Knorr's leadership, the society produced its own English translation of the Bile entitled *The New World Translation of Holy Scriptures.*

Claims of the Jehovah's Witnesses

Jehovah's Witnesses are zealous and sincere, and they claim to accept the Bible as their only authority. However, their theology denies every cardinal belief of historic Christianity including the Trinity, the divinity of Jesus Christ, His bodily resurrection, salvation by grace through faith, and eternal punishment of the wicked.

The Watchtower has this to say about itself:

> It is God's sole collective channel for the flow of biblical truth to men on earth. 53/439

Source of Authority

Note the following statement by "Pastor" Russell:

> If the six volumes of *Scripture Studies* are practically the Bible, topically arranged with Bible proof texts given, we might not improperly name the volumes "the Bible in an arranged form," that is to say, they are not mere comments on the Bible, buy they are practically the Bible itself.
>
> Furthermore, not only do we find that people cannot see the divine plan in studying the Bible by itself, but we see, also, that if anyone lays the *Scripture Studies* aside, even after he has used them, after he has became familiar with them, after he has read them for ten years—if he then lays them aside and ignores them and goes to the Bible alone, though he has understood his Bible for ten years, our experience shows that within two years he goes into darkness. On the other hand, if he had merely read the *Scripture Studies* with their references and had not read a page of the Bible as

such, he would be in the light at the end of two years, because he would have the light of the Scriptures. 42/298

Although the Watchtower contends that the Scriptures are their final authority, we find they constantly misuse the Scriptures to establish their own peculiar beliefs. This is accomplished chiefly by quoting texts out of context while omitting other passages relevant to the subject. For all practical purposes their publications take precedence over the Scriptures.

Trinity

The Watchtower makes it clear they do not believe in the doctrine of the Trinity. "The trinity doctrine was not conceived by Jesus or the early Christians. . . .The plain truth is that this is another of Satan's attempts to keep the God-fearing person from learning the truth of Jehovah and His Son Christ Jesus." 20/92-93

In Watchtower theology neither Jesus Christ nor the Holy Spirit is God.

Jesus Christ

In the theological system of the Jehovah's Witnesses, Jesus Christ is not God in human flesh, but rather a created being.

"Jesus, the Christ, a created individual, is the second greatest personage of the Universe. Jehovah God and Jesus together constitute the superior authorities." 25/207

"He was a god, but not the Almighty God, who is Jehovah." 20/33

"If Jesus were God, then during Jesus' death God was dead in the grave." 19/91

"The truth of the matter is that the word is Christ Jesus, who did have a beginning." 19/88

The denial of the deity of Christ is nothing new in the history of the church. It is a revival of the ancient heresy known as Arianism (named after the fourth-century A.D. heretic Arius.) Arianism teaches that the Son was of a substance different from the Father and was, in fact, created.

The Jehovah's Witnesses, in an attempt to demonstrate that Jesus Christ is not Jehovah God, appeal to the Bible to substantiate their beliefs. However, it is the Bible that contradicts their theology, revealing it to be both unbiblical and non-Christian.

JOHN 14:28

One favorite passage used by Jehovah's Witnesses to prove Christ is less than God is John 14:28: "My Father is greater than I." This verse refers to the voluntary subordination of Jesus during His earthly life when

He willingly placed Himself in submission to the Father. It says nothing about His nature, only His temporary rank on earth. Thus, the "greater than" refers to His position rather than His person.

COLOSSIANS 1:15

Jesus is called the "firstborn" of all creation in Colossians 1:15. The Watchtower takes this to mean "first created." However, the passage itself states that Christ is the Creator of all things (verses 16 and 17), not a created being. The title firstborn refers to His preeminent position, not that He is Jehovah's "first creation."

In Revelation 1:5 and Colossians 1:8, Christ is referred to as the "firstborn from the dead." It is obvious that the literal sense of the word cannot be used here. Also it cannot be used as the first to be raised from the dead. It can only mean preeminence or sovereignty, in that Christ was the first to be raised from the dead by His own power and to be exalted to immortality, 13/382 as the context in both cases corroborates.

The Witnesses try to substantiate their doctrine of Christ being one of the creation by deliberate insertion of a word for which there is no basis in the Greek text. A clear example occurs here in *The New World Translation of the Christian Greek Scriptures,* Colossians 1:16,17, which is pertinent to this discussion . . .

> because by means of him all [other] things were created in the heavens and upon the earth, the things visible and the things invisible, no matter whether they are thrones or lordships or governments or authorities. All [other] things have been created through him and for him. Also, he is before all [other] things and by means of him all [other] things were made to exist.

The word *other* has been inserted all the way through the passage unjustly. There is no equivalent word in the Greek text and no reputable translation includes it. When it is considered that the Jehovah's Witnesses assume Jesus Christ to be a created being, it is easy to understand why they insert "other."

The Greek solely states, "He is before all things and by him all things hold together," which is interpreted logically by Stedman to plainly teach that "Christ is the Creator of everything that has existence, material or immaterial, and therefore He cannot Himself be a creature." 47/50:32

However, when the word *other* is unwarrantedly interjected four times, it alters the thought to imply that Christ is the author of all created things, with the exception of one, Himself, who the Watchtower Society says was created. A footnote in the *New World Translation* reads: "All other: as at Luke 13:2,4 and elsewhere." 36/3385

The reference here to Luke 13:2,4 corresponds to the Lord's question about the Galileans whom Pilate had killed, and the eighteen men who were slain by the falling tower of Siloam. He asks, "Do you suppose that these Galilean were greater sinners than all *other* Galileans?" and, "Or do you suppose that these 18 . . . were worse culprits than all [the other—NWT] men who live in Jerusalem?" (NASB)

Stedman, in his article, "The New World Translation of the Christian Greek Scriptures," set forth clearly the reason for the inclusion of "other" here and its exclusion in Colossians 1:15-18.

> Now here, though the original has no word for "other," it is plainly implied in the context, for, of course, these dead men were being put in contrast with all their fellow-citizens. However, there is no such implication in Colossians 1:15-17 *unless one presupposes that Christ Himself was nothing but a creature.* But no translator has the right thus to presuppose on a doctrinal issue. If the text were simply rendered as it is, leaving out the inserted word *other,* it would agree exactly with other New Testament passages that declare plainly that the Lord Jesus Christ is Creator of everything that has been created (Hebrews 1:10; John 1:3).
>
> Again it is evident that the translators have taken special care to make the text say what they suppose it ought to say rather than to let it speak plainly for itself. 47/33

Therefore, in light of the historical, literal and metaphorical meanings of "firstborn" the Jehovah's Witnesses are unscriptural in the application of it to Christ as created.

Jesus Christ, as taught in Colossians 1:15-18, is prior to, distinct from and sovereign over the universe.

JOHN 1:1

One of the readings of the *New World Translation* that has caused considerable outrage among Greek scholars is its totally unsupportable rendering of the last clause of John 1:1, "The word was a god." This translation makes Jesus Christ less than God, relegating Him to the position of a "created being" in accordance with Watchtower theology. There is no basis whatsoever for this rendering, although the Watchtower would have people believe the contrary:

> How are we to understand John 1:1,2, of which there are differing translations? Many translations read: "And the Word was with God, and the Word was God." Others read: "And the Word (The Logos) was divine." Another: "and the Word was God." Others, "And the Word was a god." Since we have examined so much of what John wrote about Jesus who was the Word made flesh, we are now in a position to determine which of those several translations is correct. It means our salvation. 55/52

This is a misleading statement because it gives the impression that other translations agree with their rendering when the opposite is true. There are no reputable authorities or translations that support the reading, "The Word was a god."

The only other translation quoted in this Watchtower publication that reads the same way is *The New Testament in an Improved Version Upon the Basis of Archbishop Newcome's New Translation: With a Corrected Text*, printed in London in 1808. Such an antiquated and obscure translation done by a Unitarian cannot be considered reputable.

GRAMMATICAL EXPLANATION OF JOHN 1:1 . . .

The grammatical explanation given by the Watchtower for its translation of John 1:1 is unsatisfactory. They contend that when *theos* (the Greek word for God) appears in John 1:1 it appears twice, once with the definite article [the] and once without. When it appears without the definite article (in the last clause of John 1:1) they feel justified in translating it, "And the Word was a god."

In the first eighteen verses of John's Gospel, the word for God—*theos*—appears six times without the definite article (vss. 1,6,12,13, and twice in 18). Yet, it is rendered God (referring to Jehovah) in each instance except for the last clause of verse one when it refers to Jesus!

If the Watchtower's translations were consistent, verse 6 should read: "There arose a man that was sent forth as a representative of a god." Moreover, verse 12 should read "to become a god's children," etc. Why only in verse 1 do they refuse to translate *theos* as God (meaning Jehovah)?

We conclude that there is no basis for translating John 1:1, "The Word was a god," as in the *New World Translation*. It is a biased rendering that cannot be justified grammatically.

They do not want to acknowledge what is clearly taught in verse 1: Jesus Christ is God. Also, it should be observed that the absence of the definite article does *not* indicate someone other than the true God. The entry on *theos* in the authoritative *Arndt and Gingrich Greek Lexicon* states *theos* is used "quite predominately of the true God, sometimes with, sometimes without, the article." 10/357

Even without going to the Greek grammar of John 1:1, we can see that the Watchtower translation of John 1:1 goes against the clear teachings of the Bible. In both the Old and New Testaments we are taught that there is only one true God (Isaiah 43:10; John 17:3; 1 Corinthians 8:4-6; etc.). All other "gods" are false gods. Those who would acknowledge any god as true except for Jehovah God are guilty of breaking the first commandment: "You shall have no other gods before me" (Exodus 20:3).

By translating the last part of John 1:1 as, "The Word was a god," the Watchtower has declared its belief in polytheism, or the belief in more than one god. According to the whole testimony of the Bible, the Word (Jesus Christ) of John 1:1 must be either the only true God, Jehovah, or a false god. The Bible knows only one true God, Jehovah.

JOHN 8:58

In the eighth chapter of the Gospel of John, Jesus is asked by the religious leaders, "Whom do you make yourself out to be?" (verse 53).

He answered, "Before Abraham was, I Am" (verse 58).

His answer is a direct reference to Exodus 3:14 where God identifies Himself from the burning bush to Moses by the designation, "I Am." The Jews, realizing that Jesus claimed to be God, attempted to stone Him for blasphemy (verse 59).

The *New World Translation* mistranslates this verse by making it read, "Before Abraham came into existence I have been." The footnote to John 8:58 in the 1950 edition is enlightening: "I have been—*'ego eimi'* after the aorist infinitive clause and hence properly rendered in the perfect indefinite tense."

This statement was completely false. So the Watchtower changed the note to read "the perfect tense," dropping the word *indefinite* (see *The Kingdom Interlinear Translation of the Greek Scriptures*, 1969). However, this is also incorrect since the verb *eimi* is in the present tense, indicative mood, and hence should properly be translated, "I Am." Moreover in the context of John 8:58 (8:42–9:12), the verb "to be," occurs 22 times in the indicative mood and the *New World Translation* correctly renders 21 out of 22. The only incorrect rendering is in John 8:58. Why?

Dr. A. T. Robertson, one of the greatest Greek scholars who ever lived, after translating *ego eimi* as "I AM," had this to say about John 8:58: "Undoubtedly here Jesus claims external existence with the absolute phrase used of God." 39/158-59

The Watchtower betrays itself in its own *Kingdom Interlinear Translation* which contains a literal English translation beneath the Greek text as well as the New World Translation reading. In John 8:58 under the Greek *ego eimi, The Kingdom Interlinear* rightly translates it, "I am," but the *New World Translation* changes it to, "I have been." This inconsistency is striking.

There is no sufficient basis for the translation, "I have been," in John 8:58. This is another example of the scholarly shortcomings of the Watchtower. It obscures the fact that Jesus Christ is Jehovah God.

Holy Spirit

According to the Watchtower Society the Holy Spirit is not part of the Godhead. Both the personality and the deity of the Holy Spirit (defined as "the invisible active force of Almighty God which moves His servants to do His will" 19/108) are denied. The personality of the Holy Spirit is consistently rejected throughout the *New World Translation* by not capitalizing the term "spirit" when referring to the Holy Spirit.

To promulgate this error they mistranslate such passages as Ephesians 4:30 ("also, do not be grieving God's holy spirit, with which you have been sealed for a day of releasing by ransom") and John 14:26 ("But the helper, the holy spirit which the Father will send in my name, that one will teach you all things and bring back to your minds all the things I told you").

However, both of these verses teach the personality of the Holy Spirit. How can one grieve something impersonal? Or how can an "impersonal force," teach all things? Competent translations substitute "with which" in Ephesians 4:30 with "by whom," and have "whom the Father will send" and "he will teach you" in John 14:26 rather than the impersonal holy spirit of the Watchtower.

Salvation

In Watchtower theology, salvation is not regarded as a free gift from God based upon Jesus Christ's work on the cross. Rather, their literature stresses a salvation by works. Russell wrote, "They must be recovered from blindness as well as from death, that they, each for himself, may have a full chance to prove, by obedience or disobedience, their worthiness of life eternal." 40/158 The Bible teaches we are saved by grace through faith alone. Man's good works can never contribute to his salvation. "For by grace you have been saved through faith; and that not of yourselves, it is the gift of God; not as a result of works, that no one should boast" (Ephesians 2:8,9, NASB). "He saved us, not on the basis of deeds which we have done in righteousness, but according to His mercy" (Titus 3:5, NASB).

False Prophecies

"When Jesus said He would come again He did not mean He would return in the flesh visible to men on earth. He has given up that earthly life as a ransom and therefore, cannot take such life back again. . . . The good news today is that Christ Jesus has come again, that God's Kingdom by Him has been set up and is now ruling in heaven . . . all the evidence shows that Jesus took up His Kingdom power and began His reign from Heaven, in the year 1914." 49/19,21

The idea that the second coming of Christ took place in 1914 is important to Watchtower theology. That was the time, they say, that God's kingdom was fully set up in heaven. However, this was not always their teaching. Before 1914, the Watchtower was predicting that God's Kingdom was to be set up on *earth* (not in heaven) in 1914!

> "The times of the Gentiles" extend to 1914. And the Heavenly Kingdom will not have full sway till then, but as a "stone" the Kingdom of God is set up "in the days of these Kings" and by consummating them it becomes a universal Kingdom—a "great mountain and fills the whole earth." 54/82

Charles Taze Russell also stated that the world would see "the full establishment of the Kingdom of God in the earth at A.D. 1914, the terminus of the times of the Gentiles." 41/126

The prophecies made by Russell and the Watchtower concerning 1914 totally failed because the Kingdom of God was not established upon the earth. Today, as already observed, the Watchtower teaches that Christ returned invisibly in 1914 and set up His Kingdom only in Heaven. However, this idea clearly opposes the scriptural teaching of the visible bodily return of Christ:

> Ye men of Galilee, why stand ye gazing up into heaven? This same Jesus which is taken up from you into heaven, shall so come in like manner as ye have seen Him go into Heaven (Acts 1:11).

Jesus warned against such false teaching about His return:

> Wherefore if they shall say unto you, Behold, he is in the desert; go not forth: Behold, he is in the secret chambers; believe it not. For as the lightning cometh out of the East, and shineth even unto the West; so shall the coming of the Son of Man be (Matthew 24:26,27).

The Scriptures also state:

> Behold, he cometh with the clouds; and every eye shall see him (Revelation 1:7).

The Watchtower is guilty of false prophecy (Deuteronomy 18:21,22) in wrongly predicting the date 1914 to be the return of Christ. They are also wrong in asserting His coming is secretly and invisibly because the Scriptures teach completely the contrary (Revelation 1:7).

Conclusion

A close examination of the Watchtower has demonstrated that it is not what it claims to be: the "sole collective channel for the flow of biblical truth." It is guilty of false prophecy, anti-biblical theology, and misrepresentation of the truth.

We heartily recommend to Jehovah's Witnesses that they act on the following instruction from the Watchtower: "We need to examine, not only what we personally believe, but also what is taught by any religious organization with which we may be associated. Are its teachings in full harmony with God's Word, or are they based on the traditions of men? If we are lovers of the Truth, there is nothing to fear from such an examination." 51/13

Such an examination will show the shortcomings of the man-made Watchtower and the all-sufficient perfection of Jesus Christ, our "great God and Saviour" (Titus 2:13).

CHAPTER 33 *Mormonism* (UC/83-102)

But even though we, or an angel from heaven, should preach to you a gospel contrary to that which we have preached to you, let him be accursed (Galatians 1:8, NASB).

History

Joseph Smith, Jr., the founder of Mormonism, or the Church of Jesus Christ of Latter-Day Saints, was born on December 23, 1805, in Sharon, Vermont. Smith was the fourth of ten children of Joseph and Lucy Mack Smith. In 1817 the family moved to Palmyra, New York (near present-day Rochester).

Most of the members of the Smith family soon joined the Presbyterian church, but young Joseph remained undecided. His argument was that all the strife and tension among the various denominations made him question which denomination was right. It was this conflict that set the stage for Joseph's alleged first vision.

In 1820 Joseph allegedly received a vision that became the basis for the founding of the Mormon Church:

> My object in going to inquire of the Lord was to know which of all the sects was right, that I might know which to join. No sooner, therefore, did I get possession of myself, so as to be able to speak, than I asked the

> personages who stood above me in the light, which of all the sects was right—and which I should join.
>
> I was answered that I must join none of them, for they were all wrong; and the personage who addressed me said that all their creeds were an abomination in His sight; that those professors were all corrupt, that, "they draw near to me with their lips, but their hearts are far from me, they teach for doctrines the commandments of men, having a form of godliness, but they deny the power thereof." 45/2:18,19

Joseph then recounts a second vision he had on September 21, 1823, in which he claims:

> I had a second vision. A personage appeared at my bedside who was glorious beyond description. He said that he was a messenger sent from the presence of God, and that his name was Moroni, that God had a work for me to do, and that my name should be had for good and evil among all nations, kindreds and tongues.
>
> He told me that a book had been deposited, written on golden plates, giving an account of the former inhabitants of this continent and containing "the fullness of the everlasting Gospel" as delivered by the Saviour to the ancient inhabitants of this land. He also said that there were two stones in silver bows—and these stones, fastened in a breastplate, constituted what is called the Urim and Thummin—deposited with the plates, adding that God had prepared these stones for the purpose of translating this book.
>
> I was shown exactly where the plates had been deposited. That same night the heavenly messenger appeared again twice, each time repeating the same message. The next day I went to a hill outside the village where we lived [now called the Hill Cumorah] and found the golden plate deposited in a stone box with the Urim and Thummin and the breastplate.
>
> I was not permitted to take them out at this time, however, but was told by the angel, who had reappeared, that I should come back to this place every year at this time for the next four years. Finally, however, on September 22, 1827, I was given the plates by the heavenly messenger with the instructions to keep them carefully until he, the angel, should call for them again. 45/50-54

Joseph then moved to his father-in-law's house in Harmony, Pennsylvania, where, with supposedly divine help, he began to copy the characters off the plates and translate them. The publication of the translation of the plates was financed by a New York farmer named Martin Harris who was told by Smith that the writing on the plates was "reformed Egyptian." The translation was finally completed and placed on sale on March 26, 1830.

A little over a week later, on April 6, 1830, at Fayette, New York, "the church of Christ" was officially organized with six members. The name was eventually changed to the Church of Jesus Christ of Latter-Day Saints. The number of members increased rapidly and a group of them moved to Kirtland, Ohio (near present-day Cleveland). It was here that Joseph supervised the first printing of the divine revelations he had received.

First known as the *Book of Commandments*, the work has undergone significant and numerous changes and now constitutes one of the Mormon sacred works, retitled *Doctrine and Covenants*. Smith also worked on a revision ("divinely aided") of the King James Version of the Bible.

Although the Mormon church began to grow in numbers while expanding westward, it was not without persecution. Battles were fought between Mormons and their non-Mormon counterparts in Far West, Missouri, a town founded by the Mormons. Here Smith was imprisoned along with some other Mormon leaders.

After escaping, he and his followers moved to Illinois to a town Smith named Nauvoo, where he organized a small army and gave himself the title of Lieutenant-General. During this time, the Mormons were busily constructing a temple and evangelizing the populace.

When a local paper, the *Nauvoo Expositor*, began publishing anti-Mormon material, Smith ordered the press destroyed and every copy of the paper burned. This act led to Smith's arrest and imprisonment. Released and then rearrested, Smith was taken to jail in Carthage, Illinois, along with his brother Hyrum.

On June 27, 1844, a mob of about 200 people, their faces blackened to avoid recognition, stormed the jail and shot and killed Joseph and Hyrum Smith. Joseph did not die without a fight. According to the church's own account he shot several of the mob members with a gun he had (see *History of the Church*, 6:617-18). The Mormons, however, considered Joseph Smith a martyr for the cause.

After the death of Joseph Smith the leadership went to Brigham Young, the President of the Twelve Apostles, who convinced the great majority of Mormons that he was the rightful successor.

Young led the group westward in a journey which saw many hardships including Indian attacks, exposure and internal strife. On July 24, 1847, they arrived at Salt Lake Valley in Utah which became the headquarters of the Mormon church. By the time of Young's death in 1877, the members numbered approximately 150,000. Today, the church has more than four million members worldwide.

The Claims of Mormonism

The Mormons claim they are the restoration of the true church established by Jesus Christ. It is not Protestant or Catholic, but claims, rather, to be the only true church. "If it had not been for Joseph Smith and the restoration, there would be no salvation outside the Church of Jesus Christ of Latter-Day Saints." **29/670**

"No salvation without accepting Joseph Smith. . . . If Joseph Smith was verily a prophet, and if he told the truth . . . then this knowledge is of the most vital importance to the entire world. No man can reject that testimony without incurring the most dreadful consequences, for he can not enter the Kingdom of God." 44/189-90

Commenting on Joseph Smith's first vision, Dr. Walter Martin puts the matter into perspective:

> With one "Special Revelation" the Mormon Church expects its intended converts to accept the totally unsupported testimony of a fifteen-year-old boy that nobody ever preached Jesus Christ's gospel from the close of the apostolic age until the "Restoration" through Joseph Smith, Jr., beginning in 1820! We are asked to believe that the church fathers for the first five centuries did not proclaim the true gospel—that Origen, Justin, Iraneaus, Jerome, Eusebius, Athanasius, Chrysostom, and then later Thomas Aquinas, Huss, Luther, Calvin, Zwingli, Tyndale, Wycliffe, Knox, Wesley, Whitefield, and a vast army of faithful servants of Jesus Christ all failed where Joseph Smith, Jr., was to succeed!
>
> With one dogmatic assertion, Joseph pronounced everybody wrong, all Christian theology an abomination, and all professing Christians corrupt—all in the name of God! How strange for this to be presented as restored Christianity, when Jesus Christ specifically promised that "the gates of Hell" would not prevail against the church (Matthew 16:18)! In Mormonism we find God contradicting this statement in a vision to Joseph Smith, Jr., some eighteen centuries later! 25/31

The Mormons make the claim that they are the "restored church of Jesus Christ" but the facts totally discount their claim.

Sources of Authority

The Mormon Church has four accepted sacred works: the Bible, the *Book of Mormon, Doctrine and Covenants,* and *The Pearl of Great Price*. The present prophet's words are also a source of authority.

The Bible

The Mormon articles of faith read: "We believe the Bible to be the Word of God in so far as it is translated correctly." 11 The *Book of Mormon* claims that a correct translation of the Bible is impossible since the Catholic Church has taken away from the Word of God "many parts which are plain and most precious; and also many covenants of the Lord have they taken away. And all this have they done that they might pervert the right ways of the Lord" (1 Nephi 13:26*b*,27).

Thus the Mormons put more trust in the other three sacred books than they do in the Bible. This opens the door for the Mormons to add their new non-biblical teachings by claiming they were doctrines deliberately removed by the Catholic Church.

The Book of Mormon

The *Book of Mormon* is also considered inspired: "We also believe the *Book of Mormon* to be the Word of God." 11 The *Book of Mormon* is supposedly an account of the original inhabitants of America to whom Christ appeared after His resurrection.

Doctrine and Covenants

Doctrine and Covenants is a record of 136 revelations revealing some of Mormonism's distinctive doctrines such as baptism for the dead and celestial marriage.

The Pearl of Great Price

The Pearl of Great Price contains the *Book of Moses*, which is roughly equivalent to the first six chapters of Genesis, and *The Book of Abraham*, a translation of an Egyptian Papyrus that later proved to be fraudulent. It also contains an extract from Joseph Smith's translation of the Bible, extracts from the *HIstory of Joseph Smith*, which is his autobiography, and the *Articles of Faith*.

The Living Prophets

The "living prophet" also occupies an important part in present-day Mormonism. Ezra Taft Benson, President of the Council of the Twelve Apostles, said in a speech on February 26, 1980, at Brigham Young University, that the living prophet (head of the church) is "more vital to us than the standard works." This echoed what was given to the ward teachers (similar to Christian Education adult teachers) in 1945.

> Any Latter-Day Saint who denounces or opposes, whether actively or otherwise, any plan or doctrine advocated by the prophets, seers, and revelators of the church is cultivating the spirit of apostasy. . . . Lucifer . . . wins a great victory when he can get members of the church to speak against their leaders and to do their own thinking. . . .
>
> When our leaders speak, the thinking has been done. When they propose a plan—it is God's plan. When they point the way, there is no other which is safe. When they give directions, it should mark the end of the controversy. 16/354

What the Bible Says

The Bible contradicts the Mormon reliance on multiple contradictory revelations. While the Mormon scriptures contradict each other and the Bible, the Bible never contradicts itself and the God of the Bible never contradicts Himself. Hebrews 1:1-3 tells us where our knowledge of God comes from:

> God, after He spoke long ago to the fathers in the prophets in many portions and in many ways, in these last days has spoken to us in His Son, whom He appointed heir of all things, through whom also He made the world. And He is the radiance of His glory and the exact representation of His nature, and upholds all things by the word of His power. When He had made purification of sins, He sat down at the right hand of the Majesty on high.

Any message that purports to be from God must agree with the message already brought by Jesus Christ in fulfillment of the Old Testament (Luke 24:27). Eternal life comes from the works and gifts of Jesus Christ, not from Joseph Smith, Brigham Young, or any other false Mormon prophet (John 20:31). Proverbs 30:5,6 warns those who try to add to God's Word, saying, "Every word of God is tested; He is a shield to those who take refuge in Him. Do not add to His words lest He reprove you, and you be proved a liar."

Mormon Doctrine

GOD

The Mormon doctrine of God is contradictory to what the Bible teaches. The Mormons believe in many gods and teach that God himself was once a man. Moreover, Mormon males have the possibility of attaining godhood. Joseph Smith made this clear in *The King Follett Discourse:*

> God was once as we are now, and is an exalted man, and sits enthroned in yonder heavens. . . . I say, if you were to see him today, you would see him like a man in a form like yourselves in all the person, image, and very form of a man.
>
> I am going to tell you how God came to be God. We have imagined and supposed that God was God from all eternity. I will refute that idea and take away the veil so that you may see.
>
> It is the first principle of the gospel to know for certainty the character of God and to know that we may converse with him as one man with another, and that he was once a man like us; yea, that God himself, the father of us all, dwelt on an earth, the same as Jesus Christ did.
>
> Here then, is eternal life—to know the only wise and true God; and you have got to learn how to be Gods yourselves, and to be kings and priests to God, the same as all Gods have done before you (pp. 8-10).

Lorenzo Snow repeated Joseph Smith's words about the Mormon idea of God:

> As Man is, God was;
> As God is, man may become.

Smith's teaching on the nature of God not only contradicts the Bible; it also contradicts the Book of Mormon!

> And Zeezrom said unto him: "Thou sayest that there is a true and living God?" And Amulek said: "Yea, there is a true and living God." Now Zeezrom said: "Is there more than one God?" And he answered, "No!" (Alma 11:26-29, *Book of Mormon).*

See also Alma 11:21,22; 2 Nephi 11:7; 31:21; 3 Nephi 11:27,36; Mosiah 15:1-5; 16:15, all in the *Book of Mormon.*

The Bible repeatedly affirms that there is only one true God. Isaiah 43:10 emphatically declares, "You are My witnesses, declares the Lord, and My servant whom I have chosen, in order that you may know and believe Me, and understand that I am He. Before Me there was no God formed, and there will be none after me."

In the New Testament we are assured that though there are false gods and idols worshipped by men, they are worthless: "We know there is no such thing as an idol in the world, and that there is no God but one" (1 Corinthians 8:4).

JESUS CHRIST

The Mormon Church teaches that Jesus Christ was a pre-existent spirit like the rest of us. Even though we are all literally brothers and sisters of Jesus, He is set apart from the rest of us by being the firstborn of God's spirit-children.

Contrary to Mormon theology, Jesus Christ is the unique Son of God. John 1:14 declares that He "became flesh, and dwelt among us, and we beheld His glory, glory as of the only begotten from the Father, full of grace and truth." Jesus Christ reflected the power of God while on earth that no other man could ever achieve; "He is the image of the invisible God, the firstborn of all creation" (Colossians 1:15).

MAN

According to Mormonism, man is a pre-existent soul who takes his body at birth in this world.

> Man is a spirit clothed with a tabernacle. The intelligent part of which was never created or made, but existed eternally—man was also in the beginning with God. 45

Speaking of man, John Widtsoe said,

> He existed before he came to earth: He was with God "in the beginning." Man's destiny is divine. Man is an eternal being. He also is "everlasting to everlasting." 56/132

To think that we can one day be God like Jesus Christ and the Father is blasphemous.

The Book of Mormon and Archaeology

Mormon scholars can be frustrated and embarrassed understandably when they realize that after all the years of work by archaeologists, both Mormon and others:

1. No *Book of Mormon* cities have been located.
2. No *Book of Mormon* names have been found in New World Inscriptions.
3. No genuine inscriptions have been found in Hebrew in America.
4. No genuine inscriptions have been found in America in Egyptian or anything similar to Egyptian, which could correspond to Joseph Smith's "reformed Egyptian."
5. No ancient copies of *Book of Mormon* scriptures have been found.
6. No ancient inscriptions of any kind in America which indicate that the ancient inhabitants had Hebrew or Christian beliefs have been found.
7. No mention of *Book of Mormon* persons, nations, or places has been found.
8. No artifact of any kind which demonstrates the *Book of Mormon* is true has been found.
9. Rather than finding supportive evidence, Mormon scholars have been forced to retreat from traditional interpretations of *Book of Mormon* statements. 15/12

Dr. Gleason Archer has done an excellent job in listing a few of the anachronisms and historical inaccuracies in the Mormon scriptures:

> In 1 Nephi 2:5-8, it is stated that the river Laman emptied into the Red Sea. Yet neither in historic nor prehistoric times has there been any river in Arabia at all that emptied into the Red Sea. Apart from an ancient canal which once connected the Nile with the coast of the Gulf of Suez, and certain wadis which showed occasional rainfall in ancient times, there were no streams of any kind emptying into the Red Sea on the western shore above the southern border of Egypt. . . .
>
> According to Alma 7:10, Jesus was to be born at Jerusalem (rather than in Bethlehem, as recorded in Luke 2:4 and predicted in Micah 5:2). . . .
>
> Alma 46:15 indicates that believers were called "Christians" back in 73 B.C. rather than at Antioch as Acts 11:26 informs us. It is difficult to imagine how anyone could have been labeled Christian so many decades before Christ was even born.
>
> Helaman 12:25,26, allegedly written in 6 B.C., quotes John 5:29 as a prior written source, introducing it by the words, "We read." It is difficult to see how a quotation could be cited from a written source not composed until eight or nine decades after 6 B.C. . . .

> Even more remarkable is the abundance of parallels of word-for-word quotations from the New Testament which are found in the Book of Mormon, which was allegedly in the possession of the Nephites back in 600 B.C. Jerald and Sandra Tanner 48/87-102 have listed no less than 400 clear examples out of a much larger number that could be adduced; and these serve to establish beyond all question that the author of the Book of Mormon was actually well acquainted with the New Testament, and specifically the KJV of 1611. . . .
>
> Most interesting is the recently exposed fraud of the so-called Book of Abraham, part of the Mormon scripture known as *The Pearl of Great Price.* This was assertedly translated from an ancient Egyptian papyrus found in the mummy wrappings of certain mummies which had been acquired by a certain Michael H. Chandler.
>
> In 1835 Joseph Smith became very much interested in these papyrus leaves, which he first saw in Kirtland, Ohio, on July 3, and arranged for the purchase of both mummies and manuscripts. Believing he had divinely received the gift of interpreting ancient Egyptian, he was delighted to find that one of the rolls contained the writings of Abraham himself, whose signature he had personally inscribed in the Egyptian language.
>
> In 1842, Smith published his translation under the title, "The Book of Abraham" in *Times and Seasons.* He even included two drawings of the pictures or vignettes appearing in the manuscript, and interpreted the meaning of these illustrations: Abraham sitting upon the throne of Pharaoh and the serpent with walking legs who tempted Eve in Eden.
>
> For many years this collection of papyri was lost, but somehow they (or else a duplicate set of them from ancient times) were presented to the Mormon Church by the Metropolitan Art Museum of New York City on November 27, 1967. This made the translation skill of Joseph Smith susceptible to objective verification.
>
> The unhappy result was that earlier negative verdicts of scholars like Theodule Devaria of the Louvre, and Samuel A. B. Mercer of Western Theological Seminary, and James H. Breasted of the University of Chicago, and W. F. Flinders Petrie of London University (who had all been shown Smith's facsimiles) were clearly upheld by a multitude of present-day Egyptologists. 2/501-4

Their finding was that not a single word of Joseph Smith's alleged translation bore any resemblance to the contents of this document.

Conclusion

When all the evidence is considered, the Mormon claim to be the restoration of Jesus Christ's church falls to the ground. We have taken up the challenge of Brigham Young who said, "Take up the Bible, compare the religion of the Latter-Day Saints with it, and see if it will stand the test." 17/46

Orson Pratt echoed the same sentiment, "Convince us of our errors of Doctrine, if we have any, by reason, by logical arguments, or by the Word of God and we will ever be grateful for the information and you will ever have the pleasing reflections that you have been instruments in the hands of God of redeeming your fellow beings." 43/15

Our conclusion is that when Mormonism is weighed in the balances it is found wanting.

CHAPTER 34 *Other Popular Cults*

NOTE: Other cults covered in *Understanding the Cults* are: Children of God, Christian Science, EST, Theosophy, The Way International and Unity.

Hare Krishna (UC/51-54)

History

The origin of The Hare Krishnas (International Society for Krishna Consciousness or ISKCON) dates back to the fifteenth century A.D., when Chaitanya Mahaprabhu developed the Doctrines of Krishnaism from the Hindu sect of Vishnuism.

Simply stated, Vishnuism believed Vishnu, the Supreme God, manifested himself at one time as Krishna. Chaitanya Mahaprabhu taught the reverse: Krishna was the chief God who had revealed himself at one time as Vishnu. The doctrinal system of Krishnaism is Hinduistic and denies personality in God's ultimate state while believing every individual must go through a series of successive lives (reincarnation) to rid himself of the debt of his actions (karma).

Krishnaism was one of the early attempts to make philosophical Hinduism appealing to the masses. While pure Hinduism's god is impersonal and unknowable, Krishnaism (and other sects) personalize their god and promote worship of and interaction with the personalized aspects of the god, such as Krishna.

In 1965 Krishnaism came to America by means of Abhay Charan De Bhaktivedanta Swami Prabhupada, an aged Indian exponent of the worship of Krishna. He founded ISKCON and remained its leader until his death in 1978. Presently, ISKCON is ruled by two different groups, one group of eleven men who rule over spiritual matters, and another group, a board of directors, who head the administrative matters. This wealthy organization presently has about ten thousand members in America. Part of ISKCON's wealth comes from soliciting funds and distributing its lavishly illustrated literature including the *Bhagavad-Gita: As It Is,* and its periodical, *Back to Godhead.*

ISKCON's beliefs are those of Hinduism and are wholly incompatible with Christianity. This can be observed by a comparison between the statements of ISKCON on matters of belief with those of the Bible.

Salvation

The Bible teaches that all of us have sinned against a holy God and are therefore in need of a Savior: "For all have sinned and come short of the glory of God" (Romans 3:23); "For the wages of sin is death but the gift of God is eternal life through Jesus Christ our Lord" (Romans 6:23).

According to ISKCON, salvation must be earned by performing a series of works. To eliminate ignorance, one must practice disciplinary devotion: chanting the name of God, hearing and singing His praises, meditating upon the divine play and deeds of KRSNA, engaging in the rites and ceremonies of worship, and repeating the name of God to the count of beads. 38/326

Cult experts, Robert and Gretchen Passantino, have done extensive research in this area, and they offer pertinent comments regarding salvation in ISKCON:

> Salvation in Hare Krishna is thoroughly entwined with the Hindu concept of karma, or retributive justice. This teaching, which requires belief in reincarnation and/or transmigration of the soul, says that one's deeds, good and bad, are measured and judged either for or against him. Only when his good deeds have "atoned" for his bad deeds (and he is thus cleansed of this

evil world) can he realize his oneness with Krishna and cease his cycles of rebirth. 37/150

Transcendental Meditation (UC/105-11)

The History of TM

The founder of Transcendental Meditation (TM), Mahesh Brasad Warma, later known as Maharishi Mahesh Yogi, was born in India around 1910. After graduating from Allahabad University in 1942 with a degree in physics, Mahesh became the disciple of the Indian religious leader Guru Dev. It was Guru Dev who taught Mahesh a meditation technique derived from the Vedas (part of the Hindu scripture).

The Maharishi (as he is referred to) was devoted to fulfilling the plan of Guru Dev in bringing his teachings to the world. In 1958 Maharishi founded the Spiritual Regeneration Movement in India. He came to America the following year and set up his organization while spreading the gospel of Guru Dev. Today, several million people in the United States and around the world have been taught the Maharishi's meditation techniques, said to be nonreligious, although thoroughly Hindu.

The Claims of TM

How would you like to have your health improved, your self-image and productivity increased, and your intelligence and creativity heightened without stress or tension?

According to its advertisements, these are some of the ways TM will benefit individuals. Allegedly all this can be done within any religious or nonreligious system since TM supposedly has no religious basis.

Under a World Plan, 350 teaching centers of the Science of Creative Intelligence have been founded in the largest cities throughout the United States and the world. In fact, resolutions drawn up by the Maharishi and promoting TM have been adopted by legislatures throughout the country.

TM can appeal to all segments of society, including the famous (such as the Beatles in the mid-'60s), the counter-culture, the business community and the intelligentsia. Stanford law professor John Kaplan testifies, "I use it the way I'd use a product of our technology to overcome nervous tension. It's a non-chemical tranquilizer with no unpleasant side effects." 18

TM, however, is not a neutral discipline that can be practiced without harm to the individual. In actuality, TM is a Hindu meditation technique that attempts to unite the meditator with Brahman, the Hindu concept of God.

The Religious Nature of TM

Despite claims to the contrary, TM is religious in nature. The following is a translation of part of the Puja, the initiation ceremony read in Sanskrit by the TM instructor.

PUJA

Whether pure or impure, whether purity or impurity is permeating everywhere, whoever opens himself to the expanded vision of unbounded awareness gains inner and outer purity.

Invocation

To Lord Narayana, to lotus-born Brahma the Creator, to Vashishta, to Shakti, and to his son, Parashar, to Vyasa, to Shukadava, to the great Gaudapada, to Govinda, ruler among yogies, to his disciple, Shri Trotika and Varttika-Kara, to others, to the tradition of our masters I bow down. To the abode of the wisdom of the Shrutis, Smritis and Puranas, to the abode of kindness, to the personified glory of the Lord, to Shankara, emancipator of the Lord, I bow down. To Sharkaracharya, the redeemer, hailed as Krishna and Badarayana, to the commentator of the Brahma Sutras, I bow down again and again. At whose door the whole galaxy of gods pray for perfection day and night, adorned with immeasurable glory, perceptor of the whole world, having bowed down to him, we gain fulfillment. Skilled in dispelling the cloud of ignorance of the people, the gentle emancipator, Bramananda Saraswati—the supreme teacher, full of brilliance, him I bring to my awareness.

From the translation of the Puja, the religious nature of TM can clearly be seen. In 1977, a New Jersey federal court barred the teaching of TM in the schools of that state, the presiding judge concluding,

> The teaching of SCI [Science of Creative Intelligence]/TM and the Puja are religious in nature, no other inference is permissible or reasonable . . . although defendants have submitted well over 1500 pages of briefs, affidavits and deposition testimony in opposing plaintiffs' motion for summary judgement, defendants have failed to raise the slightest doubt as to the facts or as to the religious nature of the teaching of the Science of Creative Intelligence and the Puja. The teaching of SCI/TM courses in New Jersey violates the establishment clause of the First Amendment, and its teaching must be enjoined. 52

Is It Harmless?

Many of the statements made by the Maharishi concerning the Science of Creative Intelligence and the Age of Enlightenment are disturbing:

> There has not been and there will not be a place for the unfit. The fit will lead, and if the unfit are not coming along, there is no place for them. In the place where light dominates there is no place for darkness. In the Age of Enlightenment there is no place for ignorant people. The ignorant

> will be made enlightened by a few orderly, enlightened people moving around. Nature will not allow ignorance to prevail. It just can't. Nonexistence of the unfit has been the law of nature. 24/47
>
> It is only childish and ridiculous to base one's life on the level of thinking. Thinking can never be a profound basis of living. Being is the natural basis . . . thinking, on the other hand, is only imaginary. 23/99

It is disturbing to think that Maharishi would eliminate opposers and that thinking is useless! The Bible says that judgment belongs only to the Lord Jesus Christ (John 5:22,27) and that one should examine and test all things by God's Word (1 John 4:1).

The Religious Beliefs of TM

We have already observed that TM is religious in nature, based upon Hinduism, consequently their theology is in direct contrast to Christianity.

GOD

This "supreme being" is identified with nature: "Everything in creation is the manifestation of the unmanifested absolute impersonal being, the omnipresent God." 23/266 "This impersonal God is that being which dwells in the heart of everyone." 23/269

Man is also identified with God: "Each individual is, in his true nature, the impersonal God." 22/276 This same God is controlling evolution: "God, the supreme almighty being, in whose person the process of evolution finds its fulfillment, is on the top level of creation." 23/270 "He [God] maintains the entire field of evolution and the different lives of innumerable beings in the whole cosmos." 23/271

Maharishi's view of God and man is not in accord with the Bible. Scripture teaches that God is infinite while man is finite. Man can never become God or attain Godhood for he is part of God's creation. Man is the creature, God is the creator.

JESUS CHRIST

The Maharishi does not have much to say about Jesus but when he does, he contradicts the Bible.

> Due to not understanding the life of Christ and not understanding the message of Christ, I don't think Christ ever suffered or Christ could suffer. . . . It's a pity that Christ is talked of in terms of suffering. . . . Those who count upon the suffering, it is a wrong interpretation of the life of Christ and the message of Christ. . . . How could suffering be associated with the one who has been all joy, all bliss, who claims all that? It's only the misunderstanding of the life of Christ. 21/123-24

It is the Maharishi who misunderstands the purpose of Christ's coming, which was to die for the sins of the world. "The next day he saw Jesus coming to him, and said, Behold, the Lamb of God who takes away the sin of the world!" (John 1:29, NASB); and, "Just as the Son of man did not come to be served, but to serve, and to give His life a ransom for many" (Matthew 20:28, NASB). Jesus Christ, contrary to the teaching of the Maharishi, suffered on the cross for our sins so we might receive forgiveness from God for our sins. His suffering was real.

The Unification Church–The "Moonies" (UC/133-39)

The founder and leader of the Unification Church is Sun Myung Moon who was born in Korea on January 6, 1920. His family converted to Christianity when he was ten and became members of the Presbyterian Church.

At age 16 young Moon experienced a vision while in prayer on a Korean mountainside. Moon claims that Jesus Christ appeared to him in the vision admonishing him to carry out the task that Christ had failed to complete. Jesus supposedly told Moon that he was the only one who could do it.

The years between his "conversion" experience and his coming to America are shrouded in much controversy. For documentation on those intervening years we would recommend *The Moon Is Not the Son* by James Bjornstad. 12

After achieving success with his new religion in the Far East, especially South Korea, Moon came to America at the end of 1971 and his cult began to flourish. Today they claim some two million members worldwide.

The Claims of Sun Myung Moon

Sun Myung Moon has made it clear that he believes himself to be the Messiah for this age.

> With the fullness of time, God has sent his messenger to resolve the fundamental questions of life and the universe. His name is Sun Myung Moon. 32/n.p.

Moon has also said, "No heroes in the past, no saints or holy men in the past, like Jesus or Confucius, have excelled us." 33/3

Even though Moon's doctrines are opposed to Christianity, he claims that it was Jesus who revealed them to him. "You may again want to ask me, 'With what authority do you weigh these things?' I spoke with Jesus Christ in the spirit world." 31/98

And, like almost all cult leaders, Moon claims exclusive knowledge. "We are the only people who truly understand the heart of Jesus, and the hope of Jesus." 35/20

Source of Authority

In the Unification Church the writings and teachings of Moon take precedence over the Bible: "It may be displeasing to religious believers, especially to Christians, to learn that a new expression of truth must appear. They believe that the Bible, which they now have, is perfect and absolute in itself." 32/9

For the members of the Unification Church, the *Divine Principle* is the ultimate authoritative work, superseding even the Bible. The *Divine Principle* is known as the completed testament because it supposedly contains the present truth for this age which heretofore had never been revealed.

The assertions of Moon are at complete odds with the Bible. The Scriptures testify that the Word of God is eternal:

> The grass withers, the flower fades, but the Word of God stands forever (Isaiah 40:8 NASB).

Jesus said,

> Heaven and earth shall pass away, but my Words shall not pass away (Matthew 24:35).

Moreover, the Bible records the strongest condemnation for those who would add to what the Scriptures have revealed:

> You shall not add to the Word which I am commanding you, nor take away from it. That you may keep the commandments of the LORD your God which I command you (Deuteronomy 4:2, NASB).

> I testify to everyone who hears the words of the prophecy of this book; if anyone adds to them, God shall add to him the plagues which are written in this book (Revelation 22:18, NASB).

Unification Doctrine

Basic to Moon's world view is the concept of dualism. All of existence is dual: Father God and Mother God; Male and Female; Light and Dark; Yin and Yang; Spirit and Flesh. Each part of existence has its dual aspect. Moon's God (with dual male/female aspects) always acts in a dual manner with his dual creation.

THE FALL OF MAN

According to the *Divine Principle,* until now no one has correctly understood the Genesis account of the fall of man. The *Divine Principle* teaches there were two falls, one physical and one spiritual. Moreover, both falls were sexual in nature. Eve supposedly had an illicit sexual relationship with Lucifer causing the spiritual fall. Afterward, her sexual relationship with spiritually immature Adam resulted in the physical fall.

JESUS CHRIST

When Jesus Christ came to earth, He was supposed to redeem mankind both physically and spiritually, but He failed in His mission: "Jesus failed in His Christly mission. His death on the cross was not an essential part of God's plan for redeeming sinful man." 32/142-43

Moon believes the major reason for Jesus' crucifixion was John the Baptist's failure. John was supposed to clear the way for Jesus to come to the people of his day but he failed because he lost faith. This caused the people to abandon Jesus and eventually resulted in His death. The crucifixion was not something God desired because the work of Christ was unfinished. It is here where Sun Myung Moon picks up where Jesus left off. Moon is supposedly the "third Adam," the one who is called to redeem mankind physically.

Moon has a non-biblical view of the person of Jesus Christ by denying the unique deity of Jesus Christ. "It is plain that Jesus is not God Himself." 32/258

Moon tells his followers that they are able to not only equal Jesus, but they can also excel Him.

"You can compare yourself with Jesus Christ, and feel you can be greater than Jesus Himself." 34/4

Speaking of the work of Christ, the writer to the Hebrews said, "For by one offering He has perfected for all time those who are sanctified" (Hebrews 10:14). The Scriptures testify that the work of Christ on the cross is complete, sufficient to secure the salvation of the individual. Jesus accomplished all that was necessary for the full salvation of mankind. He was not a failure.

The Scriptures teach that "God was in Christ reconciling the world to Himself" (2 Corinthians 5:19). But Moon declares, "The physical body of Jesus was invaded by Satan through the cross." 32/438

Conclusion

Rev. Moon has stated, "God is now throwing Christianity away and is establishing a new religion, and this new religion is the Unification Church." 50/n.p.

Although the Unification Church makes astounding claims for itself, the facts speak otherwise. The teaching of the *Divine Principle* is at odds with the Bible at all of its central points and therefore cannot be a completion of God's revelation. Moon has no messianic credentials and must be considered as a false prophet, of which Jesus warned us:

> Beware of false prophets, who come to you in sheep's clothing, but inwardly are ravenous wolves. You will know them by their fruits (Matthew 7:15,16, NASB).

The Worldwide Church of God—"Armstrongism"

(UC/153-61)

History

The founder of the Worldwide Church of God was Herbert W. Armstrong, born on July 31, 1892, in Des Moines, Iowa. As a young man, Armstrong worked in the advertising business and showed little interest in spiritual things. In a dispute with his wife over the issue of keeping the seventh-day Sabbath, Armstrong began an intensive personal study of the Bible. This resulted in his agreeing with his wife on observing the Saturday Sabbath. Further Bible study convinced Armstrong that much of what he had been taught in traditional churches was wrong.

> I found that the popular church teachings and practices were not based on the Bible. They had originated, as research in history had revealed, in paganism. Numerous Bible prophecies foretold it; the amazing unbelievable truth was, the SOURCE of these popular beliefs and practices of professing Christianity, was quite largely paganism, and human reasoning and custom, NOT the Bible! 4/298-99

According to Armstrong, the Worldwide Church of God began in January 1934.

Armstrong at this time began his radio broadcast and the publishing of the magazine *The Plain Truth*. Since its inception, the Worldwide Church of God has experienced significant growth reaching into millions of homes through the distribution of its magazine and the "World Tomorrow" radio broadcast.

The Claims of Armstrong

Herbert W. Armstrong makes no small claim for his work in the Worldwide Church of God.

> A.D. 69, the apostles and the church fled to Pella from Jerusalem according to Jesus' warning (Matthew 24:15,16). That was the END of the organized proclaiming of Christ's gospel by His church to the world! . . . For eighteen and one-half centuries, all worldwide organized proclaiming of Christ's gospel was stamped out. 4/502-3

> And listen again! Read this twice! Realize this, incredible though it may seem—no other work on earth is proclaiming this true gospel of Christ to the whole world as Jesus foretold in Matthew 24:14 and Mark 13:10! This is the most important activity on earth today! 27/35-36

GOD

Like the Mormons, Armstrong believed in a plurality of personal gods, based upon the Hebrew word for God, "Elohim."

> And as I have explained previously, God is not a single person, but the Hebrew word for God portrays God as a FAMILY of persons. 6/7
>
> "Elohim" is a uniplural or collective noun, such as "church" or "family" or "kingdom." In other words, Elohim stands for a single class composed of TWO or MORE individuals. Elohim, then, is the "God Kingdom" or "God Family." 9/5

THE TRINITY

There is no biblical Trinity in Armstrong's theology. Presently the Godhead is limited to the Father and the Son but in the future more persons will be added to the Godhead. "God is a family—not a trinity. God's family will not be limited to an intractably closed circle of three . . . God's family is open." 30/31

Simply stated, the Bible teaches there exists one God who is three separate persons; the Father, the Son, and the Holy Spirit, and these three persons are the one God. There is no teaching whatever in Scripture that suggests God is a family.

MAN

The final destiny of man is to become God: "You are setting out on a training to become creator—to become God!" 8/22

> The PURPOSE OF LIFE is that in us God is really recreating His own kind—reproducing Himself after His own kind—for we are, upon real conversion, actually begotten as sons (yet unborn) of God . . . we grow spiritually more and more like God, until, at the time of the resurrection we shall be instantaneously changed from mortal to immortal—we shall be born of God—WE SHALL THEN BE GOD! 14/27

The idea that man will someday be God can be found nowhere in the Bible. God is God by nature. He was, is and always will be God. Man cannot attain Godhood for he is finite, limited by his nature. There is no other God, neither will there be any other God:

> "You are my witnesses," declares the LORD, "and my servant whom I have chosen, in order that you may know and believe me and understand that I am He. Before Me there was no God formed, and there will be none after me" (Isaiah 43:10, NASB).

SALVATION BY WORKS

As is the case with all non-Christian cults, Armstrongism teaches that salvation is achieved by the individual's self-effort rather than relying only on God's grace.

> Salvation, then is a process! But how the God of this world would blind your eyes to that!!! He tries to deceive you into thinking all there is to it is just "accepting Christ" with "no works"—and presto-chango, you are

pronounced "saved." But the Bible reveals that none is yet "saved." 8/11

Armstrongism claims salvation consists of repentance, faith and water baptism. No one is saved in this life. It rejects, in the strongest of terms, the doctrine of "simply" coming to Christ for salvation:

> People have been taught, falsely, that "Christ completed the plan of salvation on the cross"—when actually it was only begun there. The popular denominations have taught, "Just believe, that's all there is to it; believe on the Lord Jesus Christ, and you are that instant saved!" That teaching is false! And because of deception, because the true gospel of Jesus Christ has been blotted out, lo these 1900 years by the preaching of a false gospel about the person of Christ—and often a false Christ at that—millions today worship Christ—and all in vain! 3/1

According to Armstrong, a person must be baptized in order to be saved: "God commands water baptism; and for one who is able to either defy the command and refuse, or neglect . . . certainly would be an act of disobedience which would impose the PENALTY of sin, and cause loss of salvation." 3/19

Moreover, the Saturday Sabbath needs to be observed to attain salvation: "Thus did God reveal which day is HIS SABBATH, and also that it DOES MAKE LIFE-AND-DEATH DIFFERENCE—for to break God's Holy Sabbath is SIN and the penalty is eternal DEATH." 7/35

Contrary to Armstrong's statements, the Scriptures teach that salvation is a free gift from God. The Scriptures further declare that salvation cannot be earned by doing any work, whether it be water baptism or the keeping of the Sabbath. Salvation comes as a result of a person simply placing his faith in Jesus Christ:

> For by grace you have been saved through faith; and that not of yourselves, it is the gift of God; not as a result of works, that no one should boast (Ephesians 2:8,9, NASB).

> He saved us, not on the basis of deeds which we have done in righteousness, but according to His mercy, by the washing of regeneration and renewing by the Holy Spirit (Titus 3:5, NASB).

THE NEW BIRTH

Armstrong and his followers have a peculiar view regarding the new birth. They believe an individual is not born of God until the resurrection. Rather, he is only "begotten" (like pregnant) of God at his conversion:

> When we are converted, our sins forgiven, we receive the Holy Spirit, we are then BEGOTTEN of God—not yet BORN of God. . . . Even as Christ was BORN AGAIN, born of God by his resurrection, even so WE—the brethren—shall be BORN AGAIN as sons of God, through the RESURRECTION of the dead. 5/40

Until now Christ is the only person who has been born again. The rest of the believers must await a future resurrection to experience the new birth.

Armstrongism is incorrect in this assertion. A person becomes born again the moment he trusts Christ. The apostle Peter, while speaking to believers, said, "For you *have been* born again not of seed which is perishable but imperishable, that is, through the living and abiding Word of God" (1 Peter 1:23, NASB, italics ours).

Part Three: Bibliography

1. Anonymous. *Qualified to Be Ministers.* n. pub., 1955.
2. Archer, Gleason L. *A Survey of Old Testament Introduction.* Chicago: Moody Press, 1973.
3. Armstrong, Herbert W. *All About Water Baptism.*
4. Armstrong, Herbert W. *The Autobiography of Herbert W. Armstrong.* Pasadena: Ambassador College Press, 1967.
5. Armstrong, Herbert W. "Was Jesus Christ Born Again?" *The Plain Truth* (February 1963).
6. Armstrong, Herbert W. "What is the True Gospel?" *Tomorrow's World* (January 1970).
7. Armstrong, Herbert W. *Which Day Is the Christian Sabbath?* Pasadena: Ambassador College Press, 1971.
8. Armstrong, Herbert W. *Why Were You Born?*
9. Armstrong, Herbert W., ed. *Ambassador College Correspondence Course.* 1972. Lesson 8.
10. Arndt, William F., and Gingrich, F. Wilbur. *Greek-English Lexicon of the New Testament.* University of Chicago Press, 1957.
11. *Articles of Faith of the Church of Jesus Christ of Latter-Day Saints,* Article 8.
12. Bjornstad, James. *The Moon Is Not the Son.* Minneapolis: Dimension Books/Bethany House Press, 1976.
13. Gill, John. *An Exposition of the New Testament, Both Doctrinal and Practical* 4. London: George Keith, 1876.
14. Hill, David Jon. "Why Is God the Father Called a Father?" *Tomorrow's World* (September 1970).
15. Hougey, Hal. *Archaeology and the Book of Mormon.*
16. *Improvement Era,* June 1945.
17. *Journal of Discourses* 16
18. Kaplan, John, testimony. *Time* Magazine (October 30, 1975).
19. *Let God Be True,* 1946.
20. *Let God Be True,* 1952.
21. Maharishi Mahesh Yogi. *Meditations of Maharishi Mahesh Yogi.*
22. Maharishi Mahesh Yogi. *Science of Being and Art of Living.* Rev. ed., 1967.
23. Maharishi Mahesh Yogi. *Transcendental Meditation.*
24. Maharishi Mahaesh Yogi. *Inauguration of the Dawn of the Age of Enlightenment.* MIU Press.
25. *Make Sure of All Things.*
26. Martin, Walter. *The Maze of Mormonism.* Santa Ana, CA: Vision House Publishers, Inc., 1977.
27. Martin, Walter. *The Rise of the Cults.* Santa Ana, CA: Vision House Publishers, 1977. Rev. ed. Quoting Herbert W. Armstrong, personal letter to Robert Sumner, November 27, 1958.

28. Martin, Walter. *The Rise of the Cults.* Santa Ana, CA: Vision House Publishers Incorporated, 1980.

29. McConkie, Bruce R. *Mormon Doctrine.*

30. McDowell, B. "Is the Holy Spirit a Person?" *Tomorrow's World* (September 1970).

31. Moon, Sun Myung. *Christianity in Crisis.* HSA Pubns.

32. Moon, Sun Myung. *Divine Principle.* The Holy Spirit Association for the Unification of World Christianity. 2nd ed., 1973.

33. Moon, Sun Myung. "Our Shame." Trans., Won Pok Choi. From *The Master Speaks* (March 11, 1973).

34. Moon, Sun Myung. "The Way." Trans., Won Pok Choi. From *The Master Speaks* (June 30, 1974).

35. Moon, Sun Myung. *The Way of the World.*

36. *New World Translation of the Holy Scriptures.* Brooklyn: Watchtower Bible and Tract Society, 1950, 1963.

37. Passantino, Robert and Gretchen. *Answers to the Cultists at Your Door.* Eugene, OR: Harvest House Publishers, 1981.

38. Prabhupada, Abhay Charan de Bhaktivedanta Swami. *Bhagavad-Gita: As It Is.*

39. Robertson, A. T. *Word Pictures in the New Testament* 5. New York: Harper & Row, 1930-33.

40. Russell, Charles Taze. *Studies in the Scriptures* 1. London: International Bible Students' Association, 1899.

41. Russell, Charles Taze, *Thy Kingdom Come,* 1891.

42. Russell, Charles Taze. *The Watchtower* (September 15, 1910).

43. *The Seer.*

44. Smith, Joseph. *Pearl of Great Price.*

45. Smith, Joseph Fielding. *Doctrines of Salvation.*

46. Smith, Joseph Fielding. *Progress of Man.*

47. Stedman, Ray C. "The New World Translation of the Christian Greek Scriptures." *Our Hope* (July 1953).

48. Tanner, Jerald and Sandra. *The Case Against Mormonism* 2. Salt Lake City: Modern Microfilm Company, 1967.

49. "This Good News of the Kingdom." Pamphlet.

50. *Time* magazine (September 20, 1974).

51. *The Truth That Leads to Eternal Life* (1968).

52. United States District Court, District of New Jersey, Civil Action No. 76-34.

53. *The Watchtower* (July 15, 1960).

54. *Watchtower Reprints* 1 (March 1880).

55. Widtsoe, John. *Varieties of American Religion.*

56. "The Word, Who Is He? According to John." *Watchtower*, n.d.

Part Four
THE OCCULT

CHAPTER 35 *The Occult Phenomena* (UO/10-24)

NOTE: Other subjects covered in the book *Understanding the Occult* but not covered here are dowsing, fire walking, fortunetelling, ghosts, magic, parapsychology, ESP, psychic surgery, Rosicrucianism, Satan, spiritism (necromancy), and superstition. Also note that *Understanding the Occult* may be consulted for additional details and bibliography on the subjects covered in the following pages.

What Is the Occult?

The word *occult* comes from the Latin word *occultus* and it carries the idea of things hidden, secret and mysterious. Hoover lists three distinct characteristics of the occult:

1. The occult deals with things secret or hidden.
2. The occult deals with operations or events which seem to depend on human powers that go beyond the five senses.
3. The occult deals with the supernatural, the presence of angelic or demonic forces. **9/8**

Under the designation occult we would class at least the following items: witchcraft, magic, palm reading, fortune telling, Ouija boards, tarot cards, satanism, spiritism, demons and the use of crystal balls. To this list we could add much more.

Avoiding Extremes

C. S. Lewis once commented,

> There are two equal and opposite errors into which our race can fall about the devils. One is to disbelieve in their existence. The other is to believe, and to feel an unhealthy interest in them. They themselves are equally pleased by both errors and hail a materialist or a magician with the same delight. 12/preface

It is our desire to avoid these common extremes in dealing with the occult. We neither see the devil in everything nor completely deny his influence and workings.

A Word of Warning

We realize that by informing people about the world of the occult, we will be exposing some of them to things of which they previously have been ignorant. However, we do not want to stimulate anyone's curiosity to the point where interest in the occult could become an obsession. Mankind already has a certain fascination about evil, so it would be prudent to take the advice of the apostle Paul: "I want you to be wise in what is good and innocent in what is evil" (Romans 16:19, NASB).

Playing around with the world of the occult can lead to serious repercussions, both psychologically and spiritually. There is a difference between knowing intellectually that taking poison will kill you and actually taking the poison to experience what you already know to be a fact. We need to be aware of the workings of the satanic realm but not to the point of unhealthy fascination or involvement.

Occultic Deception

Another thing we must be careful of is that although we admit the reality of the supernatural, we must not place all unexplained phenomena into that category. Much goes on under the guise of the supernatural that is nothing but fakery. These pseudo-occult phenomena have fooled many people into believing in their legitimacy.

In an excellent book entitled *The Fakers,* Danny Korem and Paul Meier list eleven principles of deception that fakers use to imitate supernatural or occultic phenomena. These include:

1. Sleight of hand
2. Psychological principles

3. Using a stooge
4. Unseen and unknown devices
5. Mathematical principles
6. Physics
7. Physical deception
8. Mechanical deception
9. Optical illusion
10. Luck and probability
11. Combination of all the principles 11/22-29

Needless to say, caution must be exercised before assuming some unexplained phenomenon is demonic.

The Bible and the Occult

The Bible categorically denounces any and all occultic practices:

> When you enter the land which the LORD your God gives you, you shall not learn to imitate the detestable things of those nations. There shall not be found among you anyone who makes his son or his daughter pass through the fire, one who uses divination, one who practices witchcraft, or one who interprets omens, or a sorcerer, or one who casts a spell, or a medium, or a spiritualist, or one who calls upon the dead. For whoever does these things is detestable to the LORD; and because of these detestable things the LORD your God will drive them out before you. You shall be blameless before the LORD your God.
>
> For those nations, which you shall dispossess, listen to those who practice witchcraft and to diviners, but as for you, the LORD your God has not allowed you to do so (Deuteronomy 18:9-14, NASB).

In the same manner, the New Testament condemns such workings (Galatians 5:20). In the city of Ephesus many who were practicing in the occult became believers in Jesus Christ and renounced their occultic practices. "Many also of those who practiced magic brought their books together and began burning them in the sight of all" (Acts 19:19).

Another encounter with the occult can be seen in Acts 13:6-12 (NASB):

> And when they had gone through the whole island as far as Paphos, they found a certain magician, a Jewish false prophet whose name was Bar-Jesus, who was with the proconsul, Sergius Paulus, a man of intelligence. This man summoned Barnabas and Saul and sought to hear the word of God. But Elymas the magician (for thus his name is translated) was opposing them, seeking to turn the proconsul away from the faith. But Saul, who was also known as Paul, filled with the Holy Spirit, fixed his gaze upon him. And he said, "You who are full of all deceit and fraud, you son of the devil, you enemy of all righteousness, will you not cease to make crooked the straight ways of the Lord? And now, behold, the hand of the Lord is

> upon you, and you will be blind and not see the sun for a time." And immediately a mist and a darkness fell upon him, and he went about seeking those who would lead him by the hand.
>
> Then the proconsul believed when he saw what happened, being amazed at the teaching of the Lord.

From the above, to which much could be added, we see how the Bible in the strongest terms condemns the occult and those who practice it. The road of the occult is broad and leads to destruction, while the way of Christ is narrow and leads to life eternal.

Hypnotism (UO/85-88)

There is a wide difference of opinion on the validity and usefulness of hypnotism. Some see hypnotism as being neutral, neither good nor bad, while others argue that hypnotism can be beneficial for diagnosis and therapy. There are yet others who see hypnotism as harmful, no matter what the case, because it is an attack on the human psyche.

Since there are so many examples of hypnosis which have ended in disaster, we would strongly warn people to stay away from all forms of either occultic or entertaining hypnosis. If a person allows himself to be hypnotized, it should be only under the most controlled situation by a qualified and experienced physician. The human mind is not something to play with or to let another person have control of. At best, hypnosis can have only limited use.

Even the secular *Encyclopedia Britannica* warns:

> While little skill is required to induce hypnosis, considerable training is needed to evaluate whether it is the appropriate treatment technique and, if so, how it should properly be employed. When used in the treatment context, hypnosis should never be employed by individuals who do not have the competence and skill to treat such problems without the use of hypnosis. For this reason hypnosis "schools" or "institutions" cannot provide the needed training for individuals lacking the more general scientific and technical qualifications of the healing professions. . . . Improperly used, hypnosis may add to the patient's psychiatric or medical difficulties. Thus, a sufferer of an undiscovered brain tumor may sacrifice his life in the hands of a practitioner who successfully relieves his headache by hypnotic suggestion, thereby delaying needed surgery. Broad diagnostic training and therapeutic skill are indispensable in avoiding the inappropriate and potentially dangerous use of hypnosis. 6/133

The Bible says, "All things are lawful for me, but not all things are profitable. All things are lawful for me, but I will not be mastered by anything" (1 Corinthians 6:12, NASB). We do not need to be mastered by the power of suggestion from some other person.

Ouija Boards (UO/95-97)

One of the most popular occultic devices in the world today is the Ouija board. What is the Ouija board and what does it claim to do? *The Dictionary of Mysticism* defines it as:

> an instrument for communication with the spirits of the dead. Made in various shapes and designs, some of them used in the sixth century before Christ. The common feature of all its varieties is that an object moves under the hand of the medium, and one of its corners, or a pointer attached to it, spells out messages by successively pointing to letters of the alphabet marked on a board which is a part of the instrument. 7/132

Our convictions concerning the Ouija board agree exactly with those of noted cult and occult observer Edmond Gruss.

> The Ouija board should be seen as a device which sometimes actually makes contact with the supernatural for several reasons:
>
> —The content of the messages often goes beyond that which can be reasonably explained as coming from the conscious or subconscious mind of the operator. Examples of such are presented in Sir William F. Barrett's *On the Threshold of the Unseen* (pp. 176-89), and in the experiences of Mrs. John H. Curran, related in the book *Singer in the Shadows.*
>
> —The many cases of "possession" after a period of Ouija board use also support the claim that supernatural contact is made through the board. Psychics and parapsychologists have received letters from hundreds of people who have experienced "possession" (an invasion of their personalities). Rev. Donald Page, a well-known clairvoyant and exorcist of the Christian Spiritualist Church, is reported as saying that most of his "possession" cases "are people who have used the Ouija board," and that "this is one of the easiest and quickest ways to become possessed." 13/2060*ff.*
>
> —The board has been subjected to tests which support supernatural intervention. The testing of the board was presented in an article by Sir William Barrett, in the September 1914 *Proceedings of the American Society for Psychical Research* (pp. 381-894). The Barrett report indicated that the board worked efficiently with the operators blindfolded, the board's alphabet rearranged and its surface hidden from the sight of those working it. It worked with such speed and accuracy under these tests that Barrett concluded:
>
> > Reviewing the results as a whole, I am convinced of their supernormal character, and that we have here an exhibition of some intelligent, disincarnate agency, mingling with the personality of one or more of the sitters and guiding their muscular movements. 8/115-16

The Ouija board is not a plaything. It is another tool often used by Satan to get people to look somewhere else besides to Jesus Christ for the answers. Whether supernatural forces are at work or not, if the person using the Ouija board thinks the supernatural is at work, he will then employ it rather than looking to God for ultimate answers.

The Black Mass (UO/36)

The black mass is said in honor of the devil at the witches' Sabbath. It is practiced by many satanic groups. The ritual reverses the Roman Catholic mass, desecrating the objects used in worship. Oftentimes a nude woman is stretched out upon the altar where the high priest ends the ritual by having sex with her.

Sometimes the participants drink the blood of an animal during the ceremony, along with the eating of human flesh in a mock communion ritual. Human sacrifices, though rare, are not unknown to the black mass.

The black mass contains many other repulsive practices that are unmentionable. It perverts and desecrates the true worship of God and is a blasphemous affront to all believers in Christ.

Witchcraft (UO/173-85)

Witchcraft is known as the "Old Religion" and is an ancient practice dating back to biblical times. Witchcraft can be defined as the performance of magic for nonbiblical ends, an activity forbidden by God. The word *witchcraft* is related to the old English word *wiccian,* the "practice of magical arts."

During the Middle Ages witchcraft experienced a great revival. Everyone believed in the supernatural, and superstition abounded.

If someone wanted to become a witch, there was an initiation process. Some of the techniques were simple and some were complicated, but there were usually two requirements. The first was that the would-be witch must join of his or her own free will. The second requirement was that the prospective witch must be willing to worship the devil.

Halloween

The day witches celebrate above all others is October 31, which is Halloween, a form of All Hallows Eve. It is believed that on this night Satan and his witches have their greatest power.

The origin of Halloween goes back two thousand years before the days of Christianity to a practice of the ancient Druids in Britain, France, Germany and the Celtic countries. The celebration honored their god Samhain, lord of the dead. The Celtic people considered November 1st as being the day of death, because it was the end of autumn and the beginning of winter for them.

The time of falling leaves seemed an appropriate time to celebrate death, which is exactly what Halloween was to them: a celebration of death honoring the god of the dead. The Druids believed that on this particular evening the spirits of the dead returned to their former home to visit the living.

If the living did not provide food for these evil spirits, all types of terrible things would happen to the living. If the evil spirits did not get a treat, then they would trick the living. This ancient practice is still celebrated today when people dress up as the dead, knock on doors and say, "Trick or treat," not realizing the origin of what they are practicing. Nevertheless, it is still considered by witches as the night on which they have their greatest power.

Before the introduction of Christianity to these lands, the celebration of death was not called Halloween. "All Hallows Eve" was a holy evening instituted by the church to honor all the saints of church history.

Some church historians allow the possibility that All Saints' Eve was designated October 31 to counteract the pagan influences of the celebration of death. While All Hallows Eve began as a strictly Christian holiday, the pagan influences from earlier traditions gradually crept in while the church's influences waned.

Today Halloween is largely a secular holiday, an excuse to get dressed up as somebody else and have a party. However, true witches and followers of witchcraft still preserve the early pagan beliefs and consider Halloween a sacred and deadly powerful time. Having turned their backs on the God of the Bible, they invoke the help of Satan, who has fallen from God's favor and been relegated to darkness.

Witchcraft Today

The modern witch does not fit the stereotype of the old hag, for many people who are practicing this art are in the mainstream of society.

Modern witchcraft is a relatively recent development (the last 200 years), embraces hundreds of beliefs and practices and has hundreds of thousands of adherents. The one common theme running through modern witchcraft is the practice of and belief in things forbidden by God in the Bible as occultic.

The Bible and Witchcraft

Both the Old and New Testaments make repeated references to the practice of witchcraft and sorcery, and whenever these practices are referred to they are always condemned by God. The Bible condemns all forms of witchcraft, including sorcery, astrology and reading human and animal entrails. The following passages describe various forms of witchcraft which are condemned by God.

> You shall not eat anything with the blood, nor practice divination or soothsaying (Leviticus 19:26, NASB).
>
> Do not turn to mediums or spiritists; do not seek them out to be defiled by them. I am the LORD your God (Leviticus 19:31, NASB).
>
> Now a man or a woman who is a medium or a spiritist shall surely be put to death. They shall be stoned with stones, their bloodguiltiness is upon them (Leviticus 20:27, NASB).
>
> You shall not behave thus toward the LORD your God, for every abominable act which the LORD hates they have done for their gods; for they even burn their sons and daughters in the fire to their gods (Deuteronomy 12:31, NASB).
>
> There shall not be found among you anyone who makes his son or his daughter pass through the fire, one who uses divination, one who practices witchcraft, or one who interprets omens, or a sorcerer, or one who casts a spell, or a medium, or a spiritist, or one who calls up the dead. . . . For those nations, which you shall dispossess, listen to those who practice witchcraft and to diviners, but as for you, the LORD your God has not allowed you to do so (Deuteronomy 18:10,11,14, NASB).
>
> Then they made their sons and their daughters pass through the fire, and practiced divination and enchantments, and sold themselves to do evil in the sight of the Lord, provoking Him (2 Kings 17:17, NASB).
>
> And he made his son pass through the fire, practiced witchcraft and used divination, and dealt with mediums and spiritists. He did much evil in the sight of the LORD provoking Him to anger (2 Kings 21:6, NASB).
>
> Moreover, Josiah removed the mediums, and the spiritists and teraphim and the idols and all the abominations that were seen in the land of Judah and in Jerusalem, that he might confirm the words of the law which were written in the book that Hilkiah the priest found in the house of the LORD (2 Kings 23:24, NASB).
>
> So Saul died for his trespass which he committed against the LORD, because of the word of the LORD which he did not keep; and also because he asked counsel of a medium, making inquiry of it, and did not inquire of the LORD. Therefore He killed him, and turned the kingdom to David the son of Jesse (1 Chronicles 10:13, NASB).
>
> And when they say to you, "Consult the mediums and the spiritists who whisper and mutter," should not a people consult their God? Should they consult the dead on behalf of the living? (Isaiah 8:19, NASB).
>
> Then the spirit of the Egyptians will
> be demoralized within them;
> And I will confound their strategy,
> So that they will resort to idols and ghosts of the dead,
> And to mediums and spiritists (Isaiah 19:3, NASB).

> Stand fast now in your spells
> And in your many sorceries
> With which you have labored from your youth;
> Perhaps you will be able to profit,
> Perhaps you may cause trembling.
> You are wearied with your many counsels;
> Let now the astrologers,
> Those who prophesy by the stars,
> Those who predict by the new moons,
> Stand up and save you from what will come upon you (Isaiah 47:12,13, NASB).

But as for you, do not listen to your prophets, your diviners, your dreamers, your soothsayers, or your sorcerers, who speak to you, saying, "You shall not serve the king of Babylon." For they prophesy a lie to you, in order to remove you far from your land; and I will drive you out, and you will perish (Jeremiah 27:9,10, NASB).

"Then I will draw near to you for judgment; and I will be a swift witness against the sorcerers and against the adulterers and against those who swear falsely, and against those who oppress the wage earner in his wages, the widow and the orphan, and those who turn aside the alien, and do not fear Me," says the LORD of Hosts (Malachi 3:5, NASB).

Now the deeds of the flesh are evident, which are: immorality, impurity, sensuality, idolatry, sorcery, enmities, strife, jealousy, outbursts of anger, disputes, dissensions, factions, envying, drunkenness, carousing, and things like these, of which I forewarn you just as I have forewarned you that those who practice such things shall not inherit the kingdom of God (Galatians 5:19-21, NASB).

But for the cowardly and unbelieving and abominable and murderers and immoral persons and sorcerers and idolaters and all liars, their part will be in the lake that burns with fire and brimstone, which is the second death (Revelation 21:8, NASB).

CHAPTER 36 *Satanism and Demon Possession*

(UO/137-41)

Satanism

The worship of Satan has deep historical roots. Known as Satanism, it is found expressed in various ways. Black magic, the Black Mass, facets of the drug culture, and blood sacrifice all have connections with Satanism.

In *Escape From Witchcraft,* Roberta Blankenship explains what two girls, both Satanists, wrote to her as part of their initiation ritual:

> They had to go to a graveyard in the dead of night, walk across a man-sized cross, and denounce any belief in Christ. Afterwards, a ritual was performed and the girls had to drink the blood of animals that had been skinned alive. 1/1

Lynn Walker comments:

> In April, 1973, the battered, mutilated body of a 17-year-old boy, Ross "Mike" Cochran, was found outside of Daytona Beach, Florida. An Associated Press story said, "The verdict of police is that Cochran was the victim of devil worshippers: killed in a frenzied sacrificial ritual."

Lynn McMillon, Oklahoma Christian College professor, reports, "One variety of Satanism consists primarily of sex clubs that embellish their orgies with Satanist rituals. Another variety of Satanists are the drug-oriented groups." 25/1

Traditional Satanism

In the past Satanism's associations have been much more secretive than they are now. The anti-religious and anti-god aspect was prevalent in all forms of Satanism. Although this is not true of modern Satanism, traditional Satanism still is associated with black magic and ritualism.

The worship of a personal and powerful devil is central to traditional Satanism. Those involved reject Christianity, yet choose the Lucifer of Scriptures as their god. The *Occult Sourcebook* comments:

> Traditionally, Satanism has been interpreted as the worship of evil, a religion founded upon the very principles which Christianity rejects. As such, Satanism exists only where Christianity exists, and can be understood only in the context of the Christian worldview. Things are, so to speak, reversed—the Christian devil becomes the Satanist's god, Christian virtues become vices, and vices are turned into virtues. Life is interpreted as a constant battle between the powers of light and darkness, and the Satanist fights on the side of darkness, believing that ultimately this will achieve victory. 5/149

Satanic witchcraft is to be found under this category of Satanism, where witches are involved in the darkest side of evil.

The recent onslaught of drugs and sexual perversion associated with the devil can be found here as well.

Modern Satanism

Traditional Satanism is still very prevalent, and growing in society today. However, in recent times, with the growing secularization of society and decline of Judeo-Christian morality, a new humanistic Satanism has emerged and drawn a strong following. The Church of Satan is the clearest example of this new emphasis.

> In modern times groups have emerged in England and Europe, and particularly in the United Sates, which, taking advantage of the permissiveness of modern society, have encouraged some publicity. The most famous of these has been the Church of Satan, founded in San Francisco in 1966 by Anton La Vey, which currently has a membership of many thousands, and has established itself as a church throughout the United States.
>
> Several other groups in America have imitated it, and some groups have also been established as "black witchcraft" covens. The Manson gang, in which a bizarre mixture of Satanism and occultism was practiced, gained a great deal of unfavorable publicity for Satanism in America, but in fact it also resulted in a greater public interest in the subject. With more people

rejecting the traditional values of morality, the Satanist movement will inevitably have greater appeal. 5/154

In a chapter on Satanism today, William Petersen in *Those Curious New Cults* comments on the fact that since the mid-1960s Satanism is making a comeback. He points to the catalyst for the strong upswing as being the box office smash of "Rosemary's Baby." Of the film he states:

> Anton Szandor La Vey, self-styled high priest of San Francisco's First Church of Satan and author of *The Satanic Bible* (1969), played the role of the devil. Later, he called the film the "best paid commercial for Satanism since the Inquisition." No doubt it was. 18/75

Many people are becoming involved in Satanism, and they come from all walks of life. They vary in age, occupation and educational background.

Church of Satan

Although the "Church of Satan" sounds like a contradiction in terms, its emphasis is on materialism and hedonism. Satan, to followers of this church, is more a symbol than a reality. In this emphasis they depart from other forms of Satanism. They are interested in the carnal and worldly pleasures mankind offers.

La Vey is of Russian, Alsatian and Rumanian descent, and his past jobs have been with the circus, an organ player in nightclubs and a police photographer. All during this time La Vey studied the occult.

Of the establishing of the church La Vey declares it was to be:

> a temple of glorious indulgence that would be fun for people. . . . But the main purpose was to gather a group of like-minded individuals together for the use of their combined energies in calling up the dark force in nature that is called Satan. 5/77

Of Satanism La Vey believes:

> It is a blatantly selfish, brutal religion. It is based on the belief that man is inherently a selfish, violent creature, that life is a Darwinian struggle for survival of the fittest, that the earth will be ruled by those who fight to win. 5/78

Emphases of the Church

La Vey is currently the High Priest of the church, which espouses any type of sexual activity that satisfies your needs, be it heterosexuality, homosexuality, adultery or faithfulness in marriage. Part of La Vey's philosophy is expressed here:

> I don't believe that magic is supernatural, only that it is supernormal. That is, it works for reasons science cannot yet understand. As a shaman or magician, I am concerned with obtaining *recipes*. As a scientist, you seek *formulas*. When I make a soup, I don't care about the chemical reactions be-

tween the potatoes and the carrots. I only care about how to get the flavor of soup I seek. In the same way, when I want to hex someone, I don't care about the scientific mechanisms involved, whether they be psychosomatic, psychological, or what-not. My concern is with how to best hex someone. As a magician, my concern is with effectively *doing* the thing, not with the scientist's job of *explaining* it. 23/631

Truzzi describes the "Church of Satan" here:

> This group is legally recognized as a church, has a developed hierarchy and bureaucratic structure which defines it as no longer a cult, and claims over 10,000 members around the world. Most of these members are, in fact, merely mail-order and geographically isolated joiners, but there are clearly at least several hundred fully participating and disciplined members in the various "grottos" (as their fellowships are called) set up around the world. Grottos are growing up rapidly around this country with about a dozen now in operation.
>
> . . . [La Vey's] *The Satanic Bible* . . . has already reportedly sold over 250,000 copies and is now in its third paperback printing. La Vey also publishes a monthly newsletter for those members who subscribe to it, conducts a newspaper column in which he advises those who write in questions, and he has recently written a book on man-catching for the would-be Satanic witch. 23/632

There are nine Satanic statements to which all members must agree. These are that Satan represents indulgence, vital existence, undefiled wisdom, kindness only to those who deserve it, vengeance, responsibility only to those who are responsible, the animal nature of man, all the "so-called sins," and "the best friend the church has ever had, as he has kept it in business all these years."

The Satanic Church is strongly materialistic as well as being anti-Christian. Pleasure-seeking could well describe their philosophy of life. What the world has to offer through the devil is taken full advantage of in the Church of Satan.

Demons and Demon Possession (UO/47-54)

The Bible not only teaches the existence of the devil but also of a great company of his followers known as demons or evil spirits. These demons originally were holy but with Satan, their leader, they fell away from God. Their ultimate end will be eternal damnation when God judges Satan and his host at the Great White Throne judgment (Revelation 20:10-15).

Since the release of the motion picture, *The Exorcist,* there has been renewed discussion about the subject of demon possession. Can demon possession, or control of a person's will by a demon, actually occur? What are the signs of a possessed person? Is it really just superstition and ignorance to believe in demon possession?

The Reality of Demon Possession

The evidence from Scripture is *unmistakable* that a human being can be possessed or controlled by a demon or evil spirit (Mark 7:24-30; 9:17-29).

From the New Testament accounts of demon possession, along with other examples, we can chart some of the phenomena that can be observed during a demonic attack.

A. Change of Personality

Including intelligence, moral character, demeanor, appearance

B. Physical Changes

1. Preternatural strength
2. Epileptic convulsions; foaming
3. Catatonic symptoms, falling
4. Clouding of consciousness, anaesthesia to pain
5. Changed voice

C. Mental Changes

1. Glossolalia; understanding unknown languages [the counterfeit gift as opposed to the biblical gift]
2. Preternatural knowledge
3. Psychic and occult powers, e.g., clairvoyance, telepathy and prediction

D. Spiritual Changes

1. Reaction to and fear of Christ; blasphemy with regret as in depression
2. Affected by prayer

E. Deliverance possible in the name of Jesus

As this is a diagnosis in retrospect it falls outside the range of pre-exorcism symptoms. 20/156

Does Demon Possession Occur Today?

Granting the fact that demon possession occurred in New Testament times, the natural question arises, "Does it occur today?" After extensive study of demonology and years of observing patients, psychiatrist Paul Meier gives his professional opinion:

> I can honestly say that I have never yet seen a single case of demon possession. The main thing I have learned about demon possession is how little we really know about it and how little the Bible says about it.
>
> I have had hundreds of patients who came to see me because they thought they were demon possessed. Scores of them heard "demon voices"

telling them evil things to do. It was at first surprising to me that all of these had dopamine deficiencies in their brains, which were readily correctable with Thorazine or any other major tranquilizer.

Don't get me wrong, I am a strict Biblicist who believes in the inerrancy of Scripture. I believe demons really do exist because the Bible says they do. I believe that there probably are some demon-possessed persons in various parts of the world. 11/160-61

However, there are many others who attest to having witnessed demon possession. Walter Martin recorded a couple of examples he encountered:

In Newport Beach, California, I encountered a case of demonic possession in which five persons, including myself, were involved. In this case the girl, who was about 5 feet 4 inches tall and weighed 120 pounds, attacked a 180-pound man and with one arm flipped him 5 or 6 feet away. It took four of us, including her husband, to hold her body to a bed while we prayed in the name of Jesus Christ for the exorcism of the demons within her.

During the course of the exorcism we found out that she was possessed because she had worshipped Satan, and because of that worship he had come with his forces and taken control of her. She was a perfect "tare in the wheat field," as Jesus said (Matthew 13:24-30). She had married a Christian, was a daughter of a Christian minister, had taught Sunday school in a Christian church, and had appeared on the surface to be perfectly consistent with Christian theology. But the whole time she was laughing inwardly at the church and at Christ. It was not until her exorcism that she was delivered and received Jesus Christ as her Lord and Savior. Today she and her husband are on the mission field serving the Lord Jesus Christ.

I have a psychologist friend who was present with me at [another] exorcism in Newport Beach, California. Before we entered the room he said, "I want you to know I do not believe in demonic possession. This girl is mentally disturbed."

I said, "That may well be. We'll find out very soon."

As we went into the room and closed the door, the girl's supernatural strength was soon revealed. Suddenly from her body a totally foreign voice said quietly, with a smirk on the face (she was unconscious—the psychologist testified to that), "We will outlast you."

The psychologist looked at me and said, "What was that?"

"That is what you don't believe in," I said.

We spent about 3½ hours exorcising what the psychologist didn't believe in!

At the end of the exorcism he was not only a devout believer in the personality of the devil, but in demonic possession and biblical exorcism as well. He now knows that there are other-dimensional beings capable of penetrating this dimension and of controlling human beings! 14/17-18,21

In conclusion, although most cases of alleged demon possession turn out to be in reality something quite different, it does not negate the fact that demon possession can and does occur today. However, one should be very careful before he considers an individual to be demon possessed when the person's problem may be physiological or psychological.

Only a mature Christian, experienced and seasoned by the Lord in counseling and spiritual warfare, should take an active part in diagnosing or treating alleged cases of demon possession. The human body, mind and spirit are so complex and interrelated that it takes spiritual discernment coupled with a great amount of knowledge to deal responsibly with what appears to be demon possession.

NOTE: See pages 395*ff.* for information on the believer's authority over the demonic realm.

CHAPTER 37 *Astrology*

(UO/25-34)

Two of the most crucial questions that haunt humanity are, "Who am I?" and "What's going to happen in the future?" Many people lose sleep at night worrying about the future, wondering what will happen tomorrow. Astrology claims to have the solution to these basic questions. They offer daily horoscopes to predict individuals' futures. "What's your sign?" crops up in many casual conversations. The ancient occultic art of astrology has become very popular in our 20th-century culture.

What Is Astrology?

Astrology is an ancient practice that assumes that the position of the stars and planets has a direct influence upon people and events. Supposedly, one's life pattern can be charted by determining the position of the stars and planets at the time of one's birth. The chart that attempts to accomplish this is known as a "horoscope." Rene Noorbergen explains how one's horoscope is charted:

> For every personal horoscope, the moment of birth is the essential starting point. This, coupled with the latitude and longitude of the individual's birthplace, provides the initial package for the usual astrologi cal chart. While this is elementary, it is not complete; a factor known as "true local time" must also be considered. This "true" time is arrived at by adding or subtracting four minutes for each degree of longitude that your birthplace lies to the east or west of the center of your time zone of birth.

Once this has been accomplished, the next step is to convert this "true" time into "sidereal" or star time. This is done with the aid of an ephemerus, a reference book showing the positions of the planets in relationship to the earth. Checking this star time in an astrological table is the last formal move, for in doing so, the theme of the individual's "ascendant"—the astrological sign that is supposed to have been rising on the eastern horizon at the moment of birth—is revealed.

Once you have developed this data—these simple steps are no more difficult than solving a seventh-grade math problem—then you are ready to "chart" your horoscope. This means you align the "ascendant" with the nine-o'clock point on the inner circle of the horoscope, and from there you are prepared to "read" the various zodiacal "houses" that control your life and fortune. 17/176-77

How Is It Justified?

How astrologers justify their practice is explained by Michael Van Buskirk:

> One's future can be forecast, allegedly, because astrology asserts the unity of all things. This is the belief that the Whole (or all of the universe put together) is in some way the same as the Part (or the individual component or man), or that the Part is a smaller reflection of the Whole (macrocosmic/microcosmic model). The position of the planets (the macro) influences and produces a corresponding reaction in man (the micro). This makes man a pawn in the cosmos with his life and actions pre-determined and unalterable. 24/6

Noorbergen concludes:

> To believe in astrology, you must support the philosophy that you are either a "born loser" or a "born winner." The stars, we are being told, do not merely forecast the course of our lives, but they also cause the events to take place. They both impel and compel. 17/178-79

Problems of Astrology

The claims astrologists have made have drawn severe criticism from the scientific community. In September, 1975, 186 prominent American scientists, along with 18 Nobel Prize winners, spoke out against "the pretentious claims of astrological charlatans," saying, among other things, that there is no scientific basis whatsoever for the assumption that the stars foretell events and influence lives. The following are some of the reasons the practice of astrology must be rejected as both unscientific and unbiblical.

Conflicting Systems

The problem of authority in astrology is graphically revealed when one realizes there are many systems of astrology which are diametrically opposed to each other. Astrologers in the West would not interpret a horoscope the same way a Chinese astrologer would.

Even in the West, there is no unanimity of interpretation among astrologers, seeing that some contend for eight zodiac signs rather than twelve, while others argue for fourteen or even twenty-four signs of the zodiac.

With these different systems employed by astrologers, an individual may go to two different astrologers and receive two totally opposed courses of behavior for the same day! This is not only a possibility, but it is also a reality—a simple comparison between astrological forecasts in daily newspapers will often reveal contradictions.

Missing Planets

One of the major misconceptions that is the basis of astrology concerns the number of planets in our solar system. Most astrological charts are based upon the assumption that there are seven planets in our solar system (including the sun and the moon).

In ancient times, Uranus, Neptune and Pluto were unobservable with the naked eye. Consequently, astrologers based their system upon the seven planets they believed revolved around the earth. Since that time, it has been proven that the sun, not the earth, is the center of the solar system and that three other planets exist in our solar system.

According to the astrological theory (that the position of planets has a definite influence upon human behavior and events), the three previously undiscovered planets should also influence behavior and must be considered for an exact horoscope to be cast. They usually are not considered, so the astrological theory breaks down, for no accurate horoscope could be charted without considering all the planets and their supposed influence.

Twins

A constant source of embarrassment for astrologers is twins. Since they are born at exactly the same time and place, they should have the same destiny. Unfortunately, experience shows this is not the case.

No Scientific Verification

Probably the most damaging criticism that can be leveled at astrological prediction is the fact that its scientific value is nil. Paul Couderc, astronomer at the Paris Observatory, concluded after examining the horoscopes of 2,817 musicians:

> The position of the sun has absolutely no musical significance. The musicians are born throughout the entire year on a chance basis. No sign of the zodiac or fraction of a sign favors or does not favor them.

> We conclude: The assets of scientific astrology are equal to zero, as is the case with commercialized astrology. 15/106

Shifting Constellations

Astrology is unscientific because of the fact of the precession or the shifting of constellations. Kenneth Boa elaborates on this problem:

> The early astronomers were not aware of precession and therefore failed to take it into account in their system. The twelve signs of the zodiac originally corresponded with the twelve constellations of the same names. But due to precession, the constellations have shifted about 30° in the last 2,000 years. This means that the constellation of Virgo is now in the sign of Libra, the constellation of Libra is now in the sign of Scorpio, and so on. 2/124-25

The Bible and Astrology

The Bible warns people against relying on astrologers and astrology:

> You are wearied with your many counsels; let now the astrologers, those who prophesy by the stars, those who predict by the new moons, stand up and save you from what will come upon you. Behold, they have become like stubble, fire burns them; they cannot deliver themselves from the power of the flame . . . there is none to save you (Isaiah 47:13-15, NASB).

Other warnings can be found in such verses as Jeremiah 10:2: "Learn not the way of the heathen, and be not dismayed at the signs of Heaven; for the heathen are not dismayed at them." Elsewhere, the Scripture says, "And beware, lest you lift up your eyes to heaven and see the sun and the moon and the stars, all the host of heaven, and be drawn away and worship them and serve them" (Deuteronomy 4:19, NASB).

The Book of Daniel gives us a comparison between the astrologers and those dedicated to the true and living God. In 1:20 we see that Daniel and his three friends were ten times better in matters of wisdom and understanding than the astrologers because they served the living and true God rather than the stars. The king had a disturbing dream, and the astrologers could not give an explanation for it. God alone had the answer. Only He can reveal the future (see Daniel 2:27,28).

The Scriptures make it clear that any type of astrological practice is severely condemned by God, for it attempts to understand the future through occultic means rather than through God's divinely inspired Word. The fatalistic approach of astrology, which says our lives are determined by the stars, is contradicted by Scripture, which holds us responsible for our destiny. Astrology and Christianity are simply incompatible.

Dangers of astrology

There are some very real dangers in trying to live your life by a horoscope. **First** is the attempt to try to run your life by following along in astrology. Since it is apparent a great deal of astrology has no basis in reality, you run the risk of great loss.

There can be the loss of money, both of what you may spend on astrology and what the astrologers may recommend for you to do. They may recommend you invest now, buy later, don't purchase this, etc. These recommended investments are no more certain than a fortune cookie, and you could suffer considerable financial loss.

Second, a person who continually tries to live his life by a horoscope can become very depressed as he begins to see life as fatalistic, predetermined since his birth, with no opportunity to break free.

Why Do People Believe in Astrology?

If astrology is both unscientific and unbiblical, why do so many people believe in it? One answer would be that it sometimes works, as one book on astrology attests:

> When the late astrological genius, Grant Lewi, was asked why he believed in astrology, his blunt answer was, "I believe in it because it works." This is as good an answer as any . . . we say that astrology works because it is based on natural law. 19/35

There is a much better explanation for the so-called accuracy of astrological predictions. If one reads a horoscope, even in a cursory manner, he will be struck with the general and ambiguous nature of the statements, which can be pointed to as fulfilling anything and everything. *Time* magazine observed:

> There are so many variables and options to play with that the astrologer is always right. Break a leg when your astrologer told you the signs were good, and he can congratulate you on escaping what might have happened had the signs been bad. Conversely, if you go against the signs and nothing happens, the astrologer can insist that you were subconsciously careful because you were forewarned. 22/56

The suggestive aspect also needs to be taken into consideration, as Koch has pointed out: "The person who seeks advice from an astrologer comes with a certain readiness to believe the horoscope. This predisposition leads to an autosuggestion to order his life according to the horoscope, and thus contribute to its fulfillment." 10/95

Astrology is bankrupt both biblically and scientifically. Since it is fatalistic in its approach, it rules out the free choice of each of us, leaving man merely as a cog in the cosmic machinery. This view of reality is at odds with Scripture, which indicates all of us have both the capacity and responsibility to choose which road in life we will take.

CHAPTER 38 *False Prophets*

Jeane Dixon (UO/55-61)

Invariably when the subject of astrology is discussed, the question of Jeane Dixon is brought up. Is Jeane Dixon a true prophetess? Do her powers come from God? What about the amazing predictions that she has made? We feel these and other questions concerning Jeane Dixon need to be addressed in light of the Bible in order to get a true picture of the situation.

Background

Jeane Dixon was born Jeane (or Lydia) Pinckert around the turn of the century in a small Wisconsin town. Her psychic abilities were either non-existent or hidden during her early years. It was not until she met a Gypsy woman who gave her a crystal ball that her psychic career began.

Supposedly, this Gypsy woman told her she had the makings of a psychic and was destined for great things. Although Jeane Dixon received recognition as early as the 1940s for her psychic powers, it was the publication of two books concerning her life, *A Gift of Prophecy* by Ruth Montgomery in 1965, and *Jeane Dixon: My Life and Prophecies* by Rene Noorbergen in 1969, that made her famous.

The Claims of Jeane Dixon

Jeane Dixon has made it clear that she believes her prophetic gift comes from God. "It is my belief God has given me a gift of prophecy for His own reasons, and I do not question them." 4/42

Furthermore, she has stated, "The future has been shown me to 2037 A.D." 4/175 She told her biographer, Rene Noorbergen, that "the same spirit that worked through Isaiah and John the Baptist also works through me." 17/114

In the foreword of her book, *The Gift of Prophecy,* Ruth Montgomery designated Mrs. Dixon as a "modern-day psychic whose visions apparently lift the curtain of tomorrow."

Fulfilled Prophecies?

Mrs. Dixon and others have made some astounding claims as to her ability to predict the future. The introductory section of one of her books reads as follows:

> If you don't believe that anyone can predict the future with a crystal ball . . . then read these startling, often frightening, precognitions of events by the phenomenal Jeane Dixon.
>
> —The assassination of President Kennedy.
> —Nehru's death and his succession by Shastri.
> —That China would go communistic.
> —The assassination of Mahatma Ghandi.
> —Russia's launching the world's first satellite.
> —Eisenhower's election; his heart attack, and his recovery.
> —The Kremlin shake-up ending with Kruschev's dismissal and Suslov's takeover. 16/preface

She also supposedly predicted the deaths of Carole Lombard and Marilyn Monroe and the assassinations of Robert F. Kennedy and Martin Luther King, Jr.

The May 13, 1956, issue of *Parade* magazine said this about one of her prophecies:

> As to the 1960 election, Mrs. Dixon thinks it will be dominated by labor and won by a Democrat. But he will be assassinated or die in office, though not necessarily in his first term.

With these examples of fulfilled prophecy, one might conclude that Jeane Dixon has a true prophetic gift. However, upon closer examination her "amazing" prophecies are not really all that amazing. Her prophecies concerning the 1960 Presidential election prompted Milbourne Cristopher to comment:

As we know now, the election was not "dominated by labor." She did not name the Democrat she said would win; no date was given for the President-to-be's end; and his announced demise was qualified with Delphic ingenuity "assassinated or die in office, though not necessarily in his first term." Thus if the president served a single term, it would be within four years; if he was re-elected there was an eight-year span.

Such a surmise was not illogical for anyone who has studied recent American history. William McKinley was assassinated a year after the turn of the century. Warren Gamaliel Harding and Franklin Delano Roosevelt died in office, and during Harry S. Truman's tenure an attempt was made on his life. Moreover, the normal burdens of the Presidency are such that it is commonly regarded as a mankilling office. Woodrow Wilson and Dwight Eisenhower were critically ill during their terms. Unfortunately for the nation, the odds against Mrs. Dixon's prophecy's being fulfilled were not too great—7-3 based on twentieth-century experience. 3/80-81

Moreover, before the 1960 election, Mrs. Dixon changed her mind, as Cristopher points out:

In January 1960 Mrs. Dixon changed her mind. Kennedy, then a contender for the Democrat nomination, would not be elected in November, she said in Ruth Montgomery's syndicated column. In June she stated that "the symbol of the Presidency is directly over the head of Vice-President Nixon" but "unless the Republican party really gets out and puts forth every effort it will topple." Fire enough shots, riflemen agree, and eventually you will hit the bull's-eye. 3/81

One of the most famous of all her prophecies was received on February 5, 1962. "A child, born somewhere in the Middle East shortly after 7 A.M. (EST) on February 5, 1962, will revolutionize the world. Before the close of the century he will bring together all mankind in one all-embracing faith. This will be the foundation of a new Christianity, with every sect and creed united through this man who will walk among the people to spread the wisdom of the Almighty Power. . . . He is the answer to the prayers of a troubled world."

This prophecy of a coming Messiah who would save the world received much criticism. Consequently, Mrs. Dixon revised the true identity of this child. Her biographer, Rene Noorbergen, notes:

For several years Jeane continued to advocate that this Christ child would guide the world in the early 1980s. The child was godly, he was divine, and he would become the salvation of the world.

Suddenly something happened. While interviewing "Mrs. D." for *My Life and Prophecies,* I became aware of the inconsistencies in the revelation. Over-sensitive to criticism, Mrs. Dixon soon changed her interpretation. "There is no doubt that he will fuse multitudes into one all-embracing doctrine," she explained in her "revised version." She continued, "He will form a new 'Christianity' based on this 'almighty power,' but leading man in a direction far removed from the teachings and life of Christ, the Son." Enlarging on her new interpretation, she called the child the "Antichrist"—

a far cry from her first prophetic evaluation. 17/121

False Prophecies

Although Jeane Dixon supposedly has made some predictions that have come true, she has made many other prophecies that have failed. These include:

1. World War III would begin in 1954.
2. Red China would be admitted to the United Nations in 1958. This did not occur until 1971.
3. The Vietnam war would end in 1966. It did not end until 1975.
4. On October 19, 1968, she predicted Jacqueline Kennedy was not thinking of marriage. The next day Mrs. Kennedy married Aristotle Onassis!
5. Union Leader, Walter Reuther, would run for President in 1964. He did not.
6. In 1970, she predicted the following events which did not occur:
   (a) Castro would be overthrown from Cuba and would have to leave the island;
   (b) new facts concerning the death of President Kennedy would be brought to light from a foreign source;
   (c) attempts would be made on the life of President Nixon.

Evaluation

There are those who believe Jeane Dixon has no supernatural power whatsoever but is rather a clever fortuneteller. Danny Korem comments:

> In a given population there will be those whose "hit" ratio (a thought and an event matching up) will be higher than others simply because of the law of probability. This is true in any game of chance. When a clever fortuneteller combines good cold-reading techniques with a chance guess or two, he or she will appear to almost unerringly pick up someone's thoughts and prognosticate the future, but there will be other times when he or she will fail.
>
> My questions is this: If such powers exist, why are they so fleeting, and why can't they be tested? The reason is a simple one. They don't exist. In the 12 years I have devoted to researching this subject, I have neither seen a valid case of prognostication, nor have I been confronted with hard-core documentation to substantiate a purported case. 11/115

Whether Mrs. Dixon possesses a supernatural ability to predict the future or not, she is definitely not a prophet of God for she fails on the following counts:

(1) *She uses occult artifacts.*

Jeane Dixon uses such things as a crystal ball, a deck of tarot cards and other occult artifacts to receive her prophecies. This type of practice is at odds with Scripture, for the biblical prophets received their prophecies directly from God without the use of any artifacts. The artifacts Mrs. Dixon uses are the same ones used by fortunetellers who attempt to predict the future through occultic means. A true prophet of God would never resort to using any occultic paraphernalia.

The true prophet of God spoke by the direct agency of God through the power of the Holy Spirit, not by means of any occultic devices. The words of the prophets are preserved for us in Holy Scripture (Romans 1:2) and their supreme testimony is always of Jesus Christ, the Son of God (Hebrews 1:1,2).

(2) *Her prophecies do not exalt Jesus Christ.*

The Bible makes it clear that all true prophecy has Jesus Christ as its central theme, "For the testimony of Jesus is the Spirit of prophecy" (Revelation 19:10, NASB).

Mrs. Dixon fails miserably in this, for there is no attempt in her prophecies to bring people to the God of the Bible and His Son, Jesus Christ. There is simply no witness to Christ in her prophecies!

The biblical prophets always prophesied in accordance with God's will and for His glory. Mrs. Dixon does not glorify God in her prophecies, and there is no room for frivolous or gossiping prophecy in God's Word.

The biblical prophets also gave their prophecies in the name of the Lord, something Jeane Dixon does not do.

Since Jeane Dixon does not prophesy in the name of the Lord, or for the purpose of bringing individuals into a personal relationship with Christ, she cannot be considered a true prophet of God.

(3) *She gives prophecies that do not come true.*

Mrs. Dixon also fails in the most important test of all: She utters prophecies which do not come true. The Bible makes it clear how one can know who is a true prophet of God:

> And you may say in your heart, "How shall we know the word which the Lord has not spoken?" When a prophet speaks in the name of the LORD, if the thing does not come about or come true, that is the thing which the LORD has not spoken. The prophet has spoken it presumptuously; you shall not be afraid of him (Deuteronomy 18:21,22, NASB).

Edgar Cayce and the Association of Research and Enlightenment (A.R.E.) (UO/38-45)

A man who caused considerable controversy in the twentieth century with his prophetic utterings was Edgar Cayce, known as the "sleeping prophet" because of the prophecies he gave while he appeared to be sleeping.

Born in Kentucky in 1877, Cayce realized at an early age that he was clairvoyant and he determined to use his gift for the betterment of mankind. At 21 Cayce was struck with paralysis of the throat, losing most of his ability to speak. After some time Cayce diagnosed his disease and prescribed a cure while in a self-induced trance. The word quickly spread of the strange ability he possessed.

Cayce began to diagnose illnesses and prescribe cures for people who were thousands of miles away. He would make remarkable diagnoses which were later verified by medical authorities. All this was accomplished in spite of the fact that Cayce had no medical training and only a grammar school education.

Sometimes during his trances he would speak about religious and philosophical issues, and occasionally he would predict the future. During his career his "readings" on medical questions totalled almost 15,000.

Cayce was active in the "Christian" church, faithfully reading his Bible from beginning to end each year for 46 years. However, at the same time, he was an occult practitioner who gained international fame for his exploits.

In 1931 Cayce formed a foundation which he named the Association of Research and Enlightenment, Inc. (A.R.E.) The purpose of his organization was to preserve and make available for study the readings of Edgar Cayce. His son, Hugh Lynn, assumed leadership of the organization upon his father's death in 1945. The A.R.E. did not stagnate after its founder's death, but instead used his readings and experiences as a vast resource for reaching the contemporary world.

Today's aggressively evangelistic A.R.E. claims to "offer a contemporary and mature view of the reality of extrasensory perception, the importance of dreams, the logic of reincarnation, and a rational or loving personal concept of God, the practical use of prayer and meditation and a deeper understanding of the Bible." 18/48 Current paid membership in the A.R.E. totals 20,000.

Cayce's readings

The readings made by Cayce over the years reveal not only cures for medical ailments, but also statements about God and the future. His readings brought out the following:

- California would fall into the Pacific Ocean in the early 1970s.
- Jesus Christ was a reincarnation of Adam, Melchizedek, Joshua and other figures who lived before Him.
- God has in His nature a male and female principle, making Him

a Father-Mother God.

- Mary, the mother of Jesus, was virgin-born like her Son.
- God does not know the future.
- Salvation is something man does on his own. It is not a work of God alone.
- Reincarnation occurs in many human beings.
- Jesus was tutored in prophecy on Mt. Carmel while He was a teenager. His teacher was a woman named Judy, a leader of the Essenes.
- Jesus grew up in Capernaum, not Nazareth.
- Luke did not write the Acts of the Apostles as traditionally believed by the Church. The true author was Cayce himself in a previous life as Lucius, Bishop of Laodicea.

Biblical Evaluation

Although the A.R.E. claims to be a study group and not a religion, the readings made by Cayce comment on God and consequently should be evaluated in the light of God's revealed Word, the Bible.

First and foremost, Edgar Cayce is a false prophet according to biblical standards. He predicted many things which did not come to pass. Deuteronomy 18:21,22 applies here as well as with Jeane Dixon.

When Cayce said God does not know the future, he clearly contradicted Scripture. In stark contrast to Cayce, the God of the Bible does know the future, telling mankind of events before they come to pass. For example:

> I declared the former things long ago and they went forth from my mouth, and I proclaimed them. Suddenly I acted, and they came to pass.... Therefore I declared them to you long ago; before they took place I proclaimed them to you, lest you should say, my idol has done them and my graven image and my molten image have commanded them (Isaiah 48:3,5, NASB).

Through His prophets, the God of the Bible revealed many things in detail before they came to pass. The predictions were specific and always accurate. Contrast that to Cayce, whose predictions were vague and often inaccurate.

Cayce and his followers have a low view of the person and work of Jesus Christ. One Cayce devotee expressed it this way:

> For almost 20 centuries the moral sense of the Western World has been blunted by a theology which teaches the vicarious atonement of sin through Christ, the Son of God.... All men and women are sons of God.... Christ's giving of his life ... is no unique event in history.... To build these two statements, therefore—that Christ was the Son of God and that he died for man's salvation—into a dogma, and then to make salvation depend upon

believing that dogma, has been the great psychological crime because it places responsibility for redemption on something external to the self; it makes salvation dependent on belief in the divinity of another person rather than on self-transformation through belief in one's own intrinsic divinity. 21/27-28

Cayce's claim to be the reincarnated author of the book of Acts rests on his fundamental belief in reincarnation. This is one of the central doctrines and greatest attractions of the A.R.E.

NOTE: See *Understanding the Occults,* pages 40-44, for a discussion of reincarnation.

William Petersen gives a thought-provoking conclusion concerning Cayce's activities:

For a good portion of his life, Cayce was a commercial photographer. He understood very well the mechanics of his trade. A blank film is developed in the dark.

The nature of a photograph, whether it is a formal family picture or pornography, depends not on the film but on the photographer who uses the camera. During his trances, Cayce's mind was like a blank film that would be developed in the dark.

I believe Cayce allowed his camera to get into the wrong hands. 18/59

CHAPTER 39 *The Authority of the Believer*

(UO/195-202)

At the center of the occult, either openly or disguised as an "angel of light," is Satan. Peter exhorts believers concerning our chief foe when he writes, "Be of sober spirit, be on the alert. Your adversary, the devil, prowls about like a roaring lion, seeking someone to devour" (1 Peter 5:8, NASB).

Christians often have the tendency to "blame it all on the devil," when in fact it was their own carelessness or fleshly nature which led to the sin or error. It can also be said, however, that even when it is our fleshly nature or the world which draws us from the Lord—and not the devil directly—it is nevertheless true that Satan and his army of demons desire that we be drawn to the world's standards.

Satan is the one who ultimately desires that we pursue the lusts of the flesh, and it is he who sits as the "god of this world" (Ephesians 2:1-10). Though not always directly involved, Satan's prime objective is the defeat of God, and for us that means our defeat.

The authority of the believer spells out the authority a believer has over Satan and his efforts to thwart God's desire for our lives and his attempts to defeat us.

For the rest of your life, one of the most important scriptural messages you'll ever consider is found here.

As you study the Old Testament, you see that men and women were in a constant struggle with Satan, fighting many spiritual battles. As you study the life of Christ, and Paul, and the other apostles, you see a constant spiritual struggle. Christians today face many spiritual battles.

I'm so glad I learned the authority of the believer before I went to South America. The authority of the believer is a possession that belongs to every true child of God. And it gives so much authority over the enemy that Satan has tried to blind most believers to the authority they have.

During Easter week at Balboa, I first learned of the authority of the believer. About 50,000 high school and college students came down for Easter. With André Kole, the illusionist, we packed out a big ballroom several nights in a row—for two or three meetings a night. So many people were coming to our meetings, in fact, that many of the bars were empty. It really irritated some of the barkeepers. The second night, one of the men from a night club came over to break up our meeting. They figured if they broke up one of them, that would finish it for us.

As André was performing, this guy pulled up with his Dodge Dart all souped up. With a deafening sound, he popped the clutch and went roaring down the street. Everyone inside, of course, turned around and looked outside to see the commotion. Finally, André got them settled down.

Then the guy went around the block again. As he stopped out front, he revved it up again and roared down the street. By this time everyone was whispering and wondering what was going on. Some stood up, trying to look out the window.

When the guy went back around the block again, I knew that if he repeated his performance one more time, it would be disastrous. Turning to Gene Huntsman, one of our staff members, I said, "I think Satan is trying to break up this meeting. Let's step out in the doorway and exercise the authority of the believer." So we stepped outside and prayed a very simple prayer.

When the guy came back, he started to rev it up again, and as he popped the clutch—pow! The rear end of his car blew all over the street. By that time, we just thanked the Lord and went over and pushed him off the street. As I shared the *Four Spiritual Laws* with him, it reminded me that Jesus said all authority is given to the believer in heaven and in earth.

The Authority

Now, to see what the authority is, let's look at Luke 10:19: "Behold, I give unto you power to tread on serpents and scorpions, and over all the power of the enemy: and nothing shall by any means hurt you" (KJV).

What It Is

Two separate Greek words are used for *power* here, but one English translation. The first one should be translated *authority,* not *power.* The Lord is saying, "Behold, I give you authority over the power of the enemy." The Christian does not have *power* over Satan; he has *authority* over Satan. Let me give you an illustration.

I used to live in Argentina. Buenos Aires, the second largest city in the western hemisphere, has six subway lines, one of the longest streets in the world (almost 60 miles long), and one of the widest streets in the world (25 lanes, almost three blocks wide). One street is called Corrente, which means *current.* It is a solid current of traffic—sometimes considered one of the longest parking lots in the world.

One intersection is so busy, about the only way you can make it across is to confess any unknown sin, make sure you are filled with the Spirit, commit your life to the Lord and dash madly! But one day we approached, and an amazing thing took place.

Out in the center of the intersection was a platform, on which stood a uniformed policeman. About 20 of us waited at the corner to cross. All of a sudden, he blew his whistle and put up his hand. As he lifted his hand, all those cars came to a screeching halt. With all of his personal power he couldn't have stopped one of those cars, but he had something far better; he was invested with the authority of the police department. And the moving cars and the pedestrians recognized that authority. So, **first**, we see that

Authority is delegated power.

Source of Authority

Second, let's examine the source of this authority. Paul writes about:

> what is the surpassing greatness of His Power toward us who believe. These are in accordance with the working of the strength of His might which He brought about in Christ, when He raised Him from the dead, and seated Him at His right hand in the heavenly places, far above all rule and authority and power and dominion, and every name that is named, not only in this age, but also in the one to come. And He put all things in subjection under His feet, and gave Him as head over all things to the Church, which is His Body, the fullness of Him who fills all in all (Ephesians 1:19-23, NASB).

When Jesus Christ was raised from the dead, we see the act of the resurrection and the surrounding events as one of the greatest workings of God manifested in the Scriptures. So powerful was the omnipotency of God that the Holy Spirit, through the apostle Paul, used four different words for power.

First, the greatness of His power—in the Greek—is *dunamis,* from which comes the English word *dynamite.* Then comes the word *working—energios,* where *energy* comes from—a working manifestation or activity. The third word is *strength—kratous*—meaning "to exercise strength." Then comes *might,* or *esquai*—a "great summation of power."

These four words signify that behind the events described in Ephesians 1:19-23 are the greatest workings of God manifested in the Scriptures—even greater than creation. This great unleashing of God's might involved the resurrection, the ascension and the seating of Jesus Christ. "When He had disarmed the rulers and authorities, He made a public display of them, having triumphed over them through Him" (Colossians 2:15, NASB). Satan was defeated and disarmed. All of this unleashing of God's might in the resurrection, the ascension and the seating of Jesus Christ was for you and me—that we might gain victory right now over Satan.

Our authority over Satan is rooted in God and His power.

Qualifications Needed to Exercise the Authority

Third, what are the qualifications you must have to be able to be consistent in exercising the authority of the believer?

First, there must be *knowledge,* a knowledge of our position in Christ and of Satan's defeat. At the moment of salvation we are elevated to a heavenly placement. We don't have to climb some ladder of faith to get there. We are immediately identified in the eyes of God—and of Satan—with Christ's crucifixion and burial, and we are co-resurrected, co-ascended and co-seated with Jesus Christ at the right hand of the Father, far above all rule and power, authority and dominion and above every name that is named.

The problem is that, though both God and Satan are aware of this, most believers are not. And if you don't understand who you are, you will never exercise that authority which is the birthright of every true believer in Jesus. So the first step is knowledge.

The *second* qualification is *belief.* A lot of people really don't comprehend one of the primary aspects of belief, which is "to live in accordance with." This is not merely mental assent, but it leads to action. You could say it like this: That which the mind accepts, the will obeys. Otherwise you are not really a true believer. Do we actually believe that we've been co-resurrected, co-ascended, co-seated with Jesus Christ? If we do, our actions will be fervent.

We should wake up each morning and say something like, "Lord, I accept my position. I acknowledge it to be at the right hand of the Father, and today, through the Holy Spirit, cause it to be a reality in me that I might experience victory."

You talk about space walking! A Christian who is filled with the Holy

Spirit and who knows his position with Christ is walking in the heavenlies. I put it this way: Before you can be any earthly good, you have to be heavenly minded. Your mind should be set at the right hand of the Father, knowing who you are.

Often, when I wake up in the morning, while my eyes are still closed, I go over my position in Christ, thanking the Holy Spirit for indwelling me, etc. But every morning, I acknowledge my position in Christ. I don't have to drum it up—I ask the Holy Spirit to make my position real in my experience.

The *third* qualification is *humility.* While belief introduces us to our place of throne power at the right hand of the Father, only humility will ensure that we can exercise that power continuously. Let me tell you, ever since Mr. and Mrs. Adam occupied the garden of Eden, man has needed to be reminded of his limitations. Even regenerated man thinks he can live without seriously considering his total dependence upon God.

Yet, humility to me is not going around saying, "I'm nothing, I'm nothing, I'm nothing. I'm just the dirt under the toenail. When I get to heaven all I want is that little old dinky cabin, that's enough for me." That's an insult to Christ. It's not humility—it's pride. Humility is knowing who you are and knowing who made you who you are and giving Him the glory for it. Sometimes, when I hear a person claim he's nothing, I say, "Look sir, I don't know about you, but I'm someone." I *am* someone. On December 19, 1959, at 8:30 at night, Jesus Christ made me a child of God, and I'm sure not going to say I'm nothing. Maybe I'm not all I should be, but I am more than I used to be, and God's not finished with me yet. I know He has made me, and I won't insult what God has made.

The next qualification, the *fourth* one, is *boldness.* Humility allows the greatest boldness. True boldness is faith in full manifestation. When God has spoken and you hold back, that is not faith, it is sin. We need men and women who have set their minds at the right hand of the Father and who fear no one but God. True boldness comes from realizing your position in Jesus Christ and being filled with the Holy Spirit.

The *fifth* and final qualification is *awareness,* a realization that being at the right hand of the Father also puts you in the place of the most intense spiritual conflict. The moment your eyes are open to the fact that you are in that place, that you have been co-resurrected, co-ascended and co-seated with Christ, Satan will do everything he possibly can to wipe you out, to discourage you. You become a marked individual. The last thing Satan wants is a Spirit-filled believer who knows his throne rights. Satan will start working in your life to cause you not to study or to appropriate the following principles which show you how to defeat him.

Principles for Defeating Satan

Going through all of the above was necessary to lay a foundation on which you can exercise the authority of the believer. Here is how I do it. Remember, authority is delegated power. Usually I speak right out loud and *address Satan directly,* "Satan, in the name of the Lord Jesus Christ . . . " I always use this point first because those three names—Lord, Jesus and Christ—describe His crucifixion, burial, resurrection and seating, and His victory over Satan. "Satan, in the name of the Lord Jesus Christ and His shed blood on the cross, I command you to stop your activities in this area." Or, "Satan, in the name of the Lord Jesus Christ and His shed blood on the cross, I acknowledge that the victory is Jesus' and all honor and glory in this situation go to Him." I speak to Satan in various ways, but I always *use those beginning phrases* because they remind him that he is already defeated.

Next, I *realize there is nothing I can do.* I have no power over Satan, I only have authority. And the more I learn of the power behind me, the force behind me, the greater boldness I have in exercising the authority of the believer.

Once the authority of the believer is exercised, though, we must *be patient.* Never have I exercised that authority that I did not see Satan defeated, but I have had to learn to wait.

Some time ago, for example, I was to speak in a university in South America. Because of the university's Marxist leanings, I was the first American to speak there in four years, and it was a tense situation. Big photographs of me had been posted all over campus and the Communist students, trying to influence the other students to stay away from the meeting, had painted "CIA Agent" in red letters across the posters. I thought CIA meant "Christ in Action." Anyway, it backfired. Most of the students had never seen a CIA agent, so they came to the meeting to see what one looked like, and the room was packed. However, as is often the case when someone speaks in that part of the world, professional Marxist agitators had also come, and their intent was to disrupt the meeting.

When I go to another country I like to speak as well as possible in the language of that country. So I pointed out to the audience that I was learning their language and that night I would be lecturing in it. Well, I started, and, oh, it was horrible! My back was against the wall—the chairs were about five inches from me. And one after another, these agitators would jump up and throw accusations at me, call me "a filthy pig," etc., and hurl words at me that I didn't even know. Right in front of the audience they twisted me around their little fingers. I couldn't answer them; I didn't even know what they were saying. I felt so sorry for the Christians who were there because they had looked forward so eagerly to my coming to the campus and to seeing people come to Christ.

After 45 minutes of this heckling, I just felt like crying. I literally wanted to crawl under the carpet. My wife asked me one time, "Honey, what's the darkest situation you've ever been in?"

I said, "It was that one."

By this time I was ready to give up. Every time I even mentioned the name of Jesus they laughed. I had exercised the authority of the believer, and now I thought, "God, why aren't you doing something? Why? Isn't Satan defeated?" Well, I wasn't walking by faith. You see, God works when it brings the greatest honor and glory to His name, not to ours.

Finally, God started to work. The secretary of the Revolutionary Student Movement stood up, and everyone else became silent. I figured she must be someone important.

She was quite an outspoken woman, and I didn't know what to expect. But this is what she said. "Mr. McDowell, if I become a Christian tonight, will God give me the love for people that you have shown for us?"

Well, I don't have to tell you what happened. It broke just about everyone's heart who was there, and we had fifty-eight decisions for Christ.

I've learned to exercise the authority of the believer and then to walk by faith and to wait. Sometimes I have had to wait six months or a year, but in the long run, when I look back on a situation and see how God has been glorified, it is beautiful.

And I *never repeat the exercise of the authority of the believer in a given situation.* Satan only needs one warning. God will take care of it from there. Jesus said, "All authority has been given to me in heaven and earth. Go therefore, and make disciples of all nations."

CHRISTIANITY
Questions Asked

CHAPTER 40 *Questions About God*

How Do You Know God Exists? (A/65-66)

Is there truly a God? How can anyone be sure such a being exists? We believe that questions relating to the existence of God can be intelligently answered. The reason we know God exists is that He has told us so, and He has revealed Himself to us. He has told us all about who He is, what He is like and what His plan is for planet earth. He has revealed these things to mankind through the Bible.

The Bible Tells Us

The Bible has demonstrated itself to be more than a mere book; it is the actual Word of God. The evidence is more than convincing to anyone who will consider its claims honestly.

Because of the boasts the Bible makes for itself, many have tried to destroy it, as related in this statement by Martin Luther:

> Mighty potentates have raged against this book and sought to destroy and uproot it—Alexander the Great and princes of Egypt and Babylon, the monarchs of Persia, of Greece and of Rome, the Emperors Julius and Augustus—but they prevailed nothing.

> They are gone while the book remains, and it will remain forever and ever, perfect and entire, as it was declared at first. Who has thus helped it—who has protected it against such mighty forces? No one, surely, but God Himself, who is master of all things. 8/n.p.

Even the French skeptic, Rousseau, saw something different in the Scriptures:

> I must confess to you that the majesty of the Scriptures astonishes me; the holiness of the evangelists speaks to my heart and has such striking characters of truth, and is, moreover, so perfectly inimitable, that if it had been the invention of men, the inventors would be greater than the greatest heroes. 5/32

The Bible, therefore, gives us sufficient reason to believe that it is the Word of the living God, who does exist and who has revealed Himself to the world.

Jesus Christ Tells Us

Another reason we know God exists is that He has appeared in human flesh. Jesus Christ was God Almighty who became a man. The Bible says, "The Word became flesh and dwelt among us" (John 1:14, RSV), and it states clearly that Jesus came to earth to reveal who God is and what He is all about (John 1:18).

If someone wants to know who God is and what He is like, he needs only to look at Jesus Christ. As Lord Byron said, "If ever man was God or God was man, Jesus Christ was both." 5/81

Instead of man reaching up to find God, God reached down to man, as Casserley explains:

> The gospel provides that knowledge of ultimate truth which men have sought through philosophy in vain, inevitably in vain, because it is essential to the very nature of God that He cannot be discovered by searching and probing of human minds, that He can only be known if He first takes the initiative and reveals Himself. 1/21

Jesus, in coming back from the dead, established Himself as having the credentials to be God, and it was this fact that demonstrated its truth to the unbelieving world. As Machen says,

> The great weapon with which the disciples of Jesus set out to conquer the world was not a mere comprehension of eternal principles; it was a historical message, an account of something that had happened; it was the message, "He is risen!" 4/28-29

Thus we have the Bible and the person of Jesus Christ as two strong arguments for the existence of God. No other religion or philosophy offers anything near those two reasons to demonstrate that God exists.

Is God Different in the Old and New Testaments?

(A/69-70)

Another of the frequent accusations against the Bible is that it contains two different concepts of God. The Old Testament allegedly presents only a God of wrath, while the New Testament alledgedly depicts only a God of love.

The Old Testament contains stories of God's commanding the destruction of Sodom and the annihilation of the Canaanites, and many other stories of God's judgment and wrath. The accusers claim this demonstrates a primitive, warlike deity in contradistinction to the advanced teachings of Jesus to love one another and to turn the other cheek, as contained in the Sermon on the Mount.

These ideas about God seem to be in direct conflict, but a moment's reflection will show otherwise. Jesus Himself declared that the Old Testament may be summed up by the commandments to love God and love your neighbor (Matthew 22:37). He also observed that, in the Old Testament, God had continually desired love and mercy rather than sacrifice (Matthew 9:13; 12:7).

This attitude can be seen with statements such as, "Have I any pleasure in the death of the wicked . . . and not rather that he should turn from his way and live?" (Ezekiel 18:23, RSV). God would not have destroyed certain nations except that He is a God of justice and their evil could not go unchecked or condoned.

In the case of the Amorites, God gave them hundreds of years to repent, yet they did not (Genesis 15:16). Noah preached 120 years to his generation before the great flood (Genesis 6:3).

The proper Old Testament picture is one of a very patient God who gives these people untold opportunities to repent and come into harmony with Him, and only when they continually refuse does He judge and punish them for their evil deeds.

Contrary to some popular belief, the strongest statements of judgment and wrath in the Bible were made by the Lord Jesus Himself. In Matthew 23, for example, He lashed out at the religious leaders of His day, calling them hypocrites and false leaders, and informing them that their destiny was eternal banishment from God's presence.

In Matthew 10:34 (KJV), Jesus says that the purpose of His mission is not to unite but to divide. "Think not that I am come to send peace on earth: I came not to send peace, but a sword." He goes on to say that His Word will cause a father to be against his son, a mother against her daughter, and a daughter-in-law against her mother-in-law (Matthew 10:35).

We find judgment as well as love scattered profusely throughout the New Testament, and love and mercy as well as judgment throughout the Old Testament. God is consistent and unchanging, but different situations call for different emphases. Therefore, when the two testaments are read the way they were intended, they reveal the same holy God who is rich in mercy, but who will not let sin go unpunished.

Isn't There More Than One Way to God? (A/62-63, C/115-16)

People are constantly asking, "What's so special about Jesus? Why is He the only way that someone can know God?"

Along with the problem of the heathen who never hear about Jesus (discussed in the next chapter), there is no question asked more often than this one. We are accused of being narrow-minded because we assert there is no other way to get to God.

The first point to make is that we did not invent the idea of Jesus being the only way. This is not our claim; it is His. We are merely relating His claim, and the claim of the writers of the New Testament.

Jesus said, "I am the way, and the truth, and the life; no one comes to the Father, but through Me" (John 14:6, NASB); and, "Unless you believe that I am He, you shall die in your sins" (John 8:24, NASB).

The apostle Peter echoed these words, "Neither is there salvation in any other: for there is none other name under heaven given among men whereby we must be saved" (Acts 4:12, KJV).

Paul concurred: "There is one God, and one mediator between God and men, the man Christ Jesus" (1 Timothy 2:5, KJV). It is therefore the united testimony of the New Testament that no one can know God the Father except through the person of Jesus Christ.

To understand why this is so, we must go back to the beginning. An infinite, personal God created the heavens and the earth (Genesis 1:1), and He created man in His own image (Genesis 1:26). When He had finished creating, everything was good (Genesis 1:31).

Man and woman were placed in a perfect environment, with all their needs taken care of. They were given only one prohibition; they were not to eat of the fruit of the tree of the knowledge of good and evil, lest they die (Genesis 2:17).

Unfortunately, they did eat of the tree (Genesis 3), and the relationship between God and man was now broken, as can be seen from Adam and Eve's attempting to hide from God (Genesis 3:8).

However, God promised that He would send a Saviour, or Messiah, who would deliver the entire creation from the bondage of sin (Genesis

3:15). The Old Testament kept repeating the theme that some day this person would come into the world and set mankind free.

God's Word did indeed come true. God became a man in the person of Jesus Christ (John 1:14,29). Jesus eventually died in our place in order that we could enjoy again a right relationship with God. The Bible says, "God was in Christ, reconciling the world unto Himself"; and, "He hath made Him to be sin for us, who knew no sin; that we might be made the righteousness of God in Him" (2 Corinthians 5:19,21, KJV).

Jesus has paved the way! God has done it all, and our responsibility is to accept that fact. We can do nothing to add to the work of Jesus; all of it has been done for us.

If mankind could have reached God any other way, Jesus would not have had to die. His death verifies the fact that there is no other way. Therefore, no other religion or religious leader can bring someone to the knowledge of the one true God.

At this point many people ask, "Why couldn't God just forgive?"

An executive of a large corporation said, "My employees often do something, perhaps break something, and I just forgive them." Then he added, "Are you trying to tell me I can do something that God can't do?"

People fail to realize that wherever there is forgiveness there's also a payment. For example, let's say my daughter breaks a lamp in my home. I'm a loving and forgiving father, so I put her on my lap, and I hug her and I say, "Don't cry, honey. Daddy loves you and forgives you."

Now usually the person I tell that story to says, "Well, that's what God ought to do."

Then I ask the question, "Who pays for the lamp?"

The fact is, I do. There's always a price in forgiveness. Let's say somebody insults you in front of others and later you graciously say, "I forgive you." Who bears the price of the insult? You do.

This is what God has done. God has said, "I forgive you"; but He was willing to pay the price Himself through the cross.

Is Belief in the Trinity Belief in Three Gods? (A/71-73)

One of the most misunderstood ideas in the Bible concerns the teaching about the Trinity. Although Christians say that they believe in one God, they are constantly accused of polytheism (worshipping more than one God).

One God/Three Persons

The Scriptures do *not* teach that there are three Gods; neither do they teach that God wears three different masks while acting out the drama of history. What the Bible does teach is stated in the doctrine of the Trinity: There is *one* God who has revealed Himself in three persons, the Father, the Son and the Holy Spirit, and these three persons are the one God.

Although this is difficult to comprehend, it is nevertheless what the Bible tells us, and this is the closest the finite mind can come to explaining the infinite mystery of the infinite God.

The Bible teaches that there is one God, and only one God:

> Hear, O Israel! The LORD is our God, the LORD is one! (Deuteronomy 6:4, NASB).

> There is one God (1 Timothy 2:5, KJV).

> Thus says the LORD, the King of Israel and his Redeemer, the LORD of hosts: "I am the first and I am the last, and there is no God besides Me" (Isaiah 44:6, NASB).

However, even though God is one in His essential being or nature, He is also three persons:

> Let us make man in our image (Genesis 1:26, KJV).

> God said, Behold, the man has become like one of us (Genesis 3:22, RSV).

God's plural nature is alluded to here, for He could not be talking to angels in these instances, because angels could not and did not help God create. The Bible teaches that Jesus Christ, not the angels, created all things (John 1:3; Colossians 1:15; Hebrews 1:2).

THE FATHER

In addition to speaking of God as one, and alluding to a plurality of God's being, the Scriptures are quite specific as to naming God in terms of three persons. There is a person whom the Bible calls the Father, and the Father is designated as God the Father (Galatians 1:1).

THE SON

The Bible talks about a person named Jesus, or the Son, or the Word, also called God. "The Word was God" (John 1:1, KJV). Jesus was "also calling God His own Father, making Himself equal with God" (John 5:18, NASB).

THE HOLY SPIRIT

There is a third person mentioned in the Scriptures called the Holy Spirit, and this person—different from the Father and the Son—is also called God ("Ananias, why has Satan filled your heart to lie to the Holy Spirit? . . . You have not lied to men, but to God" (Acts 5:3,4, RSV).

THE TRINITY

The facts of the biblical teaching are these: There is one God. This one God has a plural nature. This one God is called the Father, the Son, the Holy Spirit, all distinct personalities, all designated God. We are therefore led to the conclusion that the Father, Son and Holy Spirit are one God, and that comprises the doctrine of the Trinity.

Dr. John Warwick Montgomery offers an analogy to help us understand this doctrine better:

> The doctrine of the Trinity is not "irrational"; what is irrational is to suppress the biblical evidence for trinity in favor of unity, or the evidence for unity in favor of trinity.
>
> Our data must take precedence over our models—or, stating it better, our models must sensitively reflect the full range of data.
>
> A close analogy to the theologian's procedure here lies in the work of the theoretical physicist: Subatomic entities are found, on examination, to possess wave properties *(W)*, particle properties *(P)*, and quantum properties *(h)*.
>
> Though these characteristics are in many respects incompatible (particles don't diffract, waves do, etc.), physicists "explain" or "model" an electron as *PWh*. They have to do this in order to give proper weight to all the relevant data.
>
> Likewise, the theologian speaks of God as "three in one." Neither the scientist nor the theologian expects you to get a "picture" by way of his model; the purpose of the model is to help you take into account *all* of the facts, instead of perverting reality through super-imposing an apparent "consistency" on it.
>
> The choice is clear: either the Trinity or a "God" who is only a pale imitation of the Lord of biblical and confessional Christianity. **6/14-15**

Why Does a Good God Allow Evil to Exist? (A/152-54)

One of the most haunting questions we face concerns the problem of evil. Why is there evil in the world if there is a God? Why isn't He doing something about it? Many assume that the existence of evil disproves the existence of God.

Sometimes the problem of evil is put to the Christian in the form of a complex question, "If God is good, then He must not be powerful enough to deal with all the evil and injustice in the world since it is still going on. If He is powerful enough to stop wrongdoing then He must be evil since He's not doing anything about it. So which is it? Is He a bad God or a God that's not all powerful?"

Evil Not Created

Even the biblical writers complained about pain and evil:

> Evils have encompassed me without number (Psalm 40:12, RSV).
>
> Why is my pain unceasing, my wound incurable, refusing to be healed? (Jeremiah 15:18, RSV).
>
> The whole creation has been groaning in travail together until now (Romans 8:22, RSV).

Thus we readily admit that evil is a problem and we also admit that if God created the world the way it is today He would not be a God of love but rather an evil God.

However, the Scriptures make it plain that God did not create the world in the state in which it is now—evil came as a result of the selfishness of man. The Bible says that God is a God of love and He desired to create a person and eventually a race that would love Him. But genuine love cannot exist unless freely given through free choice and will, and thus man was given the choice to accept God's love or to reject it. This choice made the possibility of evil become very real. When Adam and Eve disobeyed God, they did not choose what God created, and, by their choice, they brought evil into the world. God is not evil nor did He create evil. Man brought evil upon himself by selfishly choosing his own way apart from God's way.

Because of the fall, the world now is abnormal. Things are not in the state they should be in. Man, as a result of the fall, has been separated from God. Nature is not always kind to man, and the animal world also can be his enemy. There is conflict between man and his fellow man. None of these conditions were true before the fall. Any solution that might be given to the problems mankind faces must take into consideration that the world as it stands now is not normal.

Evil Not Permanent

Although evil is here and it is real, it is also temporary. It eventually will be destroyed. This is the hope the believer has. There is a new world coming in which there will be no more tears or pain because all things will be made new (Revelation 21:5). Paradise lost will be paradise regained. God will right every wrong and put away evil once for all, in His time.

In the meantime, however, Christians have a justification for fighting evil, immorality, and corruption. The world was not designed with evil in mind; God does not desire evil nor does He ever condone it—He hates evil. The Christian is not only to despise evil along with God, but he is also obligated to do something about it. By identifying with Jesus, the believer has a duty to call things wrong that are wrong and to speak out when evil is overtaking good. Natural disasters, crime, and mental retardation should not be accepted as the order of things, because they were never meant to be, and they will not be in God's future kingdom.

Some people, however are still bothered that God even allows evil in the first place. They question His wisdom in giving man a choice in the matter.

Dorothy Sayers put the problem of evil in the proper perspective:

> For whatever reason God chose to make man as he is—limited and suffering and subject to sorrows and death—[God] had the honesty and the courage to take His own medicine. Whatever game He is playing with His creation, He has kept His own rules and played fair. He can exact nothing from man that He has not exacted from Himself. He has Himself gone through the whole of human experience, from the trivial irritations of family life and the cramping restrictions of hard work and lack of money to the worst horrors of pain and humiliation, defeat, despair and death. When He was a man, He played the man. He was born in poverty and died in disgrace and thought it well worth while. 9/4

CHAPTER 41 *Questions About Faith and Reason*

What About All the Hypocrites in the Church? (A/127-28)

One major excuse that people use in their refusal to embrace Christianity concerns hypocrites in the church, both past and present. People like to point to past misdeeds done in the name of Christ, such as the Spanish Inquisition, witch trials and other horrible acts.

Then, there are the present-day examples of preachers, deacons or church leaders who have been caught in alcoholism, adulterous relationships or some other inconsistency with what they say they believe. This type of behavior has led many to say, "If that's what Christianity is all about, then I don't want any part of it."

It must be admitted that there has been hypocrisy in the church, and today we are not exempt from people who are hypocritical. A hypocrite is an actor, one who puts on a false face. He says one thing but does another.

However, just because the church contains hypocrites does not mean that all Christians are hypocrites. With every example of hypocrisy that can be pointed to in the church, a counter example can be pointed out showing people living consistently with the teaching of Jesus Christ.

It is important not to confuse hypocrisy with sin. All Christians are sinners, but not all Christians are hypocrites. There is a misconception that a Christian is a person who claims that he does not sin, but the truth is that to call oneself a Christian is to admit to being a sinner (1 John 1:5–2:2).

All believers, including the clergy, are fallible human beings who are prone to all types of sin. Just because a person is not perfect does not mean he is a phony. The distinction between the two is important. The failures of the believers do not invalidate the truth.

Jesus Christ had very harsh words for people who were committing the sin of hypocrisy, especially the religious leaders of His day. He denounced them in no uncertain terms:

> Woe unto you, scribes and Pharisees, hypocrites! for ye compass sea and land to make one proselyte, and when he is made, ye make him twofold more the child of hell than yourselves (Matthew 23:15, KJV).

People can and do enter the ministry for the wrong reasons, or they can compromise the convictions of the faith. When people do this they are wrong, and the Bible denounces this clearly.

Christianity does not stand or fall on the way Christians have acted throughout history or are acting today. Christianity stands or falls on the person of Jesus, and Jesus was not a hypocrite. He lived consistently with what He taught, and at the end of His life He challenged those who had lived with Him night and day, for more than three years, to point out any hypocrisy in Him. His disciples were silent, because there was none.

Since Christianity depends on Jesus, it is incorrect to try to invalidate the Christian faith by pointing to horrible things done in the name of Christianity.

Let's look at one illustration of the reasoning involved in this question. For example, let's say the president of a large car company is always advertising and telling his friends that a certain make of car in his company is the best in the country and the only car we should be driving.

In fact, a number of automotive magazines and consumer groups have backed up some of his claims. But yet, when you see this man, he is driving the competition's leading model! (Perhaps he likes their colors better.)

You say, what a hypocrite! If he believed all that stuff about his own car, and he's in a position to know, then he'd be driving one. That is probably true. Yet his being a hypocrite does *not* invalidate the claim that his car may be the best one in the country.

The same is true of Christianity. People may claim it's true, yet have lives inconsistent with their claim, but this does not mean Christianity is not true.

What About Those Who Have Never Heard the Gospel? (A/129-32)

The Bible is very clear that no one can come to God except through Jesus Christ.

Jesus said, "No one comes to the Father except through Me" (John 14:6, MLB). The only basis for forgiveness of sin and life everlasting is the way made by Jesus. Many people think this implies that those who have never heard about Jesus automatically will be damned. However, we do not know this is the case.

Although the Scriptures never explicitly teach that someone who has never heard of Jesus can be saved, we do believe that it infers this. We do believe that every person will have an opportunity to repent, and that God will not exclude anyone because he happened to be born at the wrong place or at the wrong time.

Jesus said, "If any man will do His will, he shall know of the doctrine, whether it be of God, or whether I speak of Myself" (John 7:17, KJV).

The Bible also reveals that no one has any excuse:

> For what can be known about God is plain to them, because God has shown it to them. Ever since the creation of the world His invisible nature, namely His eternal power and deity, has been clearly perceived in the things that have been made. So they are without excuse (Romans 1:19,20, RSV).

It is a fact that all of mankind can tell that a creator does exist, because His creation testifies to it. This testimony is universal. Although people have enough information that God does exist, they become willfully ignorant of the things of God because their hearts are evil.

The Bible teaches that the unbelieving individual is "holding down the truth in unrighteousness" (Romans 1:18, Lit. Trans.). Moreover, the Scriptures relate that man is not seeking after God but actually running from Him. "There is none that seeketh after God" (Romans 3:11, KJV). Therefore, it is not a case of God refusing to get His Word to someone who is desperately searching for the truth.

We also know that it is God's desire that "none should perish but that all should come to repentance" (2 Peter 3:9). This indicates that God also cares for those persons who have not heard the gospel. He had demonstrated this by sending His Son to die in their place. "While we were yet sinners, Christ died for us" (Romans 5:8, KJV).

The Bible teaches that God is going to judge the world fairly and righteously. "Because he hath appointed a day, in which He will judge the world in righteousness" (Acts 17:31, KJV). This means that when all the facts are in, God's name will be vindicated and no one will be able to accuse Him of unfairness.

Even though we may not know how He is going to deal with these people specifically, we know His judgment will be fair. This fact alone should satisfy anyone who wonders how God will deal with people who never have heard of Jesus Christ.

The Bible itself testifies to the fact that, out of every people on the earth, some will hear and respond. "For you were killed, and have redeemed us to God by your blood out of every kindred, and tongue, and people, and nation" (Revelation 5:9).

The Bible gives an example of a man who was in a situation not unlike many today. His name was Cornelius. He was a very religious man who constantly prayed to God. He had not heard of Jesus Christ, but he was honestly asking God to reveal Himself to him.

God answered the prayer of Cornelius by sending the apostle Peter to him to give him the full story of Jesus. When Peter preached to Cornelius, Cornelius put his trust in Christ as his Savior. This example demonstrates that anyone who sincerely desires to know God will hear about Jesus.

There are people today, like Cornelius, who pray the same prayer to know the true and living God, and they are being reached no matter where they might live. Simon Peter stated, "I perceive that God is no respecter of persons: But in every nation he that feareth Him, and worketh righteousness, is accepted with Him" (Acts 10:34,35, KJV).

The Scriptures contain other examples of individuals who were accepted by God, even though their knowledge of Him was limited.

- Rahab, the prostitute, had only the smallest amount of knowledge about God, but the Bible refers to her as a woman of faith, and her actions were commended (Joshua 2:9; Hebrews 11:31).
- Naaman, the Syrian, was granted peace with God because he exercised faith, even though he was living in the midst of a pagan culture (2 Kings 5:15-19).
- Jonah, the prophet, was sent to Nineveh, a heathen society, and they repented at his preaching (Jonah 3:5).

No one will be condemned for not ever hearing of Jesus Christ. Based on the above examples from Scripture, it can be seen that God will judge all mankind fairly and that no one can claim he or she received an unfair hearing. Therefore, the people who ask this question should be very careful not to use this as an excuse for not coming to Christ.

What you think might happen or might not happen to someone else does not release you from your responsibility on Judgment Day. Although we might not be able to answer the question about those who haven't heard to the satisfaction of everyone, the Bible has made certain things clear.

One person put it this way, "Many things in the Bible I cannot understand; many things in the Bible I only think I understand; but there are many things in the Bible I cannot misunderstand" (Anonymous).

Isn't It Enough Just to Be Sincere? (A/133-34)

A person can be sincere, but he also can be sincerely wrong. The Bible says, "There is a way which seems right to a man, but its end is the way of death" (Proverbs 16:25, NASB).

There are many cases each year when someone jokingly points a gun at someone else, sincerely believing it is empty. The gun goes off and the other individual is killed—and the person who pulled the trigger says, "I didn't know it was loaded."

That person might be 100 percent sincere in the fact that he did not want to harm the other individual, but he was sincerely believing something that just was not true. Sincerity is not enough if the object of belief is not true, and all the sincerity in the world will not bring that person who has been shot back to life.

The apostle Paul teaches that simply practicing religion does not excuse anyone; rather, it may compound the person's guilt. In examining the pagan's religion, Paul points out that it is a distortion of the truth. He says, "They exchanged the truth of God for a lie" (Romans 1:25, NASB).

The glory of God is substituted and replaced by the glory of the creature. Their religion is one of idolatry, and to worship idols is an insult to the dignity of God. This is something God has always detested.

> You shall have no other gods before Me. You shall not make for yourself an idol, or any likeness of what is in heaven above or on the earth beneath or in the water under the earth. You shall not worship them or serve them; for I, the LORD your God, am a jealous God (Exodus 20:3-5, NASB).

Thus a religious person has no advantage if he is worshiping the wrong God, no matter how sincere.

If a person attempts to get into a movie theater and the price is $4, it does not matter whether he has $3.90 or 25¢; he is still short. If someone is believing the wrong thing, it does not matter how sincere he is, for he is short of what God requires of men for them to reach Him.

God sets the standard, and He will accept only those who come to Him through Jesus Christ. "Neither is there salvation in any other: for there is none other name under heaven given among men, whereby we must be saved" (Acts 4:12, KJV).

Is Christianity Merely a Psychological Crutch? (A/125-26)

Every college, it seems, has the campus atheist who says, "Christianity is for the weaklings; it is just a crutch."

Karl Marx's famous line, "Religion is the opiate of the masses," is still a common view of many. Those who call themselves Christians are seen as people who need something to enable them to cope with the problems of life. Some people use alcohol, some drugs, others Christianity to get themselves through this difficult world.

The fact of the matter is we all *do* need a crutch to get by in this world. We are all crippled in some sense, and down deep inside there is a desire for something to sustain us. The real issue is, "Is this crutch we call Christianity true, or is it something on the same level as drugs or alcohol, invented to meet an admitted need?"

There are definite psychological needs—fear of danger, disease or death, for example—that might prompt us to invent God so we could feel secure. However, there are also psychological needs that might lead us to deny that God exists. The agnostic or atheist may be using agnosticism or atheism as a crutch to avoid the responsibility of God's demands.

The God of the Bible is awesome and a threat to mankind. A God who is all-powerful, all-knowing, righteous, holy and just, and who is going to judge the world for its sin, is an extremely imposing figure. Thus it is only fair to point out that some people need the crutch of denying God's existence in order to live their lives as they please without fear of judgment.

Aldous Huxley articulated this thought in *Ends and Means:* "For myself, the philosophy of meaninglessness was essentially an instrument of liberation, sexual and political." 3/270*ff.*

The truth of the Christian faith is not based upon psychological needs for or against God. Yes, it is possible that Christianity could have started because people needed something to lean on, but the question is not how it *could* have started but how it *did* start.

We again are brought back to the real issue, which is the person of Jesus Christ. Does mankind need to lean on Him, or can we lean on something else?

Jesus made the issue very clear:

> Therefore whosoever heareth these sayings of Mine, and doeth them, I will liken him unto a wise man, which built his house upon a rock: And the rain descended, and the floods came, and the winds blew, and beat upon that house; and it fell not: for it was founded upon a rock.
>
> And every one that heareth these sayings of Mine, and doeth them not, shall be likened unto a foolish man, which built his house upon the sand: And the rain descended, and the floods came, and the winds blew, and beat upon that house; and it fell; and great was the fall of it (Matthew 7:24-27, KJV).

One could also state it this way. A crutch presupposes two things: (1) that there is a disease, sickness or hurt; and (2) that a person has been given some type of a remedy (this is why he has the crutch).

Two questions immediately arise. **First**, what is this disease? Is it real or imagined? And **second**, is the remedy the correct one for the disease?

With Christianity, God clearly states that the disease is sin, and that the disease is real. It is not a psychological, imaginary hang-up in need of a religious fix as Marx would propound. Rather, the remedy, instead of being a religious crutch, is a relationship with Jesus Christ.

Therefore, Christianity in one sense is a crutch. But it is more than a crutch; it is the sure foundation, the truth of life.

If Jesus Christ be God, and if He died on the cross for our sins, and if He created us to be in fellowship with God the Father through Him, then to call Him a crutch would be like a light bulb saying to an electrical socket, "You are my crutch." As a light bulb was created to function properly when inserted into the socket, so we have been created to function properly in a personal relationship with God through Jesus Christ.

I'm a Good Person; Won't God Accept Me? (A/143-44)

In the early sixties, a song came out by J. Frank Wilson and the Cavaliers, entitled "The Last Kiss." The song is about a couple out on a date who get into a car accident. The girl dies in her boyfriend's arms. He mourns her death singing:

> Oh, where, oh where, can my baby be?
> The Lord took her away from me.
> She's gone to heaven so I got to be good,
> So I can see my baby when I leave this world.

This song sums up the attitude of a lot of people. They think if they can live a good life, if the good works they do outweigh the bad, then they will have earned their way to heaven.

Unfortunately, the Bible does not allow anyone to earn his way to heaven. The Scriptures teach that good works have nothing to do with one entering into a right relationship with God. This relationship is nothing we can earn, because God has done everything for us.

> Not by works of righteousness which we have done, but according to His mercy He saved us (Titus 3:5, KJV).

> For by grace are ye saved through faith, and that not of yourselves: it is the gift of God: Not of works, lest any man should boast (Ephesians 2:8,9, KJV).

> But without faith it is impossible to please Him (Hebrews 11:6, KJV).

If our eternal salvation was on the basis of works and we could earn it successfully, God would be our debtor: He would owe us something (Romans 4:1-3). The Bible teaches that God owes no man anything, and our own righteousness is as filthy rags (Isaiah 64:6).

The simple reason is that God has a perfect standard, and all of us have sinned and come short of this mark (Romans 3:23). We like to compare ourselves to others, and thus we feel that we are not so bad after all. But God compares us to Jesus Christ, and next to Him we cannot help but fall far short, all of us, without exception.

This can be illustrated by the following example. Out in Southern California, there is an island off the coast called Catalina, 26 miles from the pier at Newport Beach. Suppose that one day three men are standing on the end of the pier.

One is an alcoholic, grubby, sick, living in the streets. The second is the average American, and the third a fine, upstanding, pillar-of-the-community person.

All of a sudden, the alcoholic leaps off the edge of the pier five feet out into the water. The other two yell, "What are you trying to do?"

The man in the water yells back, "I'm jumping to Catalina!"

The second man, the average man on the street, says "Watch me. I can do better than that!" He proceeds to jump, landing ten feet out, twice as far as the alcoholic. The third man, moral, upright, outstanding person that he is, laughs disdainfully at the two men in the water.

He moves back about fifty yards, takes a running leap and lands twenty feet out, twice as far as Mr. Average, and four times as far as Mr. Alcoholic.

The Coast Guard fishes them out of the water and asks what they are doing, to which they all reply, "We are jumping to Catalina." Mr. Average boasts of his beating Mr. Alcoholic, and Mr. Great boasts of his accomplishment in beating both of them.

The Coast Guard officer could only shake his head and exclaim, "You fools! You are all *still* 26 miles short of your mark."

Although modern man considers himself better than—or at least as good as—others, he is still far from the target God has set for us. It is impossible for anyone to jump from the pier to Catalina, and it is impossible for anyone to reach heaven by his own deeds—apart from Jesus Christ. As Jesus Himself puts it, "No man cometh unto the Father, but by Me" (John 14:6, KJV).

Can You Prove Christianity Scientifically? (C/36-40)

Many people try to put off personal commitment to Christ by voicing the assumption that if you cannot prove something scientifically, it is not true or worthy of acceptance. Since one cannot prove scientifically the deity of Jesus or the resurrection, then (these people feel) twentieth-century individuals should know better than to accept Christ as Savior or to believe in the resurrection.

Often in a philosophy or history class I am confronted with the challenge, "Can you prove it scientifically?"

I usually say, "Well, no, I'm not a scientist."

You can hear the class chuckle, and usually several voices can be heard saying, "Don't talk to me about it"; or, "See, you must take it all by faith" (meaning blind faith).

Recently on a flight to Boston I was talking with the passenger next to me about why I personally believe Christ is who He claimed to be. The pilot, making his public relations rounds greeting the passengers, overheard part of our conversation.

"You have a problem," he said.

"What is that?" I asked.

"You can't prove it scientifically," he replied.

The mentality that modern humanity has descended to is amazing. Somehow, here in the twentieth century we have so many who hold to the opinion that if you can't prove it scientifically, it's not true. Well, *that* is not true! There's a problem with proving anything scientifically about a person or event in history. We need to understand the difference between scientific proof and what I call legal-historical proof. Let me explain these two.

Scientific proof is based on showing that something is a fact by repeating the event in the presence of the person questioning the fact. There is a controlled environment where observations can be made, data drawn, and hypotheses empirically verified.

The "scientific method, however it is defined, is related to measurement of phenomena and experimentation or repeated observation." 7/985

Dr. James B. Conant, former president of Harvard, writes:

> Science is an interconnected series of concepts and conceptual schemes that have developed as a result of experimentation and observation, and are fruitful of further experimentation and observation. 2/25

Testing the truth of a hypothesis by the use of controlled experiments is one of the key techniques of the modern scientific method. For example, somebody says, "Ivory soap doesn't float." So I take the person to the kitchen, put eight inches of water in the sink at 82.7°, and drop in the soap. Plunk. Observations are made, data are drawn, and a hypothesis is empirically verified: Ivory soap floats.

Now if the scientific method were the only method of proving something, you couldn't prove that you went to your first hour class this morning or that you had lunch today. There's no way you can repeat those events in a controlled situation.

Now let's look at legal-historical proof, which is based on showing beyond a reasonable doubt that something is fact. In other words, a verdict is reached on the basis of the weight of the evidence. That is, there's no reasonable basis for doubting the decision. It depends upon three types of testimony: oral testimony, written testimony, and exhibits (such as a gun, bullet, notebook, etc.). Using the legal method of determining what happened, you could pretty well prove beyond a reasonable doubt that you were in class this morning: Your friends saw you; you have your notes; the professor remembers you.

The scientific method can be used only to prove repeatable things; it isn't adequate for proving or disproving many questions about a person or event in history. The scientific method isn't appropriate for answering questions like, "Did George Washington live?" "Was Martin Luther King a civil rights leader?" "Who was Jesus of Nazareth?" "Was Robert Kennedy attorney general of the U.S.A.?" "Was Jesus Christ raised from the dead?" These are out of the realm of scientific proof, and we need to put them in the realm of legal proof. In other words, the scientific method, which is based on observation, the gathering of data, hypothesizing, deduction, and experimental verification to find and explain empirical regularities in nature, doesn't have the final answers to such questions as, "Can you prove the resurrection?" or, "Can you prove that Jesus is the Son of God?" When men and women rely upon the legal-historical method, they need to check out the reliability of the testimonies.

One thing that has especially appealed to me is that the Christian faith is not a blind, ignorant belief but rather an intelligent faith. Every time in the Bible when a person is called upon to exercise faith, it's an intelligent faith. Jesus said in John 8, "You shall know the truth," not ignore it.

Christ was asked, "What is the greatest commandment of all?"

He answered, "To love the Lord your God with all your heart and all your mind."

The problem with most people is that they seem to stop with their hearts. The facts about Christ never get to their minds. We've been given **a mind** innovated by the Holy Spirit to know God, as well as a **heart** to love him and a **will** to choose him. We need to function **in all three areas** to have a maximum relationship with God and to glorify him. I don't know about you, but my heart can't rejoice in what my mind has rejected. My heart and mind were created to work in harmony together. Never has an individual been called upon to commit intellectual suicide in trusting Christ as Savior and Lord.

Part Four: Bibliography

1. Casserley, J. V. Langmead. *The Christian in Philosophy.* New York: Charles Scribner's Sons, 1951.

2. Conant, James B. *Science and Common Sense.* New Haven: Yale University Press, 1951.

3. Huxley, Aldous. *Ends and Means: An Inquiry into the Nature of Ideals and into the Methods Employed for Their Realization.* Des Plaines, IL: Greenwood Publishing, 1970. Reprint of 1937 ed.

4. Machen, J. G. *Christianity and Liberalism.* Grand Rapids, MI: Wm. B. Eerdmans Publishing Co., 1923.

5. Mead, Frank. *Encyclopedia of Religious Quotations.*

6. Montgomery, John. *How Do We Know There is a God?* Minneapolis, MN: Bethany Fellowship, 1972.

7. *The New Encyclopedia Britannica,* vol. VIII.

8. Ridenour, Fritz. *Who Says?* Ventura, CA: Gospel Light Publications, Regal Books, 1967.

9. Sayers, Dorothy. *Creed or Chaos?* New York: Harcourt, Brace and Co, 1949.

THE CHRISTIAN EXPERIENCE

Its Uniqueness

CHAPTER 42 *Is the Christian Experience Just a Delusion?* (E/327-28)

I was giving my testimony during a debate in a history class recently, and just as I was finishing, the professor spoke up and remarked, "Look, McDowell, we're interested in facts, not testimonies. Why, I have met scores of people around the world who have been transformed by Christ."

I interrupted and said, "Thank you, let me wrap up what I am sharing, and then I will concentrate my remarks on your statement."

After my testimony of how Christ changed my life, I outlined the following to the class: "Many of you are saying, 'Christ changed your life, so what?' One thing that has confirmed to me the resurrection of Jesus Christ two thousand years ago is the transformation of the lives of millions of people when they become related by faith to the person of Jesus. Although they are from every walk of life and from all the nations of the world, they are changed in remarkably similar ways. From the most brilliant professor to the most ignorant savage, when one puts his trust in Christ, his life begins to change.

"Some say it is just wishful thinking, or they simply excuse it by saying it doesn't prove a thing. For a Christian, behind his subjective experience is an objective reality as its basis. This objective reality is the person of Jesus Christ and His resurrection.

"For example, let's say a student comes into the room and says, 'Guys, I have a stewed tomato in my right tennis shoe. This tomato has changed my life. It has given me a peace and love and joy that I never experienced before, not only that, but I can now run the 100-yard dash in 10 seconds flat.'

"It is hard to argue with a student like that if his life backs up what he says (especially if he runs circles around you on the track). A personal testimony is often a subjective argument for the reality of something. Therefore, don't dismiss a subjective experience as being irrelevant.

"There are two questions or tests I apply to a subjective experience. **First:** *What is the objective reality for the subjective experience?* **Second:** *How many other people have had the same subjective experience from being related to the objective reality?*

"Let me apply this to the student with the 'stewed tomato' in his right tennis shoe. To the first question he would reply, 'A stewed tomato in my right tennis shoe.'

"Then the second question would be put this way: 'How many people in this classroom, in this university, in this country, on this continent, etc., have experienced the same love, peace, joy and increased track speed as the result of a stewed tomato in their right shoes?' "

At this point, most of the history students laughed. I didn't blame them, for it was obvious that the answer to the second question was, "No one!"

Now I had to apply these same two questions to my own subjective experience:

1. *What is the objective reality or basis for my subjective experience—a changed life?*

Answer: the person of Christ and His resurrection.

2. *How many others have had this same subjective experience from being related to the objective reality, Jesus Christ?*

The evidence is overwhelming. Truly millions of people, from all backgrounds, nationalities and professions, have seen their lives elevated to new levels of peace and joy by turning their lives over to Christ. Indeed, the professor confirmed this when he said, "I have met scores of people around the world who have been transformed by Christ."

To those who say it is a delusion, then WOW! What a powerful delusion! E. Y. Mullins writes:

> A redeemed drunkard, with vivid memory of past hopeless struggles and new sense of power through Christ, was replying to the charge that

> "his religion was a delusion." He said: "Thank God for the delusion; it has put clothes on my children and shoes on their feet and bread in their mouths. It has made a man of me and it has put joy and peace in my home, which had been a hell. If this is a delusion, may God send it to the slaves of drink everywhere, for their slavery is an awful reality." 23/294-95

From the first century A.D. down to the present, Jesus Christ has been radically changing the lives of millions of individuals from all walks of life. The following pages of this section highlight a sampling of people who have come to experience the life-transforming power of "Christ in the inner man."

CHAPTER 43 *Did You Hear What Happened to Saul?*

(C/78-87)

One of the most influential testimonies to Christianity was when Saul of Tarsus, perhaps Christianity's most rabid antagonist, became the apostle Paul. Saul was a Hebrew zealot, a religious leader. Being born in Tarsus gave him the opportunity to be exposed to the most advanced learning of his day. Tarsus was a university city known for its stoic philosopers and culture. Strabo, the Greek geographer, praised Tarsus for being so interested in education and philosophy. 10/17:469

Paul, like his father, possessed Roman citizenship, a high privilege. He seemed to be well versed in Hellenistic culture and thought. He had great command of the Greek language and displayed dialectic skill. He quoted from less familiar poets and philosophers:

> For in him we live and move and exist [Epimenides], as even some of your own poets have said, "For we also are His offspring" [Aratus, Cleanthes] (Acts 17:28).

> Do not be deceived: "Bad company corrupts good morals" [Menander] (1 Corinthians 15:33).

> One of themselves, a prophet of their own, said, "Cretans are always liars, evil beasts, lazy gluttons" [Epimenides] (Titus 1:12).

Paul's education was Jewish and took place under the strict doctrines of the Pharisees. At about age fourteen, he was sent to study under Gamaliel, one of the great rabbis of the time, the grandson of Hillel. Paul asserted that he was not only a Pharisee but the son of Pharisees (Acts 23:6). He could boast: "I was advancing in Judaism beyond many of my contemporaries among my countrymen, being more extremely zealous for my ancestral traditions" (Galatians 1:14).

If one is to understand Paul's conversion, it is necessary to see why he was so vehemently anti-Christian: The reason was his devotion to the Jewish law. That devotion triggered his adamant discontent with Christ and the early church.

Paul's "offence with the Christian message was not," as Jacques Dupont writes:

> With the affirmation of Jesus' messiahship [but] . . . with the attributing to Jesus of a saving role which robbed the law of all its value in the purpose of salvation . . . [Paul was] violently hostile to the Christian faith because of the importance which he attached to the law as a way of salvation. 9/177

So Paul began his pursuit to death of "the sect of the Nazarenes" (Acts 26:9-11). He literally "laid waste the church" (Acts 8:3). He set out for Damascus with documents authorizing him to seize the followers of Jesus and bring them back to face trial.

Then something happened to Paul.

> And it came about that as he journeyed, he was approaching Damascus, and suddenly a light from heaven flashed around him; and he fell to the ground, and heard a voice saying to him, "Saul, Saul, why are you persecuting Me?" And he said, "Who art Thou, Lord?" And He said, "I am Jesus whom you are persecuting, but rise, and enter the city, and it shall be told you what you must do." And the men who traveled with him stood speechless, hearing the voice, but seeing no one. And Saul got up from the ground, and though his eyes were open, he could see nothing; and leading him by the hand, they brought him into Damascus. And he was three days without sight, and neither ate nor drank.
>
> Now there was a certain disciple at Damascus, named Ananias; and the Lord said to him in a vision, "Ananias." And he said, "Behold, here am I, Lord." And the Lord said to him "Arise and go to the street called Straight, and inquire at the house of Judas for a man from Tarsus named Saul, for behold, he is praying, and he has seen in a vision a man named Ananias come in and lay his hands on him, so that he might regain his sight" (Acts 9:1-12).

At this point one can see why the Christians feared Paul. Ananias answered:

> "Lord, I have heard from many about this man, how much harm he did to Thy saints at Jerusalem; and here he has authority from the chief priests to bind all who call upon Thy name." But the Lord said to him, "Go, for he

> is a chosen instrument of Mine, to bear My name before the Gentiles and kings and the sons of Israel; for I will show him how much he must suffer for My name's sake." And Ananias departed and entered the house, and after laying his hands on him said, "Brother Saul, the Lord Jesus, who appeared to you on the road by which you were coming, has sent me so that you may regain your sight, and be filled with the Holy Spirit." And immediately there fell from his eyes something like scales, and he regained his sight, and he arose and was baptized; and he took food and was strengthened (Acts 9:13-19*a*).

Paul said, "Have I not seen Jesus our Lord?" (1 Corinthians 9:1). He compared Christ's appearance to him with Christ's postresurrection appearances among the apostles. "And last of all . . . He appeared to me also" (1 Corinthians 15:8).

Notice that Paul's encounter with Jesus and subsequent conversion were sudden and unexpected. "A very bright light suddenly flashed from heaven all around me" (Acts 22:6). Paul had no idea who this heavenly person could be. The announcement that it was Jesus of Nazareth left him trembling and astonished.

We might not know all the details, chronology, or psychology of what happened to Paul on the road to Damascus but we do know this: It radically affected every area of his life.

First, Paul's character was drastically transformed. The *Encyclopedia Britannica* describes him before his conversion as an intolerant, bitter, persecuting, religious bigot—proud and temperamental. After his conversion he is pictured as patient, kind, enduring and self-sacrificing.

Second, Paul's relationship with the followers of Jesus was transformed. "Now for several days he was with the disciples who were at Damascus" (Acts 9:19). And when Paul went to the apostles, he received the "right hand of fellowship."

Third, Paul's message was transformed. Though he still loved his Jewish heritage, he had changed from a bitter antagonist to a determined protagonist of the Christian faith. "Immediately he began to proclaim Jesus in the synagogues, saying, 'He is the Son of God' " (Acts 9:20). Paul's intellectual convictions had changed. His experience compelled him to acknowledge that Jesus was the Messiah, in direct conflict with the Pharisees' messianic ideas. His new concept of Christ meant a total revolution in his thought. 34/185-86

Jacques Dupont acutely observes that after Paul "had passionately denied that a crucified man could be the Messiah, he came to grant that Jesus was indeed the Messiah, and, as a consequence, rethought all his messianic ideas." 9/76

Also he could now understand that Christ's death on the cross, which appeared to be a curse of God and a deplorable ending of someone's life, was actually God, through Christ, reconciling the world to himself. Paul came to understand that, through the crucifixion, Christ became a curse for us (Galatians 3:13) and was "made . . . to be sin on our behalf" (2 Corinthians 5:21). Instead of a defeat, the death of Christ was a great victory, being capped by the resurrection. The cross was no longer a "stumbling block" but the essence of God's messianic redemption. Paul's missionary preaching can be summarized as "explaining and giving evidence that the Christ had to suffer and rise again from the dead . . . 'This Jesus whom I am proclaiming to you is the Christ,' " he said (Acts 17:30).

Fourth, Paul's mission was transformed. He was changed from a Gentile-hater to a missionary to Gentiles. He was changed from a Jewish zealot to an evangelist to Gentiles. As a Jew and Pharisee, Paul looked down upon the despised Gentile as someone inferior to God's chosen people. The Damascus experience changed him into a dedicated apostle, with his life's mission aimed toward helping the Gentile. Paul saw in the Christ who appeared to him the Savior for all people. Paul went from being an orthodox Pharisee whose mission was to preserve strict Judaism to being a propagator of that new radical sect called Christianity which he had so violently opposed. There was such a change in him that "all those hearing him continued to be amazed, and were saying, 'Is this not he who in Jerusalem destroyed those who called on this [Jesus'] name, and who had come here for the purpose of bringing them bound before the chief priests?' " (Acts 9:21).

Historian Philip Schaff states:

> The conversion of Paul marks not only a turning-point in his personal history, but also an important epoch in the history of the apostolic church, and consequently in the history of mankind. It was the most fruitful event since the miracle of Pentecost, and secured the universal victory of Christianity. 31/296

During lunch at the University of Houston, I sat down next to a student. As we discussed Christianity he made the statement that there wasn't any historical evidence for Christianity or Christ. He was a history major and I noticed that one of his books was a Roman history textbook. He acknowledged that there was a chapter dealing with the apostle Paul and Christianity. After reading the chapter, the student found it interesting that the section on Paul started by describing the life of Saul of Tarsus and ended with a description of the life of the apostle Paul. In the next to the last paragraph the book observed that what happened in between was not clear. After I turned to the book of Acts and explained Christ's postresurrection appearance to Paul, this student saw that it was the most logical explanation of Paul's conversion. Later he also trusted Christ as his Savior.

Elias Andrews comments:

> Many have found in the radical transformation of this "Pharisee of the Pharisees" the most convincing evidence of the truth and the power of the

religion to which he was converted, as well as the ultimate worth and place of the Person of Christ. 10/469

Archibald MacBride, professor at the University of Aberdeen, writes of Paul: "Beside his achievements . . . the achievements of Alexander and Napoleon pale into insignificance." 5/10:516 Clement says that Paul "bore chains seven times; preached the gospel in the East and West; came to the limit of the West; and died a martyr under the rulers." 31/I:340

Paul stated again and again that the living, resurrected Jesus had transformed his life. He was so convinced of Christ's resurrection from the dead that he, too, died a martyr's death for his beliefs.

Two professors at Oxford, Gilbert West and Lord Lyttleton, were determined to destroy the basis of the Christian faith. West was going to demonstrate the fallacy of the resurrecton and Lyttleton was going to prove that Saul of Tarsus had never converted to Christianity. Both men came to the opposite conclusion and became ardent followers of Jesus.

Lord Lyttleton writes: "The conversion and apostleship of Saint Paul alone, duly considered, was of itself a demonstration sufficient to prove Christianity to be a Divine Revelation." 19/467 He concludes that if Paul's twenty-five years of suffering and service for Christ were a reality, then his conversion was true, for everything he did began with that sudden change. And if his conversion was true, Jesus Christ rose from the dead, for everything Paul was and did he attributed to the sight of the risen Christ.

CHAPTER 44 *Martyrs and Confessors*

(HW/71-87)

In the Early Church

In the first two centuries after Jesus' birth, things were somewhat different from today in much of the western world. An atheist was someone who did not believe in the gods of the Roman empire—the emperor being one of those gods. Other religions were tolerated from time to time, but inevitably they were subject to restriction and at times banishment. The Roman policy generally allowed other religions, especially in newly conquered lands, to practice their beliefs as long as they didn't cause problems for the Romans.

The Christians, however, caused problems.

The Christians did not cause problems out of contempt or resistance, though. They had a different message for the world, and when Roman cultists were attracted to it, attendance at pagan temples decreased. Former cult members stopped buying statues of the pagan gods. They stopped buying and offering sacrifices to those gods. In some areas virtual economic crisis occurred.

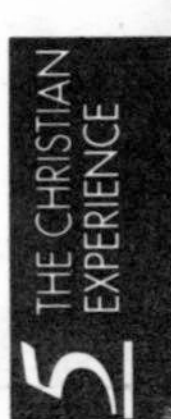

These and other disturbances motivated Roman authorities to do something about the Christians. Christians were rounded up and commanded to deny Christ, bow down to the gods of the Roman empire, and burn incense to them. Christians who would not were tortured and put to death. Thousands were burned alive or fed to the starved lions in the Colosseum at Rome, all for the "amusement" of the people. It is hard to imagine an arena full of high-class Romans cheering wildly, as at a spectator sport, while other human beings were being slaughtered, burned or torn apart before their eyes.

It began, of course, with the original apostles. Tradition tells us that many of Jesus' apostles and almost all of the New Testament writers were martyred for their faith. They chose death at the hands of persecutors rather than deny the facts of the life of Jesus which they were passing on to a new generation of Christians. Eusebius, considered to be generally accurate in what he reports, records the martyrdoms of Peter (crucified upside down), Paul (beheaded), James the brother of Jesus (stoned and clubbed), and James the brother of John (killed by the sword). Acts 12:2 is a much earlier source for the death of James the brother of John, and Josephus is a much earlier source for the death of James the brother of Jesus. Tradition holds that Thomas was killed by a spear and that Thaddaeus was put to death by arrows. Bartholomew is reported to have been flayed alive and crucified upside down. Tradition from the fourth century holds Luke to be a martyr. Other tradition has Mark dying a martyr's death in the eighth year of Nero. John is reported to have been boiled in oil but miraculously survived.

For Christians, however, suffering was not a tragedy, but an opportunity. It was the very opportunity which eventually secured victory for Christianity over the entire Roman Empire. The martyrdom, torture, and threats of death suffered by Christians actually attracted others to the Christian faith. Those who witnessed their peaceful surrender to, and in some cases eager anticipation of, suffering for Jesus were confronted with the reality of what it meant to know the true God personally. Historian Philip Schaff states:

> The final victory of Christianity over Judaism and heathenism, and the mightiest empire of the ancient world, a victory gained without physical force but by the moral power of patience and perseverance, of faith and love, is one of the sublimest spectacles in history, and one of the strongest evidences of the divinity and indestructible life of our religion. 30/2:8

It does not appear to have been a conscious realization at the time, but the willful suffering of the Christians also verified for succeeding generations their solid conviction that the writings and oral testimony passed to them about Jesus were the truth.

It was a well-known saying among those early Christians that the blood of the martyrs was the seed of the church. For all who fell, more came to take their place. Tertullian even challenged the heathen governors:

> But go zealously on. . . . Kill us, torture us, condemn us, grind us to dust. . . . The oftener we are mown down by you, the more in number we grow; the blood of Christians is seed. . . . For who that contemplates it is not excited to inquire what is at the bottom of it? Who, after inquiry, does not embrace our doctrines? And when he has embraced them, desires not to suffer? 36/50

Others confessed Jesus under the threat of death but were not executed. These were held in honor as "confessors."

Certainly it is true that many people throughout history have died for what they thought to be true, even though it may not have been. But the Christian martyrs of the first two centuries A.D. confirm at least three important facts. **First**, whatever doubts might be raised from late tradition being unreliable as to whether certain apostles endured martyrdom, the testimony of second- and third-generation martyrs indicates that most of the apostles before them died for their testimony. If the students were willing to die for their faith, how much more the teachers?

Further, the voluntary sufferings and deaths of the original eyewitnesses and disciples of Jesus confirm that the basic historical information they passed on was true. If they knew, for example, that Jesus had not performed miracles or had not risen from the dead, because they themselves had stolen the body, what possible motivation would they have had to go out and die martyrs' deaths for spreading these lies?

Second, the continued suffering and martyrdom of second-, third- and fourth-generation Christians confirms that, at the very least, any thinking person would make every possible effort to verify the accuracy of the gospel reports. From the very beginning, such a vast Christian network of multiplication spread out across the empire that it would have been easy enough to verify the historical events of Jesus' life. Even 120 years after the death of Christ, at least one godly Christian, Polycarp, was still living who could verify what some of the original disciples of Jesus had reported.

A **third** fact confirmed by the early reports is that the early Christians considered moral and ethical integrity more important than life itself. These Christians do not appear to be wild-eyed fanatics. Nor are they simply zealously devoted to a particular philosophy of life. They are men and women who, at the very least, are saying by their shed blood, "I cannot deny that Jesus of Nazareth lived, taught and died, and has been raised from the dead to demonstrate that He is Messiah and Lord and God."

CLEMENT OF ROME (Died ca A.D. 102)

He may be the Clement mentioned by Paul in Philippians 4:3. Origen calls him a disciple of the apostles. 23 According to Eusebeus, he was bishop of Rome from A.D. 92 to A.D. 101. Tertullian writes that he was appointed by Peter. Late tradition says he was a martyr, but the earliest writers up to Eusebeus and Jerome mention nothing of it. At the very least he would have felt the pressure of leadership over a *religio illicita,* or unlicensed religion, in the Roman Empire. He would have been the congregation's leader during the persecutions under Domitian. "In striking contrast with the bloody cruelties practiced by Domitian, he exhorts to prayer for the civil rulers, that God 'may give them health, peace, concord, and stability for the administration of the government he has given them.' " 30/2:643

Clement's letter to the Corinthians is the only extant work from him which is accepted as genuine. It was written about A.D. 95 or 96. In it he tells of the martyrdom of Paul and Peter. Significantly, he also quotes from Matthew, Mark, Luke and Acts, as well as 1 Corinthians, 1 Peter, Hebrews, and Titus.

IGNATIUS (Died ca A.D. 117)

On his way to certain martyrdom at Rome, Ignatius wrote seven letters, six to churches and one to his friend, Polycarp. He had been the bishop of the church at Antioch before his arrest and condemnation to death. His letters reflect a victorious faith which looks forward to the opportunity of suffering for Christ. Some details of his martyrdom are questioned, but the fact of his martyrdom is not. Polycarp's report of it around A.D. 135 confirms that he was thrown to the lions in the Colosseum at Rome for the amusement of the people. Tradition calls him a disciple of Peter, Paul and John.

Ignatius writes of a number of historical facts, and quotes from Matthew, John and Acts as well as many of Paul's letters, James and 1 Peter.

POLYCARP (ca A.D. 69–155)

Polycarp, disciple of John, maintained a relentless devotion to Christ and the Scriptures. His famous death as a martyr demonstrated his trust in the accuracy of the Scriptures. He was the chief presbyter (bishop) over the church at Smyrna and the teacher of Irenaeus of Lyons. The account of his martyrdom is given in a letter from the church at Smyrna to other churches. Except for a few insertions, the letter is held by scholars to be genuine and substantially correct in what it reports. At one point it tells of Polycarp being led into the stadium and questioned before the proconsul. The crowds were said to be in a great tumult, hearing that it was "the atheist" Polycarp.

The proconsul demanded that he "swear by the genius of Caesar; repent and say, Away with the Atheists."

Polycarp looked out on the masses, gestured toward them with his hand, and looking up to heaven said, "Away with the atheists." When it was demanded the he revile Christ, Polycarp responded, "Fourscore and six years have I been His servant, and He has done me no wrong. How then can I blaspheme my King who saved me?" After further threats Polycarp responded, "You threaten that fire which burns for a season and after a while is quenched: for you are ignorant of the fire of the future judgment and eternal punishment, which is reserved for the ungodly. But why do you delay? Come, do what you will." 27 At this point Polycarp was burned at the stake and thrust through with a sword.

JUSTIN MARTYR (ca A.D. 100–166)

Born in Flavius Neapolis, formerly Shechem, Justin grew up well educated but ignorant of Moses and Christianity. He called himself a Samaritan. During his early manhood he sought successively to become a Stoic, a Peripatetic, a Pythagorean, and finally a Platonist. When almost convinced of the truth of Platonism, he met a dignified and gentle old Christian man on a walk not far from the coast. He reports that as he investigated the Christian faith, he was moved by the fearless courage of the Christians and their steadfastness in the face of death. After becoming a Christian he became a fearless and energetic defender of the Christian faith at a time when it was most under attack. Schaff judges that as a lay preacher he "accomplished far more for the good of the church than any known bishop or presbyter of his day." 30/2:714 In A.D. 166, along with six others in Rome, he sealed his testimony with his own blood. There he was scourged and beheaded at the instigation of a Cynic philosopher, Crescens, whom he had confronted with the truth of the gospel. 30/2:715

ORIGEN (A.D. 185–ca 254)

Origen lived one of the most intense Christian lives of history. He was born in Egypt and educated by his father, Leonides, probably a rhetorician. While still a boy, Origen had memorized vast portions of Scripture. In A.D. 202 his father was martyred under the persecution of Septimus Severus. Origen wanted to die with his father but was prevented from leaving his house when his mother hid his clothes during the night. Origen went on to a brilliant career as a writer, teacher and preacher. One opponent of his said that he had written six thousand books. Jerome says he wrote more books than others could read. Admittedly many were tracts, letters, and homilies, as well as lectures which others recorded and published. In his writings, he quotes the New Testament more than eighteen thousand times.

Origen, intense defender of the Christian faith, took the words of Jesus literally and seriously. He owned only one set of clothes and no shoes. He took no thought for the morrow. During the persecution of Decius in A.D. 250, Origen was "put in chains and tortured, suffered the experience of the iron collar, was placed in stocks and confined to a dungeon." 24/S.V.

"Origen" He died shortly after—at least a "confessor" if not a martyr.

Twentieth-Century Suffering (E/357-59)

RICHARD WURMBRAND

The Rev. Richard Wurmbrand is an evangelical minister who spent 14 years in communist imprisonment and torture in his homeland of Rumania. He is one of Rumania's most widely known Christian leaders, authors and educators. Few names are better known in his homeland.

In 1945, when the communists seized Rumania and attempted to control the churches for their purposes, Richard Wurmbrand immediately began an effective, vigorous "underground" ministry to his enslaved people and the invading Russian soldiers. He was eventually arrested in 1948, along with his wife Sabina. His wife was a slave-laborer for three years. Richard Wurmbrand spent three years in solitary confinement—seeing no one but his communist torturers. After three years he was transferred to a mass cell for five years, where the torture continued.

Due to his international stature as a Christian leader, diplomats of foreign embassies asked the communist government about his safety. They were told he had fled Rumania. Secret police, posing as released fellow-prisoners, told his wife of attending his burial in the prison cemetery. His family in Rumania and his friends abroad were told to forget him since he was now dead.

After eight years he was released and promptly resumed his work with the underground church. Two years later, in 1959, he was re-arrested and sentenced to 25 years in prison.

Mr. Wurmbrand was released in a general amnesty in 1964, and again continued his underground ministry. Realizing the great danger of a third imprisonment, Christians in Norway negotiated with the communist authorites for his release from Rumania. The communist government had begun "selling" their political prisoners. The going price for a prisoner was $1,900. Their price for Wurmbrand was $10,000.

In May, 1966, he testified in Washington before the Senate's Internal Security Subcommittee and stripped to the waist to show 18 deep torture wounds covering his body. His story was carried across the world in newspapers in the United States, Europe and Asia. Wurmbrand was warned in September, 1966, that a decision had been made by the communist regime of Rumania to assassinate him. Yet he is not silent in the face of these death threats. He has been called "the voice of the Underground Church." Christian leaders have called him "a living martyr" and "the Iron Curtain Paul." 40/5,6

The following is an excerpt from Wurmbrand's book, *Tortured for Christ.*

A pastor by the name of Florescu was tortured with red-hot iron pokers and with knives. He was beaten very badly. Then starving rats were driven into his cell through a large pipe. He could not sleep, but had to defend himself all the time. If he rested a moment, the rats would attack him.

He was forced to stand for two weeks, day and night. The communists wished to compel him to betray his brethren, but he resisted steadfastly. In the end, they brought his 14-year-old son and began to whip the boy in front of his father, saying that they would continue to beat him until the pastor said what they wished him to say. The poor man was half mad. He bore it as long as he could.

When he could not stand it any more, he cried to his son; "Alexander, I must say what they want! I can't bear your beating any more!"

The son answered, "Father, don't do me the injustice to have a traitor as a parent. Withstand! If they kill me, I will die with the words, 'Jesus and my fatherland.' "

The communists, enraged, fell upon the child and beat him to death, with blood spattered over the walls of the cell. He died praising God. Our dear brother Florescu was never the same after seeing this. 40/36

Missionaries to the Auca Indians

On January 8, 1956, the whole world was stunned by the word that a band of Auca Indians, the fiercest of Ecuador's aborigines, had fatally speared an American missionary pilot, Nate Saint, and his four co-workers, Jim Elliot, Roger Youderian, Ed McCully and Peter Fleming. After official investigation confirmed the tragedy, Ecuadorian troops and missionaries serving adjoining tribes formed an expedition upriver to bury the victims. They found the plane demolished, its fabric torn to shreds.

The pilot was my brother. He and his companions were engaged in what has since become known as "Operation Auca," a mission to carry the gospel of Jesus Christ to this unlettered, Stone Age tribe in the fastnesses of the Amazon.

Through one miracle after another, as told in *The Dayuma Story,* all five killers confessed Christ as Savior. I believe it is significant that the first to believe among the Auca men were the five living killers—Kimo, Minkayi, Gikita, Dyuwi and Nimonga. When the first baptismal service was held in Tiwaeno, a little more than two years after our entry into the tribe, four of the five were baptized. The fifth was in the second group of baptisms. In this case my brother Phil did the baptizing. Each of the wives also opened her heart to the Lord Jesus Christ and received baptism. 29

Reverend Joon Gon Kim

The Rev. Joon Gon Kim is director of Korean Campus Crusade for Christ.

Dr. Kim's experience with the communists has been personal and tragic. When campus srikes broke out in Korea in 1950, Communists swept over all the colleges except one Christian university. Well over 70 percent of the students were in favor of Communism. Thousands of them were financially supported on the campuses by the Russian Communists. These turned out to be the active leaders during the Korean War.

Dr. Kim says, "One night I was awakened by the noise of men calling my name. My family and I were taken where 60 human beings, including the old, and women and children, were being killed. Ten military men, all familiar villagers, were assigned to execute my family. My wife and father were slaughtered before my eyes. I was beaten and left for dead."

Kim survived the savage beating of the Communists, and asked God to give him a love for the souls of his enemies. Kim led 30 of the Communists to Christ, including the leader responsible for the death of his loved ones.

Dr. Kim has first-hand knowledge that Jesus Christ is the answer to Communism, as He is the answer to every other problem in life. 18

CHAPTER 45 *Still Changing Lives*

(E/329-57)

The following testimonies of men and women from all walks of life demonstrate the unity of Christian experience. While each one embraces a different background, profession or culture, each points to the same object as the source of new power for transformed lives—Jesus Christ. Multiply these testimonies by the hundreds of thousands and you would begin to approach something like the impact Christ has had on the world in the past two thousand years.

Is the Christian experience valid? These and millions more believe so, and have new lives to back up their statement.

POLICEMAN, Melvin Floyd

"I've been on both sides of the fence: a gang member as well as a policeman. I have seen tragedy, permanent injury, property damage, wasted lives and even death as a result of sin.

"My whole outlook on life has changed since Christ came into my life and, being a Christian policeman, I view things much differently. In all my duties I am constantly aware that I must share God's wonderful plan of salvation with others as I continue 'on patrol for God.' "

Melvin Floyd was voted by the National Jaycees as one of 1969's "Ten Outstanding Young Men in America." 25

NAZI PILOT IN WORLD WAR II, Werner Moelders

Moelders was a colonel in the Luftwaffe, ace of all Germany's aces, holder of the highest decoration his country awards her fighters—the Knight's Cross of the Iron Cross, with Oak Leaves and Diamonds.

He climbed from his riddled plane; his eyes were glassy; his frozen hands trembled; his body still shook with emotion. Werner Moelders had looked on the face of Death, and he was changed. In those terrible moments, almost unknown to himself, he had whispered: "God, God Almighty in heaven—help me out of this. YOU alone can save me!" His words had echoed in the cockpit of the plane—"Only God can help . . . "

Back in his quarters, Moelders shut himself up alone. He had to have time to think. Clearly, faith in Hitler and Naziism could not sustain him. His mind flew back to his home in Stettin, to his godly parents, to the kindly pastor. He remembered the story of the cross and the redeeming love of God in Christ Jesus, who died for sinners like him. And he knew he could never have survived that dreadful danger out there if he had not called on the everlasting God. Fear had taught him faith.

Now, freed forever from the nightmare of Naziism, he felt relieved, happy; a sense of the reality of God filled his heart with peace. He sat down and wrote out his thoughts in a letter to the Stettin pastor . . .

Day after day Moelders spoke with his comrades about his faith and about the love of God in Christ Jesus. But that did not suit his masters. In a mysterious accident Germany's famous Number 1 ace was killed—silenced forever, the Nazi leaders thought . . .

The Gestapo went into action against the faithful friends of Moelders who copied and distributed his letter. A reward of $40,000 was offered to anyone who would denounce a friend who believed what Moelders believed and passed on his letter. 8/22-25

FORMER CRIMINAL, Leo D'Arcangelo

Pacing back and forth in his prison cell, Leo D'Arcangelo was deeply disturbed. Who wouldn't be, facing what was ahead of him?

As a boy of eleven, he had picked a lady's handbag on a crowded trolley car. That was the start.

Five years of stealing followed before his first arrest at sixteen in a Philadelphia department store.

Shortly after release he started mainlining heroin. Then began the seemingly endless arrests: November, 1954, for use and possession of drugs; January, 1955, for picking pockets. Shortly after, in Los Angeles,

Leo was arrested for jumping bail.

. . . As he paced his cell he noticed a few lines crudely scrawled on the wall:

> "When you come to the end of your journey
> and this trouble is racked in your mind,
> and there seems no other way out than by just mourning,
> turn to Jesus, for it is Him that you must find."

This started him thinking: *This is the end of my journey. What have I got to show for it? Nothing except a lousy past and a worse future. Jesus, I need Your help. I've made a mess of my life and this is the end of the journey, and all the crying isn't going to change my past. Jesus, if You can change my life, please do it. Help me make tomorrow different.*

. . . For the first time Leo felt something besides despair.

Released from prison in September 1958, Leo earned his high school diploma and then went on to graduate from West Chester State College and the Reformed Episcopal Seminary in Philadelphia.

He is presently active in prison work and as a speaker in church and youth meetings. 17

MINISTER, Dr. Don E. Schooler

"In my first two churches I preached all that I knew, honesty, faith (not knowing what it meant), good habits, church attendance, honor, and a continual exhortation to be 'good,' to serve God. I talked about the fruits without knowing the roots. Enthusiasm carried me in those days—enthusiasm and youth. These two proved not to be enough.

"The marriage was getting difficult. My wife believed one thing. I believed another. We decided to study Jesus, without any helps of any kind, which we did with a small group for seven weeks in Canada. . . . It began to dawn upon me that if I would put my will into God's hands . . . this would be equal to doing God's will. . . . I was committing myself to all of God I could see in Jesus, plus all of God that would be revealed tomorrow and the next day and the next. . . . The light broke upon me. I wept like a child calling out to my wife: 'I have missed it. Utterly missed it.' All these years I had preached only ethics, social and personal, but not the gospel. . . . The gospel is the living Christ who has come to dwell in me. He has liberated me. He assured me my sins were forgiven. . . . There was a new center for all my social passion—it is not centered in human striving—it is centered in Christ. . . . Power in some measure has come." 16/125-27

COACH—DALLAS COWBOYS, Tom Landry

"St. Augustine said, 'Thou hast made us for Thyself, O God, and our hearts are restless until they find their rest in Thee.'

"Well, I discovered that truth at the age of 33. The most disappointing fact in my life, I believe, is that I waited so long before I discovered the fellowship of Jesus Christ. How much more wonderful my life would have been if I had taken this step many years earlier!" 14

GOLFER, Rik Massengale

In 1974, professional golfer Rik Massengale was ready to exchange his clubs for farmer's overalls. Life, like his golf game, had lost its zip. Massengale contemplated leaving the sport to go into the dairy business.

Thin from the strain of the Professional Golfers Association tour, his marriage beginning to sour, Massengale suffered through his fifth season, a year in which his earnings dipped to $14,193.

But one night at home with his wife Cindy, Rik began to watch *The Greatest Story Ever Told,* a movie on the life of Christ. The Massengales' lives—and Rick's erratic golf game—underwent a dramatic change thereafter.

"We started questioning and decided to go to the Bible study on the tour," recalls Massengale, a former University of Texas star. Evangelist Billy Graham was the guest speaker the first night they attended.

"I realized afterward that intellectually I had always believed Christ was the Son of God," Rik says. "That week, after Graham spoke, I asked Christ to come into my life."

With a new outlook on life, Massengale began to play like a new golfer. "Before, if I blew a shot, I'd be torn up inside. Now Christ has given me self-control and peace. A bogey is no longer the end of the world."

Since Massengale's spiritual and mental turnabout, he has captured several tournament titles, including the 1977 Bob Hope Desert Classic. In the Hope Classic, he broke Arnold Palmer's longstanding record by one stroke with a 23-under-par 337. The win boosted him high among the tour's top money winners. 21/38

TENNIS PLAYER, Stan Smith

"I began meeting with a group of athletes at the University of Southern California. These were different guys than I had known before—and they told me about a Person who was very new and exciting to me—Jesus Christ. Toward the end of that year, I put my life into His hands. I asked Him to give my life more meaning. He helped me find myself and He gave me self-confidence.

"My frustration seemed to drain off. I was confident again.

"Christ helped me win over myself. It's so clear to me now why in all things I must be the mirror of His teachings." 33/22-23

FOOTBALL PLAYER, Roger Staubach

"My future reaches far beyond football, of course, and this is what really excites me. Christianity is the most important part of my life and I'll always speak out about it. I am fortunate to have been blessed with certain talents and skills and they are the reason I have become a public figure, in a position to attract attention and be heard. I would be rejecting God's love and blessings if I didn't use my opportunities to the utmost, to talk about my faith, and why it is precious to me. To enjoy something beautiful like this to the fullest, you must share it." 35/274-75

MISS AMERICA 1973, Terry Meeuwsen Camburn

"From the time I was a small child, I dreamed of being a professional singer and actress and seeing my name up on a marquee. After a year of college, I had my first chance to sing with a small group in nightclubs throughout the Midwest. On the road I was hit with a lot of things that I wasn't prepared to handle: alcoholism, bad marriages and a lot of lonely people who were trying to escape reality.

"Then in 1970, I joined the New Christy Minstrels. But I was disillusioned with this experience, too, as we performed 50 weeks out of the year under all kinds of conditions. Still, I became increasingly determined that, if I had to scratch my way to the top, I would.

"This all changed after a performance at a Baptist college in Kansas. During the concert, the kids would clap every time we mentioned anything about God or Jesus Christ. I thought they were crazy at the time, but afterward, at a drive-in, one of the Christian students came up and started talking to me.

"We small-talked about show business and life on the road for awhile. Then she asked me a question that no one had ever asked me in my 22 years: 'Are you a Christian?' When I replied that I believed in God, she said, 'No, you don't understand,' and briefly explained about God's love and His desire to have a relationship with me through Jesus Christ.

"She gave me a Four Spiritual Laws booklet and told me to read it that night so we could talk about it over breakfast the next morning. I was willing to do that because I saw that she had a peace that I didn't have and was looking for. I started to just skim the booklet until I noticed how brief and to the point it was. Before I knew it, I was reading the suggested prayer at the end and asking God to forgive me and give me the peace that I'd never found in show business.

"The next day, the Christian girl showed genuine excitement about my decision and more love for me personally than I'd seen in a long time. And as our group was about to leave, she gave me a Bible and said, 'I don't care how busy you get—if you read a chapter a day, I promise you your life will change.'

"And it did. I began to realize that Jesus was someone who understood me and my insecurities and feelings about show business. Specific things changed in my life, too. I was very overweight at the time and smoked a pack and a half of cigarettes a day. That changed, and with it changed the low self-image I'd always had.

"Soon after I left the Christies, I found myself back home in DePere, Wisconsin, with no money and no way to get the professional training I needed to sing and act. That's when a friend of mine encouraged me to enter the Miss America pageant—even though I was feeling 'old' at 22. She argued that, because it was a good, clean program, I wouldn't have to compromise what I believed in and might even win the scholarship I needed.

"From that point on, God began opening doors, working out His plan for my life. That plan included becoming Miss America 1973. Then, during my reign, God worked more changes—in my outlook on my career and future. I realized that, though I'd been praying for God's direction in my career, I wasn't really listening for *His* answers. Now I understand that my first responsibility is to God, my second is to my husband (Tom) and children as they come. After that I can begin to think about a career.

"It's funny how God has also given me a desire to conform to His will. He still may lead me into a full-time career—just as He's led me to put out a gospel album and begin writing a book. Only now my motivation is different. I don't care about being in the limelight anymore—because I've found that the only lasting things we do are the things we do for Christ."
4/15-16

MOVIE ACTOR, Dean Jones

"I had attained many of my goals. I had a beautiful lady who loved me, three wonderful kids, a $23,000 Ferrari, a garage crowded with four racing motorcycles, a California avocado ranch, and I made between $15,000 and $20,000 a week when I was working on films. Yet there was no sense of fulfillment.

"In frustration I had driven my Ferrari at 100-plus miles per hour over the winding Malibu Canyon roads at night, not with any desire to kill myself, but with a feeling that if I did lose control of the car, so what? No great loss. I really played with the line at which the car could stay glued to the pavement around the curves."

He once took a motorcycle trip with two friends into Mexico's Baja Peninsula, miles from civilization. They stopped to buy some beer from an incredibly poor Mexican family. Dean gave a machete to an old man and a pair of levis to one of the young men. But what really shook him was a little girl with open sores on her face. Flies were all over her, picking at the sores.

"I was so angry that I jumped on my bike and opened up the throttle wide—too wide for the rough terrain," Dean says. "With total abandon, I cursed God and screamed out at the wind, 'God, if You exist, which I doubt, why do You let little children go through that kind of misery?'

"Tears blinded my eyes. The last thing I remember was a small gully ahead of me. It triggered the thought, *Twist that throttle and get that front wheel up!*

"I didn't make it. When I came to, one of my friends had his fist in my hip, trying to stop me from bleeding to death. The rear foot peg of the cycle had shot through my hip, shattering my pelvis in 13 places. I had a brain concussion (with partial amnesia) and a separated right shoulder. In addition, almost every inch of my body was sandpapered by the desert floor. I lay there in shock for a day and a half before arrangements could be made to transport me to a hospital in Burbank."

All of this hopelessness came to a head the summer of 1973 in Cherry Hill, New Jersey, when Dean was doing a stage production of *1776*.

"I felt so empty that I went to the lodge one night and stood at the window gazing out at the sumptuous landscape," he says.

"I realized I had been motivated by self all my years. But I had come to the point where self could no longer carry me through life. There would come a time when I would not have enough motivation to stay alive. I might even take a shotgun to the top of my head like Ernest Hemingway. I turned from the window, walked to the edge of the bed, knelt and began to pray.

" 'God, You probably don't exist. I'm probably just talking to the walls here, but . . . '

"I began to pour out my doubts, weaknesses, failures to God. I wept like a child.

"Finally I said something like, 'If You do exist, if You are real, and if You will make Yourself known to me in some way, I'll serve You the rest of my life.' It was a total commitment.

"Suddenly my soul was flooded with a peace that passed understanding. It filled that emptiness. It was as though Bambi, the little deer in the forest, heard everything go silent. The birds stopped singing, the crickets stopped chirping, and all the other sounds just ended. There was such a silence that it became something I listened to. I listened to the calm. I had an inner spirit without agitation or anxiety."

At the time, Dean didn't fully understand what had happened to him, but he and Lory . . . began searching for a church. Finally God led them to one in the San Fernando Valley, and February 10, 1974, both he and Lory publicly confessed their faith in Jesus Christ. 38/16*ff*.

SINGER, B. J. Thomas

By 1970 he had made $13 million. By 1976, despite his success in selling more than 32 million records, including the hit recording, "Raindrops Keep

Falling on My Head," B. J. Thomas was $800,000 in debt.

His life was bankrupt in more ways than financial. In spite of his successful singing career, for years B. J. was about as miserable as a man could be. He was a drug addict with a $3,000-a-week cocaine habit. In addition, he was so hooked on uppers and downers that he was taking 40 to 50 pills at a time just to keep going.

"At 15, I started in music and almost immediately I got involved with drugs," Thomas said.

"Eleven years later," Thomas added, "I was an addict. I couldn't go to sleep without it. I couldn't do anything without it."

Thomas was so doped up he barely remembers recording his 1969 hit, "Raindrops." And its success helped catapult him even deeper into drugs. Cocaine was ruling his life. His marriage was broken and he could barely function.

Once he took 80 pills and was taken unconscious off a plane in Hawaii. He was rushed to a hospital. He almost died of the overdose, and at the time he didn't care if he died or not.

When he came to he asked the sister attending him in the Catholic hospital if "it had been close."

She said, "Very close," and told him he had been on the machine for an hour and 40 minutes, which was the only reason he pulled through.

"I don't understand why I made it," he told the nurse. "I really didn't want to make it."

She asked him to bow his head and she prayed for him. She said, "God must have something He wants to do with your life."

On a later tour he realized that he was losing his mind. When his brother and his road man—the people who loved him—looked at him in pity he hated them. "I wanted to kill them," said Thomas. "In fact, I was afraid I would."

B. J. became so saturated with drugs he couldn't sleep for days. He could not get high. There was nothing he could do to get that euphoric feeling any more. In desperation he called his wife, Gloria. He thought maybe if he went home he could get a little sleep there.

"We had separated several times over the years," Thomas explained, "because I was acting so crazy." But lately when he had called he had sensed a peace and calmness coming from Gloria on the phone. She had asked him to come home, saying, "There's help here," but she would not explain what the help was . . .

When he arrived he found his wife had become a Christian and that there were a lot of people praying for him and wanting to talk to him about the Lord.

"That was the last thing I wanted to do," Thomas said. But one evening his wife got him to drop by the home of the friends who had led her to the Lord.

The husband, Jim Reeves, was gone, but the wife asked them to stay for dinner. With the husband away B. J. felt safe from religious talk, and they stayed. "I felt such peace in that home," B. J. said, "that I knew they must know God. When Jim came home I asked him about it, and he began to tell me about the Lord.

"Jim Reeves told me that as he talked with me there was something about me, or about my face or eyes that frightened him," B. J. said. "He could tell I wanted to listen, but one minute I was receptive and the next minute I was not. The strangeness startled him. He asked if he could pray for a minute. He bowed his head right there at the dining room table, and asked that if there were any forces of Satan or any power of Satan in that room that were interfering with B. J. hearing the word of God that by the shed blood of Jesus Christ they would leave."

"As he prayed," B. J. related, "there was a disturbance in my chest. I felt for a minute a sharp pain and I thought I might have a broken rib. Then I had the illusion that something was 'just going' and a peace came over me. I had a receptive attitude and I listened intently to all they told me. Then I put my head down and began to pray. I prayed for about 20 minutes, and I prayed all the good things they told me I should pray.

"When I raised my head these guys were crying, and I was so happy I was just jumping around. That conversion experience to me was just a miraculous thing. I had been such a bad person."

What happened that night caused a mental change and a physical change in B. J. Thomas. He had some marijuana, but he went home and threw it away. He had been dependent upon valium for years. He needed that more than all the other pills. But that night he stopped taking it.

B. J. expected terrible withdrawal pains. He was willing to go through it. He had done so before, but had always gone back to drugs. But this time he went through no withdrawal symptoms: no shakes, no bad illusions or dreams. His deliverance from drugs was just as miraculous as his salvation and from that day, January 29, 1976, to this, he has never doubted his experience with the Lord or that his salvation was real. 39/1,34

AUTHOR, Eugenia Price

"At the age of thirty-three, I had almost lost interest in finding the key to why I am here. My study of the philosophies had stimulated my mind but had left my heart empty. My study of many of the religions of the world left me exhausted. I knew that somehow I didn't have enough desire to 'know righteousness,' to go through the elaborate intellectual and spiritual gyrations required by them to 'reach God.'

"My life was won by Ellen Riley, a childhood friend whom I saw again while in Charleston after those 18 years. Ellen had become a dynamic Christian. Christ was a Person to her. She was home from New York City on her vacation at the same time I was there from Chicago. When she saw me again she was horrified to see the girl she had known as a bubbling, happy teenager, now a tired, bored, would-be sophisticate. She said I looked as though I was warding off a blow.

" ' . . . What do you really believe about God?' I asked her.

" 'I believe God came to earth in the Person of Jesus Christ to show us what He is really like and to save us from sin.'

" . . . And so, on Sunday afternoon, October 2, 1949, after quite an argument on my part I just suddenly looked at her and said: 'Okay, I guess you're right.' And that was it. God doesn't require any big, formal introduction.

"Since then, day by day, life with Christ has been a continuous experience of one new discovery after another. Now I like to get up in the morning. He is my reason for waking up!" 28/6-7

MEDICAL DOCTOR, Vernon R. Phillips

"After the war, I started general practice in the Harrisburg, Pennsylvania, area. I was introduced to a social life that I thought necessary to be successful. This included frequent cocktail parties and country club dances. I thought this was fine, because I relaxed from the problems of the day and got away from reality for short periods.

"By 1952 I had to do more relaxing by attending parties two and three times a week. Before this time I would have considered myself a heavy drinker, but now my drinking became uncontrollable.

"I suffered a decline in my medical practice, and worst of all, the loss of the respect of my wife and family. I finally admitted my desperate need of help.

" . . . A brother of mine had trusted Christ as his Savior a year earlier. He invited me one day to go along with him to a banquet of the Christian Business Men's Committee. At this meeting I heard testimonies in which men told how their lives had been changed. One man had had a life quite similar to mine, until Christ transformed him.

" . . . These men were different from the men I was associating with, and they were willing to help me when I was in serious trouble. Greatest of all, they told me my need was knowing the Lord Jesus Christ.

" . . . On May 21, 1959, while on a business trip, I was under deep conviction as I drove along. I prayed to God to save me. I realized that I was lost and needed God's help. But it was not until I said, 'Anything You want me to do, Lord, I will do,' that I could believe, and the indescribable experience occurred. Tears of joy ran down my cheeks as the tremendous load of sin was lifted. God gave me the assurance that I was a new creature in Christ Jesus. I have not been tempted since to take another drink of alcohol. My main problem was not alcoholism, but that I did not know Jesus Christ." 11/65-69

FORMER WHITE HOUSE AIDE, Charles Colson

"I felt a strange deadness when I left the White House. I should have been exhilarated because I'd done all the things I'd ever set out to do, and in a hurry. I'd gone to law school nights, worked days, earned scholarships, been the youngest company commander in the Marine Corps, and the youngest administrative assistant on Capitol Hill. I had gotten to the top of the mountain and I couldn't think of any other mountains.

"And then I saw Tom Phillips, an old friend. He's a guy much like myself in that he was born to immigrant parents, he went to school nights, he became an engineer at Raytheon when he was twenty-five and by age thirty-six was executive vice president. By age forty, he was president—a tremendous success story. A busy, frantic worker, barking orders, very aggressive, very dynamic.

"When I saw him in the spring of '73, he seemed totally different. He was smiling; he was radiant, caring about me. I asked him what had happened. He told me he'd committed his life to Jesus Christ.

"I'd . . . learned about Jesus Christ as an historical figure, a prophet, a cut above His time. But the whole idea of an intelligent, educated, successful businessman saying, 'I've accepted Him and committed my life,' just threw me. I thought Tom had had some sort of strange experience—I changed the subject.

"The months went by, very tough months in Washington. And everything that Tom represented, Washington wasn't. I marveled at it and wanted to find out for myself, so I called him and spent an evening on his porch. He read to me from C. S. Lewis' *Mere Christianity,* the chapter on pride. It was a torpedo. I could just see my whole life. I felt unclean. Then Tom told me he had had a real spiritual longing until he went to a Billy Graham rally in New York and accepted Christ.

"It was such a beautiful story, but I wouldn't admit it to him. I was the big-time Washington lawyer.

"That night I couldn't get the keys into the ignition because I was crying so hard. I didn't like to cry because I never liked to show weakness. I prayed in the car, and thought. It was sort of an eerie feeling sitting by the side of the road alone, and yet not alone now. There was a tremendous cleansing feeling that night. Then I spent a week on the Maine Coast, and later that week, the case for Christ became obvious to me.

"My biggest problem had always been the intellectual reservations. I knew there was a God, but I could never see how man could have a personal relationship with Him. But the intellectual case for Christianity became powerful to me after reading *Mere Christianity.* At the end of the week I could not imagine how you could not believe in Jesus Christ." **32/n.p.**

FORMER PRESIDENT OF THE
U. N. GENERAL ASSEMBLY, Charles Malik

"Having fully realized that the whole world is as it were dissolving before our very eyes, it is impossible then to ask more far-reaching questions than these three: What is then emerging? Where is Christ in it? And what difference are we making to the whole thing?

"In one word: the life of the spirit is life in Jesus Christ. In Him and through Him we can raise and answer these three fundamental questions. In Him and through Him we can be saved from the universal dissolution of the world.

"These are great days and what is being decided in them is absolutely historic. But all these things are going to pass, and with them life itself. What, then, is the life that does not pass? What, then, is life eternal? This is the first and last question. I believe that 'this is life eternal, that they might know Thee the only true God, and Jesus Christ, whom Thou has sent' (John 17:3). . . . Faith in Jesus Christ is the first and last meaning of our life. I do not care who or what you are; I put only one question to you: Do you believe in Jesus Christ?" **20/32-35**

Dr. Charles Malik served as President of the United Nations General Assembly in 1959. He is now a professor at The American University in Beirut, Lebanon.

PHILOSOPHER, Cyril E. M. Joad

Dr. Cyril E. M. Joad, head of the philosophy department of the University of London . . . believed that Jesus was only a man, that God was a part of the universe and that, should the universe be destroyed, God would be destroyed. He believed that there is no such thing as sin, that man was destined for Utopia; that given a little time, man would have heaven on earth.

In 1948, in the magazine section of the *Los Angeles Times,* there was a picture of that venerable old scholar, and with it was a statement concerning the dramatic change that had taken place in his life. He told how for many years he had been antagonistic toward Christianity. Now he had come to believe that sin was a reality.

Two world wars and the imminence of another had demonstrated conclusively to him that man was sinful. Now he believed that the only explanation for sin was found in the Word of God, and the only solution was found in the cross of Jesus Christ. Before his death, Dr. Joad became a zealous follower of the Savior. **3/2-3**

PSYCHOLOGIST, Ruda

The professor was too polite to say that the landlord had warned him about his Protestant neighbor. "He is a very zealous Protestant," the owner of the apartment building had said. "He will try to convert you."

Professor Ruda's face then had creased with a soft Latin smile. "Let him. I will match wits with him. Perhaps I can convert him to be a freethinker like me. No?"

The Professor felt that he had little to fear from a zealous Protestant. He knew something about religion and psychology himself. Had he not been raised in the Catholic faith, even though he no longer accepted the old dogmas? He had his doctorate in psychology and was professor of logic and researcher in psychology in the Argentine University of the South. His major field of study and teaching was in personality development. *Perhaps,* he thought, *I will learn something by analyzing the personality of a Protestant missionary.*

After attending the missionary's church and after exchanging beliefs hoping to show him his error, Ruda finally made the decision for Christ. He explains it his way:

"As a research psychologist in the field of personality development I analyzed hundreds of people. I sought to discover the inner motivation which governs the basic attitudes of living.

"But when I met Charles Campbell I knew that here was someone whose personality I could not rationally explain. Then when I became a Christian I understood that the life-changing ingredient in his life was Christ. Today, the most important proof to me of Christianity is the amazing change that has come into my own life. Peace and confidence in God have taken the place of anxiety and worry. My troubles increased when I became a Christian, but Christ gave me power to have victory over all of them." 15/59-64

UNIVERSITY LECTURER, Carsten Thiede

"From the beginning of my time at school I was very interested in religion. I read many of the major religious writings of mankind, including the Bible, the Koran, the Bhagavad-Gita (Hindu) and the Tao Te Ching (Taoism), wanting to make up my own mind, to form my personal opinion from an intellectual point of view as to what I would believe.

"In 1966 Billy Graham held a Crusade in Berlin, and along with 10,000-15,000 other people, I sat in a large hall and listened as he explained the Jesus Christ of the Bible. As he spoke, I realized that all of my attempts to form a personal opinion were a preparation for this very moment when I needed to confess my sins and give myself to Christ. From my own readings and Dr. Graham's message, I was able to judge that the gospel of Jesus Christ was the real truth for me.

"At first I did not regard the other religions as false, believing that they might have *part* of the truth or have another way of expressing the truth. But later, as I continued my studies in comparative literature at the Universities of Berlin and Geneva, I realized that there is *no* alternative to the historical truth of the resurrection of Jesus Christ. Under the most careful scrutiny, no scientist, no historian, no literacy critic, if he is honest to his science, will be able to deny the basic truth of the gospel of the New Testament. No other religion or philosophy of mankind can claim this kind of historical support.

"There are hardly any universities now where true Christian belief is taught. Modern German theologians and philosophers claim to use objective methods of literacy analysis in determining that much of the New Testament is legendary. But as I compare the writings of these critics, I find that they are working with pre-formed biases, leaving out any historical truth which might contradict their own beliefs.

"I believe it can be shown that everything written in the New Testament has historical and literary proof to back it up. I would like to introduce a Christian method of analyzing literature, mainly to provide students with an alternative to common methods of interpreting literature (positivism, structuralism, new criticsm, existentialism, etc.). It seems like a mammoth task, but it is not merely I trying to do it, but Christ working in me, giving me the ideas.

"Through the years I have grown stronger and more certain of my beliefs. My desire to find the truth through the examination of various religions and philosophies was satisfied in the words and person of Jesus Christ. Within myself I am certain that my faith is based on facts that can never be proved false." 37/11

Carsten Thiede is assistant lecturer in German and Comparative Literature at the University of Geneva.

FORMER GANG LEADER, Nicky Cruz

This excerpt from Nicky Cruz's autobiography, *Run Baby Run,* tells of his conversion:

"Wilkerson was speaking again. He said something about repenting for your sin. I was under the influence of a power a million times stronger than any drug. I was not responsible for my movements, actions or words. It was as though I had been caught in a wild torrent of a rampaging river. I was powerless to resist. I didn't understand what was taking place within me. I only knew the fear was gone.

"Wilkerson was speaking again. 'He's here! He's in this room. He's come especially for you. If you want your life changed, now is the time.' Then he shouted with authority: 'Stand up! Those who will receive Jesus Christ and be changed—stand up! Come forward!'

"I felt Israel stand to his feet. 'Boys, I'm going up. Who's with me?'

"I was on my feet; I turned to the gang and waved them on with my hand. 'Let's go.' There was a spontaneous movement out of the chairs and toward the front. More than 25 of the Mau Maus responded. Behind us about 30 boys from other gangs followed our example.

" . . . I wanted to be a follower of Jesus Christ.

"I . . . was happy, yet I was crying. Something was taking place in my life that I had absolutely no control over . . . and I was happy about it."

Since his conversion and subsequent college training, Nicky has spent almost every weekend criss-crossing the United States, sharing his faith in Jesus Christ with the youth of America.

One year in city-wide crusades, church services, high school and college assemblies and other meetings, Nicky spoke to over 200,000 young people. 7/126-27

DEATH ROW PRISONER, Ernest Gaither

"I'm a Negro, just 23 years of age, but I'm ready to go, you see. Why, if my number were up this very minute, I'd be ready to meet God. I'm really happy. Just this week I had a dream that I'll carry with me to the chair. I was on my way to heaven. Jesus was with me. But I was taking four steps to His two. He asked me why I was going so fast. I told Him I was eager to get there. Then I was there, surrounded by numerous angels.

"Some folks might think that's strange talk from a man who came to jail an atheist. But that's just the way I feel. You'll understand better when I tell you how I met God early one morning.

"Not long after I was placed behind the bars last March 23, a woman of my own race—Mrs. Flora Jones, of Olivet Baptist Church—invited me to attend a prisoner's gospel service. I was playing cards with some other fellows at the time and laughed at her. 'Why, I don't even believe there's a God,' I boasted, and went on playing cards, the woman still pleading with me. Actually I felt so sinful, that I didn't want to know about God even if He existed—so I ignored her.

"Suddenly, something she was saying caught my attention. 'If you don't believe in God,' she called from outside the bars, 'just try this little experiment. Before you go to sleep tonight ask Him to awaken you at any time; then ask Him to forgive you your sins.' She had real faith. It got ahold of me.

"I didn't go to the service but I remembered the experiment. 'God,' I mumbled as I lay on my cot, 'wake me up at 2:45 if You're real.'

"Outside it was wintery. Windows on the inside were frosted. For the first few hours I slept soundly, then my sleep became restless. Finally, I was wide awake. I was warm and sweating, although the cell was cool. All was quiet except for the heavy breathing of several prisoners and the snoring of a man near by. Then I heard footsteps outside my cell. It was a guard, making his regular check. As he was passing, I stopped him. 'What time is it?' I asked.

"He looked at his pocket watch. 'Fifteen to three.'

" 'That's the same as 2:45, ain't it?' I asked, my heart taking a sudden leap.

"The guard grunted and passed on. He didn't see me climb from my cot and sink to my knees. I don't remember just what I told God but I asked Him to be merciful to me, an evil murderer and sinner. He saved me that night I know. I've believed on His Son Jesus ever since.

"I'd promised a whipping to another prisoner the next day. That morning I went to him. He backed off. 'I don't want to fight you; you used to be a boxer,' he said.

" 'I don't want to fight,' I said. 'I just came to see you.' Several prisoners had gathered for a fight and were disappointed.

"But God had saved me from my sins—why should I want to fight? Later it was whispered around that I was putting on an act, trying to get out of going to the chair.

"My case did later come up before the Illinois Supreme Court, but they upheld the death sentence. Sure, that jolted me some, but I haven't lost faith in God. I know He will go with me. So, you see, I'm really not afraid."

(Pete Tanis, then a prison-gate missionary from Chicago's Pacific Garden Mission, takes up the story here and describes Ernest Gaither's last hours on earth.)

"I was admitted to Ernest's cell about an hour before midnight. The atmosphere seemed charged and guards who stood about his cell kept talking to keep his mind off the midnight journey. But things they said were strained and meaningless, like the things you say when you don't know what to say.

"As I entered, Ernest smiled and greeted me. A Negro chaplain was reading with him from the Bible. He gave me the Book and asked me to read. I selected the first chapter of Philippians. Ernest leaned forward intently as I read:

" 'For to me to live is Christ, and to die is gain . . . For I am in a strait betwixt two, having a desire to depart, and to be with Christ; which is far better.'

" . . . A moment later a black hood was slipped over his head and he began the last mile. At each side were guards, both noticeably nervous. Ernest sensed it: 'What are you fellows shaking for? I'm not afraid.'

"Finally, at 12:03 A.M., the first of three electrical shocks flashed through his body.

"By 12:15 five doctors had paraded up, and one by one, confirmed the death.

"But I knew that the real Ernest Gaither still lived—only his body was dead. As I left the jail, I thought of the verse he liked so well: 'For to me to live is Christ, but to die is gain.' " 1/149-55

FORMER NATIONAL COMMUNIST
YOUTH PRESIDENT OF CZECHOSLOVAKIA, Jan Chelcicky

"At 16 I was an atheist. At 18 I was organizer of Communist Youth in our factory. Now today I had been elected national president of the Communist Youth. I drifted off to sleep and dreamed.

" . . . Out of the sky came a voice: 'Take heed that ye be not deceived; for many shall come in my name, saying, I am Christ . . . and then shall they see the Son of Man coming in a cloud with power and great glory.'

" . . . I awoke with a start. My heart was pounding fiercely. I tried to tell myself it was only a dream. But God's presence was there in the room. Dropping off the side of the bed onto my knees, I prayed, 'Oh, Lord, forgive me. Accept me.'

"I spent the rest of the night in prayer. Then as the first light of dawn appeared, another voice spoke inside me. 'What have you done? You will have to give up everything you worked for. Your former friends will mock you, despise you, persecute you. Turn back now before it is too late.'

"I was full of fear, but inside God said, 'Have no fear; my Spirit shall witness for you.'

" ' . . . I am resigning my functions as your leader for I can no longer be a Communist,' I said.

" 'You are a fool,' they replied. 'Why do you wish to take such stupid action?'

" 'I can no longer follow Marx and Lenin,' I said, 'because I am now a follower of Jesus Christ.'

" . . . Today I am pastor of a small church near the Russian border. If I go to prison, it matters not; for wherever I am I serve Him, and He strengthens me.

"Lenin taught that you change man by changing society. Jesus, however, teaches that you change society by changing man. I serve in God's 'new world order,' introduced by the greatest revolutionary of all time—Jesus Christ." 6

A CONVERT FROM ISLAM, John A. Subhan

Bishop John A. Subhan of the Methodist Episcopal Church at Hyderabad was a convert from Islam. He was born in Calcutta into a well-to-do

Muslim family whose ancestors were of the Moghul race and who had served at the Great Moghul's court.

The new stage originated in a simple event; a Muslim friend gave him a copy of the Gospel. When the same thing had happened a few years earlier, he had torn it to pieces in spite of an unsatisfied longing. This longing, to know and understand the revelation given in Jesus, had never subsided. On the contrary, his close acquaintance with Sufism had intensified it. Now, he decided to study the book. He still considered it corrupt, but he argued that it must contain at least parts of the original revelation. As for its blasphemous contents, surely they could be easily detected and discarded as interpolations or inventions by wicked Christians!

The result of his initial reading was startling. First, he did not find a single blasphemous or Satanic clause, though he had read it with vigilance. Second, his common sense told him that the deliberate corruption of sacred books must have a sufficient motive behind it. His close examination of the Gospel yielded no adequate ground for such an act. The high ethical teaching of the Gospel, for example, bore no mark of tampering; there was no ethic of convenience here. He reached the same conclusion in the study of the Gospel narratives. No disciple would have invented the crucifixion story with its shameful treatment of the founder of Christianity. Even if true, the crucifixion would have been the first thing to be removed or modified. How plainly it refuted the claim that Jesus was the Son of God! This wrestling of the young Muslim with his preconceived ideas of the New Testament is revealing.

His second reading of the Gospel produced a deep conviction that it was the true *Injil,* that it was God's Word and His revelation. The effect of reading the Gospel was markedly different from that produced by the recitation of the Qur'an.

Upon this second reading Subhan decided to become a Christian. He was convinced that Christianity was the only true religion. The conviction and decision are remarkable, for apart from the Gospel he had no knowledge of the Christian faith. All the time he had been moving with Islam. He had no Christian friends; the Gospel was given to him by a Muslim.

He sums up his experience of Christianity in these words: "It is not a mere acceptance of certain beliefs and dogmas, though they are necessary, but essentially it is living in close fellowship with Christ. It is not only a religion to be practiced, but also a life to be lived." 12/51-61

FORMER SATANIST, Anonymous

"My parents were church members, and I had gone to church fairly regularly with them. But it was an empty thing. Jesus Christ was some vague, far-off figure, with little meaning for me. When I asked my parents questions about God, they turned them aside. 'You're a regular question box,' they'd say. 'Just accept it as we do.' I couldn't do that, and as far as I was concerned the church offered nothing.

"I was constantly searching, however, for something to fill the void in my life. At the age of 17 I met a spiritist medium.

" 'The only way to live,' said my new friend, 'is by the cards and your horoscope. Come, let me show you.'

"I was fascinated. She seemed ruled by a strange spirit, and in a trance-like vision she laid out my cards and unfolded to me past happenings with an eerie accuracy. She also demonstrated a strange ability to cure diseases. Often doctors sent patients to her.

" 'Here's a deck of cards,' she offered one day. 'You must always start your day off by laying the cards.' Deftly she laid my cards and showed me how to interpret them. I learned the different combinations and their meanings. Soon I was able to spell out future events, it appeared.

"In the months that followed I found myself controlled more and more by this mysterious woman. Step by step she led me into the spirit world until one day she declared, 'You're one of us now. Will you take the oath?'

"Powerless, I nodded agreement. Hardly knowing what I was doing, I cut my finger and with my own blood wrote, 'I give to thee, O Satan, my heart, body and soul.'

"I now lived completely by the cards and my horoscope. I hardly dared to breathe without first consulting them.

"The devil, who now had claim to my soul, tormented me incessantly. I did things that can't be told publicly. By the age of 19 I was utterly demoralized.

"Melancholy and depression filled me. I had fits of temper. I couldn't concentrate on my nursing work because of the turmoil of soul, and my job suffered.

"In March, 1960, I signed the horoscope chart that forecast I would take my life on July 26. According to the horoscope, my life was no longer of any use. And so on the night of July 25 I wandered the dark streets searching for a way out. I was terrified at the thought of dying.

"Beautiful music penetrated my troubled soul, and I was drawn toward a religious meeting being held in a large tent. Furtively I entered the tent. The music ended and the speaker, Leander Penner of the Greater Europe Mission stood up. 'Tonight I'm going to tell you about the wonderful power of the gospel,' he said.

"I wanted to run, but I was drained of energy. In all my years of churchgoing I had never heard of this Christ—a personal Savior who had died for me personally. Oh, how I longed to break Satan's hold.

" 'Only Christ can break the power of Satan,' the preacher said. He invited the hearers to come forward and confess Christ. I pushed myself to the front and asked: 'Is there hope for a sinner such as I? Preacher, if what you say is true, I want deliverance. Pray for me.'

"The evangelist prayed, and then assured me that Christ could forgive the greatest of sinners if only He is asked. 'For him that cometh to Me I will in no wise cast out,' he quoted from John 6:37.

"But I couldn't ask Christ for help. Each time I tried I felt an invisible hand clutching my throat.

" 'Go home,' the preacher advised me, 'and we'll have a special prayer group for you. Come back tomorrow night.' "

"I wanted to cry: 'But that will be too late!' Fearfully I went home.

"The long night of terror passed. I couldn't sleep; I could only dread the approaching day. Slowly daylight seeped into my room, and I mechanically laid my cards and got ready for work.

"I shuddered as I crossed the river on my way to the hospital; I would soon be down there. I arrived at work and tried once more to escape my tormentor. With trembling finger I dialed the evangelist's number. 'Can you come right over?' I asked. 'It's a matter of life and death.'

"When he came hurrying in I demanded, 'Does your Christ really have power over Satan?'

" 'Yes, of course,' he assured me.

"I handed him the box with my horoscope and the neatly folded pledge of death inside. 'Read it,' I urged. 'If your Christ can't rescue me now, I'll have to jump in the river this afternoon. The time, place, and method have already been picked out for me.'

"Fervently he prayed, and I felt as if I were being torn apart. I twitched and shook uncontrollably. Tears cooled my cheeks. In vain I tried to reach out for Christ. I tried to pray, but an invisible power choked me just as before. 'It's no use, I can't do it,' I cried.

" 'You can't, but Christ can,' came the earnest reply. For a half-hour the preacher prayed, and the battle within me raged. With a violent twist I suddenly threw myself on my knees and beseeched the Lord to take this awful devil obsession from me. Christ's power won, and a feeling of peace flooded my soul. I knew that I could live.

"For a week after that I struggled to get up the courage to live without my occult crutches. At last I apprehensively put them all in a bag and surrendered them to Mr. Penner. Then I began climbing the long road to spiritual stability and serenity. I have had setbacks along the way, and sometimes I feel a sinister presence, but Christ's strength is always sufficient when I ask for it.

"Today, thanks to God's grace, I'm working in a Bible conference center, helping to print and distribute gospel tracts. My daily prayer is, 'Please, Lord, let me be a blessing to someone still bound by Satan.' " 2/68-71

FORMER ATHEIST, Giovanni Papini

Although Giovanni Papini was one of the foremost Italian men of letters, the publication of his *Life of Christ,* in 1921 came as a stunning surprise to many of his friends and admirers. For Papini had been an atheist, a vocal enemy of the Church and a self-appointed debunker of any form of mysticism. A more unlikely source for a reverent portrait of Jesus could hardly be imagined.

What brought about his sudden conversion—so reminiscent of Saul's on the road to Damascus? Like many cynics he was, under the surface, a tormented soul, disgusted with a humanity that could accept the first World War, unable to see hope for better things unless, somehow, the hearts of men could be changed. And he craved, as he later said, 'a crumb of certitude.'

During that war he took his family to live in a mountain village. There, living with the peasants, observing their devotions, something began to happen to him. Sometimes in the evenings, he was asked to read aloud stories from the New Testament. This rediscovery of the Bible, against the background of his own uncertainties, became a revelation to him, and soon he determined to write his own version of the life of Christ. Before long he became convinced that the only power that could change the hearts of men was the teaching of Jesus.

This conviction pervades [Papini's] *Life of Christ,* a book which, in the words of a distinguished critic, "will stand for many years as a rallying sign for thousands making their way painfully to a less inhuman, because a more Christlike, world." 13/8

THE MAN WHO MASTERED 45 LANGUAGES AND DIALECTS, Robert Dick Wilson

The story of Dr. Robert Dick Wilson stands as a remarkable testimony to the reliability of the Bible. Wilson's scholarship, in many ways still unsurpassed, gave the world compelling evidence that the Old Testament is an accurate and trustworthy document. Robert Dick Wilson was born in 1856 in Pennsylvania. In 1886 Wilson received the Doctor's degree. He received training at Western Theological Seminary in Pittsburg, followed by two years in Germany at the University of Berlin.

Upon his arrival in Germany, Professor Wilson made a decision to dedicate his life to the study of the Old Testament. He recounted his decision, "I was twenty-five then; and I judged from the life of my ancestors that I should live to be seventy; so that I should have forty-five years to work. I divided the period into three parts. The first fifteen years I would devote to the study of the languages necessary. For the second fifteen I was going to devote myself to the study of the text of the Old Testament; and I reserved the last fifteen years for the work of writing the results of my previous studies and investigations, so as to give them to the world." Dr. Wilson's plans were carried out almost to the very year he had projected, and his scholastic accomplishments were truly amazing.

As a student in seminary he would read the New Testament in nine different languages including a Hebrew translation which he had memorized syllable for syllable! Wilson also memorized large portions of the Old Testament in the original Hebrew. Incredible as it may seem, Robert Dick Wilson mastered forty-five languages and dialects. Dr. John Walvoord, President of Dallas Theological Seminary, called Dr. Wilson "probably the outstanding authority on ancient languages of the Middle East."

Dr. Wilson commented on his scholastic achievements, relating why he devoted himself to such a monumental task: "Most of our students used to go to Germany, and they heard professors give lectures which were the results of their own labours. The students took everything because the professor said it. I went there to study so that there would be no professor on earth that could lay down the law for me, or say anything without my being able to investigate the evidence on which he said it.

"Now I consider that what was necessary in order to investigate the evidence was, first of all, to know the languages in which the evidence is given. So I . . . determined that I would learn all the languages that throw light upon the Hebrew, and also the languages into which the Bible had been translated down to A.D. 600, so that I could investigate the text myself.

"Having done this I claim to be an expert. I defy any man to make an attack upon the Old Testament on the ground of evidence that I cannot investigate. I can get at the facts if they are linguistic. If you know any language that I do not know, I will learn it."

Wilson challenged other so-called "experts" in the Old Testament field demanding that they prove their qualifications before making statements concerning its history and text. "If a man is called an expert, the first thing to be done is to establish the fact that he is such. One expert may be worth more than a million other witnesses that are not experts. Before a man has the right to speak out about the history, the language, and the paleography of the Old Testament, the Christian church has the right to demand that such a man establish his ability to do so."

Dr. Wilson met his own challenge. For 46 years Wilson had devoted himself to this great task of studying the Old Testament, carefully investigating the evidence that had a bearing upon its historical reliability. His findings drove him to the firm conviction that "in the Old Testament we have a true historical account of the history of the Israelite people."

As a professor at Princeton Dr. Wilson won international fame as a scholar and defender of the historic Christian faith. The emphasis of professor Wilson's teaching was to give his students "such an intelligent faith in the Old Testament Scriptures that they will never doubt them as long as they live." 22/i,ii

Bibliography

1. Adair, James R. *Saints Alive.* Wheaton, IL: Van Kampen Press, 1951.

2. Adair, James R., and Miller, Ted, eds. *We Found Our Way Out.* Grand Rapids, MI: Baker Book House, 1964.

3. Bright, Bill. *Jesus and the Intellectual.* Campus Crusade for Christ, Int., 1968.

4. Camburn, Terry Meeuwsen. "Miss America 1973." *Worldwide Challenge* 3:2 (February 1976).

5. *Chamber's Encyclopedia.* London: Pergamon Press, 1966.

6. Chelcicky, Jan. "My Last Days as a Communist." *Guideposts.* 1971.

7. Cruz, Nicky. *Run Baby Run.* Plainfield, NJ: Logos Books, 1968.

8. Dennis, Clyde H., ed. *These Live On.* Westchester, IL: Good News Publishers, 1966.

9. Dupont, Jacques. "The Conversion of Paul, and Its Influence on His Understanding of Salvation by Faith." *Apostolic History and the Gospel.* Edited by W. Ward Gasque and Ralph P. Martin. Grand Rapids, MI: Wm. B. Eerdmans Publishing Co., 1970.

10. *The Encyclopedia Britannica.* William Benton, Publisher. Chicago: Encyclopedia Britannica, Inc., 1970.

11. Enlow, David R. *Men Made New.* Grand Rapids, MI: Zondervan Publishing House, 1964.

12. Estborn, S. *Gripped by Christ.* London: Lutterworth Press, 1965.

13. *Family Treasury of Great Biographies* 3. Pleasantville, NJ: Reader's Digest Association, 1970.

14. *Football Was the Name of the Game* (tract). Oradell, NJ: American Tract Society.

15. Hefley, James C. *Living Miracles.* Grand Rapids, MI: Zondervan Publishing House, 1964.

16. Jones, E. Stanley. *Conversion.* New York: Abingdon Press, 1959.

17. *Journey's End* (tract). Oradell, NJ: American Tract Society.

18. Kim, Joon Gon. Photocopy of personal testimony from International Office, Campus Crusade for Christ, International.

19. Lyttleton, George. *The Conversion of St. Paul.* New York: American Tract Society, 1929.

20. Malik, Charles. "Hope for a World in Crisis." *Collegiate Challenge* 7:2 (1968).

21. Massengale, Rick. *Athletes in Action.* 1977.

22. McDowell, Josh, and Stewart, Don. *Answers to Tough Questions Skeptics Ask About the Christian Faith.* San Bernardino, CA: Here's Life Publishers, 1980.

23. Mullins, E. Y. *Why Is Christianity True?* Chicago: Christian Culture Press, 1905.

24. *The New International Dictionary of the Christian Church.* J. D. Douglas, ed. Revised edition. Grand Rapids, MI: Zondervan Publishing House, 1974.

25. *On Patrol for God* (tract). Oradell, NJ: American Tract Society.

26. Origen. *De Principiis,* 2. 3. 6.

27. Polycarp. *Philippians* 8.

28. Price, Eugenia. "Personally Involved . . . and Transformed." *Collegiate Challenge* 1:4 (1962).

29. Saint, Rachel. "Ten Years After the Massacre." *Decision.* January 1966.

30. Schaff, Philip. *History of the Christian Church.* New York: Charles Scribner's Sons, 1882.

31. Schaff, Philip. *History of the Christian Church* 1 (Apostolic Christianity, A.D. 1-100). Grand Rapids, MI: Wm. B. Eerdmans Publishing Co., 1910.

32. Short, Shirl. "Exclusive Interview with Charles Colson." *Moody Monthly.* February 1976.

33. Smith, Stan. "My Way of Playing." *Guideposts.* 1972.

34. Sparrow-Simpson, W. J. *The Resurrection and the Christian Faith.* Grand Rapids, MI: Zondervan Publishing House, 1968.

35. Staubach, Roger. *Staubach: First Down, Lifetime to Go.* Waco, TX: Word Incorporated, 1974.

36. Tertullian. *Apology* 50.

37. Thiede, Carsten. *Collegiate Challenge* 16 (1977).

38. White, Lona A. "How the Shaggy D. A. Became a Lamb." *Christian Life* 39.

39. Willems, Betty. "B. J. Thomas: Home Where He Belongs." *Contemporary Christian Acts.* January 1978.

40. Wurmbrand, Richard. *Tortured for Christ.* Glendale, CA: Diane Books, 1967.

Index

AUTHORS

Index

SUBJECTS

Index

SCRIPTURE REFERENCES

Old Testament

New Testament

Evidence That Demands A Verdict
Volume One

by Josh McDowell

A Classic Defense of Christian belief.

- Is the Christian faith built upon good solid evidence?
- Can the Bible withstand the onslaught of the most scholarly sceptics?
- Is the Bible a reliable historical record?
- Was the resurrection a hoax or one of the greatest historical events?
- Were the events surrounding the life of Jesus Christ accurately foretold centuries before his birth?
- Why was Jesus Christ profoundly different from any other man who ever lived?

There are answers—scholarly, intelligent, well-grounded answers. Answers backed by solid evidence. Answers that span over six thousand years of history. Answers which will satisfy anyone who is willing to honestly weigh the evidence.

Price £6.50 UK Product Code HK058

Also available:
Evidence That Demands A Verdict
Volume 2

Know Your Bible

by Josh McDowell

Josh McDowell uses 5 simple steps to bring the excitement of God's Word to your life! Clearly explained and illustrated.

Know Your Bible will help you:

- Become more consistent in your Bible Study.
- Use key questions to discover the full meaning of a verse, chapter or entire book.
- Remember and review what you've studied through simple charts.
- Have a more stimulating group Bible Study.
- Handle personal emergencies more effectively through a special chapter on 'Crisis Bible Study'.

Price £5.50 UK Product Code HK082

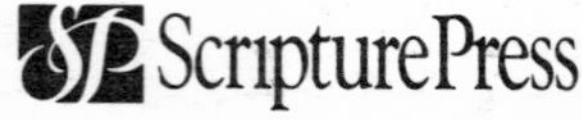